THEOSOPHY
THE WISDOM RELIGION

Other Theosophy Trust Books

Mahatma Gandhi and Buddha's Path to Enlightenment
by Raghavan Iyer

The Yoga Sutras of Patanjali
by Raghavan Iyer

Meditation and Self-Study
Essays on the Spiritual Life
by Raghavan Iyer

The Origins of Self-Consciousness
in *The Secret Doctrine*
by H.P. Blavatsky

Wisdom in Action
Essays on the Spiritual Life
by Raghavan Iyer

The Dawning of Wisdom
Essays on Walking the Path
by Raghavan Iyer

Teachers of the Eternal Doctrine
From Tsong-Ka-Pa to Nostradamus
by Elton Hall

Symbols of the Eternal Doctrine
From Shamballa to Paradise
by Helen Valborg

The Key to Theosophy
An Exposition of the Ethics, Science, and Philosophy
by H. P. Blavatsky

Evolution and Intelligent Design
in *The Secret Doctrine*
by H.P. Blavatsky

THEOSOPHY
THE WISDOM RELIGION

COMPILED BY THE

EDITORIAL BOARD OF THEOSOPHY TRUST

THEOSOPHY TRUST BOOKS

NORFOLK, VA

Theosophy – The Wisdom Religion

Theosophy Trust books may be ordered through Amazon.com, CreateSpace.com, and other retail outlets, or by visiting:

http://www.theosophytrust.org/online_books.php

ISBN-13: 978-0-9916182-4-8
ISBN-10: 0991618246

Library of Congress Control Number: 2015933717

Printed in the United States of America

Dedicated to the "seeker after truths undying",

that they may reach the goal,

with their "Soul-gaze centred on the One Pure Light,

the Light that is free from affection",

to "use their golden Key . . . "

The central tenets of *Theosophia* are not derived from any ancient or modern sect but represent the accumulated wisdom of the ages, the unrecorded inheritance of humanity. Its vast scheme of cosmic and human evolution furnishes all true seekers with the symbolic alphabet necessary to interpret their recurrent visions as well as the universal framework and metaphysical vocabulary, drawn from many mystics and seers, which enable them to communicate their own intuitive perceptions. All authentic mystical writings are enriched by the alchemical flavour of Theosophical thought. Theosophy is an integrated system of fundamental verities taught by Initiates and Adepts across millennia. It is the *Philosophia Perennis*, the philosophy of human perfectibility, the science of spirituality and the religion of responsibility. It is the primeval fount of myriad religious systems as well as the hidden essence and esoteric wisdom of each. Man, an immortal monad, has been able to preserve this sacred heritage through the sacrificial efforts of enlightened and compassionate individuals, or *Bodhisattvas*, who constitute an ancient Brotherhood. They quietly assist in the ethical evolution and spiritual development of the whole of humanity. *Theosophia* is Divine Wisdom, transmitted and verified over aeons by the sages who belong to this secret Brotherhood.

Spritual Evolution
Hermes, August 1979
Raghavan Iyer

CONTENTS

INTRODUCTION

IT may seem strange to the reader, but this book began in response to many requests we received from prison inmates in the U.S. – especially in Texas, North Carolina, South Carolina, Florida and Missouri – for books on Theosophy. Those requests began in August of 2009 with an inmate in the Texas Department of Criminal Justice prison system, Casey Myers, incarcerated in the McConnell Unit in Beeville, Texas, who was subsequently killed in prison in a knife attack in 2012 by a gang to whom he refused to show obeisance. Casey was a dedicated student of Theosophy who labored to spread the Teachings to his fellow inmates. His work contributed to the spread of awareness of Theosophy to many of the 108 Units of the Texas Department of Criminal Justice prison system, as well as state prisons in North and South Carolina, Florida and Missouri (for more on Theosophy Trust's Prisoner Book Donation initiative, see http://www.theosophytrust.org/PrisonerDonation.html). Looking around at the vast literature of the theosophical movement, we could find no one volume that would satisfy the need behind these requests. The only work that came close was Mr. W.Q. Judge's *The Ocean of Theosophy*, a splendid work from the 19th Century Cycle, but which, we thought, needed to be augmented with other writings to be most useful to the first-time enquirer. Surveying the books on Theosophy on amazon.com and other online resources convinced us that there was a glaring lack in the available publications; there were many authors who published their own thoughts and interpretations of these sacred Teachings, but no one had put together a compendium of the most relevant selections and articles from the accredited Founders of the Movement and those who labored after their passing to maintain the purity of the original teachings and the impulse behind them; hence, the present work.

The idea behind this book was to provide a single volume that would draw from a multiplicity of sources of the Theosophical Movement and introduce the reader (whether incarcerated or not) to a very complex universe of thought, one that seems to many – justifiably or not – to be intimidating if not forbidding because of its complexity and rich vocabulary. That this perception is incorrect was made plain by William Q. Judge in the introduction to his work, *The Ocean of Theosophy*. Likening Theosophy to an ocean was meant to illustrate that although its unfathomable depths give the fullest scope to the most intrepid thinkers, at its shore, the philosophy of Theosophy is gentle and placid enough to "not overwhelm the understanding of a child". The reader will find that the present work is similar to Mr. Judge's in that many of the articles are remarkably easy to understand, while others require a concentration and ability to think which we do not normally bring to our daily tasks.

This work introduces the reader to that complex universe of thought called Theosophy, or *theosophia*, by drawing from works penned by the original founders of the Theosophical Movement of the 19th Century, H.P. Blavatsky and William Q. Judge, as well as the man who rescued the original message of the Founders from confusion, chaos and degradation, Robert Crosbie, and the latest representative of the Theosophical Movement of the 20th Century, Professor Raghavan Iyer. Forty articles were chosen from the enormous collection of Theosophical literature that were thought to best exemplify and explain some particular aspect of the Wisdom Religion. These were arranged into three themes: Theosophy Generally Stated (also the title of one of Mr. Judge's articles); Universal Ideas of Theosophy; and Practical Theosophy. The thinking behind this arrangement was to first give the reader an introduction to the theme of what is Theosophy (and correspondingly, what are the theosophists?) through a series of 12 articles that were chosen because of their remarkably clear explanations. The next section of 15 essays deals with the theme of the universal ideas of Theosophy, those conceptions and archetypes that comprise the foundation stones of the world's religions and philosophies. Finally, any treatment of the philosophy of Theosophy would be deficient if it did not explain how Theosophy can be applied in daily life to one's perceptions of the world surrounding us, our ethical behavior, and the meaning we bring to our lives. Thus, the final 13 articles in the section on Practical Theosophy show the reader how the idea of Universal Brotherhood, for example, can be applied in practice, every day and in nearly every situation we find ourselves in. The entire work is therefore built upon a stable triangle of references to the Source of universal ideation, the ideas manifested from that potency, and the channel through which those ideas can be brought down into the most mundane plane of manifestation, daily life. It is analogous to the bridge between Heaven and Earth described in Mr. Crosbie's essay, What Reincarnates?, in which he notes "Humanity now is building the bridge of thought, the bridge of ideas that connects the lower with the higher. The whole purpose of incarnation, or our descent into matter, was not only to gain further knowledge of matter, but to impel the lower kingdoms to come up to where we are."

From our vantage point of some 50 years of study of the philosophy of Theosophy, no introductory work would be complete if it did not include that most remarkable personage of Prof. Raghavan Iyer, who founded HERMES, a journal of Theosophical Wisdom, just prior to the beginning of the 1975 Cycle in Santa Barbara, California, as one of several vehicles for the current behind the 7th Century Impulse. In that journal, he illustrated the ways in which *Mahatmas* have worked and continue to work in the world. In the HERMES article, "The Seventh Impulse: 1963-2000", Prof. Iyer made clear that the Mahatmic impulsions were concentrated in the last quarter of each century, but that preparations for them occurred earlier, and that their reverberations lasted far beyond the conclusion of each quarter-century cycle in an unfailing continuous stream.

Although this work began as a way to transmit the unadulterated teachings of Theosophy to an imprisoned population, it will be equally useful to the wider population of spiritual seekers who are responding to the promptings of their inmost selves to take up the search again for an authentic spiritual life. From a Theosophical perspective, these souls are answering the call behind the powerful impulse of the 1975 Cycle, an impulse which reaches far beyond the narrow confines of organizations and sects. Individuals all over the globe are prompted by this impulse to take up the search for those truths that will lead them to a deeper comprehension of their own spiritual nature and the spiritual identity of all beings. In this regard, some of the articles in this volume will undoubtedly raise questions about the relation between the original Theosophical Society (formed by Madame H.P. Blavatsky, along with H.S. Olcott and William Q. Judge, in New York in 1875) and the current Society in America, England and other places, as well as the United Lodge of Theosophists. There is a very complex history to this question, one that this work does not address, but the issue can be boiled down to one simple point – the primary aim of H.P.B.'s Society was to create the nucleus of a Universal Brotherhood. Whether the original impulse and brilliance of the Founders in establishing this ideal as the foundation of the Society remains active in any current organization is a question best left to each reader to answer for themselves.

In her magnificent work, *The Key to Theosophy*, Madame Blavatsky declared that "Theosophy, in its abstract meaning, is Divine Wisdom, or the aggregate of the knowledge and wisdom that underlie the Universe – the homogeneity of eternal GOOD; and in its concrete sense it is the sum total of the same as allotted to man by nature, on this earth, and no more." That the universe might have an unfathomable knowledge and wisdom at its core, not as an artificial human invention but something integral to its very existence, is an idea that perplexes many enquirers, as it seems to imply that there is a universal mind in the cosmos that can be apprehended by human understanding. That the universe might have "eternal GOOD" at its very core seems to run counter to our suspicions that there is a fundamental indifference to the cosmos that results in a sense of separation and alienation from much of what we perceive beyond us. If this volume helps the reader to deepen their insight into these themes, it will have served its purpose.

Editor, Theosophy Trust

NOTE: All of the articles and readings in this work can be found in their original forms on the Theosophy Trust website at theosophytrust.org.

PART I:

THEOSOPHY GENERALLY STATED

WHAT IS THEOSOPHY?

THIS question has been so often asked, and misconception so widely prevails, that the editors of a journal devoted to an exposition of the world's Theosophy would be remiss were its first number issued without coming to a full understanding with their readers. But our heading involves two further queries: What is the Theosophical Society; and what are the Theosophists? To each an answer will be given.

According to lexicographers, the term *theosophia* is composed of two Greek words – *theos*, "god," and *sophos*, "wise." So far, correct. But the explanations that follow are far from giving a clear idea of Theosophy. Webster defines it most originally as "a supposed intercourse with God and superior spirits, and consequent attainment of superhuman knowledge, by *physical processes,* as by the theurgic operations of some ancient Platonists, or by the *chemical processes* of the German fire-philosophers."

This, to say the least, is a poor and flippant explanation. To attribute such ideas to men like Ammonius Saccas, Plotinus, Iamblichus, Porphyry, Proclus – shows either intentional misrepresentation, or Mr. Webster's ignorance of the philosophy and motives of the greatest geniuses of the later Alexandrian School. To impute to those whom their contemporaries as well as posterity styled "theodidaktoi," god-taught – a purpose to develop their psychological, spiritual perceptions by "physical processes," is to describe them as materialists. As to the concluding fling at the fire-philosophers, it rebounds from them to fall home among our most eminent modern men of science; those, in whose mouths the Rev. James Martineau places the following boast: "matter is all we want; give us atoms alone, and we will explain the universe."

Vaughan offers a far better, more philosophical definition. "A Theosophist," he says – "is one who gives you a theory of God or the works of God, which has not revelation, but an inspiration of his own for its basis." In this view every great thinker and philosopher, especially every founder of a new religion, school of philosophy, or sect, is necessarily a Theosophist. Hence, Theosophy and Theosophists have existed ever since the first glimmering of nascent thought made man seek instinctively for the means of expressing his own independent opinions.

There were Theosophists before the Christian era, notwithstanding that the Christian writers ascribe the development of the Eclectic theosophical system to the early part of the third century of their Era. Diogenes Laertius traces Theosophy to an epoch antedating the dynasty of the Ptolemies; and names as its founder an Egyptian Hierophant called Pot-Amun, the name being Coptic and signifying a priest consecrated to Amun, the god of Wisdom. But history shows it revived by Ammonius Saccas, the founder of the Neo-Platonic School. He and his disciples called themselves "Philalethians" – lovers of the truth; while others termed them the "Analogists," on account of their method of interpreting all sacred legends, symbolical myths and mysteries, by a rule of analogy or correspondence, so that events which had occurred in the external world were regarded as expressing operations and experiences of the human soul. It was the aim and purpose of Ammonius to reconcile all sects, peoples and nations under one common faith – a belief in one Supreme Eternal, Unknown, and Unnamed Power, governing the Universe by immutable and eternal laws. His object was to prove a primitive system of Theosophy, which at the beginning was essentially alike in all countries; to induce all men to lay aside their strifes and quarrels, and unite in purpose and thought as the children of one common mother; to purify the ancient religions, by degrees corrupted and obscured, from all dross of human element, by uniting and expounding them upon pure philosophical principles. Hence, the Buddhistic, Vedantic and Magian, or Zoroastrian, systems were taught in the Eclectic Theosophical School along with all the philosophies of Greece. Hence also, the preeminently Buddhistic and Indian feature among the ancient Theosophists and Alexandria, of due reverence for parents and aged persons; a fraternal affection for the whole human race; and a compassionate feeling for even the dumb animals. While seeking to establish a system of moral discipline which enforced upon people the duty to live according to the laws of their respective countries; to exalt their minds by the research and contemplation of the one Absolute Truth; his chief object in order, as he believed, to achieve all others, was to extract from the various religious teachings, as from a many-chorded instrument, one full and harmonious melody, which would find response in every truth-loving heart.

Theosophy is, then, the archaic *Wisdom-Religion,* the esoteric doctrine once known in every ancient country having claims to civilization. This "Wisdom" all the old writings show us as an emanation of the divine Principle; and the clear comprehension of it is typified in such names as the Indian Buddh, the Babylonian Nebo, the Thoth of Memphis, the Hermes of Greece; in the appellations, also, of some goddesses – Metis, Neitha, Athena, the Gnostic *Sophia,* and finally the *Vedas,* from the word "to know." Under this designation, all the ancient philosophers of the East and West, the Hierophants of old Egypt, the Rishis of Aryavart, the Theodidaktoi of Greece, included all knowledge of things occult and essentially divine. The *Mercavah* of the Hebrew Rabbis, the secular and popular series, were thus designated as only the vehicle, the outward shell which contained the higher esoteric knowledge. The Magi of Zoroaster received instruction and were initiated in the caves and secret lodges of Bactria; the Egyptian and Grecian hierophants had their *apporrheta,* or secret discourses, during which the *Mysta* became an *Epopta* – a Seer.

The central idea of the Eclectic Theosophy was that of a simple Supreme Essence, Unknown and *Unknowable* – for – "How could one know the knower?" as enquires *Brihadaranyaka Upanishad*. Their system was characterized by three distinct features: the theory of the above-named Essence; the doctrine of the human soul – an emanation from the latter, hence of the same nature; and its theurgy. It is this last science which has led the Neo-Platonists to be so misrepresented in our era of materialistic science. Theurgy being essentially the art of applying the divine powers of man to the subordination of the blind forces of nature, its votaries were first termed magicians – a corruption of the word "*Magh,*" signifying a wise, or learned man, and – derided. Skeptics of a century ago would have been as wide of the mark if they had laughed at the idea of a phonograph or telegraph. The ridiculed and the "infidels" of one generation generally become the wise men and saints of the next.

As regards the Divine essence and the nature of the soul and spirit, modern Theosophy believes now as ancient Theosophy did. The popular *Diu* of the Aryan nations was identical with the *Iao* of the Chaldeans, and even with the Jupiter of the less learned and philosophical among the Romans; and it was just as identical with the *Jahve* of the Samaritans, the *Tiu* or "Tiusco" of the Northmen, the *Duw* of the Britains, and the Zeus of the Thracians. As to the Absolute Essence, the One and all – whether we accept the Greek Pythagorean, the Chaldean Kabalistic, or the Aryan philosophy in regard to it, it will lead to one and the same result. The Primeval Monad of the Pythagorean system, which retires into darkness and is itself Darkness (for human intellect) was made the basis of all things; and we can find the idea in all its integrity in the philosophical systems of Leibnitz and Spinoza. Therefore, whether a Theosophist agrees with the *Kabala* which, speaking of *En-Soph* propounds the query: "Who, then, can comprehend It since It is formless, and Non-existent?" – or, remembering that magnificent hymn from the *Rig-Veda* (Hymn 129th, Book 10th) – enquires:

> "Who knows from whence this great creation sprang?
> Whether his will created or was mute.
> He knows it – or perchance *even He knows not;*"

or again, accepts the Vedantic conception of Brahma, who in the *Upanishads* is represented as "without life, without mind, pure," *unconscious,* for – Brahma is "Absolute Consciousness"; or, even finally, siding with the Svabhâvikas of Nepaul, maintains that nothing exists but "*Svabhâvat*" (substance or nature) which exists by *itself* without any creator; any one of the above conceptions can lead but to pure and absolute Theosophy – that Theosophy which prompted such men as Hegel, Fichte and Spinoza to take up the labors of the old Grecian philosophers and speculate upon the One Substance – the Deity, the *Divine All* proceeding from the Divine Wisdom – incomprehensible, unknown and *unnamed* – by any ancient or modern religious philosophy, with the exception of Christianity and Mohammedanism. Every Theosophist, then, holding to a theory of the Deity "which has not revelation, but an inspiration of his own for its basis," may accept any of the above definitions or belong to any of these religions, and yet remain strictly within the boundaries of Theosophy. For the latter is belief in the Deity as the ALL, the source of all existence, the infinite that cannot be either comprehended or known, the universe alone revealing *It*, or, as some prefer it, Him, thus giving a sex to that, to anthropomorphize which is *blasphemy*. True, Theosophy shrinks from brutal materialization; it prefers believing that, from eternity retired within itself, the Spirit of the Deity neither wills nor creates; but that, from the infinite effulgency everywhere going forth from the Great Centre, that which produces all visible and invisible things, is but a Ray containing in itself the generative and conceptive power, which, in its turn, produces that which the Greeks called *Macrocosm*, the Kabalists *Tikkun* or Adam Kadmon – the archetypal man, and the Aryans *Purusha*, the manifested Brahm, or the Divine Male. Theosophy believes also in the *Anastasis* or continued existence, and in transmigration (evolution) or a series of changes in the soul[1] which can be defended and explained on strict philosophical principles; and only by making a distinction between *Paramâtma* (transcendental, supreme soul) and *Jivâtma* (animal, or conscious soul) of the Vedantins.

To fully define Theosophy, we must consider it under all its aspects. The interior world has not been hidden from all by impenetrable darkness. By that higher intuition acquired by *Theosophia* – or God-knowledge, which carried the mind from the world of form into that of formless spirit, man has been sometimes enabled in every age and every country to perceive things in the interior or invisible world. Hence, the "*Samadhi*," or *Dyan Yog Samadhi*, of the Hindu ascetics; the "*Daimonion-photi*," or spiritual illumination of the Neo-Platonists; the "sidereal confabulation of soul," of the Rosicrucians or Fire-philosophers; and, even the ecstatic trance of mystics and of the modern mesmerists and spiritualists, are identical in nature, though various as to manifestation. The search after man's diviner "self," so

---

[1] In a series of articles entitled "*The World's Great Theosophists*," we intend showing that from Pythagoras, who got his wisdom in India, down to our best known modern philosophers and theosophists – David Hume, and Shelley, the English poet – the Spiritists of France included – many believed and yet believe in metempsychosis or reincarnation of the soul; however unelaborated the system of the Spiritists may fairly be regarded.

often and so erroneously interpreted as individual communion with a personal God, was the object of every mystic, and belief in its possibility seems to have been coeval with the genesis of humanity, each people giving it another name. Thus Plato and Plotinus call "Noetic work" that which the Yogin and the Shrotriya term *Vidya*. "By reflection, self-knowledge and intellectual discipline, the soul can be raised to the vision of eternal truth, goodness, and beauty – that is, to the *Vision of God* – this is the *epopteia*," said the Greeks. "To unite one's soul to the Universal Soul," says Porphyry, "requires but a perfectly pure mind. Through self-contemplation, perfect chastity, and purity of body, we may approach nearer to It, and receive, in that state, true knowledge and wonderful insight." And Swami Dayanand Saraswati, who has read neither Porphyry nor other Greek authors, but who is a thorough Vedic scholar, says in his *Veda Bhâshya* (*opasna prakaru ank.* 9):

> "To obtain *Diksh* (highest initiation) and *Yog,* one has to practise according to the rules . . . The soul in human body can perform the greatest wonders by knowing the Universal Spirit (or God) and acquainting itself with the properties and qualities (occult) of all the things in the universe. A human being (a *Dikshit* or initiate) can thus *acquire a power of seeing and hearing at great distances.*"

Finally, Alfred R. Wallace, F.R.S., a spiritualist and yet a confessedly great naturalist, says, with brave candour: "It is 'spirit' that alone feels, and perceives, and thinks – that acquires knowledge, and reasons and aspires . . . there not unfrequently occur individuals so constituted that the spirit can perceive independently of the corporeal organs of sense, or can perhaps, wholly or partially, quit the body for a time and return to it again . . . the spirit . . . communicates with spirit easier than with matter." We can now see how, after thousands of years have intervened between the age of Gymnosophists[2] and our own highly civilized era, notwithstanding, or, perhaps, just because of such an enlightenment which pours its radiant light upon the psychological as well as upon the physical realms of nature, over twenty millions of people today believe, under a different form, in those same spiritual

---

[2] The reality of the Yog power was affirmed by many Greek and Roman writers, who call the Yogins Indian Gymnosophists; by Strabo, Lucan, Plutarch, Cicero (*Tusculum*), Pliny (vii,2), etc.

powers that were believed in by the Yogins and the Pythagoreans, nearly 3,000 years ago. Thus, while the Aryan mystic claimed for himself the power of solving all the problems of life and death, when he had once obtained the power of acting independently of his body, through the *Atman* – "self," or "soul"; and the old Greeks went in search of *Atmu* – the Hidden one, or the God-Soul of man, with the symbolical mirror of the Thesmophorian mysteries; – so the spiritualists of today believe in the faculty of the spirits, or the souls of the disembodied persons, to communicate visibly and tangibly with those they loved on earth. And all these, Aryan Yogins, Greek philosophers, and modern spiritualists, affirm that possibility on the ground that the embodied soul and its never embodied spirit – the real *self,* are not separated from either the Universal Soul or other spirits by space, but merely by the differentiation of their qualities; as in the boundless expanse of the universe there can be no limitation. And that when this difference is once removed – according to the Greeks and Aryans by abstract contemplation, producing the temporary liberation of the imprisoned Soul; and according to spiritualists, through mediumship – such an union between embodied and disembodied spiritst becomes possible. Thus was it that Patanjali's Yogins and, following in their steps, Plotinus, Porphyry and other Neo-Platonists, maintained that in their hours of ecstasy, they had been united to, or rather become as one with God, several times during the course of their lives. This idea, erroneous as it may seem in its application to the Universal Spirit, was, and is, claimed by too many great philosophers to be put aside as entirely chimerical. In the case of the *Theodidaktoi,* the only controvertible point, the dark spot on this philosophy of extreme mysticism, was its claim to include that which is simply ecstatic illumination, under the head of sensuous perception. In the case of the Yogins, who maintained their ability to see *Iswara* "face to face," this claim was successfully overthrown by the stern logic of Kapila. As to the similar assumption made for their Greek followers, for a long array of Christian ecstatics, and, finally, for the last two claimants to "God-seeing" within these last hundred years – Jacob Boehme and Swedenborg – this pretension would and *should* have been philosophically and logically questioned, if a few of our great men of science who are spiritualists had had more interest in the philosophy than in the mere phenomenalism of spiritualism.

The Alexandrian Theosophists were divided into neophytes, initiates, and masters, or hierophants; and their rules were copied from the ancient Mysteries of Orpheus, who, according to Herodotus, brought them from India. Ammonius obligated his disciples by oath not to divulge his *higher* doctrines, except to those who were proved thoroughly worthy and initiated, and who had learned to regard the gods, the angels, and the demons of other peoples, according to the esoteric *hyponia*, or under-meaning. "The gods exist, but they are not what the *hoi polloi*, the uneducated multitude, suppose them to be," says Epicurus. "He is not an atheist who denies the existence of the gods whom the multitude worship, but he is such who fastens on these gods the opinions of the multitude." In his turn, Aristotle declares that of the "Divine Essence pervading the whole world of nature, what are styled the *gods* are simply the first principles."

Plotinus, the pupil of the "God-taught" Ammonius, tells us that the secret *gnosis* or the knowledge of Theosophy, has three degrees – opinion, science, and *illumination*. "The means or instrument of the first is sense, or perception; of the second, dialectics; of the third, intuition. To the last, reason is subordinate; it is *absolute knowledge*, founded on the identification of the mind with the object known." Theosophy is the exact science of psychology, so to say; it stands in relation to natural, uncultivated mediumship, as the knowledge of a Tyndall stands to that of a school-boy in physics. It develops in man a direct beholding; that which Schelling denominates "a realization of the identity of subject and object in the individual"; so that under the influence and knowledge of *hyponia* man thinks divine thoughts, views all things as they really are, and, finally, "becomes recipient of the Soul of the World," to use one of the finest expressions of Emerson. "I, the imperfect, adore my own perfect" – he says in his superb *Essay on the Oversoul*. Besides this psychological, or soul-state, Theosophy cultivated every branch of sciences and arts. It was thoroughly familiar with what is now commonly known as mesmerism. Practical theurgy or "ceremonial magic," so often resorted to in their exorcisms by the Roman Catholic clergy – was discarded by the theosophists. It is but Iamblichus alone who, transcending the other Eclectics, added to Theosophy the doctrine of Theurgy. When ignorant of the true meaning of the esoteric divine symbols of nature, man is apt to miscalculate the powers of his soul, and, instead of communing spiritually and mentally with the higher, celestial beings, the good spirits (the gods of the theurgists of the Platonic school), he will unconsciously call forth the evil, dark powers which lurk around humanity – the undying, grim creations of human crimes and vices – and thus fall from *theurgia* (white magic) into *gäetia* (or black magic, sorcery). Yet, neither white, nor black magic are what popular superstition understands by the terms. The possibility of "raising spirits" according to the key of Solomon, is the height of superstition and ignorance. Purity of deed and thought can alone raise us to an intercourse "with the gods" and attain for us the goal we desire. Alchemy, believed by so many to have been a spiritual philosophy as well as physical science, belonged to the teachings of the theosophical school.

It is a noticeable fact that neither Zoroaster, Buddha, Orpheus, Pythagoras, Confucius, Socrates, nor Ammonius Saccas, committed anything to writing. The reason for it is obvious. Theosophy is a double-edged weapon and unfit for the ignorant or the selfish. Like every ancient philosophy it has its votaries among the moderns; but, until late in our own days, its disciples were few in numbers, and of the most various sects and opinions. "Entirely speculative, and founding no school, they have still exercised a silent influence upon philosophy; and no doubt, when the time arrives, many ideas thus silently propounded may yet give new directions to human thought" – remarks Mr. Kenneth R. H. Mackenzie IX . . . himself a mystic and a Theosophist, in his large and valuable work, *The Royal Masonic Cycloepædia*[3] (articles *Theosophical Society of New York* and *Theosophy*, p. 731). Since the days of the fire-philosophers, they had never formed themselves into societies, for, tracked like wild beasts by the Christian clergy, to be known as a Theosophist often amounted, hardly a century ago, to a death-warrant. The statistics show that, during a period of 150 years, no less than 90,000 men and women were burned in Europe for

---

[3] *The Royal Masonic Cycloepædia of History, Rites, Symbolism, and Biography.* Edited by Kenneth R. H. Mackenzie IX (Cryptonymous), Hon. Member of the Canongate KD-winning Lodge, No. 2, Scotland. New York, J. W. Bouton, 706 Broadway, 1877.

alleged witchcraft. In Great Britain only, from A.D. 1640 to 1660, but twenty years, 3,000 persons were put to death for compact with the "Devil." It was but late in the present century – in 1875 – that some progressed mystics and spiritualists, unsatisfied with the theories and explanations of Spiritualism, started by its votaries, and finding that they were far from covering the whole ground of the wide range of phenomena, formed at New York, America, an association which is now widely known as the Theosophical Society. And now, having explained what is Theosophy, we will, in a separate article, explain what is the nature of our Society, which is also called the "Universal Brotherhood of Humanity."

Theosophist, October, 1879
H.P. Blavatsky

IS THEOSOPHY A RELIGION?

"Religion *is* the best armour that man can have, but it is the worst cloak."

– Bunyan

It is no exaggeration to say that there never was – during the present century, at any rate – a movement, social or religious, so terribly, nay, so absurdly misunderstood, or more blundered about than THEOSOPHY – whether regarded theoretically as a code of ethics, or practically, in its objective expression, *i.e.*, the Society known by that name.

Year after year, and day after day had our officers and members to interrupt people speaking of the theosophical movement by putting in more or less emphatic protests against Theosophy being referred to as a "religion," and the Theosophical Society as a kind of church or religious body. Still worse, it is as often spoken of as a "new sect"! Is it a stubborn prejudice, an error, or both? The latter, most likely. The most narrow-minded and even notoriously unfair people are still in need of a plausible pretext, of a peg on which to hang their little uncharitable remarks and innocently-uttered slanders. And what peg is more solid for that purpose, more convenient than an "ism" or a "sect." The great majority would be very sorry to be disabused and finally forced to accept the fact that Theosophy is neither. The name suits them, and they pretend to be unaware of its falseness. But there are others, also, many more or less friendly people, who labour sincerely under the same delusion. To these, we say: Surely the world has been hitherto sufficiently cursed with the intellectual extinguishers known as dogmatic creeds, without having inflicted upon it a new form of faith! Too many already wear their faith, truly, as Shakespeare puts it, "but as the fashion of his hat," ever changing "with the next block." Moreover, the very *raison d'être* of the Theosophical Society was, from its beginning, to utter a loud protest and lead an open warfare against dogma or any belief based upon blind faith.

It may sound odd and paradoxical, but it is true to say that, hitherto, the most apt workers in practical Theosophy, its most devoted members were those recruited from the ranks of agnostics and even of materialists. No genuine, no sincere searcher after truth can ever be found among the *blind* believers in the "Divine Word," let the latter be claimed to come from Allah, Brahma or Jehovah, or their respective *Kuran, Purana* and *Bible*. For:

Faith is not *reason's* labour, but repose.

He who believes his own religion on faith, will regard that of every other man as a lie, and hate it on that same faith. Moreover, unless it fetters reason and entirely blinds our perceptions of anything outside our own particular faith, the latter is no faith at all, but a temporary belief, the delusion we labour under, at some particular time of life. Moreover, "faith without principles is but a flattering phrase for willful positiveness or fanatical bodily sensations," in Coleridge's clever definition.

What, then, is Theosophy, and how may it be defined in its latest presentation in this closing portion of the XIXth century?

Theosophy, we say, is not *a* Religion.

Yet there are, as everyone knows, certain beliefs, philosophical, religious and scientific, which have become so closely associated in recent years with the word "Theosophy" that they have come to be taken by the general public for Theosophy itself. Moreover, we shall be told these beliefs have been put forward, explained and defended by those very Founders who have declared that Theosophy is *not* a Religion. What is then the explanation of this *apparent* contradiction? How can a certain body of beliefs and teachings, an elaborate doctrine, in fact, be labelled "Theosophy" and be tacitly accepted as "Theosophical" by nine-tenths of the members of the T.S., if Theosophy is not a Religion? – we are asked.

To explain this is the purpose of the present protest.

It is perhaps necessary, first of all, to say, that the assertion that "Theosophy is not *a* Religion," by no means excludes the fact that "Theosophy *is* Religion" itself. A Religion in the true and only correct sense, is a bond uniting men together – not a particular set of dogmas and beliefs. Now Religion, *per se,* in its widest meaning is that which binds not only *all* MEN, but also *all* BEINGS and all *things* in the entire Universe into one grand whole. This is our theosophical definition of religion; but the same definition changes again with every creed and country, and no two Christians even regard it alike. We find this in more than one eminent author. Thus Carlyle defined the Protestant Religion in his day, with a remarkable prophetic eye to this ever-growing feeling in our present day, as:

For the most part a wise, prudential feeling, grounded on mere calculation; a matter, as all others now are, of expediency and utility; whereby some smaller *quantum* of earthly enjoyment may be exchanged for a far larger *quantum* of celestial enjoyment. Thus religion, too, is profit, a working for wages; not reverence, but vulgar hope or fear.

In her turn Mrs. Stowe, whether consciously or otherwise, seemed to have had Roman Catholicism rather than Protestantism in her mind, when saying of her heroine that:

Religion she looked upon in the light of a ticket (with the correct number of indulgences bought and paid for), which, being once purchased and snugly laid away in a pocket-book, is to be produced at the celestial gate, and thus secure admission to heaven. . . .

But to Theosophists (the genuine Theosophists are here meant) who accept no mediation by proxy, no salvation through innocent bloodshed, nor would they think of "working for wages" in the *One Universal* religion, the only definition they could subscribe to and accept in full is one given by Miller. How truly and theosophically he describes it, by showing that

. . . true Religion
Is always mild, propitious and humble;
Plays not the tyrant, plants no faith in blood,
Nor bears destruction on her chariot wheels;
But stoops to polish, succour and redress
And builds her grandeur on the public good.

The above is a correct definition of what true Theosophy *is*, or ought to be. (Among the creeds Buddhism alone is such a true heart-binding and men-binding philosophy, because it is not a dogmatic religion.) In this respect, as it is the duty and task of every genuine theosophist to accept and carry out these principles, Theosophy is RELIGION, and the Society its one Universal Church; the temple of Solomon's wisdom, in building which "there was neither hammer, nor axe, *nor* any tool of iron heard in the house while it was building" (I Kings, vi.); for this "temple" is made by no human hand, nor built in any locality on earth – but, verily, is raised only in the inner sanctuary of man's heart wherein reigns alone the awakened soul.

Thus Theosophy is not *a* Religion, we say, but RELIGION itself, the one bond of unity, which is so universal and all-embracing that no man, as no speck – from gods and mortals down to animals, the blade of grass and atom – can be outside of its light. Therefore, any organization or body of that name must necessarily be a UNIVERSAL BROTHERHOOD.

Were it otherwise, Theosophy would be but a word added to hundreds other such words as high sounding as they are pretentious and empty. Viewed as a philosophy, Theosophy in its practical work is the alembic of the Mediæval alchemist. It transmutes the apparently base metal of every ritualistic and dogmatic creed (Christianity included) into the gold of fact and truth, and thus truly produces a universal panacea for the ills of mankind. This is why, when applying for admission into the Theosophical Society, no one is asked what religion he belongs to, nor what his deistic views may be. These views are his own personal property and have nought to do with the Society. Because Theosophy can be practiced by Christian or Heathen, Jew or Gentile, by Agnostic or Materialist, or even an Atheist, provided that none of these is a bigoted fanatic, who refuses to recognize as his brother any man or woman outside his own special creed or belief. Count Leo N. Tolstoy does not believe in the Bible, the Church, or the divinity of Christ; and yet no Christian surpasses him in the practical bearing out of the principles alleged to have been preached on the Mount. And these principles are those of Theosophy; not because they were uttered by the Christian Christ, but because they are universal ethics, and were preached by Buddha and Confucius, Krishna, and all the great Sages, thousands of years before the Sermon on the Mount was written. Hence, once that we live up to such Theosophy, it becomes a universal *panacea* indeed, for it heals the wounds inflicted by the gross asperities of the Church "isms" on the sensitive soul of every naturally religious man. How many of these, forcibly thrust out by the reactive impulse of disappointment from the narrow area of blind belief into the ranks of arid disbelief, have been brought back to hopeful aspiration by simply joining our Brotherhood – yea, imperfect as it is.

If, as an offset to this, we are reminded that several prominent members have left the Society disappointed in Theosophy as they had been in other associations, this cannot dismay us in the least. For with a very, *very few* exceptions, in the early stage of the T.S.'s activities when some left because they did not find mysticism practiced in the General Body as *they* understood it, or because "the leaders lacked Spirituality," were "untheosophical, hence, untrue to the rules," you see, the majority left because most of them were either half-hearted or too self-opinioned – a church and infallible dogma in themselves. Some broke away, again under very shallow pretexts indeed, such, for instance, as "because Christianity (to say Churchianity, or *sham* Christianity, would be more just) was too roughly handled in our magazines" – just as if other fanatical religions were ever treated any better or upheld! Thus, all those who left have done well to leave, and have never been regretted.

Furthermore, there is this also to be added: the number of those who left can hardly be compared with the number of those who found everything they had hoped for in Theosophy. Its doctrines, if seriously studied, call forth, by stimulating one's reasoning powers and awakening the *inner* in the animal man, every hitherto dormant power for good in us, and also the perception of the true and the real, as opposed to the false and the unreal. Tearing off with no uncertain hand the thick veil of dead-letter with which every old religious scriptures were cloaked, scientific Theosophy, learned in the cunning symbolism of the ages, reveals to the scoffer at old wisdom the origin of the world's faiths and sciences. It opens new vistas beyond the old horizons of crystallized, motionless and despotic faiths; and turning blind belief into a reasoned knowledge founded on mathematical laws – the only *exact* science – it demonstrates to him under profounder and more philosophical aspects the existence of that which, repelled by the grossness of its dead-letter form, he had long since abandoned as a nursery tale. It gives a clear and well-defined object, an ideal to live for, to every sincere man or woman belonging to whatever station in Society and of whatever culture and degree of intellect. Practical Theosophy is not *one* Science, but embraces every science in life, moral and physical. It may, in short, be justly regarded as the universal "coach," a tutor of world-wide knowledge and experience, and of an erudition which not only assists and guides his pupils toward a successful examination for every scientific or moral service in earthly life, but fits them for *the lives* to come, if those pupils will only study the universe and its mysteries *within themselves*, instead of studying them through the spectacles of orthodox science and religions.

And let no reader misunderstand these statements. It is Theosophy *per se*, not any individual member of the Society or even Theosophist, on whose behalf such a universal omniscience is claimed. The two – Theosophy and the Theosophical Society – as a vessel and the *olla podrida* it contains, must not be confounded. One is, as an ideal, *divine* Wisdom, perfection itself; the other a poor, imperfect thing, trying to run *under*, if not *within*, its shadow on Earth. No man is perfect; why, then, should any member of the T.S. be expected to be a paragon of every human virtue? And why should the whole organization be criticized and blamed for the faults, whether real or imaginary, of some of its "Fellows," or even its Leaders? Never was the Society, as a concrete body, free from blame or sin – *errare humanum est* – nor were any of its members. Hence, it is rather those members most of whom will not be led by Theosophy, that ought to be blamed. Theosophy is the soul of its Society; the latter the gross and imperfect body of the former. Hence, those modern Solomons who *will* sit in the Judgment Seat and talk of that they know nothing about, are invited before they slander Theosophy or any theosophists to first get acquainted with both, instead of ignorantly calling one a "farrago of insane beliefs" and the other a "sect of impostors and lunatics."

Regardless of this, Theosophy is spoken of by friends and foes as a religion when not a *sect*. Let us see how the special beliefs which have become associated with the word have come to stand in that position, and how it is that they have so good a right to it that none of the leaders of the Society have ever thought of disavowing their doctrines.

We have said that we believed in the absolute unity of nature. Unity implies the possibility for a unit on one plane, to come into contact with another unit on or from another plane. We believe in it.

The just published "*Secret Doctrine*" will show what were the ideas of all antiquity with regard to the *primeval instructors* of primitive man and his three earlier races. The genesis of that WISDOM-RELIGION in which all theosophists believe, dates from that period. So-called "Occultism," or rather Esoteric Science, has to be traced in its origin to those Beings who, led by Karma, have incarnated in our humanity, and thus struck the key-note of that secret Science which countless generations of subsequent adepts have expanded since then in every age, while they checked its doctrines by personal observation and experience. The bulk of this knowledge – which no man is able to possess in its fullness – constitutes that which we now call Theosophy or "divine knowledge." Beings from other and higher worlds may have it entire; we can have it only approximately.

Thus, unity of everything in the universe implies and justifies our belief in the existence of a knowledge at once scientific, philosophical and religious, showing the necessity and actuality of the connection of man and all things in the universe with each other; which knowledge, therefore, becomes essentially RELIGION, and must be called in its integrity and universality by the distinctive name of WISDOM-RELIGION.

It is from this WISDOM-RELIGION that all the various individual "Religions" (erroneously so called) have sprung, forming in their turn offshoots and branches, and also all the minor creeds, based upon and always originated through some personal experience in psychology. Every such religion, or religious offshoot, be it considered orthodox or heretical, wise or foolish, started originally as a clear and unadulterated stream from the Mother-Source. The fact that each became in time polluted with purely human speculations and even inventions, due to interested motives, does not prevent any from having been pure in its early beginnings. There are those creeds – we shall not call them religions – which have now been overlaid with the human element out of all recognition; others just showing signs of early decay; not one that escaped the hand of time. But each and all are of divine, because natural and true origin; aye – Mazdeism, Brahmanism, Buddhism as much as Christianity. It is the dogmas and human element in the latter which led directly to modern Spiritualism.

Of course, there *will* be an outcry from both sides, if we say that modern Spiritualism *per se*, cleansed of the unhealthy speculations which were based on the *dicta* of two little girls and their very unreliable "Spirits" – is, nevertheless, far more true and philosophical than any church dogma. *Carnalised* Spiritualism is now reaping its Karma. Its primitive *innovators*, the said "two little girls" from Rochester, the Mecca of modern Spiritualism, have grown up and turned into old women since the first raps produced by them have opened wide ajar the gates between this and the other world. It is on their "innocent" testimony that the elaborate scheme of a sidereal Summer-land, with its active astral population of "Spirits," ever on the wing between their "Silent Land" and our very loud-mouthed, gossiping earth – has been started and worked out. And now the two female Mahommeds of Modern Spiritualism have turned self-apostates and play false to the "philosophy" they have created, and have gone over to the enemy. They expose and denounce *practical* Spiritualism as the humbug of the ages. Spiritualists – (save a handful of fair exceptions) – have rejoiced and sided with *our* enemies and slanderers, when these, *who had never been Theosophists,* played us false and showed the cloven foot denouncing the Founders of the Theosophical Society as frauds and impostors. Shall the Theosophists laugh in their turn now that the original "revealers" of Spiritualism have become its "revilers"? Never! for the phenomena of Spiritualism are facts, and the treachery of the "Fox girls" only makes us feel new pity for all mediums, and confirms, before the whole world, our constant declaration that no medium can be relied upon. No true theosophist will ever laugh, or far less rejoice, at the discomfiture even of an opponent. The reason for it is simple:

Because we know that beings from other, higher worlds do confabulate with some elect mortals now as ever; though *now* far more rarely than in the days of old, as mankind becomes with every civilized generation worse in every respect.

Theosophy – owing, in truth, to the *levée in arms* of all the Spiritualists of Europe and America at the first words uttered against the idea that every communicating *intelligence* is necessarily the Spirit of some ex-mortal from this earth – has not said its last word about Spiritualism and "Spirits." It may one day. Meanwhile, an humble servant of Theosophy, the Editor, declares once more her belief in Beings, grander, wiser, nobler than any *personal* God, who are beyond any "Spirits of the dead," Saints, or winged Angels, who, nevertheless, *do* condescend in all and every age to occasionally overshadow rare sensitives – often entirely unconnected with Church, Spiritualism or even Theosophy. And believing in high and holy Spiritual Beings, she must also believe in the existence of their opposites – lower "spirits," good, bad and indifferent. Therefore does she believe in spiritualism and its phenomena, some of which are so repugnant to her.

This, as a casual remark and a digression, just to show that Theosophy includes Spiritualism – as it should be, not as it is – among its sciences, based on knowledge and the experience of countless ages. There is not a religion worthy of the name which has been started otherwise than in consequence of such *visits* from Beings on the higher planes.

Thus were born all prehistoric, as well as all the historic religions, Mazdeism and Brahmanism, Buddhism and Christianity, Judaism, Gnosticism and Mahomedanism; in short every more or less successful "ism." All are true at the bottom, and all are false on their surface. The Revealer, the artist who impressed a portion of the Truth on the brain of the Seer, was in every instance a true artist, who gave out genuine truths; but the instrument proved also, in every instance, to be *only a man*. Invite Rubenstein and ask him to play a sonata of

Beethoven on a piano left to *self-tuning,* one-half of the keys of which are in chronic paralysis, while the wires hang loose; then see whether, the genius of the artist notwithstanding, you will be able to recognize the sonata. The moral of the *fabula is* that a man – let him be the greatest of mediums or natural Seers – is but a man; and man left to his own devices and speculations *must* be out of tune with absolute truth, while even picking up some of its crumbs. For Man is but a *fallen* Angel, a god within, but having an animal brain in his head, more subject to cold and wine fumes while in company with other men on Earth, than to the faultless reception of divine revelations.

Hence the multi-coloured dogmas of the churches. Hence also the thousand and one "philosophies" so-called (some contradictory, theosophical theories included); and the variegated "Sciences" and schemes, Spiritual, Mental, Christian and Secular; Sectarianism and bigotry, and especially the personal vanity and self-opinionatedness of almost every "Innovator" since the mediæval ages. These have all darkened and hidden the very existence of TRUTH – the common root of all. Will our critics imagine that we exclude theosophical teachings from this nomenclature? Not at all. And though the esoteric doctrines which our Society has been and is expounding, are not *mental* or *spiritual* impressions from some "unknown, *from above,*" but the fruit of teachings given to us by living men, still, except that which was dictated and written out by those Masters of Wisdom themselves, these doctrines may be in many cases as incomplete and faulty as any of our foes would desire it. The "Secret Doctrine" – a work which gives out all that can be given out during this century, is an attempt to lay bare *in part* the common foundation and inheritance of all – great and small religious and philosophical schemes. It was found indispensable to tear away all this mass of concreted misconceptions and prejudice which now hides the parent trunk of (*a*) all the great world-religions; (*b*) of the smaller sects; and (*c*) of Theosophy as it stands now – however veiled the great Truth, by ourselves and our limited knowledge. The crust of error is thick, laid on by whatever hand; and because we *personally* have tried to remove some of it, the effort became the standing reproach against all theosophical writers and even the Society. Few among our friends and readers have failed to characterize our attempt to expose error in the *Theosophist* and *Lucifer* as "very uncharitable attacks on Christianity," "untheosophical assaults," etc., etc. Yet these are necessary, nay, indispensable, if we wish to plough up at least *approximate* truths. We have to lay things bare, and are ready to suffer for it – as usual. It is vain to promise to *give* truth, and then leave it mingled with error out of mere faint-heartedness. That the result of such policy could only muddy the stream of facts is shown plainly. After twelve years of incessant labour and struggle with enemies from the four quarters of the globe, notwithstanding our four theosophical monthly journals – the *Theosophist, Path, Lucifer,* and the French *Lotus* – our wish-washy, tame protests in them, our timid declarations, our "masterly policy of inactivity," and playing at hide-and-seek in the shadow of dreary metaphysics, have only led to Theosophy being seriously regarded as a religious SECT. For the hundredth time we are told – "What good is Theosophy doing?" and "See what good the Churches are doing!"

Nevertheless, it is an averred fact that mankind is not a whit better in morality, and in some respects ten times worse now, than it ever was in the days of Paganism. Moreover, for the last half century, from that period when Freethought and Science got the best of the Churches – Christianity is yearly losing far more adherents among the cultured classes than it gains proselytes in the lower *strata*, the scum of Heathendom. On the other hand, Theosophy has brought back from Materialism and blank despair to belief (based on logic and evidence) in man's *divine* Self, and the immortality of the latter, more than one of those whom the Church has lost through dogma, exaction of faith and tyranny. And, if it is proven that Theosophy saves one man only in a thousand of those the Church has lost, is not the former a far higher factor for good than all the missionaries put together?

Theosophy, as repeatedly declared in print and *viva voce by* its members and officers, proceeds on diametrically opposite lines to those which are trodden by the Church; and Theosophy rejects the methods of Science, since her inductive methods can only lead to crass materialism. Yet, *de facto*, Theosophy claims to be both "RELIGION" and "SCIENCE," for Theosophy is the essence of both. It is for the sake and love of the two divine abstractions – *i.e.*, theosophical religion and science, that its Society has become the volunteer *scavenger* of both orthodox religion and modern science; as also the relentless Nemesis of those who have degraded the two noble truths to their own ends and purposes, and then divorced each violently from the other, though the two are and *must be one. To* prove this is also one of our objects in the present paper.

The modern Materialist insists on an impassable chasm between the two, pointing out that the "Conflict between Religion and Science" has ended in the triumph of the latter and the defeat of the first. The modern Theosophist refuses to see, on the contrary, any such chasm at all. If it is claimed by both Church and Science that each of them pursues the truth and *nothing but the truth,* then either one of them is mistaken, and accepts falsehood for truth, or both. Any other impediment to their reconciliation must be set down as purely *fictitious.* Truth is one, even if sought for or pursued at two different ends. Therefore, Theosophy claims to reconcile the two foes. It premises by saying that the *true* spiritual and primitive Christian religion is, as much as the other great and still older philosophies that preceded it – *the light of Truth –* "*the* life and the light of men."

But so is the *true* light of Science. Therefore, darkened as the former is now by dogmas examined through glasses smoked with the superstitions artificially produced by the Churches, this light can hardly penetrate and meet its sister ray in a science, equally as cobwebbed by paradoxes and the materialistic sophistries of the age. The teachings of the two are incompatible, and cannot agree so long as both Religious philosophy and the Science of physical and external (in philosophy, *false)* nature, insist upon the infallibility of their respective "will-o'-the wisps." The two lights, having their beams of equal length in the matter of false deductions, can but extinguish each other and produce still worse darkness. Yet, they can be reconciled on the condition that both shall clean their houses, one from the human dross of the ages, the other from the hideous excrescence of modern materialism and atheism. And as both decline, the most meritorious and best thing to do is precisely what Theosophy alone can and *will* do: *i.e.,* point out to the innocents caught by the glue of the two waylayers – verily two dragons of old, one devouring the intellects, the other the souls of men – that their supposed chasm is but an optical delusion; that, far from being one, it is but an immense garbage mound respectively erected by the two foes, as a fortification against mutual attacks.

Thus, if Theosophy does no more than point out and seriously draw the attention of the world to the fact that the *supposed* disagreement between religion and science is conditioned, on the one hand by the intelligent materialists rightly kicking against absurd human dogmas, and on the other by blind fanatics and interested churchmen who, instead of defending the souls of mankind, fight simply tooth and nail for their personal bread and butter and authority – why, even then, Theosophy will prove itself the saviour of mankind.

And now we have shown, it is hoped, what real Theosophy is, and what are its adherents. One is divine Science and a code of Ethics so sublime that no theosophist is capable of doing it justice; the others weak but sincere men. Why, then, should Theosophy ever be judged by the personal shortcomings of any leader or member of our 150 branches? One may work for it to the best of his ability, yet never raise himself to the height of his call and aspiration. This is his or her misfortune, never the fault of Theosophy, or even of the body at large. Its Founders claim no other merit than that of having set the first theosophical wheel rolling. If judged at all they must be judged by the work they have done, not by what friends may think or enemies say of them. There is no room for *personalities* in a work like ours; and all must be ready, as the Founders are, if needs be, for the car of Jaggennath to crush them *individually* for *the good of all*. It is only in the days of the dim Future, when death will have laid his cold hand on the luckless Founders and stopped thereby their activity, that their respective merits and demerits, their good and bad acts and deeds, and their theosophical work will have to be weighed on the Balance of Posterity. Then only, after the two scales with their contrasted loads have been brought to an equipoise, and the character of the net result left over has become evident to all in its full and intrinsic value, then only shall the nature of the verdict passed be determined with anything like justice. At present, except in India, those results are too scattered over the face of the earth, too much limited to a handful of individuals to be easily judged. Now, these results can hardly be perceived, much less heard of amid the din and clamour made by our teeming enemies, and their ready imitators – the indifferent. Yet however small, if once proved good, even now every man who has at heart the moral progress of humanity, owes his thankfulness to Theosophy for those results. And as Theosophy was revived and brought before the world, *viâ* its unworthy servants, the "Founders," if their work was useful, it alone must be their vindicator, regardless of the present state of their balance in the petty cash accounts of Karma, wherein social "respectabilities" are entered up.

Lucifer, November, 1888
H. P. Blavatsky

AN EPITOME OF THEOSOPHY

Theosophy, the Wisdom-Religion, has existed from immemorial time. It offers us a theory of nature and of life which is founded upon knowledge acquired by the Sages of the past, more especially those of the East; and its higher students claim that this knowledge is not imagined or inferred, but that it is a knowledge of facts seen and known by those who are willing to comply with the conditions requisite for seeing and knowing.

Theosophy, meaning knowledge of or about God (not in the sense of a personal anthropomorphic God, but in that of divine "godly" wisdom), and the term "God" being universally accepted as including the whole of both the known and the unknown, it follows that "Theosophy" must imply wisdom respecting the absolute; and, since the absolute is without beginning and eternal, this wisdom must have existed always. Hence Theosophy is sometimes called the Wisdom-Religion, because from immemorial time it has had knowledge of all the laws governing the spiritual, the moral, and the material.

The theory of nature and of life which it offers is not one that was at first speculatively laid down and then proved by adjusting facts or conclusions to fit it; but is an explanation of existence, cosmic and individual, derived from knowledge reached by those who have acquired the power to see behind the curtain that hides the operations of nature from the ordinary mind. Such Beings are called Sages, using the term in its highest sense. Of late they have been called *Mahatmas* and Adepts. In ancient times they were known as the *Rishis* and *Maha-Rishis* – the last being a word that means Great *Rishis*.

It is not claimed that these exalted beings, or Sages, have existed only in the East. They are known to have lived in all parts of the globe, in obedience to the cyclic laws referred to below. But as far as concerns the present development of the human race on this planet, they now are to be found in the East, although the fact may be that some of them had, in remote times, retreated from even the American shores.

There being of necessity various grades among the students of this Wisdom-Religion, it stands to reason that those belonging to the lower degrees are able to give out only so much of the knowledge as is the appanage of the grade they have reached, and depend, to some extent, for further information upon students who are higher yet. It is these higher students for whom the claim is asserted that their knowledge is not mere inference, but that it concerns realities seen and known by them. While some of them are connected with the Theosophical Society, they are yet above it. The power to see and absolutely know such laws is surrounded by natural inherent regulations which must be complied with as conditions precedent; and it is, therefore, not possible to respond to the demand of the worldly man for an immediate statement of this wisdom, insomuch as he could not comprehend it until those conditions are fulfilled. As this knowledge deals with laws and states of matter, and of consciousness undreamed of by the "practical" Western world, it can only be grasped, piece by piece, as the student pushes forward the demolition of his preconceived notions, that are due either to inadequate or to erroneous theories. It is claimed by these higher students that, in the Occident especially, a false method of reasoning has for many centuries prevailed, resulting in a universal habit of mind which causes men to look upon many effects as causes, and to regard that which is real as the unreal, putting meanwhile the unreal in the place of the real. As a minor example, the phenomena of mesmerism and clairvoyance have, until lately, been denied by Western science, yet there have always been numerous persons who know for themselves, by incontrovertible introspective evidence, the truth of these phenomena, and, in some instances, understand their cause and rationale.

The following are some of the fundamental propositions of Theosophy:

The spirit in man is the only real and permanent part of his being; the rest of his nature being variously compounded. And since decay is incident to all composite things, everything in man but his spirit is impermanent.

Further, the universe being one thing and not diverse, and everything within it being connected with the whole and with every other thing therein, of which upon the upper plane (below referred to) there is a perfect knowledge, no act or thought occurs without each portion of the great whole perceiving and noting it. Hence all are inseparably bound together by the tie of Brotherhood.

This first fundamental proposition of Theosophy postulates that the universe is not an aggregation of diverse unities but that it is one whole. This whole is what is denominated "Deity" by Western Philosophers, and "*Para-Brahma*" by the Hindu Vedantins. It may be called the Unmanifested, containing within itself the potency of every form of manifestation, together with the laws governing those manifestations. Further, it is taught that there is no creation of worlds in the theological sense; but that their appearance is due strictly to evolution. When the time comes for the Unmanifested to manifest as an objective Universe, which it does periodically, it emanates a Power or "The First Cause" so called because it itself is the rootless root of that Cause, and called in the East the "Causeless Cause." The first Cause we may call *Brahma*, or Ormazd, or Osiris, or by any name we please. The projection into time of the influence or so-called "breath of *Brahma*" causes all the worlds and the beings upon them to gradually appear. They remain in manifestation just as long as that influence continues to proceed forth in evolution. After long aeons the outbreathing, evolutionary influence slackens, and the universe begins to go into obscuration, or *Pralaya*, until, the "breath" being fully indrawn, no objects remain, because nothing *is* but *Brahma*. Care must be taken by the student to make a distinction between *Brahma* (the impersonal *Parabrahma*) and *Brahma* the manifested *Logos*. A discussion of the means used by this power in acting would be out of place in this Epitome, but of those means Theosophy also treats.

This breathing-forth is known as a *Manvantara*, or the Manifestation of the world between two *Manus* (from *Manu*, and *Antara* "between") and the completion of the inbreathing brings with it *Pralaya*, or destruction. It is from these truths that the erroneous doctrines of "creation" and the "last judgment" have sprung. Such *Manvantaras* and *Pralayas* have eternally occurred, and will continue to take place periodically and forever.

For the purpose of a *Manvantara* two so-called eternal principles are postulated, that is, *Purusha* and *Prakriti* (or spirit and matter), because both are ever present and conjoined in each manifestation. Those terms are used here because no equivalent for them exists in English. *Purusha* is called "spirit," and *Prakriti* "matter," but this *Purusha* is not the unmanifested, nor is *Prakriti* matter as known to science; the Aryan Sages therefore declare that there is a higher spirit still, called *Purushottama*. The reason for this is that at the night of *Brahma*, or the so-called indrawing of his breath, both *Purusha* and *Prakriti* are absorbed in the Unmanifested; a conception which is the same as the idea underlying the Biblical expression – "remaining in the bosom of the Father."

This brings us to the doctrine of Universal Evolution as expounded by the Sages of the Wisdom-Religion. The Spirit, or *Purusha*, they say, proceeds from *Brahma* through the various forms of matter evolved at the same time, beginning in the world of the spiritual from the highest and in the material world from the lowest form. The lowest form is one unknown as yet to modern science. Thus, therefore, the mineral, vegetable and animal forms each imprison a spark of the Divine, a portion of the indivisible *Purusha*.

These sparks struggle to "return to the Father," or in other words, to secure self-consciousness and at last come into the highest form, on Earth, that of man, where alone self-consciousness is possible to them. The period, calculated in human time, during which this evolution goes on embraces millions of ages. Each spark of divinity has, therefore, millions of ages in which to accomplish its mission – that of obtaining complete self-consciousness while in the form of man. But by this is not meant that the mere act of coming into human form of itself confers self-consciousness upon this divine spark. That great work may be accomplished during the *Manvantara* in which a Divine spark reaches the human form, or it may not; all depends upon the individual's own will and efforts. Each particular spirit thus goes through the *Manvantara*, or enters into manifestation for its own enrichment and for that of the Whole. *Mahatmas* and *Rishis* are thus gradually evolved during a *Manvantara*, and become, after its expiration, planetary spirits, who guide the evolutions of other future planets. The planetary spirits of our globe are those who in previous *Manvantara*s – or days of *Brahma* – made the efforts, and became in the course of that long period *Mahatmas*.

Each *Manvantara* is for the same end and purpose, so that the *Mahatmas* who have now attained those heights, or those who may become such in the succeeding years of the present *Manvantara*, will probably be the planetary spirits of the next *Manvantara* for this or other planets. This system is thus seen to be based upon the identity of Spiritual Being, and, under the name of "Universal Brotherhood," constitutes the basic idea of the Theosophical Society, whose object is the realization of that Brotherhood among men.

The Sages say that this *Purusha* is the basis of all manifested objects. Without it nothing could exist or cohere. It interpenetrates everything everywhere. It is the reality of which, or upon which, those things called real by us are mere images. As *Purusha* reaches to and embraces all beings, they are all connected together; and in or on the plane where that *Purusha* is, there is a perfect consciousness of every act, thought, object, and circumstance, whether supposed to occur there, or on this plane, or any other. For below the spirit and above the intellect is a plane of consciousness in which experiences are noted, commonly called man's "spiritual nature"; this is frequently said to be as susceptible of culture as his body or his intellect.

This upper plane is the real register of all sensations and experiences, although there are other registering planes. It is sometimes called the "subconscious mind." Theosophy, however, holds that it is a misuse of terms to say that the spiritual nature can be cultivated. The real object to be kept in view is to so open up or make porous the lower nature that the spiritual nature may shine through it and become the guide and ruler. It is only "cultivated" in the sense of having a vehicle prepared for its use, into which it may descend. In other words, it is held that the real man, who is the higher self – being the spark of the Divine before alluded to – overshadows the visible being, which has the possibility of becoming united to that spark. Thus it is said that the higher Spirit is not in the man, but above him. It is always peaceful, unconcerned, blissful, and full of absolute knowledge. It continually partakes of the Divine state, being continually that state itself, "conjoined with the Gods, it feeds upon Ambrosia." The object of the student is to let the light of that spirit shine through the lower coverings.

This "spiritual culture" is only attainable as the grosser interests, passions, and demands of the flesh are subordinated to the interests, aspirations and needs of the higher nature; and this is a matter of both system and established law.

This spirit can only become the ruler when the firm intellectual acknowledgment or admission is first made that IT alone is. And, as stated above, it being not only the person concerned but also the whole, all selfishness must be eliminated from the lower nature before its divine state can be reached. So long as the smallest personal or selfish desire even for spiritual attainment for our own sake remains, so long is the desired end put off. Hence the above term "demands of the flesh" really covers also demands that are not of the flesh, and its proper rendering would be "desires of the personal nature, including those of the individual soul."

When systematically trained in accordance with the aforesaid system and law, men attain to clear insight into the immaterial, spiritual world, and their interior faculties apprehend truth as immediately and readily as physical faculties grasp the things of sense, or mental faculties those of reason. Or, in the words used by some of them, "They are able to look directly upon ideas"; and hence their testimony to such truth is as trustworthy as is that of scientists or philosophers to truth in their respective fields.

In the course of this spiritual training such men acquire perception of, and control over, various forces in Nature unknown to other men, and thus are able to perform works usually called "miraculous," though really but the result of larger knowledge of natural law. What these powers are may be found in Patanjali's *"Yoga Philosophy."*

Their testimony as to super-sensuous truth, verified by their possession of such powers, challenges candid examination from every religious mind.

Turning now to the system expounded by these sages, we find, in the first place, an account of cosmogony, the past and future of this earth and other planets, the evolution of life through elemental, mineral, vegetable, animal and human forms, as they are called.

These "passive life elementals" are unknown to modern science, though sometimes approached by it as a subtle material agent in the production of life, whereas they are a form of life itself.

Each *Kalpa*, or grand period, is divided into four ages or *yugas*, each lasting many thousands of years, and each one being marked by a predominant characteristic. These are the *Satya-Yuga* (or age of truth), the *Treta-Yuga*, the *Dvapara-Yuga*, and our present *Kali-Yuga* (or age of darkness), which began five thousand years back. The word "darkness" here refers to spiritual and not material darkness. In this age, however, all causes bring about their effects much more rapidly than in any other age – a fact due to the intensified momentum of "evil," as the course of its cycle is about rounding towards that of a new cycle of truth. Thus a sincere lover of the race can accomplish more in three incarnations during *Kali-Yuga*, than he could in a much greater number in any other age. The darkness of this age is not absolute, but is greater than that of other ages; its main tendency being towards materiality, while having some mitigation in occasional ethical or scientific advance conducive to the well-being of the race, by the removal of immediate causes of crime or disease.

Our Earth is one of a chain of seven planets, it alone being on the visible plane, while the six others are on different planes, and therefore invisible. (The other planets of our solar system belong each to a chain of seven.) And the life-wave passes from the higher to the lower in the chain until it reaches our earth, and then ascends and passes to the three others on the opposite arc, and thus seven times. The evolution of forms is coincident with this progress, the tide of life bearing with it the mineral and vegetable forms, until each globe in turn is ready to receive the human life wave. Of these globes our Earth is the fourth.

Humanity passes from globe to globe in a series of Rounds, first circling about each globe, and reincarnating upon it a fixed number of times. Concerning the human evolution on the concealed planets or globes little is permitted to be said. We have to concern ourselves with our Earth alone. The latter, when the wave of humanity has reached it for the last time (in this, our Fourth Round), began to evolute man, subdividing him into races. Each of these races when it has, through evolution, reached the period known as "the moment of choice" and decided its future destiny as an individual race, begins to disappear.

The races are separated, moreover, from each other by catastrophes of nature, such as the subsidence of continents and great natural convulsions. Coincidently with the development of races the development of specialized senses takes place; thus our fifth race has so far developed five senses.

The Sages further tell us that the affairs of this world and its people are subject to cyclic laws, and during any one cycle the rate or quality of progress appertaining to a different cycle is not possible. These cyclic laws operate in each age. As the ages grow darker the same laws prevail, only the cycles are shorter; that is, they are the same length in the absolute sense, but go over the given limit in a shorter period of time. These laws impose restrictions on the progress of the race. In a cycle, where all is ascending and descending, the Adepts must wait until the time comes before they can aid the race to ascend. They cannot, and must not, interfere with Karmic law. Thus they begin to work actively again in the spiritual sense, when the cycle is known by them to be approaching its turning point.

At the same time these cycles have no hard lines or points of departure or inception, inasmuch as one may be ending or drawing to a close for some time after another has already begun. They thus overlap and shade into one another, as day does into night; and it is only when the one has completely ended and the other has really begun by bringing out its blossoms, that we can say we are in a new cycle. It may be illustrated by comparing two adjacent cycles to two interlaced circles, where the circumference of one touches the center of the other, so that the moment where one ended and the other began would be at the point where the circumferences intersected each other. Or by imagining a man as representing, in the act of walking, the progress of the cycles; his rate of advancement can only be obtained by taking the distance covered by his paces, the points at the middle of each pace, between the feet, being the beginning of cycles and their ending.

The cyclic progress is assisted, or the deterioration further permitted, in this way; at a time when the cycle is ascending, developed and progressed Beings, known in Sanskrit by the term "*Jnanis*," descend to this earth from other spheres where the cycle is going down, in order that they may also help the spiritual progress of this globe. In like manner they leave this sphere when our cycle approaches darkness. These *Jnanis* must not, however, be confounded with the *Mahatmas* and Adepts mentioned above. The right aim of true Theosophists should, therefore, be so to live that their influence may be conducive for the dispelling of darkness to the end that such *Jnanis* may turn again towards this sphere.

Theosophy also teaches the existence of a universal diffused and highly ethereal medium, which has been called the "Astral Light" and "*Akasa*." It is the repository of all past, present, and future events, and in it are recorded the effects of spiritual causes, and of all acts and thoughts from the direction of either spirit or matter. It may be called the Book of the Recording Angel.

Akasa, however, is a misnomer when it is confused with Ether or the astral light of the Kabalists. *Akasa* is the noumenon of the phenomenal Ether or astral light proper, for *Akasa* is infinite, impartite, intangible, its only production being Sound. (*Akasa* in the mysticism of the Esoteric Philosophy is, properly speaking, the female "Holy Ghost"; "Sound" or speech being the *Logos* – the manifested *Verbum* of the unmanifested Mother. (See *Sankhyasara* by Vijnana Bhikshu, Preface, p. 33, et seq.)

And this astral light is material and not spirit. It is, in fact, the lower principle of that cosmic body of which *Akasa* is the highest. It has the power of retaining all images. This includes a statement that each thought as well as word and act makes an image there. These images may be said to have two lives. First. Their own as an image. Second. The impress left by them in the matrix of the astral light. In the upper realm of this light there is no such thing as space or time in the human sense. All future events are the thoughts and acts of men; these are producers in advance of the picture of the event which is to occur. Ordinary men continually, recklessly, and wickedly, are making these events sure to come to pass, but the Sages, *Mahatmas*, and the Adepts of the good law, make only such pictures as are in accordance with Divine law, because they control the production of their thought. In the astral light are all the differentiated sounds as well. The elementals are energic centers in it. The shades of departed human beings and animals are also there. Hence, any seer or entranced person can see in it all that anyone has done or said, as well as that which has happened to anyone with whom he is connected. Hence, also, the identity of deceased persons – who are supposed to report specially out of this plane – is not to be concluded from the giving of forgotten or unknown words, facts, or ideas. Out of this plane of matter can be taken the pictures of all who have ever lived, and then reflected on a suitable magneto-electrical surface, so as to seem like the apparition of the deceased, producing all the sensations of weight, hardness, and extension.

Through the means of the Astral Light and the help of Elementals, the various material elements may be drawn down and precipitated from the atmosphere upon either a plane surface or in the form of a solid object; this precipitation may be made permanent, or it may be of such a light cohesive power as soon to fade away. But the help of the elementals can only be obtained by a strong will added to a complete knowledge of the laws which govern the being of the elementals. It is useless to give further details on this point; first, because the untrained student cannot understand; and second, the complete explanation is not permitted, were it even possible in this space.

The world of the elementals is an important factor in our world and in the course of the student. Each thought as it is evolved by a man coalesces instantly with an elemental, and is then beyond the man's power.

It can easily be seen that this process is going on every instant. Therefore, each thought exists as an entity. Its length of life depends on two things: (*a*) The original force of the person's will and thought; (*b*) The power of the elemental which coalesced with it, the latter being determined by the class to which the elemental belongs. This is the case with good and bad thoughts alike, and as the will beneath the generality of wicked thoughts is usually powerful, we can see that the result is very important, because the elemental has no conscience and obtains its constitution and direction from the thought it may from time to time carry.

Each human being has his own elementals that partake of his nature and his thoughts. If you fix your thoughts upon a person in anger, or in critical, uncharitable judgment, you attract to yourself a number of those elementals that belong to, generate, and are generated by this particular fault or failing, and they precipitate themselves upon you. Hence, through the injustice of your merely human condemnation, which cannot know the source and causes of the action of another, you at once become a sharer of his fault or failing by your own act, and the spirit expelled returns "with seven devils worse than himself."

This is the origin of the popular saying that "curses, like chickens, come home to roost," and has its root in the laws governing magnetic affinity.

In the *Kali-Yuga* we are hypnotized by the effect of the immense body of images in the Astral Light, compounded of all the deeds, thoughts, and so forth of our ancestors, whose lives tended in a material direction. These images influence the inner man – who is conscious of them – by suggestion. In a brighter age the influence of such images would be towards Truth. The effect of the Astral Light, as thus molded and painted by us, will remain so long as we continue to place those images there, and it thus becomes our judge and our executioner. Every universal law thus contains within itself the means for its own accomplishment and the punishment for its violation, and requires no further authority to postulate it or to carry out its decrees.

The Astral Light by its inherent action both evolves and destroys forms. It is the universal register. Its chief office is that of a vehicle for the operation of the laws of *Karma*, or the progress of the principle of life, and it is thus in a deep spiritual sense a medium or "mediator" between man and his Deity – his higher spirit.

Theosophy also tells of the origin, history, development and destiny of mankind.

Upon the subject of Man it teaches:

- First. That each spirit is a manifestation of the One Spirit, and thus a part of all. It passes through a series of experiences in incarnation, and is destined to ultimate reunion with the Divine.

- Second. That this incarnation is not single but repeated, each individuality becoming re-embodied during numerous existences in successive races and planets of our chain, and accumulating the experiences of each incarnation towards its perfection.
- Third. That between adjacent incarnations, after grosser elements are first purged away, comes a period of comparative rest and refreshment, called *Devachan* – the soul being therein prepared for its next advent into material life.

The constitution of man is subdivided in a septenary manner, the main divisions being those of body, soul and spirit. These divisions and their relative development govern his subjective condition after death. The real division cannot be understood, and must for a time remain esoteric, because it requires certain senses not usually developed for its understanding. If the present seven-fold division, as given by Theosophical writers is adhered to strictly and without any conditional statement, it will give rise to controversy or error. For instance, Spirit is not a seventh principle. It is the synthesis, or the whole, and is equally present in the other six. The present various divisions can only be used as a general working hypothesis, to be developed and corrected as students advance and themselves develop.

The state of spiritual but comparative rest known as *Devachan* is not an eternal one, and so is not the same as the eternal heaven of Christianity. Nor does "hell" correspond to the state known to Theosophical writers as *Avichi*.

All such painful states are transitory and purificatory states. When those are passed the individual goes into *Devachan*.

"Hell" and *Avichi* are thus not the same. *Avichi* is the same as the "second death," as it is in fact annihilation that only comes to the "black Magician" or spiritually wicked, as will be seen further on.

The nature of each incarnation depends upon the balance as struck of the merit and demerit of the previous life or lives – upon the way in which the man has lived and thought; and this law is inflexible and wholly just.

"*Karma*" – a term signifying two things, the law of ethical causation (Whatsoever a man soweth, that shall he also reap); and the balance or excess of merit or demerit in any individual, determines also the main experiences of joy and sorrow in each incarnation, so that what we call "luck" is in reality "desert" – desert acquired in past existence.

Karma is not all exhausted in a single life, nor is a person necessarily in this life experiencing the effect of all his previous *Karma*; for some may be held back by various causes. The principle cause is the failure of the Ego to acquire a body which will furnish the instrument or apparatus in and by which the meditation or thoughts of previous lives can have their effect and be ripened. Hence it is held that there is a mysterious power in the man's thoughts during a life, sure to bring about its results in either an immediately succeeding life or in one many lives distant; that is, in whatever life the Ego obtains a body capable of being the focus, apparatus, or instrument for the ripening of past *Karma*. There is also a swaying or diverging power in *Karma* in its effects upon the soul, for a certain course of life – or thought – will influence the soul in that direction for sometimes three lives, before the beneficial or bad effect of any other sort of *Karma* can be felt. Nor does it follow that every minute portion of *Karma* must be felt in the same detail as when produced, for several sorts of *Karma* may come to a head together at one point in the life, and, by their combined effect, produce a result which, while, as a whole, accurately representing all the elements in it, still is a different *Karma* from each single component part. This may be known as the nullification of the postulated effect of the classes of *Karma* involved.

The process of evolution up to reunion with the Divine is and includes successive elevation from rank to rank of power and usefulness. The most exalted beings still in the flesh are known as Sages, *Rishis*, Brothers, Masters. Their great function being the preservation at all times, and when cyclic laws permit, the extension of spiritual knowledge and influence.

When union with the Divine is effected, all the events and experiences of each incarnation are known.

As to the process of spiritual development, Theosophy teaches:

- First. That the essence of the process lies in the securing of supremacy, to the highest, the spiritual, element of man's nature.

- Second. That this is attained along four lines, among others, –

  (a) The entire eradication of selfishness in all forms, and the cultivation of *broad, generous* sympathy in, and effort for the good of others.

  (b) The absolute cultivation of the inner, spiritual man by meditation, by reaching to and communion with the Divine, and by exercise of the kind described by Patanjali, i.e., incessant striving to an ideal end.

  (c) The control of fleshly appetites and desires, all lower, material interests being deliberately subordinated to the behests of the spirit.

  (d) The careful performance of every duty belonging to one's station in life, without desire for reward, leaving results for Divine law.

- Third. That while the above is incumbent on and practicable by all religiously disposed men, a yet higher plane of spiritual attainment is conditioned upon a specific course of training, physical, intellectual and spiritual, by which the internal faculties are first aroused and then developed.

- Fourth. That an extension of this process is reached in Adeptship, Mahatmaship, or the states of *Rishis*, Sages and Dhyani-Chohans, which are all exalted stages, attained by laborious self-discipline and hardship, protracted through possibly many incarnations, and with many degrees of initiation and preferment, beyond which are yet other stages ever approaching the Divine.

As to the rationale of spiritual development it asserts:

- First. That the process takes place entirely within the individual himself, the motive, the effort, and the result proceeding from his own inner nature, along the lines of self-evolution.

- Second. That, however personal and interior, this process is not unaided, being possible, in fact, only through close communion with the supreme source of all strength.

As to the degree of advancement in incarnations it holds:

1. First. That even a mere intellectual acquaintance with Theosophic truth has great value in fitting the individual for a step upwards in his next earth-life, as it gives an impulse in that direction.

2. Second. That still more is gained by a career of duty, piety and beneficence.

3. Third. That a still greater advance is attained by the attentive and devoted use of the means to spiritual culture heretofore stated.

4. Fourth. That every race and individual of it reaches in evolution a period known as "the moment of choice," when they decide for themselves their future destiny by a deliberate and conscious choice between eternal life and death, and that this right of choice is the peculiar appanage of the free soul. It cannot be exercised until the man has realized the soul within him, and until that soul has attained some measure of self-consciousness in the body.

The moment of choice is not a fixed period of time; it is made up of all moments. It cannot come unless all the previous lives have led up to it. For the race as a whole it has not yet come. Any individual can hasten the advent of this period for himself under the previously stated law of the ripening of *Karma*. Should he then fail to choose right he is not wholly condemned, for the economy of nature provides that he shall again and again have the opportunity of choice when the moment arrives for the whole race. After this period the race, having blossomed, tends towards its dissolution. A few individuals of it will have outstripped its progress and attained Adeptship or Mahatmaship.

The main body, who have chosen aright, but who have not attained salvation, pass into the subjective condition, there to await the influx of the human life wave into the next globe, which they are the first souls to people; the deliberate choosers of evil, whose lives are passed in great spiritual wickedness (for evil done for the sheer love of evil *per se*), sever the connection with the Divine Spirit, or the Monad, which forever abandons the human Ego. Such Egos pass into the misery of the eighth sphere, as far as we understand, there to remain until the separation between what they had thus cultivated and the personal Isvara or divine spark is complete. But this tenet has never been explained to us by the Masters, who have always refused to answer and to explain it conclusively. At the next *Manvantara* that Divine Spark will probably begin again the long evolutionary journey, being cast into the stream of life at the source and passing upward again through all the lower forms.

So long as the connection with the Divine Monad is not severed, this annihilation of personality cannot take place. Something of that personality will always remain attached to the immortal Ego. Even after such severance the human being may live on, a man among men – a soulless being. This disappointment, so to call it, of the Divine Spark by depriving it of its chosen vehicle constitutes the "sin against the Holy Ghost," which its very nature forbade it to pardon, because it cannot continue an association with principles which have become degraded and vitiated in the absolute sense, so that they no longer respond to cyclic or evolutionary impulses, but, weighted by their own nature, sink to the lowest depths of matter. The connection, once wholly broken, cannot in the nature of Being be resumed. But innumerable opportunities for return offer themselves throughout the dissolving process, which lasts thousands of years.

There is also a fate that comes to even Adepts of the Good Law which is somewhat similar to a loss of "heaven" after its enjoyment for incalculable periods of time. When the Adept has reached a certain very high point in his evolution he may, by a mere wish, become what the Hindus call a "*Deva*" – or lesser god. If he does this, then, although he will enjoy the bliss and power of that state for a vast length of time, he will not at the next *Pralaya* partake of the conscious life "in the bosom of the Father," but has to pass down into matter at the next new "creation," performing certain functions that could not now be made clear, and has to come up again through the elemental world; but this fate is not like that of the Black Magician who falls into *Avichi*. And again between the two he can choose the middle state and become a *Nirmanakaya* – one who gives up the bliss of Nirvana and remains in conscious existence outside of his body after its death; in order to help Humanity. This is the greatest sacrifice he can do for mankind. By advancement from one degree of interest and comparative attainment to another as above stated, the student hastens the advent of the moment of choice, after which his rate of progress is greatly intensified.

It may be added that Theosophy is the only system of religion and philosophy which gives satisfactory explanation of such problems as these:

- First. The object, use, and inhabitation of other planets than this earth, which planets serve to complete and prolong the evolutionary course, and to fill the required measure of the universal experience of souls.

- Second. The geological cataclysms of earth; the frequent absence of intermediate types in its fauna; the occurrence of architectural and other relics of races now lost, and as to which ordinary science has nothing but vain conjecture; the nature of extinct civilizations and the causes of their extinction; the persistence of savagery and the unequal development of existing civilizations; the differences, physical and internal, between the various races of men; the line of future development.

- Third. The contrasts and unisons of the world's faiths, and the common foundation underlying them all.

- Fourth. The existence of evil, of suffering, and of sorrow – a hopeless puzzle to the mere philanthropist or theologian.

- Fifth. The inequalities in social condition and privilege; the sharp contrasts between wealth and poverty, intelligence and stupidity, culture and ignorance, virtue and vileness; the appearance of men of genius in families destitute of it, as well as other facts in conflict with the law of heredity; the frequent cases of unfitness of environment around individuals, so sore as to embitter disposition, hamper aspiration, and paralyze endeavor; the violent antithesis between character and condition; the occurrence of accident, misfortune and untimely death – all of them problems solvable only by either the conventional theory of Divine caprice or the Theosophic doctrines of *Karma* and Reincarnation.

- Sixth. The possession by individuals of psychic powers – clairvoyance, clairaudience, etc., as well as the phenomena of psychometry and statuvolism.

- Seventh. The true nature of genuine phenomena in spiritualism, and the proper antidote to superstition and to exaggerated expectation.

- Eighth. The failure of conventional religions to greatly extend their areas, reform abuses, reorganize society, expand the idea of brotherhood, abate discontent, diminish crime, and elevate humanity; and an apparent inadequacy to realize in individual lives the ideal they professedly uphold.

William Q. Judge

THEOSOPHY GENERALLY STATED

The claim is made that an impartial study of history, religion and literature will show the existence from ancient times of a great body of philosophical, scientific and ethical doctrine forming the basis and origin of all similar thought in modern systems. It is at once religious and scientific, asserting that religion and science should never be separated. It puts forward sublime religious and ideal teachings, but at the same time shows that all of it can be demonstrated to reason, and that authority other than that has no place, thus preventing the hypocrisy which arises from asserting dogmas on authority which no one can show as resting on reason. This ancient body of doctrine is known as the "Wisdom Religion" and was always taught by adepts or initiates therein who preserve it through all time. Hence, and from other doctrines demonstrated, it is shown that man, being spirit and immortal, is able to perpetuate his real life and consciousness, and has done so during all time in the persons of those higher flowers of the human race who are members of an ancient and high brotherhood who concern themselves with the soul development of man, held by them to include every process of evolution on all planes. The initiates, being bound by the law of evolution, must work with humanity as its development permits. Therefore from time to time they give out again and again the same doctrine which from time to time grows obscured in various nations and places. This is the wisdom religion, and they are the keepers of it. At times they come to nations as great teachers and 'saviours," who only re-promulgate the old truths and system of ethics. This therefore holds that humanity is capable of infinite perfection both in time and quality, the saviours and adepts being held up as examples of that possibility.

From this living and presently acting body of perfected men H.P. Blavatsky declared she received the impulse to once more bring forward the old ideas, and from them also received several keys to ancient and modern doctrines that had been lost during modern struggles toward civilization, and also that she was furnished by them with some doctrines really ancient but entirely new to the present day in any exoteric shape. These she wrote among the other keys furnished by her to her fellow members and the world at large. Added, then, to the testimony through all time found in records of all nations we have this modern explicit assertion that the ancient learned and humanitarian body of adepts still exists on this earth and takes an interest in the development of the race.

Theosophy postulates an eternal principle called the unknown, which can never be cognized except through its manifestations. This eternal principle is in and is everything and being; it periodically and eternally manifests itself and recedes again from manifestation. In this ebb and flow evolution proceeds and itself is the progress of the manifestation. The perceived universe is the manifestation of this unknown, including spirit and matter, for Theosophy holds that those are but the two opposite poles of the one unknown principle. They coexist, are not separate nor separable from each other, or, as the Hindu scriptures say, there is no particle of matter without spirit, and no particle of spirit without matter. In manifesting itself the spirit-matter differentiates on seven planes, each more dense on the way down to the plane of our senses than its predecessor, the substance in all being the same, only differing in degree. Therefore from this view the whole universe is alive, not one atom of it being in any sense dead. It is also conscious and intelligent, its consciousness and intelligence being present on all planes though obscured on this one. On this plane of ours the spirit focalizes itself in all human beings who choose to permit it to do so, and the refusal to permit it is the cause of ignorance, of sin of all sorrow and suffering. In all ages some have come to this high state, have grown to be as gods, are partakers actively in the work of nature, and go on from century to century widening their consciousness and increasing the scope of their government in nature. This is the destiny of all beings, and hence at the outset Theosophy postulates this perfectibility of the race, removes the idea of innate unregenerable wickedness, and offers a purpose and an aim for life which is consonant with the longings of the soul and with its real nature, tending at the same time to destroy pessimism with its companion, despair.

In Theosophy the world is held to be the product of the evolution of the principle spoken of from the very lowest first forms of life guided as it proceeded by intelligent perfected beings from other and older evolutions, and compounded also of the egos or individual spirits for and by whom it emanates. Hence man as we know him is held to be a conscious spirit, the flower of evolution, with other and lower classes of egos below him in the lower kingdoms, all however coming up and destined one day to be on the same human stage as we now are, we then being higher still. Man's consciousness being thus more perfect is able to pass from one to another of the planes of differentiation mentioned. If he mistakes any one of them for the reality that he is in his essence, he is deluded; the object of evolution then is to give him complete self-consciousness so that he may go on to higher stages in the progress of the universe. His evolution after coming on the human stage is for the getting of experience, and in order to so raise up and purify the various planes of matter with which he has to do, that the voice of the spirit may be fully heard and comprehended.

He is a religious being because he is a spirit encased in matter, which is in turn itself spiritual in essence. Being a spirit he requires vehicles with which to come in touch with all the planes of nature included in evolution, and it is these vehicles that make of him an intricate, composite being, liable to error, but at the same time able to rise above all delusions and conquer the highest place. He is in miniature the universe, for he is as spirit, manifesting himself to himself by means of seven differentiations. Therefore is he known in Theosophy as a sevenfold being. The Christian division of body, soul, and spirit is accurate so far as it goes, but will not answer to the problems of life and nature, unless, as is not the case, those three divisions are each held to be composed of others, which would raise the possible total to seven. The spirit stands alone at the top, next comes the spiritual soul or *Buddhi* as it is called in Sanskrit. This partakes more of the spirit than any below it, and is connected with *Manas* or mind, these three being the real trinity of man, the imperishable part, the real thinking entity living on the earth in the other and denser vehicles by its evolution. Below in order of quality is the plane of the desires and passions shared with the animal kingdom, unintelligent, and the producer of ignorance flowing from delusion. It is distinct from the will and judgment, and must therefore be given its own place. On this plane is gross life, manifesting, not as spirit from which it derives its essence, but as energy and motion on this plane. It being common to the whole objective plane and being everywhere, is also to be classed by itself, the portion used by man being given up at the death of the body. Then last, before the objective body, is the model or double of the outer physical case. This double is the astral body belonging to the astral plane of matter, not so dense as physical molecules, but more tenuous and much stronger, as well as lasting. It is the original of the body permitting the physical molecules to arrange and show themselves thereon, allowing them to go and come from day to day as they are known to do, yet ever retaining the fixed shape and contour given by the astral double within. These lower four principles or sheaths are the transitory perishable part of man, not him-self, but in every sense the instrument he uses, given up at the hour of death like an old garment, and rebuilt out of the general reservoir at every new birth. The trinity is the real man, the thinker, the individuality that passes from house to house, gaining experience at each rebirth, while it suffers and enjoys according to its deeds – it is the one central man, the living spirit-soul.

Now this spiritual man, having always existed, being intimately concerned in evolution, dominated by the law of cause and effect, because in himself he is that very law, showing moreover on this plane varieties of force of character, capacity, and opportunity, his very presence must be explained, while the differences noted have to be accounted for. The doctrine of reincarnation does all this. It means that man as a thinker, composed of soul, mind and spirit, occupies body after body in life after life on the earth which is the scene of his evolution, and where he must, under the very laws of his being, complete that evolution, once it has been begun. In any one life he is known to others as a personality, but in the whole stretch of eternity he is one individual, feeling in himself an identity not dependent on name, form, or recollection.

This doctrine is the very base of Theosophy, for it explains life and nature. It is one aspect of evolution, for as it is re- embodiment in meaning, and as evolution could not go on without re-embodiment, it is evolution itself, as applied to the human soul. But it is also a doctrine believed in at the time given to Jesus and taught in the early ages of Christianity, being now as much necessary to that religion as it is to any other to explain texts, to reconcile the justice of God with the rough and merciless aspect of nature and life to most mortals, and to throw a light perceptible by reason on all the problems that vex us in our journey through this world. The vast, and under any other doctrine unjust, difference between the savage and the civilized man as to both capacity, character, and opportunity can be understood only through this doctrine, and coming to our own stratum the differences of the same kind may only thus be explained. It vindicates Nature and God, and removes from religion the blot thrown by men who have postulated creeds which paint the creator as a demon. Each man's life and character are the outcome of his previous lives and thoughts. Each is his own judge, his own executioner, for it is his own hand that forges the weapon which works for his punishment, and each by his own life reaches reward, rises to heights of knowledge and power for the good of all who may be left behind him. Nothing is left to chance, favour, or partiality, but all is under the governance of law. Man is a thinker, and by his thoughts he makes the causes for woe or bliss; for his thoughts produce his acts. He is the centre for any disturbance of the universal harmony, and to him as the centre the disturbance must return so as to bring about equilibrium, for nature always works towards harmony. Man is always carrying on a series of thoughts, which extend back to the remote past, continually making action and reaction. He is thus responsible for all his thoughts and acts, and in that his complete responsibility is established; his own spirit is the essence of this law and provides for ever compensation for every disturbance and adjustment for all effects. This is the law of Karma or justice, sometimes called the ethical law of causation. It is not foreign to the Christian scriptures, for both Jesus and St. Paul clearly enunciated it. Jesus said we should be judged as we gave judgment and should receive the measure meted to others. St. Paul said: "Brethren, be not deceived, God is not mocked, for whatsoever a man soweth that also shall he reap." And that sowing and reaping can only be possible under the doctrines of Karma and reincarnation.

But what of death and after? Is heaven a place or is it not? Theosophy teaches, as may be found in all sacred books, that after death the soul reaps a rest. This is from its own nature. It is a thinker, and cannot during life fulfil and carry out all nor even a small part of the myriads of thoughts entertained. Hence when at death it casts off the body and the astral body, and is released from the passions and desires, its natural forces have immediate sway and it thinks its thoughts out on the soul plane, clothed in a finer body suitable to that existence. This is called Devachan. It is the very state that has brought about the descriptions of heaven common to all religions, but this doctrine is very clearly put in the Buddhist and Hindu religions. It is a time of rest, because the physical body being absent the consciousness is not in the completer touch with visible nature which is possible on the material plane. But it is a real existence, and no more illusionary than earth life; it is where the essence of the thoughts of life that were as high as character permitted, expands and is garnered by the soul and mind. When the force of these thoughts is fully exhausted the soul is drawn back once more to earth, to that environment which is sufficiently like unto itself to give it the proper further evolution. This alternation from state to state goes on until the being rises from repeated experiences above ignorance, and realizes in itself the actual unity of all spiritual beings. Then it passes on to higher and greater steps on the evolutionary road.

No new ethics are presented by Theosophy, as it is held that right ethics are forever the same. But in the doctrines of Theosophy are to be found the philosophical and reasonable basis for ethics and the natural enforcement of them in practice. Universal brotherhood is that which will result in doing unto others as you would have them do unto you, and in your loving your neighbour as yourself – declared as right by all teachers in the great religions of the world.

Lucifer, December, 1893
W.Q. Judge

SPIRITUAL EVOLUTION

The universe is even as a great temple.
Claude de St. Martin

The central tenets of *Theosophia* are not derived from any ancient or modern sect but represent the accumulated wisdom of the ages, the unrecorded inheritance of humanity. Its vast scheme of cosmic and human evolution furnishes all true seekers with the symbolic alphabet necessary to interpret their recurrent visions as well as the universal framework and metaphysical vocabulary, drawn from many mystics and seers, which enable them to communicate their own intuitive perceptions. All authentic mystical writings are enriched by the alchemical flavour of Theosophical thought. Theosophy is an integrated system of fundamental verities taught by Initiates and Adepts across millennia. It is the *Philosophia Perennis*, the philosophy of human perfectibility, the science of spirituality and the religion of responsibility. It is the primeval fount of myriad religious systems as well as the hidden essence and esoteric wisdom of each. Man, an immortal monad, has been able to preserve this sacred heritage through the sacrificial efforts of enlightened and compassionate individuals, or *Bodhisattvas*, who constitute an ancient Brotherhood. They quietly assist in the ethical evolution and spiritual development of the whole of humanity. *Theosophia* is Divine Wisdom, transmitted and verified over aeons by the sages who belong to this secret Brotherhood.

The supreme presupposition of theosophical thought is an eternal substance-principle postulated as the ineffable Ground of all being. It is called a substance-principle because it becomes increasingly substantial and differentiated on the plane of manifestations while it essentially remains a homogeneous principle in abstract space and eternal duration. The perceived universe is a complex mirroring of this Unknown Source, all finite conceptions of which are necessarily incomplete. It is the Absolute Negation of all that exists. It is Be-ness or *Sat*, the Secondless Reality, the No-thing of ancient philosophy, the Boundless Lir, the Unknown Beginning of Celtic cosmogony.

Compared with It, all manifestation is no more than an impermanent illusion or maya, a kaleidoscopic medium through which the one Reality shows itself in a series of reflections. Spirit and matter are the two facets of this indivisible principle, and only seem to be separate during a vast period of cosmic manifestation. They radiate from this transcendent source, yet are not causally related to It, since neither quality nor mode may properly be ascribed to It. They appear periodically on the objective plane as the opposite poles of this Reality yet they are not inherently separate, but mutually coexist as spirit-matter. In manifestation this substratum differentiates itself into seven planes of increasing density, reaching towards the region of sense data. Everywhere the root essence of homogeneous substance is the same, transforming itself by minute degrees from the most ethereal to the most gross.

The seven planes of manifestation may be seen as condensations of rarefied matter and also as living streams of intelligences – primordial rays proceeding from an invisible Spiritual Sun. All modes of activity in the universe are internally guided by powers and potencies arrayed in an almost endless series of hierarchies, each with its exact function and precise scope of action. They are called *Dhyan Chohans* in Tibetan cosmogony and bear many other titles in the rich panoply of religious traditions – Angels, *Devas*, Gods, *Elohim*, etc. All these are transmitting agents of cosmic Law *(Rta)* which guides the evolution of each atom on every plane in space, the hierarchies varying enormously in their respective degrees of creative consciousness and monadic intelligence. As an aggregate, this immense host of forces forms the manifesting *Verbum* of an unmanifest Presence, constituting simultaneously the active Mind of the cosmos and its immutable Law. The idea of myriad hierarchies of intelligences animating visible Nature is a vital key to understanding all true mysticism. Many flashes of intuitive perception reveal multitudes of radiant beings elaborating the interior architecture of matter. Great mystics show a reverential recognition of the Logos or *Verbum*, the Army of the Voice, operating behind the screen of surface events as the noumenal cause of natural phenomena. This involves deciphering the signs of these intelligent forces by following the traces of their effects. The natural world bears the signatures of a divine archetypal world. With proper keys to archaic symbolism, the true seeker can read these signatures and recover the lost knowledge which would restore a primeval state of gnosis equivalent to that of the gods. The letters composing the Sanskrit language are the phenomenal expressions of these finer forces, and by understanding them one could discover the root vibration, the ineffable Word, reverberating throughout the sentient world of visible Nature.

The arcane teaching concerning the Great Chain of Being in the supernatural realm continually reappears in human history as the inexhaustible fountain-head of aesthetic expression, heroic action and mystic illumination. The Candle of Vision, the Magician of the Beautiful, the Mount of Transfiguration, the Mighty Mother, are all different faces of the divine *Logos*. The diverse expressions of creativity in the arts, religion and philosophy stem from this common unseen source, and the search for its origin is the hallowed mission of many a mystic and artist. The problem of tracing particulars to universals is as crucial to art as to psychology. The sevenfold classification of man's inner constitution corresponds to seven cosmic planes of being. Man is truly a microcosm and miniature copy of the macrocosm. Like the macrocosm, the individual is divine in essence, a direct radiation from the central Spiritual Sun. As pure spirit, every human being needs the vestures through which life may be experienced on differentiated planes of existence, so that one can become fully conscious of individual immortality and one's indissoluble identity with the whole. Every person is a complete reflection of the universe, revealing oneself to oneself by means of seven differentiations. In one's deepest self, the individual is *Atman,* the universal Spirit which is mirrored in the luminous soul or *Buddhi.* The light of *Buddhi* is focussed through *Manas* or impersonal intellect the source of human individuation. These three together constitute the imperishable fire in man, the immortal Triad that undertakes an immense pilgrimage through successive incarnations to emerge as an effortlessly self-conscious agent of the divine will, the Light of the *Logos, Brahma Vach.*

Below this overbrooding Triad is the volatile quaternary of principles drawn from the lower planes of cosmic matter: they are *kama,* the force of blind passion and chaotic desire shared by man with animal life; *prana,* the life-current energizing the whirling atoms on the objective plane of existence; the astral paradigmatic body (*linga sarira*) the original form around which the physical molecules shape themselves, and hence the model for the physical frame (*sthula sarira*). This quaternary of principles is evanescent and changeable, established for man's use at the time of incarnation and dissolved at death into its primary constituents on their corresponding planes. The real man, the higher Triad, recedes from the physical plane to await the next incarnation. The function of each of these sheaths differs from one individual to another according to the level of spiritual development of the incarnated soul. The astral body of the Adept is of a much higher degree of resilience and purity than that of the average man. In visionaries and mystics, the sheaths intervening between the spiritual man and the brain-mind are sufficiently transparent so that they can receive communications from the overbrooding Triad in a relatively lucid manner. Man is a compound being simultaneously experiencing two worlds, inner and outer. Each person's present life-experience is but a minute portion of what was witnessed by the immortal individuality in previous incarnations. Thus if men and women assiduously search within themselves, they can recover a vast heritage of knowledge spanning aeons. These memories are locked in mansions of the soul which only ardent desire and strong discipline can penetrate.

Memory is integral to consciousness, and since all matter is alive and conscious, all beings from cells to deities have memory of some type. In man, memory is generally divided into four categories: physical memory, remembrance, recollection and reminiscence. In remembrance, an idea impinges upon the mind from the past by free association; in recollection, the mind deliberately searches it out. Reminiscence, however, is of another order altogether. Called "soul-memory", it links every human being to previous lives and assures each that he or she will live again. In principle, any man or woman may recover the knowledge gained in previous incarnations and maintain continuity with the *sutratman*, the thread-soul, the eternal witness to every incarnation. There are also types of memory which are indistinguishable from prophecy, since the more one progresses towards homogeneous and rarefied planes of existence, the more past, present and future collapse into eternal duration, within the boundless perspective of which an entire cycle of manifestation may be surveyed.

Such was the level of insight reached by the great seers who recorded their findings in what is known as *Gupta Vidya* or the Secret Doctrine. Some mystics have penetrated deeply into the realms of reminiscence bringing back the fruits of knowledge in previous lives. Greater still is the ability to enter into former and more spiritual epochs of humanity and to make those visions come alive for those who had lost all but a faint intuition of a larger sense of self.

The source and destiny of the soul's inward life fundamentally involve the entire scope of evolution. Coeval with the manifestation of the seven worlds of the cosmic plenum is the re-emergence of beings who assume once more the evolutionary pilgrimage after an immense period of rest. The emanation of matter and spirit into the objective plane of existence is but half the cycle. Its return brings all beings and forms to the bosom of absolute darkness. The period of manifestation covering trillions of years is called a *manvantara* and the corresponding period of rest, called *pralaya,* lasts for an equal duration. They are the Days and Nights of Brahma, which were reckoned with meticulous precision by the ancient Aryans. The whole span of the *manvantara* is governed by the law of periodicity, which regulates rates of activity on all planes of being. This is sometimes spoken of as the Great Breath which preserves the cosmos. The essence of life is motion, growth and expansion of awareness in every atom. Each atom is at its core a monad, an expression of the highest self (*Atman*), and its vesture is the spiritual soul (*Buddhi*). Prior to the monad's emergence in the human family, it undergoes aeons of experience in the lower kingdoms of Nature, developing by natural impulse (metempsychosis) until the latent thinking faculty of *Manas* is awakened by the sacrificial efforts of beings who have risen far above the human state in *manvantaras* past. They kindle the spark of self-consciousness, making the unconscious monad a true man (*Manushya*), capable of thought, reflection and deliberate action. The soul embarks upon a long cycle of incarnations in human form to prepare itself for entry into still greater planes of existence.

The evolutionary tide on earth is regulated by the unerring hand of cyclic law. Man passes through a series of Rounds and Races, which allows him to assimilate the knowledge of every plane of existence, from the most ethereal to the most material. Man's planetary evolution describes a spiral passing from spirit into matter and returning to spirit again with a wholly self- conscious mastery of the process. Each Round is a major evolutionary period lasting many millions of years. Each Race in turn witnesses the rise and fall of continents, civilizations and nations. An earlier Race than our own, the Lemurian, lived in an idyllic Golden Age, an epoch ruled by natural religion, universal fraternity and spontaneous devotion to spiritual teachers. Many of the myths regarding an era of childlike purity and unsullied trust in humanity's early flowering preserve the flavour of this period. As man evolved more material vestures, *kama* or passion tainted his power of thought and inflamed his irrational tendencies. The nightmare tales of Atlantean sorcerers are the heavy heirloom of contemporary humanity. The destruction of Atlantis ushered in the Aryan race of our own epoch. The Indian Sages who inaugurated this period are among the torch-bearers for the humanity of our time. Intuitive mystics recognize the sacred role of ancient India as mother and preserver of the spiritual heritage of present humanity. The classical Indian scriptures resonate with the authentic voice of the *Verbum,* uncorrupted by time and human ignorance.

Pertinent to historical insight is the doctrine of the *yugas,* the cycle of four epochs through which every Race passes: the Golden, Silver, Bronze and Iron ages. The *yugas* indicate a broad sweep of karmic activity at any point in the life of an individual or collection of individuals. The entire globe may not be undergoing the same age simultaneously nor may any one individual be necessarily in the same epoch as his social milieu. According to Hindu calculations, *Kali Yuga* began over five thousand years ago and will last altogether for a total of four hundred thirty-two thousand years. This Dark Age is characterized by widespread confusion of roles, inversion of ethical values and enormous suffering owing to spiritual blindness. A.E. celebrated the myth of the Golden Age as extolling the plenitude of man's creative potential. The doctrine of the *yugas* is not deterministic. It merely suggests the relative levels of consciousness which most human beings tend to hold in common. Thus a Golden Age vibration can be inserted into an Iron Age to ameliorate the collective predicament of mankind. The Golden Age surrounded human beings as a primordial state of divine consciousness, but their own pride and ignorance precluded its recovery. In the wonder of childhood, in archaic myths, in the sporadic illuminations of great artists and in mystical visions, one may discern shimmering glimpses of the Golden Age of universal *eros*, the rightful original estate of humanity.

The progress of man in harmony with cyclic law is facilitated by a mature grasp of karma and rebirth. These twin doctrines of responsibility and hope unravel many of the riddles of life and Nature. They show that every person's life and character are the outcome of previous lives and thought-patterns, that each one is his or her own judge and executioner, and that all rise or fall strictly by their own merits and misdeeds. Nothing is left to chance or accident in life but everything is under the governance of a universal law of ethical causation. Man is essentially a thinker, and all thoughts initiate causes that generate suffering or bliss. The immortal Triad endures the mistakes and follies of the turbulent quaternary until such time as it can assume its rightful stature and act freely in consonance with cosmic order and natural law. As man is constantly projecting a series of thoughts and images, individual responsibility is irrevocable. Each person is the centre of any disturbance of universal harmony and the ripples of effects must return to him. Thus the law of karma or justice signifies moral interdependence and human solidarity. Karma must not be seen as a providential means of divine retribution but rather as a universal current touching those who bear the burden of its effects. This has been called the law of spiritual gravitation. The entire scope of man's affairs – his environment, friends, family, employment and the like – are all dictated by the needs of the soul. Karma works on the soul's behalf to provide those opportunities for knowledge and experience which would aid its progress. This concept could be expanded so as to encompass all connections with other human beings of even the most casual kind, seeing them as karmically ordained not for one's own progress but for the sake of those who struggle with the dire limitations of ignorance, poverty or despair. A deeply moving account of this trial is given in *The Hero in Man*, wherein, while walking among the wretched outcasts of Dublin, A.E. rejoiced in the conviction that the benevolence he felt for each benighted soul would forge a spiritual bond through which he might help them in the future. Karma means a summons to the path of action and duty. As one cannot separate one's own karma from that of one's fellow-men, one may determine to devote one's life to the remission of the karmic burden of others.

At death the true Self or immortal Triad casts off the physical and astral bodies and is released from the thraldom of passions and desires. Its natural tropism to gravitate upwards allows it to enter the rarefied plane of consciousness where its thoughts are carried to culmination, clothed in a finer body suited to that sublime existence. This state, *Devachan*, is a period of rest and assimilation between lives and the basis of the popular mythology of heaven. On the other hand, the lower quaternary languishes after death in *Kamaloka*, the origin of theological dogmas concerning hell and purgatory. There it dissolves by degrees back into its primary elements at a rate determined by the cohesion given them by the narcissistic personality during life on earth. Inflamed passions and poisonous thoughts sustained for long periods of time endow this entity with a vivid, vicarious and ghoulish existence. This plane of consciousness, termed "the astral light" by Eliphas Levi, is intimately connected with the lives and thoughts of most of mankind. It is the vast slag-heap of Nature into which all selfish and evil thoughts are poured and then rebound back to pollute and contaminate human life on earth. This plane of carnalized thought tends to perpetuate the horrors of the Iron Age and condemn man to a state of spiritual darkness.

The crucial difference between individuals lies in whether they are enslaved by the astral light (the region of *psyche*) or whether they are capable of rising above it to a calm awareness of the wisdom and compassion latent in their higher nature, the realm of *nous*. Beyond the region of psychic action lies the pristine sphere of noetic awareness called *Akasha*, from which empyrean individuals could derive the inspiration needed to go forth and inaugurate a Golden Age by laying down the foundations of a regenerated civilization. Sages, past and present, have accomplished the arduous transformation of their own natures, overcoming every vice and limitation and perfecting themselves in noetic ideation and sacrificial action. *Mahatmas* or Hierophants renounce everything for the sake of suffering humanity. Solitary mystics on the ancient path of service salute them as guides and preceptors and acknowledge their invisible presence behind their own modest labours for mankind. These wise beings are the noble trustees of the *Philosophia Perennis* and the compassionate Teachers of the human family. The mystical pilgrimage of mankind is an authentic reflection of their ageless Wisdom.

> For countless generations hath the adept builded a fane of imperishable rocks, a giant's Tower of INFINITE THOUGHT, wherein the Titan dwelt, and will yet, if need be, dwell alone, emerging from it but at the end of every cycle, to invite the elect of mankind to co-operate with him and help in his turn enlighten superstitious man.

Hermes, August 1979
Raghavan Iyer

THE SYNTHESIS OF OCCULT SCIENCE

I – THE impassable gulf between mind and matter discovered by modern science is a logical result of the present methods of so-called scientific investigation. These methods are analytical and hypothetical, and the results arrived at are necessarily tentative and incomplete. Even the so-called "Synthetic Philosophy" of Spencer is, at best, an effort to grasp the entire method and modulus of nature within one of its processes only. The aim is at synthesis, but it can hardly deserve the name of philosophy, for it is purely speculative and hypothetical. It is as though the physiologist undertook to study the function of respiration in man through the single process of expiration, ignoring the fact that every expiratory act must be supplemented by inspiration or respiration cease altogether.

Taking, therefore, the facts of experience derived from the phenomena of nature and viewing both cosmic and organic processes purely from their objective side, the "missing links," "impassable gulfs", and "unthinkable gaps" occur constantly. Not so in Occult Science. So far as the science of occultism is concerned, it is both experimental and analytical, but it acknowledges no "missing links," "impassable gulfs," or "unthinkable gaps," because it finds none. Back of occult science there lies a complete and all-embracing Philosophy. This philosophy is not simply synthetical in its methods, for the simplest as the wildest hypothesis can claim that much; but it is *synthesis itself.* It regards Nature as one complete whole, and so the student of occultism may stand at either point of observation. He may from the stand-point of Nature's wholeness and completeness follow the process of segregation and differentiation to the minutest atom conditioned in space and time; or, from the phenomenal display of the atom, he may reach forward and upward till the atom becomes an integral part of cosmos, involved in the universal harmony of creation. The modern scientist may do this incidentally or empirically, but the occultist does it systematically and habitually, and hence philosophically. The modern scientist is confessedly and boastfully *agnostic.* The occultist is reverently and progressively *gnostic.*

Modern science recognizes matter as "living" and "dead," "organic" and "inorganic," and "Life" as merely a phenomenon of matter. Occult science recognizes, "foremost of all, the postulate that there is no such thing in Nature as *inorganic* substances or bodies. Stones, minerals, rocks, and even chemical '*atoms*' are simply organic units in profound lethargy. Their coma has an end, and their inertia becomes activity." (*Secret Doctrine*, Vol. I, p. 626 fn.) Occultism recognizes ONE UNIVERSAL, ALL-PERVADING LIFE. Modern science recognizes life as a special phenomenon of matter, a mere transient manifestation due to temporary conditions. Even logic and analogy ought to have taught us better, for the simple reason that so-called "inorganic" or "dead" matter constantly becomes organic and living, while matter from the organic plane is continually being reduced to the inorganic. How rational and justifiable, then, to suppose that the capacity or "potency" of life is latent in all matter!

The "elements," "atoms," and "molecules" of modern science, partly physical and partly metaphysical, though altogether hypothetical, are, nevertheless, seldom philosophical, for the simple reason that they are regarded solely as phenomenal. The Law of Avogadro involved a generalization as to physical structure and number, and the later experiments of Prof. Neumann deduced the same law mathematically from the first principles of the mechanical theory of gases, but it remained for Prof. Crookes to perceive the philosophical necessity of a primordial substratum, *protyle*, and so, as pointed out in the *Secret Doctrine*, to lay the foundations of "*Metachemistry*"; in other words, a complete philosophy of physics and chemistry that shall take the place of mere hypothesis and empiricism, if one or two generalizations deduced as logical or mathematical necessities from the phenomena of physics and chemistry have been able to work such revolutions in the old chemistry, what may we not expect from a complete synthesis that shall grasp universals by a law that compasses the whole domain of matter? And yet this complete synthesis has been in the possession of the true occultist for ages. Glimpses of this philosophy have been sufficient to give to minds like Kepler, Descartes, Leibnitz, Kant, Schopenhauer, and, lastly, to Prof. Crookes, ideas that claimed and held the interested attention of the scientific world. While, at certain points, such writers supplement and corroborate each other, neither anywhere nor altogether do they reveal the complete synthesis, for none of them possessed it, and yet it has all along existed.

> Let the reader remember these "Monads" of Leibnitz, every one of which is a living mirror of the universe, every monad reflecting every other, and compare this view and definition with certain Sanskrit stanzas (*Slokas*) translated by Sir William Jones, in which it is said that the creative source of the Divine Mind, . . . "Hidden in a veil of thick darkness, formed *mirrors of the atoms* of the world, and *cast reflection from its own face on every atom*".

> *Secret Doctrine.*, Vol. 1, p. 623.

It may be humiliating to "Modern Exact Science" and repugnant to the whole of Christendom to have to admit that the Pagans whom they have despised, and the "Heathen Scriptures" they long ridiculed or ignored, nevertheless possess a fund of wisdom never dreamed of under Western skies. They have the lesson, however, to learn, that Science by no means originated in, nor is it confined to, the West, nor are superstition and ignorance confined to the East.

It can easily be shown that every real discovery and every important advancement in modern science have already been anticipated centuries ago by ancient science and philosophy. It is true that these ancient doctrines have been embodied in unknown languages and symbols, and recorded in books inaccessible to western minds till a very recent date. Far beyond all this inaccessibility, however, as a cause preventing these old truths from reaching modern times, has been the prejudice, the scorn and contempt of ancient learning manifested by the leaders of modern thought.

Nor is the lesson yet learned that bigotry and scorn are never the mark of wisdom or the harbingers of learning; for still, with comparatively few exceptions, any claim or discussion of these ancient doctrines is met with contempt and scorn. The record has, however, been at least outlined and presented to the world. As the authors of the *Secret Doctrine* have remarked, these doctrines may not be largely accepted by the present generation, but during the twentieth century they will become known and appreciated.

The scope and bearing of philosophy itself are hardly yet appreciated by modern thought, because of its materialistic tendency.

A complete science of metaphysics and a complete philosophy of science are not yet even conceived of as possible; hence the ancient wisdom by its very vastness has escaped recognition in modern times. That the authors of ancient wisdom have spoken from at least two whole planes of conscious experience beyond that of our every-day "sense-perception" is to us inconceivable, and yet such is the fact; and why should the modern advocate of evolution be shocked and staggered by such a disclosure? It but justifies his hypothesis and extends its theatre. Is it because the present custodians of this ancient learning do not scramble for recognition on the stock exchange, and enter into competition in the marts of the world? If the practical outcome of such competition needed illustration, Mr. Keely might serve as an example. The discoveries of the age are already whole centuries in advance of its ethical culture, and the knowledge that should place still further power in the hands of a few individuals whose ethical code is below, rather than above, that of the ignorant, toiling, suffering masses, could only minister to anarchy and increase oppression. On these higher planes of consciousness the law of progress is absolute; knowledge and power go hand in hand with beneficence to man, not alone to the individual possessors of wisdom, but to the whole human race. The custodians of the higher knowledge are equally by both motive and development almoners of the divine. These are the very conditions of the higher consciousness referred to. The synthesis of occult science becomes, therefore, the higher synthesis of the faculties of man. What matter, therefore, if the ignorant shall scout its very existence, or treat it with ridicule and contempt? Those who know of its existence and who have learned something of its scope and nature can, in their turn, afford to smile, but with pity and sorrow at the willing bondage to ignorance and misery that scorns enlightenment and closes its eyes to the plainest truths of experience.

Leaving, for the present, the field of physics and cosmogenesis, it may be profitable to consider some of the applications of these doctrines to the functions and life of man.

The intellect derived from philosophy
is similar to a charioteer; for it
is present with our desires, and
always conducts them to the beautiful.

Demophilus

II – "In reality, as Occult philosophy teaches us, everything which changes is organic; it has the life principle in it, and it has all the potentiality of the higher lives. If, as we say, all in nature is an aspect of the one element, and life is universal, how can there be such a thing as an inorganic atom!" [1] Man is a perfected animal, but before he could have reached perfection even on the animal plane, there must have dawned upon him the light of a higher plane. Only the perfected animal can cross the threshold of the next higher, or the human plane, and as he does so there shines upon him the ray from the suprahuman plane. Therefore, as the dawn of humanity illumines the animal plane, and as a guiding star lures the Monad to higher consciousness, so the dawn of divinity illumines the human plane, luring the monad to the supra-human plane of consciousness. This is neither more nor less than the philosophical and metaphysical aspect of the law of evolution. Man has not one principle more than the tiniest insect; he is, however, "the vehicle of a fully developed *Monad,* self-conscious and deliberately following its own line of progress, whereas in the insect, and even the higher animal, the higher triad of principles is absolutely dormant." The original *Monad* has, therefore, locked within it the potentiality of divinity. It is plainly, therefore, a misnomer to call that process of thought a "Synthetic Philosophy" that deals only with phenomena and ends with matter on the physical plane. These two generalizations of Occult philosophy, endowing every atom with the potentiality of life, and regarding every insect or animal as already possessing the potentialities of the higher planes though these powers are yet dormant, add to the ordinary Spencerian theory of evolution precisely that element that it lacks, *viz,* the metaphysical and philosophical; and,

---

[1] Quotations are from the *Secret Doctrine* and other writings of H. P. Blavatsky.

thus endowed, the theory becomes synthetical.

The *Monad*, then, is essentially and potentially the same in the lowest vegetable organism, up through all forms and gradations of animal life to man, *and beyond*. There is a gradual unfolding of its potentialities from "Monera" to man, and there are two whole planes of consciousness, the sixth and the seventh "senses," not yet unfolded to the average humanity. Every monad that is enclosed in a form, and hence limited by matter, becomes conscious on its own plane and in its own degree. Consciousness, therefore, no less than sensitiveness, belongs to plants as well as to animals. Self-consciousness belongs to man, because, while embodied in a *form*, the higher triad of principles, Atma-Buddhi-*Manas*, is no longer dormant, but active. This activity is, however, far from being fully developed. When this activity has become fully developed, man will already have become conscious on a still higher plane, endowed with the sixth and the opening of the *seventh* sense, and will have become a "god" in the sense given to that term by Plato and his followers.

In thus giving this larger and completer meaning to the law of evolution, the Occult philosophy entirely eliminates the "missing links" of modern science, and, by giving to man a glimpse of his nature and destiny, not only points out the line of the higher evolution, but puts him in possession of the means of achieving it.

The "atoms" and "monads" of the *Secret Doctrine* are very different from the atoms and molecules of modern science. To the latter these are mere particles of matter endowed with blind force: to the former, they are the "dark nucleoles," and potentially "Gods," conscious and intelligent from their primeval embodiment at the beginning of differentiation in the dawn of the Manvantara. There are no longer any hard and fast lines between the "organic" and the "inorganic"; between the "living" and "dead" matter. Every atom is endowed with and moved by intelligence, and is conscious in its own degree, on its own plane of development. This is a glimpse of the *One Life* that –

> Runs through all time, extends through all extent,
> Lives undivided, operates unspent.

It may be conceived that the "Ego" in man is a monad that has gathered to itself innumerable experiences through aeons of time, slowly unfolding its latent potencies through plane after plane of matter. It is hence called the *"eternal pilgrim."*

The Manasic, or mind principle, is cosmic and universal. It is the creator of all forms, and the basis of all law in nature. Not so with consciousness. Consciousness is a condition of the monad as the result of embodiment in matter and the dwelling in a physical form. Self-consciousness, which from the animal plane looking upward is the beginning of perfection, from the divine plane looking downward is the perfection of selfishness and the curse of separateness. It is the "world of illusion" that man has created for himself. "Maya is the perceptive faculty of every Ego which considers itself a Unit, separate from and independent of the One Infinite and Eternal Sat or "be-ness." The "eternal pilgrim" must therefore mount higher, and flee from the plane of self-consciousness it has struggled so hard to reach.

The complex structure that we call "Man" is made up of a congeries of almost innumerable "Lives." Not only every microscopic cell of which the tissues are composed, but the molecules and atoms of which these cells are composed, are permeated with the essence of the "One Life." Every so-called organic cell is known to have its nucleus, a center of finer or more sensitive matter. The nutritive, all the formative and functional processes consist of flux and re-flux, of inspiration and expiration, to and from the nucleus.

The nucleus is therefore in its own degree and after its kind a "monad" imprisoned in a "form." Every microscopic cell, therefore, has a consciousness and an intelligence of its own, and man thus consists of innumerable "lives." This is but physiological synthesis, logically deduced no less from the known facts in physiology and histology than the logical sequence of the philosophy of occultism. Health of the body as a whole depends on the integrity of all its parts, and more especially upon their harmonious association and cooperation. A diseased tissue is one in which a group of individual cells refuse to cooperate, and wherein is set up discordant action, using less or claiming more than their due share of food or energy. Disease of the very tissue of man's body is neither more nor less than the "sin of separateness." Moreover, the grouping of cells is upon the principle of hierarchies. Smaller groups are subordinate to larger congeries, and these again are subordinate to larger, or to the whole. Every microscopic cell therefore typifies and epitomizes man, as man is an epitome of the Universe. As already remarked, the "Eternal Pilgrim," the Alter-Ego in man, is a monad progressing through the ages. By right and by endowment the ego is king in the domain of man's bodily life. It descended into matter in the cosmic process till it reached the mineral plane, and then journeyed upward through the "three kingdoms" till it reached the human plane. The elements of its being, like the cells and molecules of man's body, are groupings of structures accessory or subordinate to it. The human monad or Ego is therefore akin to all below it and heir to all above it, linked by indissoluble bonds to spirit and matter, "God" and "Nature." The attributes that it gathers, and the faculties that it unfolds, are but the latent and dormant potentialities awaking to conscious life. The tissue cells constitute man's bodily structure, but the order in which they are arranged, the principle upon which they are grouped, constituting the human *form,* is not simply an evolved shape from the lower animal plane, but an *involved* principle from a higher plane, an older world, viz, the "Lunar Pitris." "Hanuman the Monkey" antedates Darwin's "missing link" by thousands of millenniums. So also the Manasic, or mind element, with its cosmic and infinite potentialities, is not merely the developed "instinct" of the animal. *Mind* is the latent or active potentiality of *Cosmic Ideation,* the essence of every form, the basis of every law, the potency of every principle in the universe. Human thought is the reflection or reproduction in the realm of man's consciousness of these forms, laws, and principles. Hence man senses and apprehends nature just as nature unfolds in him. When, therefore, the Monad has passed through the form of the animal ego, involved and unfolded the human form, the higher triad of principles awakens from the sleep of ages and over-shadowed by the "*Manasa-putra*" and *built into* its essence and substance. How could man epitomize Cosmos if he did not touch it at every point and involve it in every principle? If man's being is woven in the web of destiny, his potencies and possibilities take hold of divinity as the woof and pattern of his boundless life. Why, then, should he grow weary or disheartened? Alas! why should he be degraded, this heir of all things!

The peculiarity also of this theology, and in which its transcendency consists, is this, that it does not consider the highest God to be the principle of beings, but the *principle of principles,* i.e. of deiform processions from itself, all which are eternally rooted in the unfathomable depths of the immensely great source of their existence, and of which they may be called supersensuous ramifications and superluminous blossoms.

Thomas Taylor
Introduction to *Mystical Hymns of Orpheus*

III – It has often been thought a strange thing that there are no dogmas and no creed in Theosophy or Occultism. Is Theosophy a religion? is often asked. No, it is *religion.* Is it a *philosophy?* No, it is *philosophy.* Is it a science? No, it is *science.* If a consensus of religion, philosophy, and science is possible, and if it has ever been reached in human thought, that thought must long since have passed the boundaries of all creeds and ceased to dogmatize. Hence comes the difficulty in answering questions. No proposition stands apart or can be taken separately without limiting and often distorting its meaning. Every proposition has to be considered and held as subservient to the synthetic whole. Really intelligent people, capable of correct reasoning, often lack sufficient interest to endeavor to apprehend the universality of these principles. They expect, where they have any interest at all in the subject, to be told "all about it" in an hours conversation, or to learn it from a column in some newspaper; all about man, all about Nature, all about Deity; and then either to reject it or to make it a part of their previous creed. These are really no wiser than the penny-a-liner who catches some point and turns it into ridicule, or makes it a butt for coarse jest or silly sarcasm, and then complacently imagines that he has demolished the whole structure! If such persons were for one moment placed face to face with their own folly, they would be amazed. The most profound thinker and the most correct reasoner might well afford to devote a life-time to the apprehension of the philosophy of occultism, and other life-times to mastering the scientific details, while at the same time his ethics and his religious life are made consistent with the principle of altruism and the Brotherhood of man. If this be regarded as too hard a task, it is, nevertheless, the line of the higher evolution of man, and, soon or late, every soul must follow it, retrograde, or cease to be.

Man is but a link in an endless chain of being; a sequence of a past eternity of causes and processes; a potentiality born into time, but spanning two eternities, his past and his future, and in his consciousness these are all one, *Duration,* the ever-present. In a former article man was shown to be a series of almost innumerable "Lives," and these lives, these living entities called "cells," were shown to be associated together on the principle of hierarchies, grouped according to rank and order, service and development, and this was shown to be the "physical synthesis" of man, and the organic synthesis as well. Disease was also shown to be the organic nutritive, or physiological "sin of separateness." Every department of man's being, every organ and cell of his body, was also shown to possess a consciousness and an intelligence of its own, held, however, subordinate to the whole. In health every action is synchronous and rhythmical, however varied and expanded, however intense and comprehensive. Enough is already known in modern physics to justify all these statements, at least by analogy. The principle of electrical induction and vibration, the quantitative and qualitative transmission of vibration and its exact registration, and their application to telegraphy, the telephone, and the phonograph, have upset all previous theories of physics and physiology. "A metallic plate, for instance, can that talk like a human being? Yea or nay? Mr. Bouillard – and he was no common man – said No; to accept such a fact were to upset all our notions of physiology. So said Mr. Bouillard, right in the face of Edison's phonograph in full Academy, and he throttled the luckless interpreter of the famous American inventor, accusing it of ventriloquism." [2]

Occultism teaches that the Ego both precedes and survives the physical body. The phenomena of man's life and the process of his thought can be apprehended and explained on no other theory. Modern physiology teaches in detail certain facts regarding the life of man. It, moreover, groups these facts and deduces certain so-called principles and laws, but such a thing as a synthesis of the *whole man* is seldom even attempted. "Psychology" is mere empiricism, represented

---

[2] Dr. J. Oehorowicz, *"Mental Suggestion,"* p. 291.

by disjointed facts, and these, of course, but little understood, and more often misinterpreted.

Ask the modern physiologist if man can *think* when unconscious and he will answer No; and if asked if man can be conscious and not think, he will as readily answer No. Both answers will be based on what is known, or supposed to be known, of memory. The idea that the real man, the Ego, is always conscious on some plane, and that it "thinks," as we ordinarily use the term, only on the lower plane through the physical brain, in terms of extension and duration, or space and time, is seldom in the least apprehended by the modern physiologist. If, however, one grasps the idea of the ego as the real man dwelling in the physical body and using it as its instrument through which it is related to space and time, perception, sensation, thought, and feeling, the gaps in physiology and psychology begin to disappear. Here again it should be particularly borne in mind that this doctrine of the ego must be considered in the light of the complete synthesis of occultism, and just to the extent that this is intelligently done will the significance of the ego appear.

The brief and concise outline of the philosophy of occultism given in the Introduction to the *Secret Doctrine* is therefore very significant, and the student who desires to apprehend that which follows in these two large volumes ought to study this outline very carefully. No subsequent proposition, no principle in the life of man, can be correctly understood apart from it. The subject-matter following is necessarily fragmentary, but the outline is both inclusive and philosophical, and if one reasons logically and follows the plainest analogies he can never go far astray. The relation of mind to brain, of thought to consciousness, of life to matter, and of man to Nature and to Deity, is there clearly defined; not, indeed, in all its details, but in a philosophical modulus, to be worked out in reason and in life. The all-pervading Life, the cyclic or periodical movements, the periods of action and of repose, and the intimate relations and inter-dependences of all things apply to Cosmos, and equally to every atom in its vast embrace.

Students sometimes complain that they cannot understand, that the subject is so vast, and so deep and intricate, and not made clear. It is because they do not realize what they have undertaken. Occultism can neither be taught nor learned in "a few easy lessons." The "object lessons" sometimes given by H.P.B., almost always misunderstood and misapplied, though often explained at the time, served as often to excite vulgar curiosity and personal abuse as to arrest attention and study. If, before the advent of the T.S. in the face of the creeds of Christendom, the materialism of science, the indifferences and supercilious scorn of Agnosticism, and the babel of spiritualism, it had been proposed to begin at the foundations and reconstruct our entire knowledge of Nature and of man; to show the unity and the foundations of the world's religions; to eliminate from science all its "missing links"; to make Agnosticism gnostic; and to place the science of psychology and the nature and laws of mind and soul over against "Mediumship"; it would have been held as an herculean task, and declared impossible of accomplishment. Now that the thing has virtually been accomplished and this body of knowledge presented to the world, people think it strange that they cannot compass it all, as the poet Burns is said to have written some of his shorter poems, "while standing on one leg!"

Again, people complain at the unfamiliar terms and the strange words imported from foreign languages. Yet if one were to undertake the study of physics, chemistry, music, or medicine, quite as great obstacles have to be overcome. Is it a strange thing, then, that the science that includes all these, and undertakes to give a synthesis of the whole realm of Nature and of life, should have its own nomenclature?

Beyond all these necessary and natural obstacles, there is another, *viz.*, that contentious spirit that disputes and opposes every point before it is fairly stated or understood. Suppose one ignorant of mathematics were to proceed in the same manner and say, "I don't *like* that proposition," "I don't see *why* they turn a six upside down to make a nine," "Why don't two and two make five?", and so on, how long would it take such a one to learn mathematics? In the study of the *Secret Doctrine* it is not a matter of likes or dislikes, of belief or unbelief, but solely a matter of intelligence and understanding. He who acknowledges his ignorance and yet is unwilling to lay aside his likes and dislikes, and even his creeds and dogmas, for the time, in order to see what is presented in its own light and purely on its merits, has neither need nor use for the *Secret Doctrine*. Even where a greater number of propositions are accepted or "believed" and a few are rejected, the synthetic whole is entirely lost sight of. But, says some one, this is a plea for blind credulity, and an attempt to bind the mind and the conscience of man to a blind acceptance of these doctrines. No one but the ignorant or the dishonest can make such an assertion in the face of the facts. Listen to the following from p. xix, Introduction to the *Secret Doctrine*. "It is above everything important to keep in mind that no theosophical book acquires the least additional value from pretended authority." If that be advocating blind credulity, let the enemies of the T.S. make the most of it. If any authority pertains to the *Secret Doctrine*, it must be sought inside, not outside. It must rest on its comprehensiveness, its completeness, its continuity and reasonableness; in other words, on its *philosophical synthesis*, a thing missed alike by the superficial and the contentious, by the indolent, the superstitious, and the dogmatic.

> O wise man: you have asked rightly. Now listen carefully. The illusive fancies arising from error are not conclusive.

> The great and peaceful ones live regenerating the world like the coming of spring, and after having themselves crossed the ocean of embodied existence, help those who try to do the same thing, without personal motives.

> *Crest Jewel of Wisdom*

IV - In the foregoing articles, necessarily brief and fragmentary, a few points have been given to show the general bearing of the *Secret Doctrine* on all problems in Nature and in Life.

Synthesis is the very essence of philosophy – "the combination of separate elements of thought into a whole" – the opposite of analysis and analysis is the very essence of science.

In the "Outline of the Secret Doctrine" by "C.J.," now running through the pages of *Lucifer*, this philosophy or synthesis of the whole is made very clear.

There have been many philosophisers in modern times, but there can be but one philosophy, one synthesis of the whole of Eternal

Nature. With the single exception of the writings of Plato, no one in modern times had given to the Western world any approximation to a complete philosophy, previous to the appearance of H. P. Blavatsky's *Secret Doctrine*. The writings of Plato are carefully veiled in the symbolical language of initiation. The *Secret Doctrine*, coming more than two millenniums later, and in an age of so-called Science, is addressed to the Scientific thought of the age, and hence considers the whole subject largely from the stand-point of Science. The present age is as deficient in philosophy as was the age of Plato in knowledge of science. It follows, therefore, that while the *Secret Doctrine* itself apprehends equally both philosophy and science, in addressing itself to the thought of an age it must recognize here, as it does everywhere, the law of cycles that rules in the intellectual development of a race no less than in the revolutions of suns and worlds, and so address the times from that plane of thought that is in the ascendant. It is just because analytical thought is in the ascendant, because it is the thought-form of the age, that the great majority of readers are likely to overlook the broad synthesis and so miss the philosophy of the *Secret Doctrine*. The only object of these brief and fragmentary papers has been to call attention to this point.

We are now in a transition period, and in the approaching twentieth century there will be a revival of genuine philosophy, and the *Secret Doctrine* will be the basis of the "New Philosophy." Science today, in the persons of such advanced students as Keely, Crookes, Lodge, Richardson, and many others, already treads so close to the borders of occult philosophy that it will not be possible to prevent the new age from entering the occult realm. H. P. Blavatsky's *Secret Doctrine* is a storehouse of scientific facts, but this is not its chief value. These facts are placed, approximately at least, in such relation to the synthesis or philosophy of occultism as to render comparatively easy the task of the student who is in search of real knowledge, and to further his progress beyond all preconception, provided he is teachable, in earnest, and intelligent. Nowhere else in English literature is the Law of Evolution given such sweep and swing. It reminds one of the ceaseless under-tone of the deep sea, and seems to view our Earth in all its changes "from the birth of time to the crack of doom." It follows man in his triple evolution, physical, mental, and spiritual, throughout the perfect circle of his boundless life. Darwinism had reached its limits and a rebound. Man is indeed evolved from lower forms. But which man? the physical? the psychical? the intellectual? or the spiritual? The *Secret Doctrine* points where the lines of evolution and involution meet; where matter and spirit clasp hands; and where the rising animal stands face to face with the fallen god; for all natures meet and mingle in man.

Judge no proposition of the *Secret Doctrine* as though it stood alone, for not one stands alone. Not "independence" here more than with the units that constitute Humanity. It is interdependence everywhere; in nature, as in life.

Even members of the T.S. have often wondered why H.P.B. and others well known in the Society lay so much stress on doctrines like Karma and Reincarnation. It is not alone because these doctrines are easily apprehended and beneficent to individuals, not only because they furnish, as they necessarily do, a solid foundation for ethics, or all human conduct, but because they are the very key-notes of the higher evolution of man. Without Karma and Reincarnation evolution is but a fragment; a process whose beginnings are unknown, and whose outcome cannot be discerned; a glimpse of what might be; a hope of what should be. But in the light of Karma and Reincarnation evolution becomes the logic of what must be. The links in the chain of being are all filled in, and the circles of reason and of life are complete. Karma gives the eternal law of action, and Reincarnation furnishes the boundless field for its display. Thousands of persons can understand these two principles, apply them as a basis of conduct, and weave them into the fabric of their lives, who may not be able to grasp the complete synthesis of that endless evolution of which these doctrines form so important a part. In thus affording even the superficial thinker and the weak or illogical reasoner a perfect basis for ethics and an unerring guide in life, Theosophy is building toward the future realization of the Universal Brotherhood and the higher evolution of man. But few in this generation realize the work that is thus undertaken, or how much has already been accomplished. The obscurity of the present age in regard to genuine philosophical thought is nowhere more apparent than in the manner in which opposition has been waged toward these doctrines of Karma and Reincarnation. In the seventeen years since the Theosophical movement has been before the world there has not appeared, from any source, a serious and logical attempt to discredit these doctrines from a philosophical basis. There have been denial, ridicule, and denunciation *ad nauseum*. There could be no discussion from such a basis, for from the very beginning these doctrines have been put forth and advocated from the logical and dispassionate plane of philosophy. Ridicule is both unanswerable and unworthy of answer. It is not the argument, but the atmosphere of weak minds, born of prejudice and ignorance.

The synthesis of occultism is therefore the philosophy of Nature and of Life; the full – or free – truth that apprehends every scientific fact in the light of the unerring processes of Eternal Nature.

The time must presently come when the really advanced thinkers of the age will be compelled to lay by their indifference, and their scorn and conceit, and follow the lines of philosophical investigation laid down in the *Secret Doctrine*. Very few seem yet to have realized how ample are these resources, because it involves a process of thought almost unknown to the present age of empiricism and induction. It is a revelation from archaic ages, indestructible and eternal, yet capable of being obscured and lost; capable of being again and again reborn, or like man himself – reincarnated.

> "He who lives in one color of the rainbow is blind to the rest. Live in the Light diffused through the entire arc, and you will know it all." – *The Path*.

> "He who knows not the common things of life is a beast among men. He who knows only the common things of life is a man among beasts. He who knows all that can be learned by diligent inquiry is a god among *men*." – *Plato*.

The Path, November, 1891; February, March, May, 1892
W.Q. Judge

THE GOLDEN THREAD

When we read what H.P. Blavatsky has written of her predecessors, those true transmitters acting in strict obedience to the Brotherhood of *Bodhisattvas* – Wise Men, Initiates, *Mahatmas* belonging to all mankind – we are naturally led to think of what she herself experienced in the nineteenth century on behalf of us all. She founded the Theosophical Society in New York with three objects, the first of which was the formation of a nucleus of Universal Brotherhood – Brotherhood *in actu* and not only in name. The second object was a comparative study of the religions, sciences and philosophies of every part of the world so that all men and women, including Americans, might come to salute every true witness in a long, largely unknown but unbroken history of accumulated wisdom. She taught the perennial philosophy and invited her true students to find in it an Ariadne's thread, a golden thread hidden behind the veil of form and symbol in every great tradition of thought, philosophy, religious aspiration and myth. It is the very basis of real science, and it is the inspiration behind the founding of the Royal Society as well as much of the significant work of men like Edison, a Fellow of the Theosophical Society, and many other scientists indirectly influenced by the wisdom of the Secret Doctrine.

When we consider the efforts of sincere Theosophists to apply this philosophy to their lives, in conformance with the third object of the Theosophical Society, we must think of those moments which are the first concern of any person of any age involved in finding meaning within the flux of experiences: the moment of birth and the moment of death. We can also think of the line that threads these moments. Each of us discovers this entirely for himself, exercising the supreme prerogative of a human being, the privilege of self-reflective consciousness, the gift of the gods, the *Dhyanis* and the *Manasaputras*, seeking out what in his or her whole life was most quintessentially sacred. A great deal happens every day, from morn to night. But even in a small town or in beautiful natural settings, much energy is dissipated. We live in a culture where fragmentation of consciousness is widespread and confusion prevails. In such times of trouble, students of *Theosophia* or *Brahma Vach* are wise in following the advice given by Merlin to Arthur: "Go back to the original moment."

Beginnings are important, endings are inevitable and change is constant in a universe of ceaseless transformation. The wheel revolves constantly faster in the Age of Iron, and everything changes so rapidly that irrelevant analyses and outmoded diagnoses crowd the scene. There are many learned tomes on the pace of change in technological society, but they are not needed by those who understand the winds of change because they recognize the timeless truth of the teachings of Lord Krishna: that a man is wise to meditate upon birth, death, decay, sickness and error. This is the most ancient wisdom, and it is as fresh today as it was five thousand years ago, thanks to the sacrificial ideation of the mighty Brotherhood of silent and eternal Teachers who worship the Nameless and Ineffable. They work in perfect harmony through willing and cheerful obedience to the *Maha Chohan*, who wanted a Brotherhood of Humanity to be initiated and knew that it would not happen at once, but that the line must and would be kept unbroken. In all theosophical assemblies and associations there are those self-determining agents who are self-elected to serve as the compassionate custodians of the living tradition of the primordial Teaching for the sake of all.

Theosophia is like that ancient Banyan tree. Some come to sit in its shade, while others come to exchange words and seek friends. Still others come to pick fruit. Nature is generous. Some come to sit in the presence of teachers to receive instruction in the mighty power of real meditation, to secure help in self-examination. All are welcome. The antiquity and enormity of the tree are beyond the capacity of any person in any period of history to enclose in a definition or formulation. Great Teachers point beyond themselves to that which is beyond formulation, which is ineffable and indefinable. They seek to make alive and to make real for every man "the priceless boon of learning truth" spoken of in *The Voice of the Silence*.

Pythagoras, in 530 B.C., with the precision of a man who had prepared himself through twenty-two years of training in the Egyptian Mysteries, came to the small town of Krotona. He spent twenty years there laying the foundations of a school and a college for the sake of establishing in the Near East, and in what subsequently became the western world, science (symbolized by the Pythagorean sphere), religion (symbolized by the tetraktis), and philosophy (a term that he devised). When asked, "Are you a wise man?" he said, "I am a man who is in love with wisdom, a philosopher, *philosophos*." Any man who loves – like a child, like a teenager, like all human beings – but loves with a wisdom sufficient to care for love itself, to treasure it, and to prize it, becomes like the blooming lotus. So he exercises the privilege and the right extended to every human being. Independent of authorities and experts, independent of the clash of rival and changing fashions, fads, isms, sects and systems, he may exercise the privilege of becoming a true philosopher, of reflecting upon the long journey. Every man is a nomad. The journey begins we know not where. It leads we know not whither. In a world which is like a stage, in which all the players are pilgrims, the pilgrimage is the thing. What is unique, precious and private to each one can only be partly known or shared imperfectly with even the closest friends. *Light on the Path* teaches that no man is our enemy, no man is our friend, but that all alike are our teachers. Our enemy is a mystery, a problem that must be solved even though it take ages. Our friend is an extension of ourself, a riddle hard to read. Only one thing is even more difficult to know, and that is one's own self. Not until the bonds of personality – the mask under which all men masquerade – is loosened, shall that Self be truly known.

Hence the great cry of the ancients, "Know thyself," and the sacred teaching in relation to self-knowledge and self-reference: that they involve and include a real love of wisdom – unmanifest and manifested, in books and brooks, in stones where there are stones, and everywhere for those who have eyes to see, and ears to listen. One of the *Mahatmas* spoke of music as the most abstract of the arts and mathematics as the most abstract of the sciences. Pythagoras was concerned with both music and mathematics. He fused in himself active and passive contemplation. This is the subject of a conversation in *The Merchant of Venice* between the newlyweds Lorenzo and Jessica, where Jessica, a Jewish girl of the time with a kind of hippie background, experiences what Lorenzo formulates. It is Lorenzo who says that the man who has no music in his soul is fit for stratagems and spoils.

We are very fortunate to have had from the beginning of the

Theosophical Society a great plan laid down in the letter of the *Maha Chohan*. He spoke of the Theosophical Society as the cornerstone, the foundation of the future religions of humanity. There is a grandeur, a magnitude, a magnificence and a breadth of love and compassion in that sacred document which few who call themselves students of Theosophy can remotely hope to emulate, but which every man or woman is invited to attempt to honour in daily life. H.P. Blavatsky said that we must honour every truth by its use, and that this is the archetypal ritual of any theosophical society. When we use those statements of the Great Master, we discover that the great plan laid down was not irrelevant then, never has been irrelevant since, nor could it ever be. Today it rings with a freshness and a contemporary relevance – especially in its reference to the struggle for existence. Everything is known to the master mathematician Hermes, who is an old man and a young boy at the same time. It is a magnanimous letter, helpful to any of us at this point of time in relation to our fellow human beings.

Each of us is potentially perfect, but each of us is like an iceberg and a mystery to himself and to everyone else. Each of us knows many marvellous volumes of mystical philosophy. When so much is known, to so little avail, clearly then what we are faced with requires more than the knowledge of the mind. It involves more than what we, as inheritors of the methods and modes of Aristotle and Bacon, regard as head-learning. We need soul-wisdom. Here we might well think of simple people walking the streets with waiting, wanting lips. Some are very old, some of them so poor in the wealth of the world that they only have what Lord Buddha called the greatest wealth – contentment. This is the simple man's golden thread. Have some of us lost that simplicity, being so overburdened with our divine discontent which sometimes takes less than human forms? Have we overlooked perhaps the importance of that which is so obvious – a measure of contentment?

We are Promethean beings. We have gaps between our limitations and our potentialities. Every one of us knows that he might have been much more than what he is or what he can show on the surface. In this society the surface has become excessively important. Appearances are lies, but we are caught in the *Mahamaya* of these lies, which then become delusions. The Buddha taught that each man makes his own prison and that within ourselves deliverance must be sought. No man can be saved by himself, and yet no man can be saved by another. In fact, the very notion of "saving" needs re-thinking. We are taught in *The Voice of the Silence* that salvation for one man has no meaning apart from the salvation of the whole of mankind and all living beings. The *Maha Chohan* spoke of mystical Christianity, of the mystical in every religion, and of self-redemption through one's own seventh principle, the liberated *paramatma.* Etymologically, it is this which ceaselessly moves and which in its movement is the source of light, and life, and joy.

If a man asks, "How can we see the Golden Thread in relation to God, Law and Man?" we might say that theosophically, God is formless, beyond colours and sounds, yet immanent in all of them. God is to be found in each of the colours of the riddle of the spectrum, which are in turn puzzles in themselves. They hide subtler hues which may only be seen by those who have the appropriate senses developed and controlled on the planes where alone those senses operate. But all can salute *Tat* – that which is like the one white colourless light, like the sacred white in rice or in the semen which gives birth to a human body within a holy receptacle. Every human being can understand that which is in the heavens, even if only in the realm of appearances, well enough to realize that there will be always some counteraction between solar wisdom – Mercury close to the Sun – and the Moon that waxes and wanes. Every human being finds that he participates in this waxing and waning, albeit not self-consciously enough since his knowledge of cyclic law is limited, his capacity to use it is less, and he usually forgets to look at the heavens. Theosophy appeals to no less an authority than the authority of the heavens, the universal wisdom from which all religions, sciences and philosophies sprang. The greatest founders of all faiths spoke in accents of great awe before That which could not be spoken about.

This profound message is relevant to seeking the Golden Thread that binds all monadic minds in the great universal pilgrimage, and to looking for that common storehouse in *akasa* where alone lies the universal solvent which no man can use unless he wishes to use it for all. In seeking the larger good, a man is able to insert his own good into the good of all – *lokasangraha*. Every man is entitled to be concerned, directly and squarely, with his own good. But his good is only supportable by the law of the universe when it is compatible with universal good. We do not fully know this. Therefore, to the extent to which either we do not know – or knowing, forget it – we have to look for clues. These clues are in the process of life, in nature and in the working of *prana*. When the force of this good comes from outside, it seems like *dharma* or fate, but when we understand it and it works within, it is always seen as our very best friend.

The Golden Thread that binds the cosmos is unveiled only in partial ways. Arising in the realm of the unmanifest, it participates in the Light of the *Logos, daiviprakriti,* which is like a veil upon the Absolute. The Absolute is beyond all relativities or absolutizations of the relative, and, in the words of the *Mandukya Upanishad,* is "unthinkable and unspeakable." But if it is unthinkable and unspeakable, can men recognize it in each other? Can men greet each other with an inward thought and an authentic reference to the absolute centre of a boundless circle within the consciousness of another man inhabiting that holy temple we call the human body? Is this possible for a human being, in the midst of the primary activities of life, in one's respect for one's parents, in one's respect for one's husband or wife, ex-husband or ex-wife, future husband or future wife? Is it possible, in relation to one s own children and the children of others, to remember, where it counts and where it hurts, but where it matters most, that all are children, all are old souls, all are fallen gods, all are men who have made mistakes, but who in the making of them deserve a chance to become self-conscious in relation to survival. Theosophy, warned the *Maha Chohan,* is for all, not for a few.

The story of the Theosophical Movement and of every group that came together in the name of the Wisdom-Religion, is that each fell below the grandeur of the universality and catholicity of the pre-ecumenical, primordial and eternal revelation which remains always in the hands of its great and mighty custodians. Though its breadth is boundless, its height is relevant throughout history and in every religion. It is relevant to every man because every man is entitled to seek and to become worthy of relationship with those men of spiritual stature whom we treat as real Teachers. They cannot be known by external marks. The Buddha's thirty-two marks were always invisible, and as *Kali Yuga* proceeds, it is only from within without that anything worthwhile may be known. All else is a kind of tomfoolery, a concession to Wall Street and Madison Avenue which the Brotherhood has never made and does not now propose to make. "Are not our beards grown?" wrote one of Them. Humanity is mature to a point where it must observe with a wise eye, with a loving heart, and with a compassion that thrills and pulses with the heart of every human being. The Theosophical Movement is for all. The contented simple man who walks the valley of life with very little, and yet smiles and laughs, is one of the teachers of the Theosophical Movement.

The Wisdom-Religion is everywhere, it assumes strange and manifold guises, but it is always sacrificial. Self-reliance is not to be thrown at others like a weapon, but rather, to be gently exemplified through love. Appeals to lesser authorities are mutually destructive, cancelled by the boundless authority of the universe, with which every man is directly linked without need of intermediary. Every man has his own access to God, as was known by the Puritans who spoke of the civil war within the breast of every human being. When we think of the very idea of God, we know that we have to negate and negate. We must negate until we begin to recognize the relevance of *No-thing* to *everything*. To see this in nature with the mind's eye takes time, but once seen, it is the Golden Thread. It shows itself in human affairs as partial representations of the mighty workings of the great wheel of the Law, which is no protector of the illusions of classes, groups, or nations, but which, as the Founding Fathers of the American Republic sensed, can ultimately be understood by all.

The American Constitution is at once a noble document and a threatening one. It is noble because it arose out of the same divine inspiration which is recalled by the third eye on the dollar bill. It is threatening to a country threatened by the magnitude of the Grand Canyon, but which offers every one of its children opportunities which they could use for the sake of all and exemplifies the meaning of the statement, "The whole of nature lies before you. Take what you can." In taking we should not forget to be thankful, not only on Thanksgiving Day, but every day. Then, Theosophy becomes a living power in the life of a man, who can ascend into the hidden realm of occultism in daily life. What is true of scientists like Einstein is even more true of the Brotherhood – that their knowledge cannot be communicated except when preliminary conditions are met. Primary among them, as Shankaracharya pointed out, is gratitude. But any and every man at any time could seek to meet them. Therefore, one of our Masters said, "Take one step in our direction and we will take one in yours."

A man may seek the Golden Thread that binds all religions, sciences and philosophies, and yet never be wholly successful unless he becomes a universal man, a Renaissance man, a man of all cultures. This is a task that is coeval with a whole lifetime. It would be good to begin it in childhood. It is never too late to start, but once started, it is not easy to pursue. Above all, it must be kept in mind with continuity of consciousness if we are to unravel the mystery of mysteries, the mystery of individuality. Who am I? Am I this or that? Am I the person who can be identified in terms of fears and hopes? Am I to be known by my likes and dislikes? Am I the person who masquerades behind a physical form of a certain age and sex, with advantages and disadvantages inherited from a whole line of remote ancestors? We know that over a thousand years every man has had a million ancestors. If a million ancestors have entered into the making of each human being, surely in the complex maze of psycho-physical ancestry there is no clue comparable to the Ariadne's Thread that Theseus used to escape the labyrinth.

Each of us is a labyrinth of complexity today. Everything is in print, but there is scarcely enough time to read or enjoy anything. We suffer from such a surfeit that it is tempting to become nominalists. Yet we know better than that, because we know that refinement of the soul and the culture of the man of the future have nothing to do with class. Therefore, Theosophy can speak to men of all kinds. It cannot be identified with the aristocracy, though H.P. Blavatsky helped them in the nineteenth century. It cannot be identified with the so-called working class, though it benefitted through the laying of the foundations of Theosophical socialism. Annie Besant founded the first trade union for girls in England, while B.P. Wadia founded the first trade union in India. Theosophists who must work in different ways must above all learn to respect diversity. We cannot have a secular fundamentalism wherein each one claims that his is the only diet, the only way. This merely creates more walls that divide men. Each must enjoy his own mode and make his own changes. A Theosophist who learns to set out on his own as an individual cannot make concessions to the conformities of a culture that is now dying. Its death throes, as well as its labour pains, are already evident both in the establishment and elsewhere. The young, with their hungers, sense that something is changing and that something has got to change. Sometimes, even though they love their parents, they cannot outwardly express their respect. In turn, sometimes parents love children so much that they cannot communicate to them the difficulty of the human enterprise. Many a man – almost every great American – knows at some level that God is not mocked, that, "As ye sow, so shall ye also reap." Nature is a teacher here. No man can teach this to another man except by the power of love and the force of example.

The modes of the future will require giving paramount emphasis to that greatest gift possessed by every human being – the most divine gift in the hands of man, treasured in the oral traditions of the past – the gift of sounding the *Logos* within the frame of the human body. It is the gift of making sound, of speech, of articulation. Appropriate articulation, with intrinsic negations, touches that which transcends all verbalization and is beyond verbal expression, that which must always baffle analysis and defy imitation. If we do not appreciate and respond to these opportunities in relation to self-discovery, it is because of the game of externalization, which people play when they come together in a variety of roles and contexts. We are all violating so constantly the most sacred commandment of the Master Jesus, "Judge not, lest ye be judged," that we are not even aware of it. Ceaseless judgment of other human beings – in small towns, in large cities, and in villages – pursued with loveless intransigence in small companionships and groups, makes us think that there is much we all have yet to do if our divine gifts ~ to become the basis of permanent well-being. What can we do – but not "do" in the sense in which "doing" is usually understood in a society which runs around too much? Can we feel what is in the hearts of the young? Of those who are aging? Can we draw larger circles? Can we learn to come together not to analyze why we cannot cooperate but to forget ourselves and to see beyond ourselves? In simple ways, can we accommodate human foibles for the sake of enhancing the good of all?

The good of all is the key to the Golden Thread. No wonder Pythagoras' disciple Plato taught that the best subject for meditation is the universal Good – *to agathon*. He who wishes to meditate on the universal Sun, the source of life and light, is invited to dwell on the sacred *mantram*, the *Gayatri*:

> *Aum bhur bhuvah svah*
> *tatsaviturvarenyam bhargo devasya dhimahi*
> *dhiyo yo nah prachodayat. Om.*

> Let us adore the supremacy of that divine sun who illuminates all, from whom all proceed, to whom all must return, whom we invoke to direct our understandings aright in our progress towards his holy seat.

Anyone who wishes to meditate upon the Sun must see beyond the planets, beyond the diversity of the myriads of galaxies, to the midnight sun in the darkness of the firmament. He must see the Sun as the source of one flame from which shoots a ray of light that kindles every spark in every atom. It is that which is differentiated into innumerable monads and is the only line that persists through its reflection within the human being. Therefore, this is the thread upon which hang like pearls all the personalities of human beings over an immensity of lives in the long journey already extending over some eighteen million years of human existence on this planet.

Every human being has played every role from Puck to Prospero. There is hardly a person who has not held the burden of kingly office. There is no human being who has not known the iniquity of poverty and deprivation. Thoreau understood this when he said, "I was in Judea once, in Greece, in Egypt, everywhere." Whitman knew this and sang of it with love in his heart in the *Song of the Open Road* so that we may all become compassionaters, brothers and lovers of all men, nations and races. It is a teaching sung throughout the history of this Republic. Theosophy is an integral part of the inheritance of the American Republic, originally conceived as a Republic of Conscience.

It has been forgotten. Men have tried to limit America. Men have tried to say that this is a three-religion country, and that each American has to choose between being a Catholic, a Protestant, or a Jew. Now, there is a great deal to learn from the Jewish tradition. It speaks of justice. It speaks of the joy of God when a man and woman come together. It is linked up with the honesty of the psychiatric tradition. Every human being is an honorary wandering Jew. But every human being can also learn from the Catholic tradition, in terms of its current emphasis upon simple decency and the beauty of simple things that can be made sacramental. Just as every boy who is born Jewish has the right of choosing to be as Jewish as he pleases, so every Catholic boy or girl must choose his or her own ways of making moments in daily life sacramental. Also, we are all Protestants because we are all protesting against the views of authority. This was at the very basis of the inspiration of the Constitution. It is imperfect, but it is too late merely to condemn the Protestant tradition. Perhaps it is not three cheers, but it is surely at least two, for the Protestant ethic. It came with the Reformation as a part of the work of Tsong-Kha-Pa and the Brotherhood for the sake of a spiritual reformation within Christianity, comparable to a concurrent spiritual reformation within Hinduism and Buddhism and earlier work within the Catholic church. The last Adept actually to work within the church was Nicolas of Cusa.

No religion or institution is exempt from the all-seeing gaze of Migmar, whose eye sweeps over slumbering Earth. Every sincere human being who seeks to become a true disciple of the divine discipline of the Wisdom-Religion has the protective aura of the hand of Lhagpa over his head. When things go wrong we cannot blame our Teachers. Accepting or assuming our own limitations, we must not limit the Brotherhood. Men have often limited and crucified those the Brotherhood sent. They did it again in a subtle psychological way in the nineteenth century. They will surely attempt to do it in this century and in the future, but will always fail because a great galaxy of Beings is involved, within a carefully designed plan providing lines of retreat to one and all. It was only the Buddha who could take the sacred decision in *Kali Yuga*, where all men have failed and no man can condemn another as a sinner, that although the rules cannot be changed (since occult laws are inviolable), nonetheless access could be made easier for more souls in every part of the world to the wisdom and its mystery temple.

The key always lies within. Tom Paine was prophetic when he anticipated the religion of the future as a trimming away of all the excrescences upon the original substratum. In the beginning was the Word, the Verbum. That was *Theosophia.* Students of Theosophy should not be sensitive to ill-considered criticisms by those non-Theosophists who are also non-everything else, due to the fear of belonging to anything. This fear has become an obsession among human beings consumed with fear for themselves and therefore of others. Instead of worrying about the opinions of others, Theosophists should display the courage of the lion wed to the gentleness of the dove.

Because Theosophy is ultimately beyond names, the Wisdom-Religion is known by many names in all times. Today, the largeness and magnificence of the Wisdom-Religion is a Golden Thread of retreat for any man who wishes to make his own contributions to the future or who wishes to come out and become separate from the cycles of the past which must run their course. He should learn from the old man in the Japanese film *Ikiru,* who, when suddenly told that he had only another week to live, said "Good heavens, what can I do in a week?" He tried everything he had tried before – drinking, doing this, doing that – but time was running out. Suddenly it occurred to him that he had never really lived, or at least that there was still something fundamental he had yet to learn about living. There was no time to make a trip to Tibet or Timbuctu. He had to find his inspiration where he was. He sat sadly, very sadly, until he saw some children playing. He saw how they were doing what Buckminster Fuller teaches – making a little go far – getting a great deal of fun out of very little. They did not even have a proper children's park, but they were having a whale of a time. Then he knew he had something which he could use, that he had tremendous gifts in certain areas. He rushed like a man on a mission and organized with all his wisdom a park where these and many more children might play and enjoy themselves. In effect, he followed the advice that the inventor of supermarkets, Edward Bellamy, gave in the nineteenth century as the secret of self-transcendence. Bellamy felt that the time would come when the only self-transcendence that people would know – and he said it would not work – would be the lesser mystery, sexual love. He predicted that men would desperately want some other mode of seeing beyond themselves, and advised that there is a joy and a thrill which every human being knows in losing himself within the welfare of others. Without this, mothers would not have brought their children to birth and suffered the trials that all mothers have suffered to see their children grow.

Life is a great teacher of the Self and of the teaching about the Self. The Golden Thread binds the various centres within the human constitution. In every human being the *sutratman,* the thread-soul, is *sutratma buddhi.* It is reflected in an innate sense of intuitive recognition, decency, fairness, kindness and minimum self-transcendence. In our culture minima have become profoundly important. They will be the foundations for the maxima of the future. Anyone who has contacted the Path of the Wisdom-Religion can, at the minimum, grasp the simple message, a reminder of what everyone already knows, that it is possible at *this* moment to make a difference to the moment of death. Follow the injunction of *The Voice of the Silence:*

> "Great Sifter" is the name of the "Heart Doctrine," O Disciple. The wheel of the Good Law moves swiftly on. It grinds by night and day. The worthless husks it drives from out the golden grain, the refuse from the flour.

Every man can sift from experience what is worth saving from what cannot be taken or must later be discarded. This was part of the training of the disciples of Pythagoras. It is part of the American Dream. Every human being can, with psychological as well as social mobility, rearrange his critical luggage in the realm of the mind. This has to do with chains of self-reproductive thought, which cannot be stilled suddenly by a dramatic attempt at meditation. Meditation involves the hindering of hindrances. Patanjali's *Yoga Sutra* defines meditation as the hindering of the modifications of the thinking principle. Each must do this in his own way. In the old traditions of Tibet, where all the various schools of Buddhism respected each other and tolerance and civility were shown between the different orders, the distinctive teaching of the Gelukpa Yellow Cap tradition was that the best thing to meditate upon is meditation.

The Golden Thread eludes us when we try too hard to think about it.

At the same time, when we do make the attempt we must think seriously about what it is and what it is not. The Golden Thread cannot be discerned in the realm of the physical body which lives through food – the *annamaya kosha,* the lowest, grossest sheath. The Golden Thread cannot be discerned in the *pranamaya kosha,* the sheath in which the lower currents of energy circulate. The Golden Thread is not to be picked up from those portions of the *manomaya kosha* which are made up of thought-patterns that come from outside and that do not originate from above. The Golden Thread can be picked up in that aspect of the *manomaya* sheath which negates externals and seeks the sheath of *Atman,* the *vignanamaya kosha,* having to do with *vignam,* discrimination or *buddhi.*

The Golden Thread can only be genuinely picked up in the realm of discriminative insight, available to every man. When it is picked up, then one must seek by negation to become self-conscious in one's awareness of continuity of consciousness. Thereby, *Manas* itself can shine and then in turn illuminate the *sutratma* thread which is *sutratma buddhi.* This, then, can become *Manas sutratman.* A person could become self-consciously a being who knows "I am I" and could proudly take his place in the cosmic scheme of things. Every human being is a unit ray reflecting the light of the *Logos.* It is the light with which every man was born, according to the gospel of St. John, and with which he may become resplendent in its fullness. It may be found by all men who choose the heroic steps outlined in the *Book of the Golden Precepts:*

> Shun ignorance, and likewise shun illusion. Avert thy face from world deceptions: mistrust thy senses; they are false. But within thy body – the shrine of thy sensations – seek in the Impersonal for the "Eternal Man"; and having sought him out, look inward: thou art Buddha.

Ojai
April 25, 1972

Hermes, November 1976
Raghavan Iyer

ARCANE KNOWLEDGE

The great and peaceful ones live regenerating
the world like the coming of the spring;
having crossed the ocean of embodied
existence themselves, they freely aid all
others who seek to cross it. The very essence
and inherent will of Mahatmas is to remove
the suffering of others, just as the ambrosia-
rayed moon of itself cools the earth heated by
the intense rays of the sun.

Shankaracharya

Only the progress one makes in the study of Arcane knowledge from its rudimental elements, brings him gradually to understand our meaning. Only thus, and not otherwise, does it, strengthening and refining those mysterious links of sympathy between intelligent men – the temporarily isolated fragments of the universal Soul and the cosmic Soul itself – bring them into full rapport. Once this established, then only will these awakened sympathies serve, indeed, to connect MAN with – what for the want of a European scientific word more competent to express the idea, I am again compelled to describe as that energetic chain which binds together the material and Immaterial Kosmos – Past, Present, and Future – and quicken his perceptions so as to clearly grasp, not merely all things of matter, but of Spirit also. I feel even irritated at having to use these three clumsy words – past, present and future! Miserable concepts of the objective phases of the Subjective Whole, they are about as ill adapted for the purpose as an axe for fine carving . . . .

Such is unfortunately the inherited and self-acquired grossness of the Western mind; and so greatly have the very phrases expressive of modern thoughts been developed in the line of practical materialism, that it is now next to impossible either for them to comprehend or for us to express in their own languages anything of that delicate seemingly ideal machinery of the Occult Kosmos. To some little extent that faculty can be acquired by the Europeans through study and meditation but – that's all. And here is the bar which has hitherto prevented a conviction of the theosophical truths from gaining wider currency among Western Nations; caused theosophical study to be cast aside as useless and fantastic by Western philosophers. How shall I teach you to read and write or even comprehend a language of which no alphabet *palpable*, or words *audible* to you have yet been invented! How could the phenomena of our modern electrical science be explained to – say, a Greek philosopher of the days of Ptolemy were he suddenly recalled to life – with such an unbridged *hiatus* in discovery as would exist between his and our age? Would not the very technical terms be to him an unintelligible jargon, an abracadabra of meaningless sounds, and the very instruments and apparatuses used, but "miraculous" monstrosities? . . .

So you see, the insurmountable difficulties in the way of attaining not only *Absolute* but even primary knowledge in Occult Science, for one situated as you are. How could you make yourself understood – *command* in fact, those semi-intelligent Forces, whose means of communicating with us are not through spoken words but through sounds and colours, in correlations between the vibrations of the two? For sound, light and colours are the main factors in forming these grades of Intelligences, these beings, of whose very existence you have no conception, nor *are you allowed* to believe in them – Atheists and Christians, materialists and Spiritualists, all bringing forward their respective arguments against such a belief – Science objecting stronger than either of these to such a "degrading superstition"! . . . Do not forget the words I once wrote to you *of those who engage themselves in the occult sciences*; he who does it "must either reach the goal or perish. Once fairly started on the way to the great Knowledge, to doubt is to risk insanity; to come to a dead stop is to fall; to recede is to tumble backward, headlong into an abyss." . . .

While the facilities of observation secured to some of us by our condition certainly give a greater breadth of view, a more pronounced and impartial, as a more widely spread humaneness – for answering Addison, we might justly maintain that it is . . . "the business of 'magic' to humanise our natures with compassion" for the whole mankind as all living beings, instead of concentrating and limiting our affections to one predilected race – yet few of us (except such as have attained the final negation of Moksha) can so far enfranchise ourselves from the influence of our earthly connection as to be insusceptible in various degrees to the higher pleasures, emotions, and interests of the common run of humanity. Until final emancipation reabsorbs the *Ego*, it *must* be conscious of the purest sympathies called out by the esthetic effects of high art, its tenderest cords respond to the call of the holier and nobler *human* attachments. Of course, the greater the progress towards deliverance, the less this will be the case, until, to crown all, human and purely individual personal feelings – blood-ties and friendship, patriotism and race predilection – all will give away, to become blended into one universal feeling, the only true and holy, the only unselfish and Eternal one – Love, an Immense Love for humanity – as a *Whole*! For it is "Humanity" which is the great Orphan, the only disinherited one upon this earth, my friend. And it is the duty of every man who is capable of an unselfish impulse, to do something, however little, for its welfare. Poor, poor humanity! It reminds me of the old fable of the war between the Body and its members: here too, each limb of this huge "Orphan" – fatherless and motherless – selfishly cares but for itself. *The* body uncared for suffers eternally, whether the limbs are at war or at rest. Its suffering and agony never cease. . . . And who can blame it – as your materialistic philosophers do – if, in this everlasting isolation and neglect it has evolved gods, unto whom "it ever cries for help but is not heard!" . . . Thus –

> Since there is hope for man *only in man*
> I would not let *one* cry whom I could save! . . .

Theosophy is no new candidate for the world's attention, but only the restatement of principles which have been recognised from the very infancy of mankind. The historic sequence ought to be succinctly yet graphically traced through the successive evolutions of philosophical schools, and illustrated with accounts of the experimental demonstrations of occult power ascribed to various thaumaturgists. The alternate breakings-out and subsidences of mystical phenomena, as well as their shiftings from one centre to another of population, show the conflicting play of the opposing forces of spirituality and animalism. And lastly it will appear that the present tidal-wave of phenomena, with its varied effects upon human thought and feeling, made the revival of Theosophical enquiry an indispensable necessity. The only problem to solve is the practical one, of how best to promote the necessary study, and give to the spiritualistic movement a needed upward impulse. It is a good beginning to make the inherent capabilities of the inner, living man better comprehended. . . . Unity always gives strength: and since Occultism in our days resembles a "Forlorn Hope," union and co-operation are indispensable. Union does indeed imply a concentration of vital and magnetic force against the hostile currents of prejudice and fanaticism.

February 1881   Mahatma K. H.

It is he alone who has the love of humanity at heart, who is capable of grasping thoroughly the idea of a regenerating practical Brotherhood who is entitled to the possession of our secrets. He alone, such a man – will never misuse his powers, as there will be no fear that he should turn them to selfish ends. A man who places not the good of mankind above his own good is not worthy of becoming our chela – he is not worthy of becoming higher in knowledge than his neighbour. If he craves for phenomena let him be satisfied with the pranks of spiritualism. Such is the real state of things. There was a time, when from sea to sea, from the mountains and deserts of the north to the grand woods and downs of Ceylon, there was but one faith, one rallying cry – to save humanity from the miseries of ignorance in the name of Him who taught first the solidarity of all men . . . . The world has clouded the light of true knowledge, and selfishness will not allow its resurrection, for it excludes and will not recognise the whole fellowship of all those who were born under the same immutable natural law.

Mahatma M.

THE CREATIVE WILL

There is no possible way of understanding or explaining the nature of any being whatever except through Evolution, which is always an unfolding from within outwards, the expression of spirit or consciousness through the intelligence acquired. The will of spirit in action has produced everything that exists.

If we understand that intelligent will lies behind everything that exists, is the cause of everything that is, is the Creator in the universe, we may perhaps gain some idea of what it is necessary for us to know in order properly to use our powers.

All stand as creators in the midst of our creations. There are creators below us in the scale of intelligence. We stand in another place, with a wider range of vision, a greater fund of experience; so we can see that below us, infinitely below us, are beings so small that many of them could be gathered on the point of a needle. Yet the scientists who have examined them under many conditions cannot deny to these infinitesimal organisms a certain intelligence, an ability to seek what they like and to avoid what they dislike. From the smallest conceivable point of perception and action there is a constantly widening range of expression, of evolution, a development more and more in the direction of a greater range of being. This evolution of intelligence, or soul, proceeds very slowly in the lower kingdoms, more rapidly in the animal kingdom, and in man has reached that stage where the being himself knows that he is, that he is conscious, that he can understand to some extent his own nature and the natures of the beings below him, and see their relation to each other.

Man has now reached a point where he begins to inquire what more there is for him to know. He has ceased to think exclusively of the material; he is sensing his own nature, and he asks, What am I, whence came I, whither do I go?

If we have these ideas, we can perceive that there must have been in the past some amongst men who asked these very questions that we are now asking, and who took the steps that carried them to a higher point of experience and knowledge than we now occupy. It is these very beings, now above us, who form a stratum of consciousness, of knowledge and power, that we have not – men who have passed through the stages we are now in. They are the very ones who come to this earth as Saviors from time to time.

As Christians, we look back to the advent of One such, and think of Him as unique. Yet He came in His time to but one small nation; He said Himself that He came but to the Jews. Do we not know that every civilization and every tribe that ever has existed has held a similar record – that of some great Personage who came amongst them?

Back of all the religions that ever have been, there is the record, the tradition, of some great Personage. And we find an astonishing fact in studying the scriptures and teachings of other days – each of these great Teachers taught the same doctrines. There is no difference between the teachings of Jesus and the teachings of Buddha, although those teachings are recorded in different languages and an interval of six hundred years separated the two great Teachers. What is true of these two is likewise true of all the other many Saviors of different times and peoples – they all taught the same fundamental ideas.

This fact suggests that there is a body of Men, of perfected men, product of past civilizations and evolution, our Elder Brothers, in fact, who have acquired and are the Custodians of the knowledge and experience gained through aeons of time. Their knowledge is actually the very Science of Life, for it enters into every department of existence, of nature. They know the natures and processes of the beings below man, and above man, as we know the processes of ordinary every-day experience. This knowledge they have preserved and recorded, and they have the memory of it, just as we have the memory of yesterday's experiences and events.

They have not extended their power to know. We have each of us the same power to know that is theirs. But they have extended the facilities of the instruments which they possess. They have improved what they have. They have better brains. They have better bodies. How did they acquire them? By fulfilling every duty which faced them, regardless of what came to themselves. They thought nothing of acquiring power and knowledge for themselves; they thought only of gaining power that they might expend it for the benefit of every living creature. In so doing they opened the doors to the full play of the power of the Spirit within.

We do the very opposite. We contract the divine power of the Spirit within us to the pin-holes of personal desires and selfishness. Do we not see that? Do we not see that we ourselves stand in the way of the use of the power within us because our ideas are selfish, small, mean?

The great work of evolution proceeds from within outwards. The Soul is the Perceiver; it looks directly on ideas. The action of the will is through ideas. The ideas give the directions. Small ideas, small force; large ideas, large force; the Force itself is illimitable, for it is the force of Spirit, infinite and exhaustless. What we lack are universal ideas. We need to arouse in ourselves that power of perception which will lay the whole field of being open to us. A stream cannot rise higher than its source.

The nature of man can never be understood in the least degree by the ideas and methods which modern psychologists and scientists and popular religions are following. They all proceed from the basis of physical life, many of them from the basis of one life only. They tabulate experiences of many kinds, without any firm basis upon which to fix their thought, their reason, and so never arrive at any definite conclusion or real knowledge of what man is, or of the powers that he may exhibit. This is their use of the creative power, but it is a limited use, a misuse. Those who follow that way usually have some selfish purpose at the base of their desire, something they wish to achieve for themselves, some benefit they desire for themselves. This is not the way. Theosophy says that if the desire or aspiration is unselfish, noble, universal, then the force which flows through the individual is grand, noble, universal in its character. Further, that every human being has in him the same elements, the same possibilities, as any other, even the noblest and highest beings in this or any solar system. This puts man in quite a different position from where our religions, our science, or our philosophy of the West place him. They all treat of man as if he were his body or his mind, as if he were the creature and not the creator.

The body changes; we change our minds; but there is a Something in us which does not change, which does not depend on change, whether of body, mind or circumstances, but which is the creator, the ruler, the experiencer of all changes of every kind. It is this portion of our nature – the real Man within us – that we need to know the nature of. If we can reach such a point of perception that we can grasp the fact of the Spirit within us, we shall have reached a point where a knowledge of ourselves is possible; and if a knowledge of ourselves, then a knowledge through that of all other beings whatsoever.

The great Teachers point to the fact that the real basis of man's nature is Divinity, Spirit, God. Deity is not some other being, however great. It is not something outside. It is the very highest in ourselves and in all others. That is the God, and all that any man may know of this Spirit is what he knows in himself, of himself, through himself. This is the idea that all the ancients put forward in saying there is but one Self, and that we are to see the Self in all things and all things in the Self. That is what we all do to some extent; we see the Self, more or less. Nothing is seen outside ourselves; everything that we see or know is within ourselves. But we think of the Self in us as mortal, perishable, having no existence apart from this body and this mind, and as separate from the Self in all other forms.

If we had within us and behind us all the power that there is in the universe, and we had no channel through which that power could flow – or only a narrow, twisted, distorted channel – that great Power would be of no use to us, would be non-existent to us. To open up the channel it is necessary for us to understand the real basis: the God within, immortal and eternal, the Source of all being, our very selves; second, that all action proceeds from that Source and Center of our being and of all being.

Then who is the constructor of all? How was all this evolution brought about? All the beings involved in it make up both the world and its inhabitants; all that exists is Self-produced, Self-evolved – the creation of Spiritual beings acting in, on, and through each other. The whole force of evolution, and the whole power behind it, is the human will, so far as humanity is concerned. We do not realize that every form occupied by any being is composed of Lives, each undergoing evolution on its own account, aided, impelled or hindered by the force of the higher form of consciousness that evolved it. For this universe is *embodied* Consciousness, or Spirit. And just as a single drop of water contains within it every element and characteristic of the whole ocean, so each being, however low in the degree of its intelligence, contains within itself the potentiality and possibilities of the highest. The will of the Spirit in action has produced all.

The great Message of Theosophy has provided for every interested enquirer the means by which he may know the truth about himself and nature. Just as the Elder Brothers have provided in the past, so They have again in our day. Everything that Humanity needs has been given to us. But can you give to anyone what he does not Want? Can you cause to enter into the mind of another what that mind will not receive?

There has to be an open mind, a pure heart, an eager intellect, an unveiled spiritual perception, before there is any hope for us. As long as we are self-centered, as long as we are satisfied with what we know and what we have, this great Message is not for us. It is for the hungry, for the weary, for those who are desirous of knowledge, for those who see the absolute paucity of what has been put before us as knowledge by those who style themselves our teachers, for those who find no explanation anywhere of the mysteries that surround us, who do not know themselves, who do not understand themselves. For them there is a way; for them there is food in abundance; for them this whole Movement is kept in being by one single will, the Will of the Elder Brothers who have carried these great eternal truths through good and evil in order that mankind may be benefited; not desiring any reward, not desiring any recognition, desiring only that Their fellow men, Their younger brothers, may know, may realize what They know.

Universal Theosophy
Robert Crosbie

THEOSOPHY AND THE MASTERS

Theosophy is that ocean of knowledge which spreads from shore to shore of the evolution of sentient beings; unfathomable in its deepest parts, it gives the greatest minds their fullest scope, yet, shallow enough at its shores, it will not overwhelm the understanding of a child. It is wisdom about God for those who believe that he is all things and in all, and wisdom about nature for the man who accepts the statement found in the Christian Bible that God cannot be measured or discovered, and that darkness is around his pavilion. Although it contains by derivation the name God and thus may seem at first sight to embrace religion alone, it does not neglect science, for it is the science of sciences and therefore has been called the wisdom religion. For no science is complete which leaves out any department of nature, whether visible or invisible, and that religion which, depending solely on an assumed revelation, turns away from things and the laws which govern them is nothing but a delusion, a foe to progress, an obstacle in the way of man's advancement toward happiness. Embracing both the scientific and the religious, Theosophy is a scientific religion and a religious science.

It is not a belief or dogma formulated or invented by man, but is a knowledge of the laws which govern the evolution of the physical, astral, psychical, and intellectual constituents of nature and of man. The religion of the day is but a series of dogmas man-made and with no scientific foundation for promulgated ethics; while our science as yet ignores the unseen, and failing to admit the existence of a complete set of inner faculties of perception in man, it is cut off from the immense and real field of experience which lies within the visible and tangible worlds. But Theosophy knows that the whole is constituted of the visible and the invisible, and perceiving outer things and objects to be but transitory it grasps the facts of nature, both without and within. It is therefore complete in itself and sees no unsolvable mystery anywhere; it throws the word coincidence out of its vocabulary and hails the reign of law in everything and every circumstance.

That man possesses an immortal soul is the common belief of humanity; to this Theosophy adds that he is a soul; and further that all nature is sentient, that the vast array of objects and men are not mere collections of atoms fortuitously thrown together and thus without law evolving law, but down to the smallest atom all is soul and spirit ever evolving under the rule of law which is inherent in the whole. And just as the ancients taught, so does Theosophy; that the course of evolution is the drama of the soul and that nature exists for no other purpose than the soul's experience. The Theosophist agrees with Prof. Huxley in the assertion that there must be beings in the universe whose intelligence is as much beyond ours as ours exceeds that of the black beetle, and who take an active part in the government of the natural order of things. Pushing further on by the light of the confidence had in his teachers, the Theosophist adds that such intelligences were once human and came like all of us from other and previous worlds, where as varied experience had been gained as is possible on this one. We are therefore not appearing for the first time when we come upon this planet, but have pursued a long, an immeasurable course of activity and intelligent perception on other systems of globes, some of which were destroyed ages before the solar system condensed. This immense reach of the evolutionary system means, then, that this planet on which we now are is the result of the activity and the evolution of some other one that died long ago, leaving its energy to be used in the bringing into existence of the earth, and that the inhabitants of the latter in their turn came from some older world to proceed here with the destined work in matter. And the brighter planets, such as Venus, are the habitation of still more progressed entities, once as low as ourselves, but now raised up to a pitch of glory incomprehensible for our intellects.

The most intelligent being in the universe, man, has never, then, been without a friend, but has a line of elder brothers who continually watch over the progress of the less progressed, preserve the knowledge gained through aeons of trial and experience, and continually seek for opportunities of drawing the developing intelligence of the race on this or other globes to consider the great truths concerning the destiny of the soul. These elder brothers also keep the knowledge they have gained of the laws of nature in all departments, and are ready when cyclic law permits to use it for the benefit of mankind. They have always existed as a body, all knowing each other, no matter in what part of the world they may be, and all working for the race in many different ways. In some periods they are well known to the people and move among ordinary men whenever the social organization, the virtue, and the development of the nations permit it. For if they were to come out openly and be heard of everywhere, they would be worshipped as gods by some and hunted as devils by others. In those periods when they do come out some of their number are rulers of men, some teachers, a few great philosophers, while others remain still unknown except to the most advanced of the body.

It would be subversive of the ends they have in view were they to make themselves public in the present civilization, which is based almost wholly on money, fame, glory, and personality. For this age, as one of them has already said, "is an age of transition," when every system of thought, science, religion, government, and society is changing, and men's minds are only preparing for an alteration into that state which will permit the race to advance to the point suitable for these elder brothers to introduce their actual presence to our sight. They may be truly called the bearers of the torch of truth across the ages; they investigate all things and beings; they know what man is in his innermost nature and what his powers and destiny, his state before birth and the states into which he goes after the death of his body; they have stood by the cradle of nations and seen the vast achievements of the ancients, watched sadly the decay of those who had no power to resist the cyclic law of rise and fall; and while cataclysms seemed to show a universal destruction of art, architecture, religion, and philosophy, they have preserved the records of it all in places secure from the ravages of either men or time; they have made minute observations, through trained psychics among their own order, into the unseen realms of nature and of mind, recorded the observations and preserved the record; they have mastered the mysteries of sound and color through which alone the elemental beings behind the veil of matter can be communicated with, and thus can tell why the rain falls and what it falls for, whether the earth is hollow or not, what makes the wind to blow and light to shine, and greater feat than all — one which implies a knowledge of the very foundations of nature — they know what the ultimate divisions of time are and what are the meaning and the times of the cycles.

But, asks the busy man of the nineteenth century who reads the newspapers and believes in "modern progress," if these elder brothers are all you claim them to be, why have they left no mark on history nor gathered men around them? Their own reply, published some time ago by Mr. A. P. Sinnett, is better than any I could write.

"We will first discuss, if you please, the one relating to the presumed failure of the 'Fraternity' to 'leave any mark upon the history of the world.' They ought, you think, to have been able, with their extraordinary advantages, to have 'gathered into their schools a considerable portion of the more enlightened minds of every race.' How do you know they have made no such mark? Are you acquainted with their efforts, successes, and failures? Have you any dock upon which to arraign them? How could your world collect proofs of the doings of men who have sedulously kept closed every possible door of approach by which the inquisitive could spy upon them? The prime condition of their success was that they should never be supervised or obstructed. What they have done they know; all that those outside their circle could perceive was results, the causes of which were masked from view. To account for these results, men have, in different ages, invented theories of the interposition of gods, special providences, fates, the benign or hostile influences of the stars. There never was a time within or before the so-called historical period when our predecessors were not moulding events and 'making history,' the facts of which were subsequently and invariably distorted by historians to suit contemporary prejudices. Are you quite sure that the visible heroic figures in the successive dramas were not often but their puppets? We never pretended to be able to draw nations in the mass to this or that crisis in spite of the general drift of the world's cosmic relations. The cycles must run their rounds. Periods of mental and moral light and darkness succeed each other as day does night. The major and minor yugas must be accomplished according to the established order of things. And we, borne along on the mighty tide, can only modify and direct some of its minor currents."

It is under cyclic law, during a dark period in the history of mind, that the true philosophy disappears for a time, but the same law causes it to reappear as surely as the sun rises and the human mind is present to see it. But some works can only be performed by the Master, while other works require the assistance of the companions. It is the Master's work to preserve the true philosophy, but the help of the companions is needed to rediscover and promulgate it. Once more the elder brothers have indicated where the truth — Theosophy — could be found, and the companions all over the world are engaged in bringing it forth for wider currency and propagation.

The Elder Brothers of Humanity are men who were perfected in former periods of evolution. These periods of manifestation are unknown to modern evolutionists so far as their number are concerned, though long ago understood by not only the older Hindus, but also by those great minds and men who instituted and carried on the first pure and undebased form of the Mysteries of Greece. The periods, when out of the Great Unknown there come forth the visible universes, are eternal in their coming and going, alternating with equal periods of silence and rest again in the Unknown. The object of these mighty waves is the production of perfect man, the evolution of soul, and they always witness the increase of the number of Elder Brothers; the life of the least of men pictures them in day and night, waking and sleeping, birth and death, "for these two, light and dark, day and night, are the world's eternal ways."

In every age and complete national history these men of power and compassion are given different designations. They have been called Initiates, Adepts, Magi, Hierophants, Kings of the East, Wise Men, Brothers, and what not. But in the Sanskrit language there is a word which, being applied to them, at once thoroughly identifies them with humanity. It is *Mahatma*. This is composed of *Maha*, great, and *Atma*, soul; so it means great soul, and as all men are souls the distinction of the *Mahatma* lies in greatness. The term *Mahatma* has come into wide use through the Theosophical Society, as Mme. H. P. Blavatsky constantly referred to them as her Masters who gave her the knowledge she possessed. They were at first known only as the Brothers, but afterwards, when many Hindus flocked to the Theosophical movement, the name *Mahatma* was brought into use, inasmuch as it has behind it an immense body of Indian tradition and literature. At different times unscrupulous enemies of the Theosophical Society have said that even this name had been invented and that such beings are not known of among the Indians or in their literature. But these assertions are made only to discredit if possible a philosophical movement that threatens to completely upset prevailing erroneous theological dogmas. For all through Hindu literature *Mahatmas* are often spoken of, and in parts of the north of that country the term is common. In the very old poem the *Bhagavad-Gita*, revered by all Hindu sects and admitted by the western critics to be noble as well as beautiful, there is a verse reading, "Such a *Mahatma* is difficult to find."

But irrespective of all disputes as to specific names, there is sufficient argument and proof to show that a body of men having the wonderful knowledge described above has always existed and probably exists today. The older mysteries continually refer to them. Ancient Egypt had them in her great king-Initiates, sons of the sun and friends of great gods. There is a habit of belittling the ideas of the ancients which is in itself belittling to the people of today. Even the Christian who reverently speaks of Abraham as "the friend of God," will scornfully laugh at the idea of the claims of Egyptian rulers to the same friendship being other than childish assumption of dignity and title. But the truth is, these great Egyptians were Initiates, members of the one great lodge which includes all others of whatever degree or operation. The later and declining Egyptians, of course, must have imitated their predecessors, but that was when the true doctrine was beginning once more to be obscured upon the rise of dogma and priesthood.

The story of Apollonius of Tyana is about a member of one of the same ancient orders appearing among men at a descending cycle, and only for the purpose of keeping a witness upon the scene for future generations.

Abraham and Moses of the Jews are two other Initiates, Adepts who had their work to do with a certain people; and in the history of Abraham we meet with Melchizedek, who was so much beyond Abraham that he had the right to confer upon the latter a dignity, a privilege, or a blessing. The same chapter of human history which contains the names of Moses and Abraham is illuminated also by that of Solomon. And thus these three make a great Triad of Adepts, the record of whose deeds can not be brushed aside as folly and devoid of basis.

Moses was educated by the Egyptians and in Midian, from both of which he gained much occult knowledge, and any clear-seeing student of the great Universal Masonry can perceive all through his books the hand, the plan, and the work of a master. Abraham again knew all the arts and much of the power in psychical realms that were cultivated in his day, or else he could not have consorted with kings nor have been "the friend of God"; and the reference to his conversations with the Almighty in respect to the destruction of cities alone shows him to have been an Adept who had long ago passed beyond the need of ceremonial or other adventitious aids. Solomon completes this triad and stands out in characters of fire. Around him is clustered such a mass of legend and story about his dealings with the elemental powers and of his magic possessions that one must condemn the whole ancient world as a collection of fools who made lies for amusement if a denial is made of his being a great character, a wonderful example of the incarnation among men of a powerful Adept. We do not have to accept the name Solomon nor the pretense that he reigned over the Jews, but we must admit the fact that somewhere in the misty time to which the Jewish records refer there lived and moved among the people of the earth one who was an Adept and given that name afterwards. Peripatetics and microscopic critics may affect to see in the prevalence of universal tradition naught but evidence of the gullibility of men and their power to imitate, but the true student of human nature and life knows that the universal tradition is true and arises from the facts in the history of man.

Turning to India, so long forgotten and ignored by the lusty and egotistical, the fighting and the trading West, we find her full of the lore relating to these wonderful men of whom Noah, Abraham, Moses, and Solomon are only examples. There the people are fitted by temperament and climate to be the preservers of the philosophical, ethical, and psychical jewels that would have been forever lost to us had they been left to the ravages of such Goths and Vandals as western nations were in the early days of their struggle for education and civilization. If the men who wantonly burned up vast masses of historical and ethnological treasures found by the minions of the Catholic rulers of Spain, in Central and South America, could have known of and put their hands upon the books and palm-leaf records of India before the protecting shield of England was raised against them, they would have destroyed them all as they did for the Americans, and as their predecessors attempted to do for the Alexandrian library. Fortunately events worked otherwise.

All along the stream of Indian literature we can find the names by scores of great adepts who were well known to the people and who all taught the same story — the great epic of the human soul. Their names are unfamiliar to western ears, but the records of their thoughts, their work and powers remain. Still more, in the quiet unmovable East there are today by the hundred persons who know of their own knowledge that the Great Lodge still exists and has its *Mahatmas*, Adepts, Initiates, Brothers. And yet further, in that land are such a number of experts in the practical application of minor though still very astonishing power over nature and her forces, that we have an irresistible mass of human evidence to prove the proposition laid down.

And if Theosophy — the teaching of this Great Lodge — is as said, both scientific and religious, then from the ethical side we have still more proof. A mighty Triad acting on and through ethics is that composed of Buddha, Confucius, and Jesus. The first, a Hindu, founds a religion which today embraces many more people than Christianity, teaching centuries before Jesus the ethics which he taught and which had been given out even centuries before Buddha. Jesus coming to reform his people repeats these ancient ethics, and Confucius does the same thing for ancient and honorable China.

The Theosophist says that all these great names represent members of the one single brotherhood, who all have a single doctrine. And the extraordinary characters who now and again appear in western civilization, such as St. Germain, Jacob Boehme, Cagliostro, Paracelsus, Mesmer, Count St. Martin, and Madame H. P. Blavatsky, are agents for the doing of the work of the Great Lodge at the proper time. It is true they are generally reviled and classed as impostors — though no one can find out why they are when they generally confer benefits and lay down propositions or make discoveries of great value to science after they have died. But Jesus himself would be called an impostor today if he appeared in some Fifth Avenue theatrical church rebuking the professed Christians. Paracelsus was the originator of valuable methods and treatments in medicine now universally used. Mesmer taught hypnotism under another name. Madame Blavatsky brought once more to the attention of the West the most important system, long known to the Lodge, respecting man, his nature and destiny. But all are alike called impostors by a people who have no original philosophy of their own and whose mendicant and criminal classes exceed in misery and in number those of any civilization on the earth.

It will not be unusual for nearly all occidental readers to wonder how men could possibly know so much and have such power over the operations of natural law as I have ascribed to the Initiates, now so commonly spoken of as the *Mahatmas*. In India, China, and other Oriental lands no wonder would arise on these heads, because there, although everything of a material civilization is just now in a backward state, they have never lost a belief in the inner nature of man and in the power he may exercise if he will. Consequently living examples of such powers and capacities have not been absent from those people. But in the West a materialistic civilization having arisen through a denial of the soul life and nature consequent upon a reaction from illogical dogmatism, there has not been any investigation of these subjects and, until lately, the general public has not believed in the possibility of anyone save a supposed God having such power.

A *Mahatma* endowed with power over space, time, mind, and matter, is a possibility just because he is a perfected man. Every human being has the germ of all the powers attributed to these great Initiates, the difference lying solely in the fact that we have in general not developed what we possess the germ of, while the Mahatma has gone through the training and experience which have caused all the unseen human powers to develop in him, and conferred gifts that look god-like to his struggling brother below. Telepathy, mind-reading, and hypnotism, all long ago known to Theosophy, show the existence in the human subject of planes of consciousness, functions, and faculties hitherto undreamed of. Mind-reading and the influencing of the mind of the hypnotized subject at a distance prove the existence of a mind which is not wholly dependent upon a brain, and that a medium exists through which the influencing thought may be sent. It is under this law that the Initiates can communicate with each other at no matter what distance. Its *rationale*, not yet admitted by the schools of the hypnotizers, is, that if the two minds vibrate or change into the same state they will think alike, or, in other words, the one who is to hear at a distance receives the impression sent by the other. In the same way with all other powers, no matter how extraordinary. They are all natural, although now unusual, just as great musical ability is natural though not usual or common. If an Initiate can make a solid object move without contact, it is because he understands the two laws of attraction and repulsion of which "gravitation" is but the name for one; if he is able to precipitate out of the viewless air the carbon which we know is in it, forming the carbon into sentences upon the paper, it is through his knowledge of the occult higher chemistry, and the use of a trained and powerful image making faculty which every man possesses; if he reads your thoughts with ease, that results from the use of the inner and only real powers of sight, which require no retina to see the fine-pictured web which the vibrating brain of man weaves about him. All that the *Mahatma* may do is natural to the perfected man; but if those powers are not at once revealed to us it is because the race is as yet selfish altogether and still living for the present and the transitory.

I repeat then, that though the true doctrine disappears for a time from among men it is bound to reappear, because first, it is impacted in the imperishable center of man's nature; and secondly, the Lodge forever preserves it, not only in actual objective records, but also in the intelligent and fully self-conscious men who, having successfully overpassed the many periods of evolution which preceded the one we are now involved in, cannot lose the precious possessions they have acquired. And because the elder brothers are the highest product of evolution through whom alone, in cooperation with the whole human family, the further regular and workmanlike prosecution of the plans of the Great Architect of the Universe could be carried on, I have thought it well to advert to them and their Universal Lodge before going to other parts of the subject.

The Ocean Of Theosophy, Chapter I
W.Q. Judge

THE LANGUAGE OF THE SOUL

The Soul is pictured in the ancient teachings as the real Self man. There are many different conceptions of what man is and what the soul. From Christian teachings we are led to believe that man has a soul, and may save it or lose it – the idea generally held in the West. But the conception of the ancients, and that of Theosophy, which is a re-presentation of this eternal idea, is different. The teaching is that Man is a Soul; that Soul is in fact the one who perceives; that it is vision itself, pure and simple, unmodified – not subject to change – and that it looks directly on ideas.

This idea presents the fact that the real Man in whatever condition he may be existing, whether asleep or awake, whether in a physical body during his lifetime, or whether in another form of body after death or before birth, or before the existence of this planet or this solar system – that this real Man was the same Perceiver, then as now, the same Soul all the time; the Creator of all the conditions that have arisen; the intelligent Creator of this universe, in connection with all the beings below him and all the beings above him. Man thus forms part of one great Brotherhood, and this bond of brotherhood extends throughout, from the lowest being to the very highest.

They are all Souls; even the very lowest forms of matter are none the less Souls, for in the lowest form of matter is the power to perceive, the power to act, the power to gain experience. The potentiality is the same in all, and that potentiality becomes a potency ever expanding as the Soul increases its range of experience. All the forms, the bodies that compose the universe, are the results of the experience and action of the souls inhabiting them. They are all the instruments of the soul, and we always act with others in any grade or class of beings. There is that unity of action which produces a similarity of instrument. In these similarities of instrument we play upon and are played upon by beings of the same class in the fullest degree, and by lower and higher classes in a greater or less degree.

So, taking this conception that the Self is the same in each being, no matter how great that being may be, nor how low, we get another idea in regard to soul – that soul also represents the acquired experience gained through evolution by each and every class of being. Each individual being is not only Self, but, in addition, the acquired experience gained through contact with all other beings. Realizing that there are individual souls, we can see that the only differences between souls are in their degrees of acquired experience. Taking the soul from this point of view, then, as the acquired experience of individuals, when we speak of God, or the Over-Soul, the Universal Over-Soul, we simply mean the acquired experiences, or wisdom, of every soul and all souls. That would be the meaning of the sentence in the Bhagavad Gita that the Self is "Wisdom itself, the object of Wisdom and that which is to be attained by Wisdom" – full consciousness of the union of all-souls, or Spiritual Identity.

If we are to try to relate these conceptions to language we would, perhaps, have to clear up many ideas which we now hold. Supposing there is a real language of the soul, what would it be capable of expressing? Undoubtedly every experience through which it had ever been.

Theosophy teaches the doctrine of reincarnation – of successive lives, both on this earth and in other states of substance and consciousness. Continuity of Consciousness, or Spirit, is preserved through all these states and environments, and the record of all that occurred in all these lives is present at all times in any one- life in manifestation, because the Self, the Spirit, is present. The language of the Soul would be capable of expressing all that we ever experienced.

In those past lives we have undoubtedly spoken different languages from those we now speak; in those personal existences we used languages now altogether deserted and forgotten by us as persons. But the memory of those languages must be there, if we are a continuing Self and preserve the continuity of experience gained, as well as the continuity of consciousness. Those old languages which we once used, in themselves amount to nothing, because any language and all languages are only the expression of the feeling and thought of the individual soul; his emotions, hopes, fears, ideas and aspirations. So there must be at all times behind any language whatever, the basis for it – the Soul and its experience. Where is that recorded? It is impacted in the imperishable part of man's nature. It cannot be any spoken tongue what ever. What, then, is its nature?

To understand these propositions we have again to consider the philosophy of Theosophy. Theosophy points out that matter is in seven states or degrees of substances, and each of these with seven sub-states, the whole ranging from the very finest, most plastic and enduring state down to the very coarsest – what we may call the material plane, or matter as it is known and suspected by us, with its many differing gradations and combinations. Man, as the highest and most evolved being concerned in the evolution of this solar system, is clothed in all these seven states of substance derived from the original primordial substance – the homogeneous matter from which every form is evolved. These degrees of substance are indicated in the seven colors of the spectrum; they are also pointed to in the seven notes of the scale of music.

The notes and colors are not exactly what we think they are: they represent the seven great distinct states of matter; sound itself, or light itself, represents the homogeneous state from which the seven notes and the seven prismatic colors are derived. Our colors and our musical notes are only replicas of these – their reflections or correspondences in this one state of matter and sound with which we are acquainted. We know there are seven colors; we know that there are other octaves of color beyond those, which our eyes are unable to transmit to us – some so high, some so low that our eyes will not register their vibrations. The same is true with sound. We are able to detect several, but there are degrees of sound beyond the highest we are able to detect, and also sounds too low for us to hear.

Let us call the Soul the Ego; perhaps that, for us, is the most compact expression for what is meant by Soul, since it includes both the one who perceives and his perceptions, both the one who knows and his experiences. Well, then, the Ego has a language of his own, and that language is one of color, sound and symbol. It is a language that may be seen; that may be heard; that may be felt. It is by means of this language of the soul that the experiences of others may become directly known to us, comprehensible to us, no matter what vocal tongues we may use. This is why it was said in old times, as mentioned in the Bible, that the Wise understood every man speaking in his own tongue, although many different languages were used, then as now. It was because these Wise men could read back of the spoken language, that they knew the very thoughts, feelings and natures of the speakers. That is why in any person's motion – even so simple an action as in moving from one chair to another – quality of the thought, the very nature of the person, is clearly shown by the assemblage of colors and shades of colors produced by the action. The same with any uttered sounds or speech, no matter what – the centers in the body are set in motion, each having its own particular tell tale colors and rates of vibration.

Strange as it may seem to us, colors may be heard, sounds may be seen, and forms may be experienced, because all are merely different rates of vibration – the motion of Intelligent Consciousness, or Spirit. They are all correlated, and one does not exist with out the others. They are merely aspects of that which is the real propulsion of the soul itself, or the conscious being. So, in our thoughts we have a great combination of colors and sounds, constantly changing their form, or appearance. Our brain is the finest material instrument we use. It, like everything else we use, is an evolution. It is the organ of thought on this plane of substance where we are now acting. If we think high and noble thoughts, then our brains become very susceptible to that kind of use. Every kind of thought has its own particular rate and range of vibration, its own particular colors. If we were acquainted with ourselves, in reality, we could read thought as we now read a book. We could read thoughts as we now hear sounds. If our brains are trained to high thoughts while we are awake; if we try to understand what we really are while occupying this physical instrument; what this body of ours represents; what it is capable of – then gradually the brain will begin to respond to something of our higher knowledge. It will carry forward and transmit more and more of the Language of the Soul, of all the garnered experience of the past.

The ideas that we have, even in regard to Spirit and Soul, to Life hitherto, here and hereafter, are those we have been taught. They are nearly all personal and keep us entirely on the personal plane – the plane of merely physical existence. They give us no true ideas whatever of the real inner self. We have not yet begun to think – in any true sense, in any true direction; and it is only true ideas that will give us knowledge of the inner nature of man. Our habits are merely memory impacted in our nature, whether they be habits of body or habits of thought. We do not store knowledge anywhere but within ourselves; but sometimes we forget where we have hidden it, or we cover it up with a lot of the useless rubbish of mere mental activity. Most of our mental activity is applied solely to the things of this life, to things of the body; so, mankind is continually moving along a false path. No being, however high, can prevent this, because each man is Soul, is Spirit, is Consciousness – is of the Highest, however he use and apply his powers.

Theosophy endeavors to present to man what his real nature is; that he is first, last, and all the time SPIRIT. Spirit means Life and Consciousness – the power to see, to know, to experience. We all have that. That is common to all of us. It is not separate in self – it is the One Life in all beings of every grade. But we, as individuals, have evolved into individuals from the great Ocean of Life. We are Individualized Spirit, and so we each have a separate individual existence, which is continuous. In that sense we are an evolution, but an evolution of Spirit, not Matter – an evolution of Knowledge, not of form only. This has been obtained through observation and experience; whatever differences exist are because of more or less experience, or a better adaptation and application of it; there is no difference in the Source or Potentialities of any being. All this we shall find out, if we move along the Path shown. For it is not an uncharted path. Remember, others have been along that path before us. They are our Elder Brothers – Jesus, for example;

Buddha for another; and all those who came at different times as Saviours to the many different peoples. They had all acquired the Language of the Soul. They all had a common body of knowledge. They come amongst men from time to time, as the intelligence of humanity progresses, and give out as much of that knowledge as the then existing state of humanity permits. They came again in our own time; and greater than Those who so came there has not been. Why should anyone say that? Because other Saviours came to separate and distinct peoples, but the Message of Theosophy is not to any one nation, not to any one class of beings, but to the whole world.

That knowledge is obtainable by any self-conscious being for himself, for it is not a question of our ideas, of our present perceptions of morality or success, nor of external power, but of Spiritual perception – of the Language of the Soul. We may make all the mistakes in the world, according to the world, in the body and through the body, and yet have a power of Spiritual perception that would do away with all "mistakes. We would not have to' have any vicarious atonement, but would be able to act in a proper relation with every being. Our thoughts and actions would be in accord. (but we would have to go through the crucifixion of the false ideas in ourselves, and arise as the Saviour did, to the right hand of the Father – the Ego free from all these delusions which have caused him to maintain himself in sin, sorrow and suffering.

All men desire Spiritual knowledge, yet the great bulk will not abate one jot or tittle of their mental and physical absorption in present and worldly things to obtain the spiritual knowledge they say they ardently long for. They will have to move on through suffering and pain till they really desire to know the truth about themselves. If any man thinks he can get that knowledge by merely desiring to possess it, or by desiring to possess it for himself alone, he is not in the position that would permit of his knowing it. The Language of the Soul can be acquired only when the being realizes that his duty is not to himself, but to the highest interests of his fellowmen; not to "save his own soul" but to lead as many of his neighbors as he possibly can in the direction of the Truth, desiring nothing for himself.

This very attitude opens the flood-gates of spiritual knowledge within himself. Then he becomes the true enjoyer, using every power he has, all the knowledge he has, to benefit others. The man who has come to that knowledge and is on the road to its realization finds "spiritual knowledge springing up spontaneously in himself in the progress of time." He requires no books to tell him; he cares not what religions have been, that now are, that ever will be. He knows the truth about himself and consequently the truth about all others.

Why do not all men take the path to this realization? Is it because they have no organs of perception, are incapable of seeing? No, it is because they will not listen; they will not take what is given and try it out. They will rather follow anything that promises some success in this life. Yet they know just as well as anyone that they cannot take a single one of the "successes" away with them from the earth. When they go, they leave on earth every earthly thing they have accumulated. And they have to go, because they do not belong here; they are of Spirit, not earth; they are only working in this matter for a while. They all know that, and yet dream of "possessions."

No one damned any of us to this condition in which we find so many. No conditions compel us to stay in a state of mental unrest, inactivity or ignorance. All these things are imposed on us by our own hard and fast conclusions as to men, things and methods. These keep us fast bound in our present conditions and will continue to hold us, as long as we maintain that attitude of mind, and cling to false ideas of God, of Nature, and of Man. We keep the doors closed of our own will. In ignorance? Yes; but who remains ignorant? Those only who will not hear, those only who doubt the Language of the Soul.

Universal Theosophy
Robert Crosbie

WHAT ARE THE THEOSOPHISTS?

Are they what they claim to be – students of natural law, of ancient and modern philosophy, and even of exact science? Are they Deists, Atheists, Socialists, Materialists, or Idealists; or are they but a schism of modern Spiritualism, – mere visionaries? Are they entitled to any consideration, as capable of discussing philosophy and promoting real science; or should they be treated with the compassionate toleration which one gives to "harmless enthusiasts"? The Theosophical Society has been variously charged with a belief in "miracles," and "miracle-working"; with a secret political object – like the Carbonari; with being spies of an autocratic Czar; with preaching socialistic and nihilistic doctrines; and, *mirabile dictu,* with having a covert understanding with the French Jesuits, to disrupt modern Spiritualism for a pecuniary consideration! With equal violence they have been denounced as dreamers, by the American Positivists; as fetish-worshippers, by some of the New York press; as revivalists of "mouldy superstitions," by the Spiritualists; as infidel emissaries of Satan, by the Christian Church; as the very types of "*gobe-mouche,*" by Professor W. B. Carpenter, F.R.S.; and, finally, and most absurdly, some Hindu opponents, with a view to lessening their influence, have flatly charged them with the employment of *demons* to perform certain phenomena. Out of all this pother of opinions, one fact stands conspicuous – the Society, its members, and their views, are deemed of enough importance to be discussed and denounced: *Men slander only those whom they hate – or fear.*

But, if the Society has had its enemies and traducers, it has also had its friends and advocates. For every word of censure, there has been a word of praise. Beginning with a party of about a dozen earnest men and women, a month later its members had so increased as to necessitate the hiring of a public hall for its meetings; within two years, it had working branches in European countries. Still later, it found itself in alliance with the Indian Arya Samaj, headed by the learned Pandit Dayanand Saraswati Swami, and the Ceylonese Buddhists, under the erudite H. Sumangala, High Priest of Adam's Peak and President of the Widyodaya College, Colombo.

He who would seriously attempt to fathom the psychological sciences, must come to the sacred land of ancient Aryâvarta. None is older than she in esoteric wisdom and civilization, however fallen may be her poor shadow – modern India. Holding this country, as we do, for the fruitful hot-bed whence proceeded all subsequent philosophical systems, to this source of all psychology and philosophy a portion of our Society has come to learn its ancient wisdom and ask for the impartation of its weird secrets. Philology has made too much progress to require at this late day a demonstration of this fact of the primogenitive nationality of Aryâvarta. The unproved and prejudiced hypothesis of modern Chronology is not worthy of a moment's thought, and it will vanish in time like so many other unproved hypotheses. The line of philosophical heredity, from Kapila through Epicurus to James Mill; from Patanjali through Plotinus to Jacob Böhme, can be traced like the course of a river through a landscape. One of the objects of the Society's organization was to examine the too transcendent views of the Spiritualists in regard to the powers of disembodied spirits; and, having told them what, in our opinion at least, a portion of their phenomena are *not*, it will become incumbent upon us now to show what they are. So apparent is it that it is in the East, and especially in India, that the key to the alleged "supernatural" phenomena of the Spiritualists must be sought, that it has recently been conceded in the Allahabad *Pioneer* (Aug. 11th, 1879), an Anglo-Indian daily journal which has not the reputation of saying what it does not mean. Blaming the men of science who "intent upon physical discovery, for some generations have been too prone to neglect super-physical investigation," it mentions "the new wave of doubt" (spiritualism) which has "latterly disturbed this conviction." To a large number of persons including many of high culture and intelligence, it adds, "the supernatural has again asserted itself as a fit subject of inquiry and research. And there are plausible hypotheses in favour of the idea that among the 'sages' of the East . . . there may be found in a higher degree than among the more modernised inhabitants of the West traces of those personal peculiarities, whatever they may be, which are required as a condition precedent to the occurrence of supernatural phenomena." And then, unaware that the cause he pleads is one of the chief aims and objects of our Society, the editorial writer remarks that it is "the only direction in which, it seems to us, the efforts of the Theosophists in India might possibly be useful. The leading members of the Theosophical Society in India are known to be very advanced students of occult phenomena, already, and we cannot but hope that their professions of interest in Oriental philosophy . . . may cover a reserved intention of carrying out explorations of the kind we indicate."

While, as observed, one of our objects, it yet is but one of many; the most important of which is to revive the work of Ammonius Saccas, and make various nations remember that they are the children "of one mother." As to the transcendental side of the ancient Theosophy, it is also high time that the Theosophical Society should explain. With how much, then, of this nature-searching, God-seeking science of the ancient Aryan and Greek mystics, and of the powers of modern spiritual mediumship, does the Society agree? Our answer is: with it all. But if asked what it believes in, the reply will be: "*As a body* – Nothing." The Society, as a body, has no creed, as creeds are but the shells around spiritual knowledge; and Theosophy in its fruition is spiritual knowledge itself – the very essence of philosophical and theistic enquiry. Visible representative of Universal Theosophy, it can be no more sectarian than a Geographical Society, which represents universal geographical exploration without caring whether the explorers be of one creed or another. The religion of the Society is an algebraical equation, in which so long as the sign of equality (=) is not omitted, each member is allowed to substitute quantities of his own, which better accord with climatic and other exigencies of his native land, with the idiosyncrasies of his people, or even with his own. Having no accepted creed, our Society is very ready to give and take, to learn and teach, by practical experimentation, as opposed to mere passive and credulous acceptance of enforced dogma. It is willing to accept every result claimed by any of the foregoing schools or systems, that can be logically and experimentally demonstrated.

Conversely, it can take nothing on mere faith, no matter by whom the demand may be made.

But, when we come to consider ourselves individually, it is quite another thing. The Society's members represent the most varied nationalities and races, and were born and educated in the most dissimilar creeds and social conditions. Some of them believe in one thing, others in another. Some incline towards the ancient *magic*, or secret wisdom that was taught in the sanctuaries, which was the very opposite of supernaturalism or diabolism; others in modern spiritualism, or intercourse with the spirits of the dead; still others in mesmerism or animal magnetism, or only an occult dynamic force in nature. A certain number have scarcely yet acquired any definite belief, but are in a state of attentive expectancy; and there are even those who call themselves materialists, in a certain sense. Of atheists and bigoted sectarians of any religion, there are none in the Society; for the very fact of a man's joining it proves that he is in search of the final truth as to the ultimate essence of things. If there be such a thing as a speculative atheist, which philosophers may deny, he would have to reject both cause and effect, whether in this world of matter, or in that of spirit. There may be members who, like the poet Shelley, have let their imagination soar from cause to prior cause *ad infinitum*, as each in its turn became logically transformed into a result necessitating a prior cause, until they have thinned the Eternal into a mere mist. But even they are not atheist in the speculative sense, whether they identify the material forces of the universe with the functions with which the theists endow their God, or otherwise; for once that they cannot free themselves from the conception of the abstract ideal of power, cause, necessity, and effect, they can be considered as atheists only in respect to a personal God, and not to the Universal Soul of the Pantheist. On the other hand the bigoted sectarian, fenced in, as he is, with a creed upon every paling of which is written the warning "No Thoroughfare," can neither come out of his enclosure to join the Theosophical Society, nor, if he could, has it room for one whose very religion forbids examination. The very root idea of the Society is free and fearless investigation.

As a body, the Theosophical Society holds that all original thinkers and investigators of the hidden side of nature whether materialists – those who find in matter "the promise and potency of all terrestrial life," or spiritualists – that is, those who discover in spirit the source of all energy and of matter as well, were and are, properly, Theosophists. For to be one, one need not necessarily recognize the existence of any special God or a deity. One need but worship the spirit of living nature, and try to identify oneself with it. To revere that *Presence*, the invisible Cause, which is yet ever manifesting itself in its incessant results; the intangible, omnipotent, and omnipresent Proteus: indivisible in its Essence, and eluding form, yet appearing under all and every form; who is here and there, and everywhere and nowhere; is ALL, and NOTHING; ubiquitous yet one; the Essence filling, binding, bounding, containing everything, contained in all. It will, we think, be seen now, that whether classed as Theists, Pantheists or Atheists, such men are near kinsmen to the rest. Be what he may, once that a student abandons the old and trodden highway of routine, and enters upon the solitary path of independent thought – Godward – he is a Theosophist; an original thinker, a seeker after the eternal truth with "an inspiration of his own" to solve the universal problems.

With every man that is earnestly searching in his own way after a knowledge of the Divine Principle, of man's relations to it, and nature's manifestations of it, Theosophy is allied. It is likewise the ally of honest science, as distinguished from much that passes for *exact*, physical science, so long as the latter does not poach on the domains of psychology and metaphysics.

And it is also the ally of every honest religion – to wit, a religion willing to be judged by the same tests as it applies to the others. Those books, which contain the most self-evident truth, are to it inspired (not revealed). But all books it regards, on account of the human element contained in them, as inferior to the Book of Nature; to read which and comprehend it correctly, the innate powers of the soul must be highly developed. Ideal laws can be perceived by the intuitive faculty alone; they are beyond the domain of argument and dialectics, and no one can understand or rightly appreciate them through the explanations of another mind, even though this mind be claiming a direct revelation. And, as this Society, which allows the widest sweep in the realms of the pure ideal, is no less firm in the sphere of facts, its deference to modern science and its just representatives is sincere. Despite all their lack of a higher spiritual intuition, the world's debt to the representatives of modern physical science is immense; hence, the Society endorses heartily the noble and indignant protest of that gifted and eloquent preacher, the Rev. O. B. Frothingham, against those who try to undervalue the services of our great naturalists. "Talk of Science as being irreligious, atheistic," he exclaimed in a recent lecture, delivered at New York, "Science is creating a new idea of God. It is due to Science that we have any conception at all of a *living* God. If we do not become atheists one of these days under the maddening effect of Protestantism, it will be due to Science, because it is disabusing us of hideous illusions that tease and embarrass us, and putting us in the way of knowing how to reason about the things we see. . . ."

And it is also due to the unremitting labors of such Orientalists as Sir W. Jones, Max Müller, Burnouf, Colebrooke, Haug, St. Hilaire, and so many others, that the Society, as a body, feels equal respect and veneration for Vedic, Buddhist, Zoroastrian, and other old religions of the world; and, a like brotherly feeling toward its Hindu, Sinhalese, Parsi, Jain, Hebrew, and Christian members as individual students of "self," of nature, and of the divine in nature.

Born in the United States of America, the Society was constituted on the model of its Mother Land. The latter, omitting the name of God from its constitution lest it should afford a pretext one day to make a state religion, gives absolute equality to all religions in its laws. All support and each is in turn protected by the State. The Society, modelled upon this constitution, may fairly be termed a "Republic of Conscience."

We have now, we think, made clear why our members, as individuals, are free to stay outside or inside any creed they please, provided they do not pretend that none but themselves shall enjoy the privilege of conscience, and try to force their opinions upon the others. In this respect the Rules of the Society are very strict: It tries to act upon the wisdom of the old Buddhistic axiom, "Honour thine own faith, and do not slander that of others"; echoed back in our present century, in the "Declaration of Principles" of the Brahmo Samaj, which so nobly states that: "no sect shall be vilified, ridiculed, or hated." In Section VI of the Revised Rules of the Theosophical Society, recently adopted in General Council, at Bombay, is this mandate:

It is not lawful for any officer of the Parent Society to express, by word or act, any hostility to, or preference for, any one section (sectarian division, or group within the Society) more than another. All must be regarded and treated as equally the objects of the Society's solicitude and exertions. All have an equal right to have the essential features of their religious belief laid before the tribunal of an impartial world.

In their individual capacity, members may, when attacked, occasionally break this Rule, but, nevertheless, as officers they are restrained, and the Rule is strictly enforced during the meetings. For, above all human sects stands Theosophy in its abstract sense; Theosophy which is too wide for any of them to contain but which easily contains them.

In conclusion, we may state that, broader and far more universal in its views than any existing mere scientific Society, it has *plus* science its belief in every possibility, and determined will to penetrate into those unknown spiritual regions which exact science pretends that its votaries have no business to explore. And, it has one quality more than any religion in that it makes no difference between Gentile, Jew, or Christian. It is in this spirit that the Society has been established upon the footing of a Universal Brotherhood.

Unconcerned about politics; hostile to the insane dreams of Socialism and of Communism, which it abhors – as both are but disguised conspiracies of brutal force and sluggishness against honest labour; the Society cares but little about the outward human management of the material world. The whole of its aspirations are directed towards the occult truths of the visible and invisible worlds. Whether the physical man be under the rule of an empire or a republic, concerns only the man of matter. His body may be enslaved; as to his soul, he has the right to give to his rulers the proud answer of Socrates to his judges. They have no sway over the *inner* man.

Such, then, is the Theosophical Society, and such its principles, its multifarious aims, and its objects. Need we wonder at the past misconceptions of the general public, and the easy hold the enemy has been able to find to lower it in the public estimation. The true student has ever been a recluse, a man of silence and meditation. With the busy world his habits and tastes are so little in common that, while he is studying, his enemies and slanderers have undisturbed opportunities. But time cures all and lies are but ephemera. Truth alone is eternal.

About a few of the Fellows of the Society who have made great scientific discoveries, and some others to whom the psychologist and the biologist are indebted for the new light thrown upon the darker problems of the inner man, we will speak later on. Our object now was but to prove to the reader that Theosophy is neither "a new-fangled doctrine," a political cabal, nor one of those societies of enthusiasts which are born today but to die tomorrow. That not all of its members can think alike, is proved by the Society having organized into two great Divisions – the Eastern and the Western – and the latter being divided into numerous sections, according to races and religious views. One man's thought, infinitely various as are its manifestations, is not all-embracing. Denied ubiquity, it must necessarily speculate but in one direction; and once transcending the boundaries of exact human knowledge, it has to err and wander, for the ramifications of the one Central and absolute Truth are infinite. Hence, we occasionally find even the greater philosophers losing themselves in the labyrinths of speculations, thereby provoking the criticism of posterity. But as all work for one and the same object, namely, the disenthralment of human thought, the elimination of superstitions, and the discovery of truth, all are equally welcome. The attainment of these objects, all agree, can best be secured by convincing the reason and warming the enthusiasm of the generation of fresh young minds, that are just ripening into maturity, and making ready to take the place of their prejudiced and conservative fathers. And, as each – the great ones as well as small – have trodden the royal road to knowledge, we listen to all, and take both small and great into our fellowship. For no honest searcher comes back empty-handed, and even he who has enjoyed the least share of popular favor can lay at least his mite upon the one altar of Truth.

Theosophist, October, 1879
H. P. Blavatsky

PART II:

UNIVERSAL IDEAS OF THEOSOPHY

CREATIVE EMANATION

Throughout these infinite orbs of mingling light,
Of which yon earth is one, is wide diffused
A spirit of activity and life,
That knows no term, cessation, or decay;
That fades not when the lamp of earthly life,
Extinguished in the dampness of the grave,
Awhile there slumbers, more than when the babe
In the dim newness of its being feels
The impulses of sublunary things,
And all is wonder to unpractised sense:
But, active, steadfast, and eternal, still
Guides the fierce whirlwind, in the tempest roars,
Cheers in the day, breathes in the balmy groves,
Strengthens in health, and poisons in disease;
And in the storm of change, that ceaselessly
Rolls round the eternal universe, and shakes
Its undecaying battlement, presides,
Apportioning with irresistible law
The place each spring of its machine shall fill;
. . . .
No atom of this turbulence fulfils
A vague and unnecessitated task,
Or acts hut as it must and ought to act.
– Percy Bysshe Shelley

Beyond conception and imagination, beyond all categories and concepts, feelings and emotions, is THAT – attributeless and without limitations. Unbounded by either frontier or horizon, It cannot be modified by anything anterior or external to It. The great teaching of the *Upanishads* and of Shri Shankaracharya is that every human being is inherently capable of cancelling all conditions of place and time. Each individual can rise to a transcendental awareness unconfined by perspectives and objects of perception. For a human being, a *Manasa*, to become self-consciously aware of the whole is to recover a primordial freedom which can neither be bought nor bartered, because it never enters into the external relations of the world, into particular forms and differentiations. A person can regain an indefinable, inalienable originality which springs from the source of all manifestation. Every human being is an original who can never be fully revealed in any finite series of concrete expressions. He can never be understood from the outside, and he is more than what he senses, feels or thinks. He is far more than all the confused and blurred vibrations arising from his brain-mind, ensnared by myriad cords of delusive desire. Every person is essentially and eternally THAT, and to affirm it in consciousness, to give it the silent strength of a potent force for regeneration, is the greatest service anyone could render for the sake of all.

With this sublime teaching, which invokes the primeval and never-ceasing power of self-regeneration in the universe and in oneself, how is one to connect it to life in the world? What is its meaning in terms of existence as a personality, a name and a form, with relationships and obligations, with debts and liabilities? If one ponders such questions, then one must intently reflect upon how entire universes could emerge from THAT. It is not adequate merely to accept the fact that these universes cannot exhaust or have any external relationship to THAT – one must ask how there could arise the staggering array of galactic clusters, galaxies, stars, solar systems, manifold forms of life-energy, light rays, and all the binding chains of causality in recorded and unrecorded history. What significance do these have, if any, in relation to THAT? Is there a cosmic basis for the decision to rearrange one's circumstances, to recreate not only one's life but one's manifesting self, allowing what is dying in oneself to die and what is gestating to be born? Out of dying embers can one kindle the fire of a new self which may find – in the realm of manifestation – meaning in life and relationships, and discover unending modes of expressing the divine within?

To begin this process of questioning, it is helpful to reflect upon an archetypal cosmic triad. Between the vast manifold of a universe of differentiations and THAT, there is the mediation of a triadic force operating ceaselessly in manifestation. One aspect of it is creative, another aspect is preservative, while a third aspect is destructive and simultaneously regenerative. This is the Trimurti of ancient Hindu tradition – Brahmâ, Vishnu, Shiva. The term "Brahmâ" derives from the root *brih*, "to expand". There is an expansive force that is ever at work in nature and in history. It manifests in certain individuals more than others because they have a proper relationship to that universal power of expansion. Anything which merely contrasts, limits, and consolidates the claustrophobic condition of self-limitation, is not protected, sustained or supported by the ever-expansive force of the creative Logos in the cosmos, the god in man. Anything in man which is not universifiable or sharable – which cannot be spread or cannot give rise to growth in others – is not of the nature of life-energy, but rather of the nature of *tamas,* inert and stagnant. The prison-house, the clay tenement of personal life, is the shadowy projection of a crippling sense of self, repeatedly involved in ossification and death. Physiologically, every human being is caught in a futile effort to beat the entropic demise of the body. It is dying faster than it can be rejuvenated. This is an extremely significant truth in the region of gross matter, dispelling the pseudo-coherence and false entitative nature of what one thinks is real and with which one identifies.

The Trimurti is continuously at work in nature and in man. In the ancient tradition of India its divine ground is called *Brahman* – without qualities, inconceivable and beyond all possible characterization. Out of *Brahman* (THAT), there emerges Brahma, the logoic force which is both spirit and matter and the fountain of creativity. It is the Invisible Sun, the transcendental source of illumination and energy, as well as the power of vivification and growth. It is the generator of electricity and magnetism and their complex transformations, working continually in a universe of constant transmutation. The creative Logos can only be cognized by those faculties which are superior to the physical sensorium, and which are capable of being activated by the powers of mental concentration and deep meditation, of controlled imagination and cool visualization. Through these faculties human beings can gain access within themselves, in the deepest recesses of thought and feeling, to their own abundant share of inexhaustible creativity. A man is as creative as he chooses or wills to be. He is as vital as is his capacity for constructive thought, which depends upon his firmness in setting aside the negative, self-cancelling and mutually contradictory mental currents which pass for thinking but are no more than chaotic cerebration. A man is as original as is his determination to replace what Shelley called "Fancy's thin creation" by seminal mental acts of the imagination carrying within themselves the sovereign power of self-sustenance. Such acts can evoke and emanate a multitude of creative energies flowing as a living, continuous stream of light from one central source of ideation, which is effectively tapped through daily meditations.

This fundamental teaching could be fruitfully applied to the extent that it is understood not only in relation to oneself but also in relation to everything that exists, especially beyond the curtain of sense-perception. One can make come alive in consciousness the invisible processes of growth in Nature and enter into an intimate relationship with what is alive, burgeoning and ceaselessly circulating. In contemporary society, people impoverish themselves through compulsive misuse of the power of speech, ignorant misdirection of the power of thought, and sad dissipation of the power of imagination in futile and sterile fancy. They thus cut off contact with their godlike resources and become like batteries that are largely drained of energy. Too many people sit and complain, hoping for some sudden miracle. One may feel compassion especially for those who know that to be self-destructive is, by definition, to be insensitive to help from outside. The tragedy of weakness of will is evident on all sides.

It is by no means unthinkable that there should be, both in principle and in practice, human beings who have perfected their faculties in relation to their vestures. For them there are no barriers in the realm of thought. They can make things happen which would baffle the boldest minds of the age. They could affect the climate at will, project themselves in many different places, materialize objects, supersede gravitational fields, and perform so-called miracles. Yet they always work under laws of Nature, with full knowledge of causes and consequences. All their doings are diverse forms of tribute to the inexhaustible power of the creative Logos. The grander their gifts, the greater their obeisance to the sacred source of creativity. They know that every human being is a god potentially, capable of viewing the universe as a vast field responsive to the powers of concentrated thought, conserved energy, chastened imagination and purified will. One could affect the whole for good or for ill. One could work with Nature to elevate all beings in accordance with the forward impulse of evolution, which excludes none and includes all in the progressive ascent of self-consciousness, culminating in enlightenment. Or one could work against Nature, and then one's creativity is a nine days' wonder, a pathetic instance of monumental waste, a pyramid of misspent energy, a tragic degradation of the prerogatives of thought and imagination.

While vast creative powers are recognized by many as potentially present, most do not understand why they are not generally accessible. Suppose one pictures a single, superhuman Creator who Jehovistically – lawlessly and arbitrarily – manufactures a universe. Then one will see the whole of Nature simply as a capricious catalogue of created things which have no innate power of creativity, but are merely inert objects spewed forth from this gigantic being, this sultan in the sky who is conceived as an anthropomorphic God. One would then view every man or woman as a helpless creature for whom the beginning of wisdom is abject fear of that almighty potentate. This is a dismal picture of the world, but it is one that cannot be discarded easily. People may say they do not believe it anymore, but it has infiltrated their consciousness. As a result, it is difficult to dislodge, especially when one takes into account previous lives of involvement with gross and degrading conceptions of this kind. Instead of rejoicing in the richness of material nature, one tends to regard it as insentient. Instead of celebrating the creative energy of the Logos, one grovels before a grotesque image and sorry substitute for the Godhead. Instead of seeing oneself as a creative being responsible for the entire stream of emanations flowing from oneself, one attempts to abdicate responsibility, seeking scapegoats because of feeling that one has lost before having started. As an original sinner, a weak worm who somehow needs to be saved, one is afraid of being damned, and pursues a frantic lifestyle unconsciously based upon a paranoid theology where Big Brother is watching and His name is interchangeably "Devil" or "Gods" – one is never quite sure which. Such human beings become so furtive that they have scarcely any relation to the dignity and stature of the mighty benefactors of mankind.

A radical revision of facile theocentric thought is necessary. If we can conceive of a realm of unmanifest, primordial matter that is ontologically prior to all energic fields, then we could view heat, light, electricity, magnetism, sound, colour and number as interrelated expressions of a single source. In its deepest and subtlest aspect, this primordial substratum of matter is suffused with a vast potential which partly manifests as what we call the universe. Thus there is much more energy in the cosmos than the whole of humanity can use. Electricity existed long before men invented ways to harness it, and is in fact coeval with manifestation. Long before men constructed thermodynamic theories, heat energy existed, subject to definite laws. It was also always true that everything that came into existence could not be easily converted into another form of energy with perfect efficiency. Every time something is given out, it cannot be taken back in its original form. Generally, before men were able to formulate theoretically their own approximations of the laws of Nature, the processes of Nature worked in accordance with archetypal principles which had a fundamental logic that was fully understood by Adepts. Their wisdom suggests that each and every person can benefit by calmly reflecting upon his own inherent potential power of creativity and also upon the fact that he has unlimited access to the undifferentiated field of primordial matter. One can activate in that homogeneous noetic substratum whatever great idea one chooses as the subject of disciplined meditation and release it as an emanation, by the force of an impersonal and unselfish desire, into a universe of manifestation.

In regard to all such acts of creative will, unselfish motive is crucial. Without an understanding of metaphysics, the precondition of altruism would appear to be an arbitrary moralistic injunction. This, however, is to be mistaken in one's comprehension of the cosmos. A person who is handling explosive material, regardless of how he acts in other contexts, must be cool and deliberate. If he is nervously thinking of himself while handling it, he is liable to be blown up. Even a selfish manipulator makes allowances for other people when driving on the road. One may say he does it out of necessity. Sometimes he may do it with panache; sometimes he may do it simply to show that he is human. There is no reason why, whatever the smallness in a person, if he has some familiarity with immense forces, he cannot summon a modicum of coolness, calm and self-forgetfulness. A man concentrated on doing a complex repair job has temporarily to forget himself. A person intent on handling potent forces has to have both knowledge and calmness at some level. It is no different in regard to the far more awesome powers of invisible Nature which operate under laws that are extraordinarily difficult to grasp, but which are known and mastered by wise beings who belong to the secret Brotherhood of *Bodhisattvas*.

For them there are no miracles: there is only law. Through self-conscious thought, will and imagination, they fuse wisdom and compassion in focussing universal, selfless desires. Their love streams forth abundantly in every direction to every being alive. They are effortlessly capable of handling the vastitude of creative possibilities of the cosmos. They always work with Nature and never against it because they have gained complete mastery over the creative will as well as the massive burden of cosmic responsibility. As long as there is an inexhaustible creative potential and, simultaneously, entropy supervenes in a law-governed realm of matter, there is need both for the capacity to harness unexplored creativity and the constant recognition that all products of creativity have limits and parameters. However grand, they must end; however great, they cannot last forever. Not only that: they entail consequences for which someone must assume responsibility, because Nature returns to human beings what they have done to and with it. If one stresses that Nature is giving back solely the consequences of other men's actions, this only means that one does not really want to take much responsibility. Masters of Wisdom and Compassion voluntarily assume responsibility without appropriating the free will of any person or atoning for anyone's sins. Taking responsibility for the whole world, they can shoulder it, and in assuming that uncircumscribed responsibility, they define themselves. The more one is responsible for the consequences of acts, the more one can recognize the practical importance of the philosophical distinction between creation and emanation.

To create is to tap the inexhaustible source of creativity, but when that creativity flows in a continuous stream in time and space, it manifests as a series of emanations. Creativity is like the tremendous energy locked within the sun, only a portion of which emanates. It streams forth in rays, and thereby gives life and light to all beings. Those who are gratefully self-conscious about what they receive, benefit more, because they come into closer relationship with thought-fields prior to the physical forms of transmission of light-energy. The physical sun is only an expression of an analogous source that generates light, life, energy and warmth through the immense power of ideation of a host of divine beings who stream forth emanations in unison. What unites them is their constant reverence and silent worship of THAT, which is beyond all, beyond the logoic source of manifestation itself, and beyond all possible worlds of manifestation. They constantly send forth streams of thought-energies which collectively constitute the highest creative potencies in the cosmos.

Any man who spends a lot of time in the heat of the sun will get sunburnt; he will find he gets a headache; he will learn that he can neither look at the brilliant light directly nor use even a little of it at any time. He will get rapidly fatigued because he does not have an adequate receptivity to solar light and energy. So too, a person may think that he seeks the company of the great *Bodhisattvas*, but would actually be unable to handle it if he were in their presence. It would be too "hot" for him. The only way in which he could manage it would be if one of them chose, out of compassion, deliberately to shield most of his light-energy, and out of the tiny portion that he manifests, helped to raise consciousness wherever needed. This voluntary self-restriction of energy is suggested in a Hindu fable about the sun. It is said that no woman could marry the sun-god because she would get burnt up if she came too close. Out of compassion, the Sun withheld most of his energy for the sake of entering into a relationship with the mythic bride who represents Nature. The Logos cannot enter into a direct relationship with Nature except through a portion or reflection of itself. This is analogous to the partial emanation of the light of the sun in a single day.

The doctrine of emanation preserves the continuity of the expressed with the unexpressed, and also the necessary finitude of what is expressed in relation to the infinity of unlimited potentiality. This philosophical idea is profoundly important for those who apply it to themselves. If one is divine in essence, then intrinsically one's energy and potentiality are inexhaustible. But at the same time, one also exists as an ever-changing physical body, where there is constant movement in complex molecular, cellular and organic structures of life-energy, and a continuous interaction with everything else. In that realm one must necessarily lose. One dies faster than one lives. Not to know this is not to grow up. But one can still make good use of one's knowledge of the inexhaustible creative energy within. Having grown up and accepted that existence as a physical body and personality is but a shadowy portion of what one really is, one can appreciate why this minute portion is mortal. Cooperating with the process of dying, one is happy to be dying every moment. Where this is understood, people can join together and aid each other. They may conspire – breathe together – to activate their latent creative wills, somewhat emulating the Brotherhood of *Bodhisattvas*, who sustain a mighty field of creative force that is benevolent and beneficent, giving appropriate channels of expression to the vast spiritual energies of the cosmos. The work of the Brotherhood of *Bodhisattvas* is to remind men of what they inwardly know but which they do not realize they have forgotten. To know it truly is to be so aware of it at all times that nothing else counts as knowledge. This is the oldest teaching in regard to creative emanation. After his compassionate enactment of the universal vision, of the incredible beauty in the universe of manifestation, springing from a single source of creativity, Krishna declares: "But what, O Arjuna, hast thou to do with so much knowledge as this? I established this whole universe with a single portion of myself, and remain separate."

Hermes, March 1978
Raghavan Iyer

THE WISDOM RELIGION ESOTERIC IN ALL AGES

ENQUIRER. Since Ammonius never committed anything to writing, how can one feel sure that such were his teachings?

THEOSOPHIST. Neither did Buddha, Pythagoras, Confucius, Orpheus, Socrates, or even Jesus, leave behind them any writings. Yet most of these are historical personages, and their teachings have all survived. The disciples of Ammonius (among whom Origen and Herennius) wrote treatises and explained his ethics. Certainly the latter are as historical, if not more so, than the Apostolic writings. Moreover, his pupils – Origen, Plotinus, and Longinus (counsellor of the famous Queen Zenobia) – have all left voluminous records of the Philaletheian System – so far, at all events, as their public profession of faith was known, for the school was divided into exoteric and esoteric teachings.

ENQUIRER. How have the latter tenets reached our day, since you hold that what is properly called the Wisdom-Religion was esoteric?

THEOSOPHIST. The Wisdom-Religion was ever one, and being the last word of possible human knowledge, was, therefore, carefully preserved. It preceded by long ages the Alexandrian Theosophists, reached the modern, and will survive every other religion and philosophy.

ENQUIRER. Where and by whom was it so preserved?

THEOSOPHIST. Among Initiates of every country; among profound seekers after truth – their disciples; and in those parts of the world where such topics have always been most valued and pursued: in India, Central Asia, and Persia.

ENQUIRER. Can you give me some proofs of its esotericism?

THEOSOPHIST. The best proof you can have of the fact is that every ancient religious, or rather philosophical, cult consisted of an esoteric or secret teaching, and an exoteric (outward public) worship. Furthermore, it is a well-known fact that the Mysteries of the ancients comprised with every nation the "greater" (secret) and "Lesser" (public) Mysteries – e.g. in the celebrated solemnities called the *Eleusinia*, in Greece. From the Hierophants of Samothrace, Egypt, and the initiated Brahmins of the India of old, down to the later Hebrew Rabbis, all preserved, for fear of profanation, their real bona fide beliefs secret. The Jewish Rabbis called their secular religious series the *Mercavah* (the exterior body), "the vehicle," or, the covering which contains the hidden soul. – i.e., their highest secret knowledge. Not one of the ancient nations ever imparted through its priests its real philosophical secrets to the masses, but allotted to the latter only the husks. Northern Buddhism has its "greater" and its "lesser" vehicle, known as the *Mahayana*, the esoteric, and the *Hinayana*, the exoteric, Schools. Nor can you blame them for such secrecy, for surely you would not think of feeding your flock of sheep on learned dissertations on botany instead of on grass? Pythagoras called his *Gnosis* "the knowledge of things that are," or , and preserved that knowledge for his pledged disciples only: for those who could digest such mental food and feel satisfied, and he pledged them to silence and secrecy. Occult alphabets and secret ciphers are the development of the old Egyptian hieratic writings, the secret of which was, in the days of old, in the possession only of the Hierogrammatists, or initiated Egyptian priests. Ammonius Saccas, as his biographers tell us, bound his pupils by oath not to divulge his higher doctrines except to those who had already been instructed in preliminary knowledge, and who were also bound by a pledge. Finally, do we not find the same even in early Christianity, among the Gnostics, and even in the teachings of Christ? Did he not speak to the multitudes in parables which had a twofold meaning, and explain his reasons only to his disciples? "To you," he says, "it is given to know the mysteries of the kingdom of heaven; but unto them that are without, all these things are done in parables" (Mark iv. 11). "The Essenes of Judea and Carmel made similar distinctions, dividing their adherents into neophytes, brethren, and the perfect, or those initiated" (*Eclectic Philosophy*). Examples might be brought from every country to this effect.

ENQUIRER. Can you attain the "Secret Wisdom" simply by study? Encyclopaedias define Theosophy pretty much as Webster's Dictionary does, i. e. as "supposed intercourse with God and superior spirits, and consequent attainment of superhuman knowledge by physical means and chemical processes." Is this so?

THEOSOPHIST. I think not. Nor is there any lexicographer capable of explaining, whether to himself or others, how superhuman knowledge can be attained by physical or chemical processes. Had Webster said "by metaphysical and alchemical processes," the definition would be approximately correct: as it is, it is absurd. Ancient Theosophists claimed, and so do the modern, that the infinite cannot be known by the finite — i.e., sensed by the finite Self – but that the divine essence could be communicated to the higher Spiritual Self in a state of ecstasy. This condition can hardly be attained, like hypnotism, by "physical and chemical means."

ENQUIRER. What is your explanation of it?

THEOSOPHIST. Real ecstasy was defined by Plotinus as "the liberation of the mind from its finite consciousness, becoming one and identified with the infinite." This is the highest condition, says Prof. Wilder, but not one of permanent duration, and it is reached only by the very very few. It is, indeed, identical with that state which is known in India as *Samadhi*. The latter is practised by the *Yogis*, who facilitate it physically by the greatest abstinence in food and drink, and mentally by an incessant endeavour to purify and elevate the mind. Meditation is silent and unuttered prayer, or, as Plato expressed it, "the ardent turning of the soul toward the divine; not to ask any particular good (as in the common meaning of prayer), but for good itself — for the universal Supreme Good" of which we are a part on earth, and out of the essence of which we have all emerged. Therefore, adds Plato, "remain silent in the presence of the divine ones, till they remove the clouds from thy eyes and enable thee to see by the light which issues from themselves, not what appears as good to thee, but what is intrinsically good."*

ENQUIRER. Theosophy, then, is not, as held by some, a newly devised scheme?

THEOSOPHIST. Only ignorant people can thus refer to it. It is as old as the world, in its teachings and ethics, if not in name, as it is also the broadest and most catholic system among all.

ENQUIRER. How comes it, then, that Theosophy has remained so unknown to the nations of the Western Hemisphere? Why should it have been a sealed book to races confessedly the most cultured and advanced?

THEOSOPHIST. We believe there were nations as cultured in days of old and certainly more spiritually "advanced" than we are. But there are several reasons for this willing ignorance. One of them was given by St. Paul to the cultured Athenians — a loss, for long centuries, of real spiritual insight, and even interest, owing to their too great devotion to things of sense and their long slavery to the dead letter of dogma and ritualism. But the strongest reason for it lies in the fact that real Theosophy has ever been kept secret.

ENQUIRER. You have brought forward proofs that such secrecy has existed, but what was the real cause for it?

THEOSOPHIST. The causes for it were: Firstly, the perversity of average human nature and its selfishness, always tending to the gratification of personal desires to the detriment of neighbours and next of kin. Such people could never be entrusted with divine secrets. Secondly, their unreliability to keep the sacred and divine knowledge from desecration. It is the latter that led to the perversion of the most sublime truths and symbols, and to the gradual transformation of things spiritual into anthropomorphic, concrete, and gross imagery – in other words, to the dwarfing of the god-idea and to idolatry.

The Key to Theosophy, pp. 7-12
H. P. Blavatsky

THE SEVENTH IMPULSION: 1963–2000

The great and peaceful ones live regenerating the world like the coming of the spring; having crossed the ocean of embodied existence themselves, they freely aid all others who seek to cross it. The very essence and inherent will of Mahatmas is to remove the suffering of others, just as the ambrosia-rayed moon of itself cools the earth heated by the intense rays of the sun.

Shankaracharya

A night of superstition, dogma and degradation descended upon the West for a millennium between the politically prudent "conversion" of Constantine and the initiation of the Seven Century Plan. In 1357 a ray of Amitabha, the Buddha of Boundless Time and Infinite Light, appeared in Tibet as the Adept-Teacher Tsong-kha-pa. To purify, preserve and promulgate the Wisdom-Religion, he founded the Gelukpa Order, the third Dalai Lama of which was recognized as a manifestation of *Avalokiteswara*, "the divine SELF perceived by Self." Tenzin Gyatso, the present Dalai Lama, is the fourteenth incarnation. Tsong-kha-pa initiated a series of seven impulsions to prepare the world through mental and spiritual revitalization to be ready to participate in the formation of the distant sixth subrace. In the last quarter of each century of the Seven Century Plan, an emissary from the Brotherhood of *Bodhisattvas* works in the West to further spiritual enlightenment and the continuity of collective growth.

In the fourteenth century two "supreme Pontiffs" were elected to the papal chair, and the resulting "great schism" cast doubt on the claims of the church to absolute spiritual and temporal authority. John Wycliffe (1320–1384) began preparing the ground for a reawakening of *Manas* by translating the Bible into English and teaching that transubstantiation and papal authority are superstitions. His disciples, the Lollards, showed in their lives the way of simple devotion and charity. Pico della Mirandola (1463–1494) led the Second Impulsion by introducing the Qabbalah to the West, deciphering the philosophical alphabet of the Hermetic teachings, and by founding human dignity upon the freedom to germinate and nourish some selection of the vast variety of seeds of possibility in plastic human nature. Paracelsus provided the transition to the sixteenth-century cycle by teaching that "everything is the product of one universal creative effort; the Microcosm and man are one." The luminous triad of Giordano Bruno (1548–1600), Robert Fludd (1575–1637) and Jacob Boehme (1575–1624) first used the term "Theosophy" in modern times. The doctrine of Paracelsus of sevenfold cosmic and human correlations was given a firm metaphysical foundation and fearless exemplification by Bruno. Fludd explained to a surprised Europe that the ancient Mysteries which preserved these doctrines had not perished with classical Greece, but flourished in the East and in secret groups in the West. For the first time in the Seven Century Plan, the central idea that Adepts worked behind the scenes to improve the human condition was intimated. Boehme demonstrated that spiritual intuition was possible, thereby giving crucial evidence for the existence of Adepts, though he made no claim for himself.

In 1675 the Rosicrucian *Instructions* were issued. Disciples who wished to serve humanity were invited to prepare quietly the ground for the public work of the Movement. In the Fifth Impulsion there arose "four heroic characters who formed a Cross of Occult Light in the eighteenth-century sky" – Saint Germain, whose life is as mysterious as his overbrooding work in history; Louis Claude de Saint-Martin (1743–1803), who purified Masonry and coined the spiritual motto "Liberty, Equality, Fraternity," distorted by the violent passions of the French revolution; Cagliostro, who offered true Masons knowledge of the Lodge of *Mahatmas*; and Franz Anton Mesmer (1734–1815), who unified the physical, mental and spiritual principles of magnetism into a single therapeutic doctrine and practice.

The Sixth Impulsion witnessed the incarnation of the enigmatic being called Helena Petrovna Blavatsky (1831–1891). Boldly announcing that she was an agent of the Great Lodge, she outlined the fundamental teachings of the Wisdom-Religion even before she founded the Theosophical Society with her associate Henry Steel Olcott and her disciple William Quan Judge. Defining true magic as divine wisdom, she identified science and theology, "the Montecchi and Capuletti of the nineteenth century," as the enemies of occultism, offering *Isis Unveiled* (1877) as evidence for her ideas and *The Secret Doctrine* (1888) as explanation of the philosophy of Theosophy. Braving the painful, though sacred, duty of openly naming the *Mahatmas* who are behind the Movement, she demonstrated the grandeur of the theosophical system and the danger of playing with its Fohatic fire. In expounding the fundamentals of *theosophia* and the basic principles of oriental *philosophia,* she pointed to the underlying roots of all individual and collective progress. Her travels from Russia to America, from India to England, cast powerful magnetic links across the world, so that the Mahatmic vibration could be tapped globally.

When H.P. Blavatsky departed on the completion of her task, W.Q. Judge continued her work in the spirit she had selflessly embodied.

> Her aim was to elevate the race. Her method was to deal with the mind of the century as she found it, by trying to lead it on step by step; to seek out and educate a few who, appreciating the majesty of the Secret Science and devoted to "the great orphan Humanity," could carry on her work with zeal and wisdom; to found a Society whose efforts – however small itself might be – would inject into the thought of the day the ideas, the doctrines, the nomenclature of the Wisdom Religion, so that when the next century shall have seen its 75th year the new messenger coming again into the world would find the Society still at work, the ideas sown broadcast, and thus to make easy the task which for her since 1875 was so difficult and so encompassed with obstacles in the very paucity of the language – obstacles harder than all else to work against.

He reminded his readers that while "at the close of each century a spiritual movement is made in the world by the *Mahatmas*," they do not wholly withdraw their current. Rather the seeds sown are allowed to germinate.

> Our destiny is to continue the wide work of the past in affecting literature and thought throughout the world, while our ranks see many changing quantities but always holding those who remain true to the programme and refuse to become dogmatic or to give up common-sense in Theosophy. Thus we will wait for the new messenger, striving to keep the organization alive that he may use it and have the great opportunity H.P.B. outlines when she says, "Think how much one, to whom such an opportunity is given, could accomplish."

As the sun simultaneously passed across the Galactic Equator and the sacred asterism Punarvarsu, the Aquarian Age began its turn as the solar month in the Great Year. Astraea, the goddess of justice, descends toward the Pit, and Aldebaran, "the eye of the Bull," surveys earth from Meru. Into this complex, chaotic and crucial period the Seventh Impulsion is sent. When speaking of this age H.P. Blavatsky warned that psychologists would have their work cut out for them, many accounts will be settled between the races and that the twentieth century would be the last of its name. The forms and traditions, the beliefs and languages which inspired Piscean man over two millennia ago are dead and decaying. Those who cling to form rather than looking to the Spiritual Sun find themselves torn asunder by the collapse of familiar patterns. Riddled with self-doubt and insecurity, not sufficiently resolute in vision to see the soft golden hues of spiritual light among the flashing beams of *maya,* many are easy prey for doomsayers, negators and cynics, and crisis becomes a mode of living. Robert Crosbie founded the United Lodge of Theosophists in 1909 to continue the Work and preserve the foundations of the coming cycle, and B.P. Wadia carried the light of U.L.T. around the world.

Into this contrasting scene of daring and despair the Magus-Teacher of the Seventh Impulsion descends. The *Guru* alone determines when, where and how he will represent himself, the levels of language he will use, the modes of teaching he will adopt, and the speed and obviousness with which he will spell out the nature of the culminating Impulsion. His work involves the *sutratmic* synthesis of the Seven Century Plan. His duty is to nothing less than the whole of humanity, and as the Voice of *Vajradhara*, the Diamond Soul, every word he speaks will be a full account of himself. His teaching will be pure *theosophia* and his expression of it will be as fresh and vivifying as are those of every *Guru* when first delivered.

The Seven Century Plan is intimately connected with the 2500-year cycle of the Buddha, and the 5000-year cycle with which Krishna inaugurated *Kali Yuga*. Robert Crosbie said that Krishna "was an administrator, while Buddha was ethical intelligence." Vinoba Bhave has reiterated that Krishna was the incarnation of pure love, the Buddha of oceanic compassion. The synthesis of the "royal art" and the science of living, of unconditional love and unerring compassion, sets the archetype for the Aquarian Man: one whose head can feel and whose heart is intelligent, "like twins upon a line" while the star which is his goal burns overhead. The New Teacher will lay down the invisible lines which are the parameters of human development for the next 2000 years.

We have the privilege of being among those who enter a New Cycle under the Seven Century Plan, bringing together East and West so fully that the distinction will fade into history. The golden impulse initiated by Krishna, Buddha and Shankara in the East, and by Pythagoras, Plato and Christ in the West, will be carried forth into the civilization of the future. Those who strive to make Theosophy by any name a living power in their lives, one-pointed in consciousness, calm and deliberate in action, may have the sacred privilege of recognizing and serving the Magus-Teacher of the Seventh Impulsion. Those who prepare themselves in the secret sanctuary of their hearts by letting go of all conditions and renouncing all wish for personal gain, may have the thrice-great privilege of working with the *Guru* for the regeneration of humanity.

Retrospective insight into the 1875 Cycle and intuitive readiness for

1975 are indissolubly wedded, with no danger of divorce in a marriage by mutual assent. The Wheel of the Good Law moves swiftly on, and those who are willing to drive out the worthless husks of feverish speculation, psychic excitement and unholy curiosity must seek the golden grain of self-validating truth in the mathematically precise marking of "the celestial dial" on the Solar Clock. 14 x 7 years and 7 months after the birth of "H.P.B.," as well as 3 x 9 years and 9 months after the Aquarian Age commenced, when the disc of the Sun crossed the galactic equator and entered the constellation of *Punarvarsu* (Pollux), an event took place on earth, under the aegis of the asterism *Punarvarsu*, containing the key to the 1975 Cycle. This says everything and nothing, in the time-honoured code language of the Wise Men of the East.

Hermes, November 1975
Raghavan Iyer

THE EVOLUTION OF THE UNIVERSE

The teachings of Theosophy deal for the present chiefly with our earth, although its purview extends to all the worlds, since no part of the manifested universe is outside the single body of laws which operate upon us. Our globe being one of the solar system is certainly connected with Venus, Jupiter, and other planets, but as the great human family has to remain with its material vehicle—the earth—until all the units of the race which are ready are perfected, the evolution of that family is of greater importance to the members of it. Some particulars respecting the other planets may be given later on. First let us take a general view of the laws governing all.

The universe evolves from the unknown, into which no man or mind, however high, can inquire, on seven planes or in seven ways or methods in all worlds, and this sevenfold differentiation causes all the worlds of the universe and the beings thereon to have a septenary constitution. As was taught of old, the little worlds and the great are copies of the whole, and the minutest insect as well as the most highly developed being are *replicas* in little or in great of the vast inclusive original. Hence sprang the saying, "as above so below" which the Hermetic philosophers used.

The divisions of the sevenfold universe may be laid down roughly as: The Absolute, Spirit, Mind, Matter, Will, Akasa or Æther, and Life. In place of "the Absolute" we can use the word Space. For Space is that which ever is, and in which all manifestation must take place. The term Akasa, taken from the Sanskrit, is used in place of Æther, because the English language has not yet evolved a word to properly designate that tenuous state of matter which is now sometimes called Ether by modern scientists. As to the Absolute we can do no more than say IT IS. None of the great teachers of the School ascribe qualities to the Absolute although all the qualities exist in It. Our knowledge begins with differentiation, and all manifested objects, beings, or powers are only differentiations of the Great Unknown. The most that can be said is that the Absolute periodically differentiates itself, and periodically withdraws the differentiated into itself.

The first differentiation – speaking metaphysically as to time – is Spirit, with which appears Matter and Mind. Akasa is produced from Matter and Spirit, Will is the force of Spirit in action and Life is a resultant of the action of Akasa, moved by Spirit, upon Matter.

But the Matter here spoken of is not that which is vulgarly known as such. It is the real Matter which is always invisible, and has sometimes been called Primordial Matter. In the Brahmanical system it is denominated *Mulaprakriti*. The ancient teaching always held, as is now admitted by Science, that we see or perceive only the phenomena but not the essential nature, body or being of matter.

Mind is the intelligent part of the Cosmos, and in the collection of seven differentiations above roughly sketched, Mind is that in which the plan of the Cosmos is fixed or contained. This plan is brought over from a prior period of manifestation which added to its ever-increasing perfectness, and no limit can be set to its evolutionary possibilities in perfectness, because there was never any beginning to the periodical manifestations of the Absolute, there never will be any end, but forever the going forth and withdrawing into the Unknown will go on.

Wherever a world or system of worlds is evolving there the plan has been laid down in universal mind, the original force comes from spirit, the basis is matter – which is in fact invisible – Life sustains all the forms requiring life, and Akasa is the connecting link between matter on one side and spirit-mind on the other.

When a world or a system comes to the end of certain great cycles men record a cataclysm in history or tradition. These traditions abound; among the Jews in their flood; with the Babylonians in theirs; in Egyptian papyri; in the Hindu cosmology; and none of them as merely confirmatory of the little Jewish tradition, but all pointing to early teaching and dim recollection also of the periodical destructions and renovations. The Hebraic story is but a poor fragment torn from the pavement of the Temple of Truth. Just as there are periodical minor cataclysms or partial destructions, so, the doctrine holds, there is the universal evolution and involution. Forever the Great Breath goes forth and returns again. As it proceeds outwards, objects, worlds and men appear; as it recedes all disappear into the original source.

This is the waking and the sleeping of the Great Being; the Day and the Night of Brahmâ; the prototype of our waking days and sleeping nights as men, of our disappearance from the scene at the end of one little human life, and our return again to take up the unfinished work in another life, in a new day.

The real age of the world has long been involved in doubt for Western investigators, who up to the present have shown a singular unwillingness to take instruction from the records of Oriental people much older than the West. Yet with the Orientals is the truth about the matter. It is admitted that Egyptian civilization flourished many centuries ago, and as there are no living Egyptian schools of ancient learning to offend modern pride, and perhaps because the Jews "came out of Egypt" to fasten the Mosaic misunderstood tradition upon modern progress, the inscriptions cut in rocks and written on papyri obtain a little more credit today than the living thought and record of the Hindus. For the latter are still among us, and it would never do to admit that a poor and conquered race possesses knowledge respecting the age of man and his world which the western flower of culture, war, and annexation knows nothing of. Ever since the ignorant monks and theologians of Asia Minor and Europe succeeded in imposing the Mosaic account of the genesis of earth and man upon the coming western evolution, the most learned even of our scientific men have stood in fear of the years that elapsed since Adam, or have been warped in thought and perception whenever their eyes turned to any chronology different from that of a few tribes of the sons of Jacob. Even the noble, aged, and silent pyramid of Gizeh, guarded by Sphinx and Memnon made of stone, has been degraded by Piazzi Smyth and others into a proof that the British inch must prevail and that a "Continental Sunday" controverts the law of the Most High. Yet in the Mosaic account, where one would expect to find a reference to such a proof as the pyramid, we can discover not a single hint of it and only a record of the building by King Solomon of a temple of which there never was a trace.

But the Theosophist knows why the Hebraic tradition came to be thus an apparent drag on the mind of the West; he knows the connection between Jew and Egyptian; what is and is to be the resurrection of the old pyramid builders of the Nile valley, and where the plans of those ancient master masons have been hidden from the profane eyes until the cycle should roll round again for their bringing forth. The Jews preserved merely a part of the learning of Egypt hidden under the letter of the books of Moses, and it is there still to this day in what they call the cabalistic or hidden meaning of the scriptures. But the Egyptian souls who helped in planning the pyramid of Gizeh, who took part in the Egyptian government, theology, science, and civilization, departed from their old race, that race died out and the former Egyptians took up their work in the oncoming races of the West, especially in those which are now repeopling the American continents. When Egypt and India were younger there was a constant intercourse between them. They both, in the opinion of the Theosophist, thought alike, but fate ruled that of the two the Hindus only should preserve the old ideas among a living people. I will therefore take from the Brahmanical records of Hindustan their doctrine about the days, nights, years and life of Brahma, who represents the universe and the worlds.

The doctrine at once upsets the interpretation so long given to the Mosaic tradition, but fully accords with the evident account in Genesis of other and former "creations," with the cabalistic construction of the Old Testament verse about the kings of Edom, who there represent former periods of evolution prior to that started with Adam, and also coincides with the belief held by some of the early Christian Fathers who told their brethren about wonderful previous worlds and creations.

The Day of Brahma is said to last one thousand years, and his night is of equal length. In the Christian Bible is a verse saying that one day is as a thousand years to the Lord and a thousand years as one day. This has generally been used to magnify the power of Jehovah, but it has a suspicious resemblance to the older doctrine of the length of Brahma's day and night. It would be of more value if construed to be a statement of the periodical coming forth for great days and nights of equal length of the universe of manifested worlds.

A day of mortals is reckoned by the sun, and is but twelve hours in length. On Mercury it would be different, and on Saturn or Uranus still more so. But a day of Brahma is made up of what are called

Manvantaras – or period between two men – fourteen in number. These include four billion three hundred and twenty million mortal, or earth, years, which is one day of Brahma.

When this day opens, cosmic evolution, so far as relates to this solar system, begins and occupies between one and two billions of years in evolving the very ethereal first matter before the astral kingdoms of mineral, vegetable, animal and men are possible. This second step takes some three hundred millions of years, and then still more material processes go forward for the production of the tangible kingdoms of nature, including man. This covers over one and one-half billions of years. And the number of solar years included in the present "human" period is over eighteen millions of years.

This is exactly what Herbert Spencer designates as the gradual coming forth of the known and heterogeneous from the unknown and homogeneous. For the ancient Egyptian and Hindu Theosophists never admitted a creation out of nothing, but ever strenuously insisted upon evolution, by gradual stages, of the heterogeneous and differentiated from the homogeneous and undifferentiated. No mind can comprehend the infinite and absolute unknown, which is, has no beginning and shall have no end; which is both last and first, because, whether differentiated or withdrawn into itself, it ever is. This is the God spoken of in the Christian Bible as the one around whose pavilion there is darkness.

This cosmic and human chronology of the Hindus is laughed at by western Orientalists, yet they can furnish nothing better and are continually disagreeing with each other on the same subject. In Wilson's translation of *Vishnu Purana* he calls it all fiction based on nothing, and childish boasting. But the Free Masons, who remain inactive hereupon, ought to know better. They could find in the story of the building of Solomon's temple from the heterogeneous materials brought from everywhere, and its erection without the noise of a tool being heard, the agreement with these ideas of their Egyptian and Hindu brothers. For Solomon's Temple means man whose frame is built up, finished and decorated without the least noise. But the materials had to be found, gathered together and fashioned in other and distant places.

These are in the periods above spoken of, very distant and very silent. Man could not have his bodily temple to live in until all the matter in and about his world had been found by the Master, who is the inner man, when found the plans for working it required to be detailed. They then had to be carried out in different detail until all the parts should be perfectly ready and fit for placing in the final structure. So in the vast stretch of time which began after the first almost intangible matter had been gathered and kneaded, the material and vegetable kingdoms had sole possession here with the Master – man – who was hidden from sight within carrying forward the plans for the foundations of the human temple. All of this requires many, many ages, since we know that nature never leaps. And when the rough work was completed, when the human temple was erected, many more ages would be required for all the servants, the priests, and the counsellors to learn their parts properly so that man, the Master, might be able to use the temple for its best and highest purposes.

The ancient doctrine is far nobler than the Christian religious one or that of the purely scientific school. The religious gives a theory which conflicts with reason and fact, while science can give for the facts which it observes no reason which is in any way noble or elevating. Theosophy alone, inclusive of all systems and every experience, gives the key, the plan, the doctrine, the truth.

The real age of the world is asserted by Theosophy to be almost incalculable, and that of man as he is now formed is over eighteen millions of years. What has become at last man is of vastly greater age, for before the present two sexes appeared the human creature was sometimes of one shape and sometimes of another, until the whole plan had been fully worked out into our present form, function, and capacity. This is found to be referred to in the ancient books written for the profane where man is said to have been at one time globular in shape. This was at a time when the conditions favored such a form and of course it was longer ago than eighteen millions of years. And when this globular form was the rule the sexes as we know them had not differentiated and hence there was but one sex, or if you like, no sex at all.

During all these ages before our man came into being, evolution was carrying on the work of perfecting various powers which are now our possession. This was accomplished by the Ego or real man going through experience in countless conditions of matter all different one from the other, and the same plan in general was and is pursued as prevails in respect to the general evolution of the universe to which I have before adverted. That is, details were first worked out in spheres of being very ethereal, metaphysical in fact. Then the next step brought the same details to be worked out on a plane of matter a little more dense, until at last it could be done on our present plane of what we miscall gross matter. In these anterior states the senses existed in germ, as it were, or in idea, until the astral plane which is next to this one was arrived at, and then they were concentrated so as to be the actual senses we now use through the agency of the different outer organs. These outer organs of sight, touch and hearing, and tasting, are often mistaken by the unlearned or the thoughtless for the real organs and senses, but he who stops to think must see that the senses are interior and that their outer organs are but mediators between the visible universe and the real perceiver within. And all these various powers and potentialities being well worked out in this slow but sure process, at last man is put upon the scene a sevenfold being just as the universe and earth itself are sevenfold. Each of his seven principles is derived from one of the great first seven divisions, and each relates to a planet or scene of evolution, and to a race in which that evolution was carried out. So the first sevenfold differentiation is important to be borne in mind, since it is the basis of all that follows; just as the universal evolution is septenary so the evolution of humanity, sevenfold in its constitution, is carried on upon a septenary Earth. This is spoken of in Theosophical literature as the Sevenfold Planetary Chain, and is intimately connected with Man's special evolution.

The Ocean of Theosophy, pp. 9-13
W.Q. Judge

THE FUNDAMENTAL TEACHINGS OF THEOSOPHY: On God

ENQUIRER. Do you believe in God?

THEOSOPHIST. That depends what you mean by the term.

ENQUIRER. I mean the God of the Christians, the Father of Jesus, and the Creator: the Biblical God of Moses, in short.

THEOSOPHIST. In such a God we do not believe. We reject the idea of a personal, or an extra-cosmic and anthropomorphic God, who is but the gigantic shadow of *man,* and not of man at his best, either. The God of theology, we say — and prove it — is a bundle of contradictions and a logical impossibility. Therefore, we will have nothing to do with him.

ENQUIRER. State your reasons, if you please.

THEOSOPHIST. They are many, and cannot all receive attention. But here are a few. This God is called by his devotees infinite and absolute, is he not?

ENQUIRER. I believe he is.

THEOSOPHIST. Then, if infinite – *i. e.,* limitless – and especially if absolute, how can he have a form, and be a creator of anything? Form implies limitation, and a beginning as well as an end; and, in order to create, a Being must think and plan. How can the ABSOLUTE be supposed to think – *i. e.,* to have any relation whatever to that which is limited, finite, and conditioned? This is a philosophical, and a logical absurdity. Even the Hebrew *Kabala* rejects such an idea, and therefore, makes of the one and the Absolute Deific Principle an infinite Unity called *Ain-Soph.*[1] In order to create, the Creator has to become active; and as this is impossible for ABSOLUTENESS, the infinite principle had to be shown becoming the cause of evolution (not creation) in an indirect way – *i.e.,* through the emanation from itself (another

---

[1] *Ain-Soph,* Hebrew אין סוף = τὸ πᾶν = ἔπειρος, the endless, or boundless, in and with Nature, the non-existent which IS, but is not a Being.

absurdity, due this time to the translators of the *Kabala*)[2] of the *Sephiroth*.

ENQUIRER. How about those Kabalists, who, while being such, still believe in Jehovah, or the *Tetragrammaton?*

THEOSOPHIST. They are at liberty to believe in what they please, as their belief or disbelief can hardly affect a self-evident fact. The Jesuits tell us that two and two are not always four to a certainty, since it depends on the will of God to make 2 X 2 = 5. Shall we accept their sophistry for all that?

ENQUIRER. Then you are Atheists?

THEOSOPHIST. Not that we know of, and not unless the epithet of "Atheist" is to be applied to those who disbelieve in an anthropomorphic God. We believe in a Universal Divine Principle, the root of ALL, from which all proceeds, and within which all shall be absorbed at the end of the great cycle of Being.

ENQUIRER. This is the old, old claim of Pantheism. If you are Pantheists, you cannot be Deists; and if you are not Deists, then you have to answer to the name of Atheists.

THEOSOPHIST. Not necessarily so. The term "Pantheism" is again one of the many abused terms, whose real and primitive meaning has been distorted by blind prejudice and a one-sided view of it. If you accept the Christian etymology of this compound word, and form it of παν, "all," and θεοσ, "god," and then imagine and teach that this means that every stone and every tree in Nature is a God or the ONE God, then, of course, you will be right, and make of Pantheists fetish-worshippers, in addition to their legitimate name. But you will hardly be as successful if you etymologise the word Pantheism esoterically, and as we do.

ENQUIRER. What is, then, your definition of it?

---

[2] How can the non-active eternal principle emanate or emit? The *Parabrahm* of the Vedantins does nothing of the kind; nor does the *Ain-Soph* of the Chaldean *Kabala*. It is an eternal and periodical law which causes an active and creative force (the *logos*) to emanate from the ever-concealed and incomprehensible one principle at the beginning of every *maha-manvantara*, or new cycle of life.

THEOSOPHIST. Let me ask you a question in my turn. What do you understand by Pan, or Nature?

ENQUIRER. Nature is, I suppose, the sum total of things existing around us; the aggregate of causes and effects in the world of matter, the creation or universe.

THEOSOPHIST. Hence the personified sum and order of known causes and effects; the total of all finite agencies and forces, as utterly disconnected from an intelligent Creator or Creators, and perhaps "conceived of as a single and separate force" – as in your cyclopædias?

ENQUIRER. Yes, I believe so.

THEOSOPHIST. Well, we neither take into consideration this objective and material nature, which we call an evanescent illusion, nor do we mean by πᾶν Nature, in the sense of its accepted derivation from the Latin *Natura* (becoming, from *nasci*, to be born). When we speak of the Deity and make it identical, hence coeval, with Nature, the eternal and uncreate nature is meant, and not your aggregate of flitting shadows and finite unrealities. We leave it to the hymn-makers to call the visible sky or heaven, God's Throne, and our earth of mud His footstool. Our DEITY is neither in a paradise, nor in a particular tree, building, or mountain: it is everywhere, in every atom of the visible as of the invisible Cosmos, in, over, and around every invisible atom and divisible molecule; for IT is the mysterious power of evolution and involution, the omnipresent, omnipotent, and even omniscient creative potentiality.

ENQUIRER. Stop! Omniscience is the prerogative of something that thinks, and you deny to your Absoluteness the power of thought.

THEOSOPHIST. We deny it to the ABSOLUTE, since thought is something limited and conditioned. But you evidently forget that in philosophy absolute unconsciousness is also absolute consciousness, as otherwise it would not be *absolute*.

ENQUIRER. Then your Absolute thinks?

THEOSOPHIST. No, IT does not; for the simple reason that it is *Absolute Thought* itself. Nor does it exist, for the same reason, as it is absolute existence, and *Be-ness*, not a Being. Read the superb Kabalistic poem by Solomon Ben Jehudah Gabirol, in the *Kether-Malchut*, and you will understand: "Thou art one, the root of all numbers, but not as an element of numeration; for unity admits not of multiplication, change, or form. Thou art one, and in the secret of thy unity the wisest of men are lost, because they know it not. Thou art one, and Thy unity is never diminished, never extended, and cannot be changed. Thou art one, and no thought of mine can fix for Thee a limit, or define Thee. Thou ART, but not as one existent, for the understanding and vision of mortals cannot attain to Thy existence, nor determine for Thee the where, the how and the why," etc., etc. In short, our Deity is the eternal, incessantly *evolving*, not *creating*, builder of the universe; that *universe itself unfolding* out of its own essence, not being *made*. It is a sphere, without circumference, in its symbolism, which has but one ever-acting attribute embracing all other existing or thinkable attributes – ITSELF. It is the one law, giving the impulse to manifested, eternal, and immutable laws, within that never-manifesting, *because* absolute LAW, which in its manifesting periods is *The ever-Becoming*.

ENQUIRER. I once heard one of your members remarking that Universal Deity, being everywhere, was in vessels of dishonour, as in those of honour, and, therefore, was present in every atom of my cigar ash! Is this not rank blasphemy?

THEOSOPHIST. I do not think so, as simple logic can hardly be regarded as blasphemy. Were we to exclude the Omnipresent Principle from one single mathematical point of the universe, or from a particle of matter occupying any conceivable space, could we still regard it as infinite?

The Key to Theosophy, pp. 61-66
H.P. Blavatsky

THE ACCUMULATED WISDOM OF THE AGES

(1.) The Secret Doctrine is the accumulated Wisdom of the Ages, and its cosmogony alone is the most stupendous and elaborate system: *e.g.,* even in the exotericism of the Purânas. But such is the mysterious power of Occult symbolism, that the facts which have actually occupied countless generations of initiated seers and prophets to marshal, to set down and explain, in the bewildering series of evolutionary progress, are all recorded on a few pages of geometrical signs and glyphs. The flashing gaze of those seers has penetrated into the very kernel of matter, and recorded the soul of things there, where an ordinary profane, however learned, would have perceived but the external work of form. But modern science believes not in the "soul of things," and hence will reject the whole system of ancient cosmogony. It is useless to say that the system in question is no fancy of one or several isolated individuals. That it is the uninterrupted record covering thousands of generations of Seers whose respective experiences were made to test and to verify the traditions passed orally by one early race to another, of the teachings of higher and exalted beings, who watched over the childhood of Humanity. That for long ages, the "Wise Men" of the Fifth Race, of the stock saved and rescued from the last cataclysm and shifting of continents, had passed their lives *in learning, not teaching.* How did they do so? It is answered: by checking, testing, and verifying in every department of nature the traditions of old by the independent visions of great adepts; *i.e.,* men who have developed and perfected their physical, mental, psychic, and spiritual organisations to the utmost possible degree. No vision of one adept was accepted till it was checked and confirmed by the visions–so obtained as to stand as independent evidence–of other adepts, and by centuries of experiences.

(2.) The fundamental Law in that system, the central point from which all emerged, around and toward which all gravitates, and upon which is hung the philosophy of the rest, is the One homogeneous divine SUBSTANCE-PRINCIPLE, the one radical cause.

> . . . "Some few, whose lamps shone brighter, have been led
> From cause to cause to nature's secret head,
> And found that one first Principle must be. . . ."

It is called "Substance-Principle," for it becomes "substance" on the plane of the manifested Universe, an illusion, while it remains a "principle" in the beginningless and endless abstract, visible and invisible SPACE. It is the omnipresent Reality: impersonal, because it contains all and everything. *Its impersonality is the fundamental conception* of the System. It is latent in every atom in the Universe, and is the Universe itself. (See in chapters on Symbolism, "Primordial Substance, and Divine Thought.")

(3.) The Universe is the periodical manifestation of this unknown Absolute Essence. To call it "essence," however, is to sin against the very spirit of the philosophy. For though the noun may be derived in this case from the verb *esse*, "to be," yet IT cannot be identified with a *being* of any kind, that can be conceived by human intellect. IT is best described as neither Spirit nor matter, but both. "*Parabrahmam and Mulaprakriti*" are One, in reality, yet two in the Universal conception of the manifested, even in the conception of the One Logos, its first manifestation, to which, as the able lecturer in the "*Notes on the Bhagavadgita*" shows, IT appears from the objective standpoint of the One Logos as Mulaprakriti and not as Parabrahmam; as its *veil* and not the one REALITY hidden behind, which is unconditioned and absolute.

(4.) The Universe is called, with everything in it, MAYA, because all is temporary therein, from the ephemeral life of a fire-fly to that of the Sun. Compared to the eternal immutability of the ONE, and the changelessness of that Principle, the Universe, with its evanescent ever-changing forms, must be necessarily, in the mind of a philosopher, no better than a will-o'-the-wisp. Yet, the Universe is real enough to the conscious beings in it, which are as unreal as it is itself.

(5.) Everything in the Universe, throughout all its kingdoms, is CONSCIOUS: *i.e.,* endowed with a consciousness of its own kind and on its own plane of perception. We men must remember that because *we* do not perceive any signs–which we can recognise–of consciousness, say, in stones, we have no right to say that *no consciousness exists there*. There is no such thing as either "dead" or "blind" matter, as there is no "Blind" or "Unconscious" Law. These find no place among the conceptions of Occult philosophy. The latter never stops at surface appearances, and for it the *noumenal* essences have more reality than their objective counterparts; it resembles therein the mediæval *Nominalists*, for whom it was the Universals that were the realities and the particulars which existed only in name and human fancy.

(6.) The Universe is worked and *guided* from *within outwards*. As above so it is below, as in heaven so on earth; and man–the microcosm and miniature copy of the macrocosm–is the living witness to this Universal Law, and to the mode of its action. We see that every *external* motion, act, gesture, whether voluntary or mechanical, organic or mental, is produced and preceded by *internal* feeling or emotion, will or volition, and thought or mind. As no outward motion or change, when normal, in man's external body can take place unless provoked by an inward impulse, given through one of the three functions named, so with the external or manifested Universe. The whole Kosmos is guided, controlled, and animated by almost endless series of Hierarchies of sentient Beings, each having a mission to perform, and who–whether we give to them one name or another, and call them Dhyan-Chohans or Angels – are "messengers" in the sense only that they are the agents of Karmic and Cosmic Laws. They vary infinitely in their respective degrees of consciousness and intelligence; and to call them all pure Spirits without any of the earthly alloy "which time is wont to prey upon" is only to indulge in poetical fancy. For each of these Beings either *was,* or prepares to become, a man, if not in the present, then in a past or a coming cycle (Manvantara). They are *perfected,* when not *incipient,* men; and differ morally from the terrestrial human beings on their higher (less material) spheres, only in that they are devoid of the feeling of personality and of the *human* emotional nature–two purely earthly characteristics. The former, or the "perfected," have become free from those feelings, because (*a*) they have no longer fleshly bodies–an ever-numbing weight on the Soul; and (*b*) the pure spiritual element being left untrammelled and more free, they are less influenced by *maya* than man can ever be, unless he is an adept who keeps his two personalities–the spiritual and the physical–entirely separated. The incipient monads, having never had terrestrial bodies yet, can have no sense of personality or EGO-ism. That which is meant by "personality," being a limitation and a relation, or, as defined by Coleridge, "individuality existing in itself but with a nature as a ground," the term cannot of course be applied to non-human entities; but, as a fact insisted upon by generations of Seers, none of these Beings, high or low, have either individuality or personality as separate Entities, *i.e.*, they have no individuality in the sense in which a man says, "*I am myself and* no one else;" in other words, they are conscious of no such distinct separateness as men and things have on earth. Individuality is the characteristic of their respective hierarchies, not of their units; and these characteristics vary only with the degree of the plane to which those hierarchies belong: the nearer to the region of Homogeneity and the One Divine, the purer and the less accentuated that individuality in the Hierarchy. They are finite, in all respects, with the exception of their higher principles–the immortal sparks reflecting the universal divine flame–individualized and separated only on the spheres of Illusion by a differentiation as illusive as the rest. They are "Living Ones," because they are the streams projected on the Kosmic screen of illusion from the ABSOLUTE LIFE; beings in whom life cannot become extinct, before the fire of ignorance is extinct in those who sense these "Lives." Having sprung into being under the quickening influence of the uncreated beam, the reflection of the great Central Sun that radiates on the shores of the river of Life, it is the inner principle in them which belongs to the waters of immortality, while its differentiated clothing is as perishable as man's body. Therefore Young was right in saying that

"Angels are men of a superior kind"

and no more. They are neither "ministering" nor "protecting" angels; nor are they "Harbingers of the Most High" still less the "Messengers of wrath" of any God such as man's fancy has created. To appeal to their protection is as foolish as to believe that their sympathy may be secured by any kind of propitiation; for they are, as much as man himself is, the slaves and creatures of immutable Karmic and Kosmic law. The reason for it is evident. Having no elements of personality in their essence they can have no personal qualities, such as attributed by men, in their exoteric religions, to their anthropomorphic God–a jealous and exclusive God who rejoices and feels wrathful, is pleased with sacrifice, and is more despotic in his vanity than any finite foolish man. Man, as shown in Book II., being a compound of the essences of all those celestial Hierarchies may succeed in making himself, as such, superior, in one sense, to any hierarchy or class, or even combination of them. "Man can neither propitiate nor command the *Devas*," it is said. But, by paralyzing his lower personality, and arriving thereby at the full knowledge of the *non-separateness* of his higher SELF from the One absolute SELF, man can, even during his terrestrial life, become as "One of Us." Thus it is, by eating of the fruit of knowledge which dispels ignorance, that man becomes like one of the Elohim or the Dhyanis; and once on *their* plane the Spirit of Solidarity and perfect Harmony, which reigns in every Hierarchy, must extend over him and protect him in every particular.

The chief difficulty which prevents men of science from believing in divine as well as in nature Spirits is their materialism. The main impediment before the Spiritualist which hinders him from believing in the same, while preserving a blind belief in the "Spirits" of the Departed, is the general ignorance of all, except some Occultists and Kabalists, about the true essence and nature of matter. It is on the acceptance or rejection of the theory of the *Unity of all in Nature, in its ultimate Essence,* that mainly rests the belief or unbelief in the existence around us of other conscious beings besides the Spirits of the Dead.

It is on the right comprehension of the primeval Evolution of Spirit-Matter and its real essence that the student has to depend for the further elucidation in his mind of the Occult Cosmogony, and for the only sure clue which can guide his subsequent studies.

In sober truth, as just shown, every "Spirit" so-called is either a *disembodied or a future man.* As from the highest Archangel (Dhyan Chohan) down to the last conscious "Builder" (the inferior class of Spiritual Entities), all such are *men*, having lived æons ago, in other Manvantaras, on this or other Spheres; so the inferior, semi-intelligent and non-intelligent Elementals–are all *future* men. That fact alone–that a Spirit is endowed with intelligence–is a proof to the Occultist that

that Being must have been a *man,* and acquired his knowledge and intelligence throughout the human cycle. There is but one indivisible and absolute Omniscience and Intelligence in the Universe, and this thrills throughout every atom and infinitesimal point of the whole finite Kosmos which hath no bounds, and which people call SPACE, considered independently of anything contained in it. But the first differentiation of its *reflection* in the manifested World is purely Spiritual, and the Beings generated in it are not endowed with a consciousness that has any relation to the one we conceive of. They can have no human consciousness or Intelligence before they have acquired such, personally and individually. This may be a mystery, yet it is a fact, in Esoteric philosophy, and a very apparent one too.

The whole order of nature evinces a progressive march towards *a higher life.* There is design in the action of the seemingly blindest forces. The whole process of evolution with its endless adaptations is a proof of this. The immutable laws that weed out the weak and feeble species, to make room for the strong, and which ensure the "survival of the fittest," though so cruel in their immediate action–all are working toward the grand end. The very *fact* that adaptations *do* occur, that the fittest *do* survive in the struggle for existence, shows that what is called "unconscious Nature" [1] is in reality an aggregate of forces manipulated by semi-intelligent beings (Elementals) guided by High Planetary Spirits, (Dhyan Chohans), whose collective aggregate forms the manifested *verbum* of the unmanifested LOGOS, and constitutes at one and the same time the MIND of the Universe and its immutable LAW.

The Secret Doctrine, I .pp. 272-278
H.P. Blavatsky

---

[1] Nature taken in its abstract sense, *cannot* be "unconscious," as it is the emanation from, and thus an aspect (on the manifested plane) of the ABSOLUTE consciousness. Where is that daring man who would presume to deny to vegetation and even to minerals *a consciousness of their own.* All he can say is, that this consciousness is beyond his comprehension.

THEOSOPHICAL DOCTRINE

Mr. Chairman; brothers and sisters; men and women; members of the Parliament of Religions: The Theosophical Society has been presenting to you but one-half of its work, but one-half of that which it has to present to the world. This is the Parliament of Religions. This is a Parliament of the Religions of the day. Theosophy is not only a religion; it is also a science; it is religious science and scientific religion, and at a Parliament of Religions it would not be possible, indeed it would not be proper, to present the science of Theosophy, which relates to so many matters outside of the ordinary domain of the religions of today. The time will come when religion will also be a science. Today it is not. The object of Theosophy is to make of religion also a science, and to make science a religion, so we have been presenting only one-half of the subject which we deal with, and I would like you to remember that. We could not go into the other part; it would be beyond the scope of this meeting.

Now, we have discovered during the last week, as many have discovered before by reading, by experience, and by travel, that the religions of the world are nearly all alike. We have discovered that Christianity is not alone in claiming a Savior. If you will go over to Japan you will find that the Buddhists of Japan have a doctrine which declares that anyone who relies upon and repeats three times a day the name "Amita Buddha," will be saved. That is one Savior of the Buddhists, who had the doctrine before Christianity was started. If you will go among the Buddhists elsewhere you will find that they also have a Savior; that by reliance upon the Lord Buddha, they claim they will be saved. If you will go to the Brahmins and the other religions of India, you will find they also have a Savior. In some parts of that mysterious land they say: "Repeat the name of Rama" – God – "and he will save you." The Brahmins themselves have in their doctrines a doctrine which is called the "Bridge Doctrine": that which has God for its aim, has God himself as the means of salvation, is itself God. And so wherever you go throughout this wide world, examining the various religions, you find they all have this common doctrine. Why should we then say that the latest of these religions is the inventor of the doctrine?

It is not. It is common property of the whole human race, and we find on further inquiry that these religions all teach, and the Christian religion also, that this Savior is within the heart of every man, and is not outside of him.

We have discovered further by examining all these religions and comparing them with the Christian religion, which is the one belonging to the foremost nation of today, that in these other religions and in Christianity are found certain doctrines which constitute the key that will unlock this vast lock made up of the different religions. These doctrines are not absent from Christianity any more than they are absent from Buddhism or from Brahminism, and now the time has come when the world must know that these doctrines are common property, when it is too late for any people West or East to claim that they have a special property in any doctrine whatever.

The two principles which unlock this great lock which bars men sometimes from getting on, are called Karma and Reincarnation. The latter doctrine bears a more difficult Sanscrit name.

The doctrine of Karma put into our language is simply and solely Justice. What is justice? Is it something that condemns alone? I say, No. Justice is also mercy. For mercy may not be dissociated from justice, and the word justice itself includes mercy within it. Not the justice of man, which is false and erring, but the justice of Nature. That is also mercy. For if she punishes you, it is in order that she may do a merciful act and show you the truth at last by discipline. That is the doctrine of Karma, and it is also called the ethical law of causation. It means that effect follows cause uniformly; not alone in mere objective nature, where if you put your hand in the fire it will surely be burned, but in your moral nature, throughout your whole spiritual and intellectual evolution. It has been too much the custom to withdraw from use this law of cause and effect the moment we look at man as a spiritual being; and the religions and philosophies of the past and the present have the proof within them that this law of cause and effect obtains on the spiritual, the moral, and the intellectual planes just as much as it does on the physical and objective. It is our object to once more bring back this law of justice to the minds of men and show them that justice belongs to God, and that he is not a God who favors people, but who is just because he is merciful.

The doctrine of reincarnation is the next one. Reincarnation, you say, what is that? Do you mean that I was here before? Yes, undoubtedly so. Do you mean to tell me that this is a Christian, a Buddhist, a Brahminical, a Japanese doctrine, and a Chinese one? Yes, and I can prove it; and if you will examine your own records with an unprejudiced and fearless mind, afraid of no man, you will prove it also. If you go back in the records of Christianity to the first year of it, you will find that for many centuries this doctrine was taught. Surely the men who lived near Jesus knew what the doctrine was. It was admitted by Jesus himself. He said on one occasion that Elias had already come back in the person of John, but had been destroyed by the ruler. How could Elias come back and be born again as John unless the law of nature permitted it? We find on examining the writers, the early Christian fathers who made the theology of the Christian churches admitting, by the greatest of them, Origen, that this doctrine was true. He, the greatest of them all, who wrote so much that men could not read all his books, believed in it. It is said in the Christian scripture that Jesus also said so much they could not record it, and if they had, the volumes could not be counted. If these teachings were not recorded, we can imagine from what he spoke and from what his early followers believed, that this doctrine was taught distinctly by him in words.

It is the doctrine of which the Reverend Mr. Beecher, brother of the famous Henry Ward Beecher, in a book called *The Conflict of Religions*, said, "It is an absolute necessity to Christianity; without it Christianity is illogical. With it it is logical." And a great writer, the Rev. William Alger, whose book, *A Critical History of the Doctrine of a Future Life,* is used in the religious educational institutions of all denominations with perhaps one exception, has written twice in two editions and said that after fifteen years study of the subject he had come to the conclusion that the doctrine was true and necessary.

Furthermore, we find that in these countries where Christianity arose – for Christianity is not a Western product – reincarnation has always been believed. You ask for human evidence. You believe in this city, not only in this city but everywhere, in a court of law, if many witnesses testify to a fact it is proven. Well, millions upon millions of men in the East testify that they not only believe in reincarnation, but that they know it is true, that they remember that they were born before and that they were here before, and hundreds and thousands of men in the West have said the same thing. That they not only believe it, but that they know it. Poets have written of it all through English literature. It is a doctrine that almost everybody believes in their hearts. The little child coming straight from the other shore, coming without any defects straight from the heavenly Father, believes that it has always lived.

If the doctrine of immortality which is taught by every religion is true, how can you split it in halves and say, you began to be immortal when you were born and you were never immortal before? How is it possible you did not live before if there is any justice in this universe? Is it not true that what happens is the result of your conduct? If you live a life of sin and wickedness, will you not suffer? If you steal, and rob, and lie, and put in operation causes for punishment, will you not be punished? Why should not that law be applied to the human being when born, to explain his state and capacity? We find children are born blind, deformed, halt, without capacity; where is the prior conduct which justifies such a thing, if they have just been born for the first time? They must have lived before. The disciples asked Jesus, "Why was this man born blind; was it for some sin he had committed?" When committed? When did he commit it if he had never been born before? Why ask Jesus, their master, this question, unless they believed the doctrine, unless, as we think, it is the true one and one then prevalent?

This doctrine of reincarnation, then, we claim is the lost chord of any religion that does not promulgate it. We say it is found in the Christian religion; it is found in every religion, and it offers to us a means whereby our evolution may be carried on, it offers an explanation to the question, Why are men born with different characters? We find one man born generous, and he will always be generous; we find another born selfish, and selfish he will be to the end of his life. We find one man born with great capacity, a great mind that can cover many subjects at once; or a special mind and capacity like that of Mozart. Why was he born so? Where did he get it if not from the character he had in the past? You may say that heredity explains it all. Then please explain how Blind Tom, born of Negro parents who never knew anything about a piano, who never knew anything about music, was able to play upon a mechanically scaled instrument like the piano? It is not a natural thing. Where did he get the capacity? Heredity does not explain that. We explain it by reincarnation. Just so with Mozart, who at four years of age was able to write an orchestral score. Do you know what that means? It means the writing down the parts for the many instruments, and not only that, but writing it in a forced scale, which is a mechanical thing. How will that be explained by heredity? If you say that among his ancestors there must have been musicians, then why not before or after him? See Bach! If Bach could look back from the grave he would have seen his musical genius fading and fading out of his family until at last it disappeared.

Heredity will not explain these great differences in character and genius, but reincarnation will. It is the means of evolution of the human soul; it is the means of evolution for every animate and inanimate thing in this world. It applies to everything. All nature is constantly being re-embodied, which is reincarnation. Go back with science. It shows you that this world was first a mass of fiery vapor; come down the years and you see this mass re-embodied in a more solid form; later still it is re-embodied as the mineral kingdom, a great ball in the sky, without life; later still animal life begins evolving until now it has all that we know of life, which is a re-embodiment over and over again, or reincarnation. It means, then, that just as you move periodically from house to house in the city, you are limited by every house you move into, so the human being, who never dies, is not subject to death, moves periodically from house to house, and takes up a mortal body life after life, and is simply limited a little more or a little less, just as the case may be, by the particular body he may inhabit.

I could not go through all this subject to answer all the objections, but Theosophy will answer them all. The differences in people are explained by the fact that the character of the individual attracts him to the family that is just like himself, and not to any other family, and through heredity he receives his discipline, punishment, and reward.

The objections to reincarnation are generally based upon the question, why we do not remember. In the West that objection arises from the fact that we have been materialists so long, we have been deceived so long, that we have forgotten; we are not able to remember anything but what makes a violent impression on our senses. In the East and in some places in the West the people remember, and the time will come when the people in the West will remember also. And I warrant you that the children of the West know this, but it is rubbed out of their minds by their fathers and mothers. They say to the child, "Don't bother me with such questions; you are only imagining things." As if a child could imagine that it had been here before if it had not been. They never could imagine a thing which has not some existence in fact or that is not built up from impressions received. As you watch the newborn child you will see it throw its arms out to support itself. Why should the child throw out its arms to support itself? You say, instinct. What is instinct? Instinct is recollection imprinted upon the soul, imprinted upon the character within a child just born, and it knows enough to remember that it must throw out its arms to save itself from being hurt. Any physician will tell you this fact is true. Whether they explain it in the same way as I do or not, I don't know. We cannot remember our past lives simply because the brain which we now have was not concerned with these past lives. You say you cannot remember a past life, and therefore you don't believe it is true. Well if we grant that kind of argument, apply it to the fact that you cannot remember the facts of your present existence here; you cannot remember what dinner you ate three weeks ago; you cannot remember one-quarter of what has happened to you. Do you mean to say that all these things did not happen because you cannot remember? You cannot remember what happens to you now, so how do you expect to remember what happened to you in another life? But the time will come when man not so immersed in materiality will form his soul to such an extent that its qualities will be impressed upon the newborn child body and he will be able to remember and to know all his past, and then he will see himself an evolving being who has come up through all the ages as one of the creators of the world, as one of those who have aided in building this world. Man, we say, is the top, the crown of evolution; not merely as one who has been out there through favor, but as one who worked himself up through nature, unconsciously sometimes to himself, but under law, the very top and key of the whole system, and the time will come when he will remember it.

Now, this being the system of evolution which we gather from all religions, we say it is necessary to show that cause and effect act on man's whole being. We say that this law of cause and effect, or Karma, explains every circumstance in life and will show the poor men in Chicago who are born without means to live, who sometimes are hunted by the upper class and live in misery, why they are born so. It will explain why a man is born rich, with opportunity which he neglects; and another man born rich, with opportunity which he does not neglect. It will explain how Carnegie, the great iron founder in America, was a poor telegraph boy before he was raised to be a great millionaire. It will explain how one is born with small brain power, and another born with great brain power. It is because we have never died; we have always been living, in this world or in some other, and we are always making causes and character for the next life as well as for this.

Do you not know that your real life is in your mind, in your thoughts? Do you not know a great deal is due to your own mind, and under every act is a thought, and the thoughts make the man, and those thoughts act upon the forces of nature? Inasmuch as all these beings come back and live together over and over again, they bring back the thoughts, the impressions of those they have met and which others have made upon them there. When you persecute and hurt a man now, you are not punished afterwards because of the act you did to him, but because of the thought under your act and the thought under his feelings when he received your act. Having made these thoughts, they remain forever with you and him, and when you come again you will receive back to yourselves that which you gave to another. And is not that Christianity as well as Brahminism and Buddhism? You say, No. I say, Yes; read it in the words of Jesus, and I would have you to show that you are right if you say, No. St. Paul I suppose is authority for you, and St. Paul says "Brethren, be not deceived; God is not mocked; for whatsoever a man soweth, that shall he also reap." I ask you where and when shall he reap that which he has sown? He must reap it where he sowed it, or there is no justice. He must come back here and help to cure that evil which he caused; he must come back here if he did cause any evil and continue to do all the good he can, so he may help to evolve the whole human race, which is waiting for him also. Jesus said; "Judge not, that ye be not judged; for with what measure ye mete, so shall it be measured out to you again." When? If you go to heaven after this life and escape all you have done, certainly not then, and you make Jesus to have said that which is not true, and make St. Paul say that which is not true.

But I believe that St. Paul and Jesus knew what they were talking about and meant what they said. So, then, we must come again here in order that God shall not be mocked and each man shall reap that which he has sowed.

It is just the absence of this explanation that has made men deny religion; for they have said: "Why, these men did not get what they sowed. Here are rich, wicked men who die in their beds, happy, with a shrive at the end of it. They have not reaped." But we know, just as Jesus and St. Paul have said, they will reap it surely, and we say according to philosophy, according to logic, according to justice, they will reap it right here where they sowed it, and not somewhere else. It would be unjust to send them anywhere else to reap it but where they did it. That has been taught in every religion ever since the world began, and it is the mission of the Theosophical Society to bring back the key to all the creeds, to show that they are really at the bottom in these essential doctrines alike, and that men have a soul in a body, a soul that is ever living, immortal and can never die, cannot be withered up, cannot be cut in two, cannot be destroyed, is never annihilated, but lives forever and forever, climbing forever and forever up the ladder of evolution, nearer and nearer, yet never reaching the full stature of the Godhead. That is what Theosophy wishes men to believe; not to believe that any particular creed is true. Jesus had no creed and formulated none. He declared the law to be, "Do unto others what you would have them do unto you." That was the law and the prophets. That is enough for any one. Love your neighbor as yourself. No more. Why, then, any creeds whatever? His words are enough, and his words and our ethical basis are the same. That is why we have no form of religion. We are not advocating religion; we are simply pointing out to men that the truth is there to pick up and prize it. Religion relates to the conduct of men; nature will take care of the results; nature will see what they will come to; but if we follow these teachings which we find everywhere, and the spirit of the philosophy which we find in all these old books, then men will know why they must do right, not because of the law, not because of fear, not because of favor, but because they must do right for rights own sake.

Parliament of Religions Address, 1893
W.Q. Judge

THE LIFE-GIVING STREAM

The Secret Doctrine is the accumulated Wisdom of the Ages, and its cosmogony alone is the most stupendous and elaborate system: e.g., even in the exotericism of the Puranas. But such is the mysterious power of occult symbolism, that the facts which have actually occupied countless generations of initiated seers and prophets to marshal, to set down and explain, in the bewildering series of evolutionary progress, are all recorded on a few pages of geometrical signs and glyphs. The flashing gaze of those seers has penetrated into the very kernel of matter, and recorded the soul of things there, where an ordinary profane, however learned, would have perceived but the external work of form.

The Secret Doctrine, i 272

The Secret Doctrine is directed to those who are devoutly seeking to bring about a fundamental transformation in embodied consciousness. Early in the book H.P. Blavatsky states: "*When* Buddhi *absorbs our EGO-tism (destroys it) with all its* Vikaras, Avalokiteshvara *becomes manifested to us, and Nirvana, or* Mukti, *is reached,*" "*Mukti*" *being the same as Nirvana, i.e., freedom from the trammels of Maya*" or illusion. "*Bodhi*" *is likewise the name of a particular state of trance condition, called* Samadhi, *during which the subject reaches the culmination of spiritual knowledge.*" If *samadhi* and *nirvana* are exalted states of consciousness, evidently the Brotherhood of *Bodhisattvas*, the Society of Sages, the Lodge of *Mahatmas* continuously resides on this cosmic plane of supreme cognition. These self-luminous beings are everywhere and nowhere, with three main sanctuaries on this globe: one beyond the Himalayas, which has existed from the most ancient times; another in the Near East, which also goes back far beyond recorded history; and the third in South America. Yet, while there are these secret centres of initiation, access to the Brotherhood has nothing to do with physical nearness or distance. *Mahatmas* are essentially beings who ceaselessly function on unseen planes of ideation mirroring universal states of consciousness. Any individual anywhere who is universal in spirit, non-sectarian in attitude, free from fixation upon place or time, who is truly devoted to universal good and human welfare, may come into the radius of influence of the Brotherhood of *Bodhisattvas* and their accredited agents in the world.

The Dedication of *The Secret Doctrine* strikes the self-validating keynote of universality:

> This Work I dedicate to all True Theosophists, in every Country, and of every Race, for they called it forth, and for them it was recorded.

In the Preface, the same keynote of universality is strongly stressed. The teachings of Theosophy are not confined to the ancient tetrad comprised by the Hindu, the Zoroastrian, the Chaldean and the Egyptian religions. Nor is it the exclusive possession of the more recent Buddhist, Islamic, Judaic and Christian faiths. The Secret Doctrine is the essence of all these. "Sprung from it in their origins, the various religious schemes are now made to merge back into their original element, out of which every mystery and dogma has grown, developed, and become materialised." Owing to the fall of all religions through false claims and creedal dogmas, true seekers everywhere today are longing to find the pristine source of Divine Wisdom, pure and unsullied. Naturally, even among such earnest seekers there is the ever-present danger of materialization. This can be minimized through close attention to the critical distinction made in the *Bhagavad Gita* between the external attributes and the immaterial essence of the Self-Governed Sage. Those who have eyes will always be able to see and will also be able to know how to come closer to the Trans-Himalayan Brotherhood, which is not to be found by external means. It has monasteries and schools and systems of initiation in secret sanctuaries which cannot be readily discovered by travel and exploration. Even the individual seeker who is able, by undertaking a pilgrimage, to come closer to the Brotherhood, is led on by the intuition of the heart, by inner guidance, and not by maps or any adventitious aids.

H.P. Blavatsky once stated that a single journey to the East undertaken in the proper spirit will do more than all the books in the world. She herself conducted such a journey but she was intensely concerned with fundamental questions: Who, where, and what is God? How can man's spirit prove God's spirit? These were the burning questions in her heart to which she devoted years of thought and enquiry. Having already had the vision of her *Guru*, asking these questions, she, as a great Teacher, re-enacted for the sake of the entire human race the archetypal quest for enlightenment. This is part of the ever-renewed sacrifice of every *Rishi* or *Mahatma*. Inquirers who have sought the Brotherhood of *Bodhisattvas* through external means are easily misled. In the Aquarian Age, especially, no encouragement can be given to people who want some kind of external and verifiable means of speeding their own growth. True spiritual growth is wholly internal, and only its efflorescence may illumine the external world through wisdom in thought, word and deed. This is the fruition of continuous meditation, and therefore one must realize, as many an ancient seeker knew, that the sacred places of pilgrimage correspond to secret centres in the human constitution. For example, Prayag, the meeting-place of rivers, corresponds to a spiritual centre in every human being. The symbolism of a sacred pilgrimage conveys clues to the inner meaning of the teaching, intimating the inward ascent through which a human being comes closer to planes of consciousness involving higher centres within the human vestures. It is possible, through deep meditation, to enter the inmost sanctuary within the tabernacle of Isis, Shekinah, Sarasvati, Kwan Yin, Brahma Vach. An indispensable pre-requisite is true devotion to the *IshtaGuru*.

The word *Theosophia* goes back to Ammonius Saccas and earlier, and there has continued an unbroken line of shining witnesses in every part of the world – even where the mystery-fires were snuffed out long ago. This line may be discerned in a few Church Fathers like Origen and Clement of Alexandria, as well as in St. Augustine. It is clearly to be seen in the neo-Platonic thinkers, as in Pythagoras and Plato, and also among the pre-Socratics. From further back than Krishna and Buddha, the ancient Egyptians and Chaldeans, and continuing all the way through recorded history, it comes down again through the last seven centuries, starting with the First Impulsion of the modern Theosophical Movement given in the fourteenth century by Tsong-Kha-Pa, who came to resuscitate the Divine Wisdom. Every century thereafter a special effort was made by the Lodge of *Mahatmas* to awaken human awareness of the accessibility as well as the enduring existence of the Wisdom Religion. Thus, as it is stated in the archetypal affirmation of the Declaration of the United Lodge of Theosophists,

"The true Theosophist belongs to no cult or sect, yet belongs to each and all."
The Secret Doctrine of H.P. Blavatsky is an encyclopaedic and talismanic
guide to that which is hidden in nature, to the sacred scriptures of the
world and to the ancient source of arcane knowledge. It points to the
great range of diverse cultures of the recorded and unrecorded past,
providing keys to many language systems, mythic maps, code
languages in mystical texts, alchemical works and ancient catechisms,
some of them orally transmitted or only partly transcribed and some
dependent upon further commentaries that are not readily available.
The two volumes encompass such a vast and varied range of material
that if one were to spend one's entire life trying to follow up on every
term and concept, on every school and system, one would find at the
end of a lifetime that one would have to start all over again in future
lives. This is truly a Himalayan pilgrimage.

Speaking of the great Transmitters of the Wisdom Religion, H.P.
Blavatsky states:

> They were the authors of new forms and interpretations, while
> the truths upon which the latter were based were as old as
> mankind. Selecting one or more of those grand verities, actualities
> visible only to the eye of the real Sage and Seer – out of the many
> orally revealed to man in the beginning, preserved and
> perpetuated in the *adyta* of the temples through initiation, during
> the MYSTERIES and by personal transmission – they revealed
> these truths to the masses. Thus every nation received in its turn
> some of the said truths, under the veil of its own local and special
> symbolism; which, as time went on, developed into a more or less
> philosophical *cultus*, a Pantheon in mythical disguise.

The Secret Doctrine, i xxxvi

In the process of transmission there is an inevitable dilution of the
life-giving stream of the eternal Wisdom. Every sincere seeker must
make an earnest effort to grasp what it would mean for these truths to
be actualities visible only to the eye of the Sage and the Seer. For
example, many Theosophists are vaguely familiar with the Sanskrit
term *Mulaprakriti*, root-matter, which is also known by the English
phrase "primordial root-substance". If one were to probe deeply into
what is currently thought about matter, one would discern that already

in contemporary physics the concept of matter is so subtle and recondite, so much an abstraction, that it has nothing to do with crude sensory conceptions of matter. If, through meditation upon the very idea of root-matter, one were to go even further, using several sections of *The Secret Doctrine* which throw light upon the philosophical problems connected with matter and forces, one could begin to comprehend what is meant by pure, noumenal matter. By experiencing even at a preliminary level that which would make the word *Mulaprakriti* sacred, one could become increasingly conscious of the ever-present cosmic sacrifice of which Shri Krishna spoke to Arjuna.

If the seeker is not living out of any concern with individual salvation, but only out of a deep desire for universal progress, then one can become a true devotee of Krishna. The *Guru* is depicted in the abstract portrait of the Self-Governed Sage given by Krishna. Persisting in true devotion to such a *Guru*, who will always be both an ideal and a fact, a veil and a presence, a person may experience subtle mutations in his vestures. The physical body changes considerably every seven years. The skin is completely renewed every seven years, and the lines on the hand change more slowly but surely. Micro-changes take place continually, affecting the blood and its circulation. The entire system renews itself so continuously that one is constantly involved in these alterations and changes. They apply not only to the gross astral that is called the physical body, but involve processes which are witnessed by and are relevant to the immortal soul. The way in which the soul sees and apprehends these processes can make a decisive difference to the whole of one's life. The common saying that "You are as young as you feel" is the mirroring of a profound truth when "feel" is understood in terms of how one thinks and breathes. Spiritual rates of metabolic transmutation, change and transformation can be affected by the *Guru* who can see into the very essence of things, and deals directly with a facet of *Mulaprakriti* which is the substratum of *Akasa*. If one genuinely tries to work through correspondences, then although one may not directly understand the process, one can at some level appreciate it by analogy to the sense of lightening and refining of the physical instrument that comes with bathing. All human souls have some glimmer of awareness of noumenal states of matter, but to be able to put that knowledge to work needs meditation, continuity of consciousness and continuous concern. Typically this quality of concentration and continuity will not be forthcoming except among those few who have such an overwhelming love for the human race, profound compassion for human suffering and pure joy in the presence of Divine Wisdom, that they would really wish to commit themselves totally and continuously to progressive self-refinement for the sake of all.

With deep concentration there is a distinct change in the quality of perception. The left eye and the right eye focus differently, not only on the physical plane, but also in ways that involve centres behind the eyes suggested in phrases like "the mind's eye", "the soul's eye" and what Krishna calls "the place between thine eyes". The eyes are the windows of the soul, and it is possible to unfold spiritual perception slowly, intermittently, but recognizably. The perception which unfolds is similar in kind, even though distant in degree, to the eye of the Sage and Seer. That is an eye for which there is no veil, an eye which can see into past, present and future though it does not see them as such but only an eternal Now. What is day to the Sage is night to the ordinary man, and what is day to the ordinary man is night, the night of ignorance, to the Sage. There is a radical difference in the perception of light and darkness, abstract and concrete, real and unreal, day and night, between the Sage or Seer and the seeker who is still fumbling and stumbling with sensory perceptions, with worldly desires, with carnal limitations, with a narrow sense of identity and personality, but who still wishes to go beyond. There is evidently a radical difference between the spiritual wisdom come alive in those who breathe it, and those who merely have it on hearsay. This is the oldest distinction in the world. In Shankara it is the distinction between *aparavidya* and *paravidya, parokshavidya* and *aparokshavidya*, indirect knowledge and direct awareness.

This is hinted at in the Preface, where the word "revelation" is used, and in different places in the book where the idea of spiritual revelation or spiritual seership is elucidated. In the beginning we are told that:

> ...the secret portions of the *"Dan"* or *"Jan-na"* (*"Dhyan"*) of Gautama's metaphysics – grand as they appear to one

unacquainted with the tenets of the Wisdom Religion of antiquity – are but a very small portion of the whole. The Hindu Reformer limited his public teachings to the purely moral and physiological aspect of the Wisdom-Religion, to Ethics and MAN alone. Things "unseen and incorporeal," the mystery of Being outside our terrestrial sphere, the great Teacher left entirely untouched in his public lectures, reserving the hidden Truths for a select circle of his Arhats. The latter received their Initiation at the famous Saptaparna cave (the *Sattapanni* of Mahavansa) near Mount Baibhar.

The Secret Doctrine i xx

And then we are told on the next page:

How the purity of these grand revelations was dealt with may be seen in studying some of the so-called "esoteric" Buddhist schools of antiquity in their modern garb, not only in China and other Buddhist countries in general, but even in not a few schools in Thibet, left to the care of uninitiated Lamas and Mongolian innovators.

The Secret Doctrine, i xxi

In India, in China and Japan, in Siam and Burma, in Egypt and Greece, in Chaldea and Mesopotamia, later in Rome and in the Arab world and among the Jews, and in the modern age in Europe and the United States of America, also in the last hundred years in the Theosophical Movement, it is the same story of partial understanding leading to misunderstanding, concretization resulting in desecration. That is the karma of the transmission of Divine Wisdom, because the uninitiated will, in the sense in which Jesus spoke of casting pearls before swine, drag down the solar teaching into the murky realm of lunar consciousness polluted by profane sense-perceptions. This is profanation, but at the same time, the immortal soul in those individuals may gain some food for *sushupti* and for *devachan* if they still have some link with the higher Triad. There would also be those who can get their mental luggage ready for another life. One may never really know how the process goes on from the outside, but one can understand why something always had to be kept secret from every person who is self-excluded from the sacred circle of initiates and ascetics. There will always be such a sacred circle, just as there will always be only a few who actually have climbed Himalayan peaks. But there will be very, very many who are fascinated by the enterprise.

Those courageous souls who are truly drawn to spiritual mountain climbing will be struck by the *Stanzas of Dzyan,* the *sutratman* of the *Gupta Vidya,* which forms the basis of the volumes of *The Secret Doctrine.* These *Stanzas* are also included as an appendix to *The Voice of the Silence,* which is derived from the same ancient source. Through their help, it is possible "to reform one's self by meditation and knowledge", but for this to happen, everything depends upon the state of mind and consciousness in which one approaches them. Those who have found them helpful take the *Stanzas* and read them silently again and again. On the whole, reading them aloud would be unwise because one may activate lower psychical forces much faster than one has gained the ability to govern them. This is a hazard with many people because of the ratios of the noetic to psychic in their lives. It is always a good practice to read quietly and absorb ideas with the mind's eye so that one receives the teaching on deeper planes than merely through the astral senses. Because in the Aquarian Age the mind is very crucial, without some understanding no such activity could be truly helpful and it may even degenerate into quasi-religious pseudo-ritual. This one does not want to encourage, and there is a constant danger that people will be pulled back through their *skandhas* into one or another form of ritualistic salvationism. The whole of *The Secret Doctrine* is a partial commentary on certain fragments of a few of many *Stanzas,* most of which are not given. If one understands all of these at some level, and tries to take a particular *Stanza,* making correlations between the *Transactions* and *The Secret Doctrine,* reading a paragraph and making a few notes, thinking deeply about it and meditating upon it, and then rereads the original *Stanza,* it would help. Clearly this is an exercise involving attention, effort, patience and calm. Anyone who has been so privileged as to have entered into the current of Divine Wisdom will have sensed that the *Stanzas of Dzyan* may be correctly intoned as the basis of noetic magic. This can only be done by initiates, a mantramic activity that is not publicized. Nevertheless, it is extremely potent and has a profound effect upon the entire globe and is solely undertaken for the benefit of all living beings.

If a person is very far from these Himalayan prospects, and has in fact gone wrong for a period of time, for a year, for three years, for ten years, for ten lives, yet would wish to begin again on the Path of *Anasakti,* selfless action, and seeks to reform his or her self by meditation and spiritual knowledge, and even hopes for a second birth, this is indeed possible. Not only is it possible, it is verily the true purpose in transmitting *The Voice of the Silence* and *The Secret Doctrine.* The sacred teaching is for those who seek to become *dwijas,* twice-born, those who wish to be born again as in the Nazarene gospel, those who ardently aspire to be spiritually regenerated. But this must be the product of a patient, persistent and yet relatively unanxious reform of the self. Knowledge only becomes wisdom through meditation acting as the basis of realization. The more one meditates, the more one's knowledge becomes real. The more it becomes real, the more it acts upon one's life-atoms and the spiritual will, transforming the sense-organs and the body, altering and elevating one's whole life. It becomes the current of a living power made free in a human being, and is highly potent. *The Secret Doctrine* is for those who devoutly seek to become Men of Meditation. As a preparation, it is helpful to gain even a little spiritual knowledge, by Buddhic intuition, of the universal, hidden, archetypal, regenerating current of spiritual life-energy referred to as the living stream of wisdom. If one can get into the current, it is bound to make a change that will work slowly but infallibly. The proper use of *The Secret Doctrine* and *The Voice of the Silence* could be like unto the study of the Vedas or of the Gospels according to John or Thomas. Even if taken in small doses but on a regular basis, the way Nature does all things, much benefit can accrue. This is really the problem: Can people learn to grow as they have seen trees grow? A little bit done regularly is of inestimably more value than doing a lot one day and nothing for weeks.

Just because the study of *The Secret Doctrine* is so vast, it does not mean that one cannot gain some benefit even from taking a single phrase or a sentence from almost anywhere in the book. One can, as sincere effort will surely demonstrate. Sometimes people suppose that they cannot come any closer to *The Secret Doctrine* because they are unworthy, but this is a great mistake and a defamation of human dignity. Some people are always making an assumption that they "belong" to themselves. This is philosophically baseless, since the mere fact that they can formulate such a claim does not in the least imply that either the body or mind is a possession of theirs. Of what is any person claiming to be the owner in this "private ownership theory" of the vestures? It is an absurd form of ignorance. One must put oneself in a learning mood or posture, and one must forget about worthiness and unworthiness. Instead, one should thrill to enter the perennial stream of supernal knowledge rendered into a living current of spiritual cleansing of the mind and purification of the heart, acting as a solvent to the lower will, and releasing the higher energies, potencies and faculties of the human being. That is what is truly intended, and those who have intuited the intention from the Preface, perhaps even from its very first words – "The Author – the writer, rather..." – will enter the stream in such a way that their lives will never be the same again. It is indeed a great shame that the golden opportunity is not taken by many more people. The reason usually is about the same, whatever the external excuses and explanations. It is a superficial entering of the stream that blocks a real entering of the stream. On the other hand, one who is afraid to enter the stream wastes this incarnation. Both of these are pointed out in *The Voice of the Silence*. Fear kills the will, leaving one paralyzed. Nothing may happen, but one will not get the golden karma, maybe for many lives, of coming any closer to such exalted teaching. Others, on the other hand, forget that the sacred teaching is for the whole of humanity, that it necessarily involves ascending planes of consciousness. Because of salvationist tendencies in previous lives, they take a Fundamentalist attitude towards *The Secret Doctrine*, supposing that through mere ritual repetition they will gain insight and find redemption. A person must, rather, choose a sentence for meditation, take a paragraph for reflection, select a page for reading as a preparation for reflection and meditation. If one has more time, and the energy and will are summoned after one's duties are done by nature and by man, one may read more for the sake of making a deep study in order to strengthen the quality of one's daily reflection and meditation.

One's whole attitude to what one can do every week is crucial. People are of differing capacities and temperaments and also have different ways of ordering their lives or of remaining disordered. It would be helpful if a person altogether avoided the "hundred per cent *or* nothing" approach, which is Atlantean and adolescent blackmail, saying, "Either I do it all or I do nothing", a sure sign of spiritual failure through pride and perversity. Just as chelas can recognize Adepts, it is only logical that Adepts can recognize failed *chelas*. Rather than become trapped in such foolish pride, one might cheerfully listen to the words of the Buddha: "Drop by drop a jar of water is filled." Choose a sentence, take a paragraph, but use it during the week to prepare for the next week. The real point is to gain greater continuity of consciousness. The Secret Doctrine is the unbroken, uninterrupted Wisdom of Those with unbroken, uninterrupted consciousness for over eighteen million years. They are the *Manushis* who became the Sons of Yoga, and those Sons of Yoga became the Sons of Wisdom. They teach under the same rule that was central to all the ancient systems of Spiritual Teaching: If you take one step in the direction of the Teaching and the Teacher, the Teacher will take one step in your direction and help you to become more capable, through meditation and practice, of spiritual regeneration, maybe even a second birth leading to further changes in lives to come.

He who would hear the voice of Nada, the "Soundless Sound",
and comprehend it, he has to learn the nature of *Dharana*.

Hermes, January 1980
Raghavan Iyer

THEOSOPHICAL TEACHINGS AS TO NATURE AND MAN
The Unity of All in All

ENQUIRER. Having told me what God, the Soul and Man are *not*, in your views, can you inform me what they *are*, according to your teachings?

THEOSOPHIST. In their origin and in eternity the three, like the universe and all therein, are one with the absolute Unity, the unknowable deific essence I spoke about some time back. We believe in no *creation*, but in the periodical and consecutive appearances of the universe from the subjective on to the objective plane of being, at regular intervals of time, covering periods of immense duration.

ENQUIRER. Can you elaborate the subject?

THEOSOPHIST. Take as a first comparison and a help towards a more correct conception, the solar year, and as a second, the two halves of that year, producing each a day and a night of six months' duration at the North Pole. Now imagine, if you can, instead of a Solar year of 365 days, ETERNITY. Let the sun represent the universe, and the polar days and nights of 6 months each – *days and nights lasting each* 182 *trillions and quadrillions of years,* instead of 182 days each. As the sun arises every morning on our *objective* horizon out of its (to us) *subjective* and antipodal space, so does the Universe emerge periodically on the plane of objectivity, issuing from that of subjectivity – the antipodes of the former. This is the "Cycle of Life." And as the sun disappears from our horizon, so does the Universe disappear at regular periods, when the "Universal night" sets in. The Hindoos call such alternations the "Days and Nights of Brahma," or the time of *Manvantara* and that of *Pralaya* (dissolution). The Westerns may call them Universal Days and Nights if they prefer. During the latter (the nights) *All is in All*; every atom is resolved into one Homogeneity.

Evolution and Illusion

ENQUIRER. But who is it that creates each time the Universe?

THEOSOPHIST. No one creates it. Science would call the process evolution; the pre-Christian philosophers and the Orientalists called it emanation: we, Occultists and Theosophists, see in it the only universal and eternal *reality* casting a periodical reflection of *itself* on the infinite Spatial depths. This reflection, which you regard as the objective *material* universe, we consider as a temporary *illusion* and nothing else. That alone which is eternal is *real*.

ENQUIRER. At that rate, you and I are also illusions.

THEOSOPHIST. As flitting personalities, to-day one person, to-morrow another – we are. Would you call the sudden flashes of the *Aurora borealis*, the Northern lights, a "reality," though it is as real as can be while you look at it? Certainly not; it is the cause that produces it, if permanent and eternal, which is the only reality, while the other is but a passing, illusion.

ENQUIRER. All this does not explain to me how this illusion called the universe originates; how the conscious *to be*, proceeds to manifest itself from the unconsciousness that *is*.

THEOSOPHIST. It is *unconsciousness* only to our finite consciousness. Verily may we paraphrase verse v, in the 1st chapter of St. John, and say "and (Absolute) light (which is darkness) shineth in darkness (which is illusionary material light); and the darkness comprehendeth it not." This absolute light is also absolute and immutable law. Whether by radiation or emanation – we need not quarrel over terms – the universe passes out of its homogeneous subjectivity on to the first plane of manifestation, of which planes there are seven, we are taught. With each plane it becomes more dense and material until it reaches this, our plane, on which the only world approximately known and understood in its physical composition by Science, is the planetary or Solar system – one *sui generis*, we are told.

ENQUIRER. What do you mean by *sui generis?*

THEOSOPHIST. I mean that, though the fundamental law and the universal working of laws of Nature are uniform, still our Solar system (like every other such system in the millions of others in Cosmos) and even our Earth, has its own programme of manifestations differing from the respective programmes of all others. We speak of the inhabitants of other planets and imagine that if they are *men, i. e.,* thinking entities, they must be as we are. The fancy of poets and painters and sculptors never fails to represent even the angels as a beautiful copy of man – *plus* wings. We say that all this is an error and a delusion; because, if on this little earth alone one finds such a diversity in its flora, fauna and mankind – from the sea-weed to the cedar of Lebanon, from the jelly-fish to the elephant, from the Bushman and negro to the Apollo Belvedere – alter the conditions cosmic and planetary, and there must be as a result quite a different flora, fauna and mankind. The same laws will fashion quite a different set of things and beings even on this our plane, including in it all our planets. How much more different then must be *external* nature in other Solar systems, and how foolish is it to judge of other *stars* and worlds and human beings by our own, as physical science does!

ENQUIRER. But what are your data for this assertion?

THEOSOPHIST. What science in general will never accept as proof – the cumulative testimony of an endless series of Seers who have testified to this fact. Their spiritual visions, real explorations by, and through, physical and spiritual senses untrammelled by blind flesh, were systematically checked and compared one with the other, and their nature sifted. All that was not corroborated by unanimous and collective experience was rejected, while that only was recorded as established truth which, in various ages, under different climes, and throughout an untold series of incessant observations, was found to agree and receive constantly further corroboration. The methods used by our scholars and students of the psycho-spiritual sciences do not differ from those of students of the natural and physical sciences, as you may see. Only our fields of research are on two different planes, and our instruments are made by no human hands, for which reason perchance they are only the more reliable. The retorts, accumulators, and microscopes of the chemist and naturalist may get out of order; the telescope and the astronomer's horological instruments may get spoiled; our recording instruments are beyond the influence of weather or the elements.

ENQUIRER. And therefore you have implicit faith in them?

THEOSOPHIST. Faith is a word not to be found in theosophical dictionaries: we say *knowledge based, on observation and experience.* There is this difference, however, that while the observation and experience of physical science lead the Scientists to about as many "working" hypotheses as there are minds to evolve them, our *knowledge* consents to add to its lore only those facts which have become undeniable, and which are fully and absolutely demonstrated. We have no two beliefs or hypotheses on the same subject.

ENQUIRER. Is it on such data that you came to accept the strange theories we find in *Esoteric Buddhism?*

THEOSOPHIST. Just so. These theories may be slightly incorrect in their minor details, and even faulty in their exposition by lay students; they are *facts* in nature, nevertheless, and come nearer the truth than any scientific hypothesis.

The Key to Theosophy, pp. 83-87
H.P. Blavatsky

WHAT REINCARNATES?

What reincarnates is a mystery to many minds because they find a difficulty in understanding such a permanency as must stand behind repeated incarnations. They know that the body is born and dies and is dissolved, but their minds are so identified with the body in its relations and surroundings that they are unable to dissociate themselves from it. They think of themselves as persons, as bodies of a physical nature, and hence cannot see where in them may reside that power of incarnating from life to life.

Theosophy presents a larger view in showing that man is *not* his body, because the body is continually changing; that man is not his mind, because he is constantly changing his mind; that there is in man a permanency which is the identity throughout all kinds of embodiments. There has been no change in our identity from childhood up to the present day. The body has changed; the surroundings have changed; but the identity remains the same and will not change from now on through all changes of body or mind or circumstance. That in us which is itself unchanging is the only real. Nothing is real that changes. It is only the real that perceives change. Change cannot see change. Only that which is constant perceives change; only the permanent can perceive impermanence. However dimly we may perceive it, there is that in us which is eternal and changeless.

This unchanging, constant, and immortal something in us is not absent from any particle or any being whatever. There is only one Life in the world to which we, as well as all other beings, pertain. We all proceeded from the same one Source - not many - and we are proceeding on the same path to the same great goal. The ancients said that the Divine Self is in all beings, but in all it does not shine forth. The real is within, and may be realized by any human being in himself. Everyone needs that realization that he may shine forth and express the God within, which all beings but partially express.

If then the Source is the same - the One Spirit - in all beings, why so many forms, so many personalities, so many individualizations? All, again Theosophy shows, are developments. In that great Ocean of Life, which is at the same time Consciousness and Spirit, we move and live and have our being. That ocean is separable into its constituent drops and the separation is effected through the great course of evolution. Even in the kingdoms below us, which are from the same Source, the tendency to separate into drops of individualized consciousness goes on in ever-increasing degree. In the animal kingdom, those species that are nearest to us make an approach to self-consciousness; but we as human beings have arrived at that stage where each is a constituent drop of the great ocean of Consciousness. As with an ocean of water, each drop of it contains all the elements of the great body, so each constituent drop of humanity - a human being - contains within its range every element of the great universe.

The same power exists in all of us, yet where we stand on the ladder of being we see many below us and others greater than we above us. Humanity now is building the bridge of thought, the bridge of ideas that connects the lower with the higher. The whole purpose of incarnation, or our descent into matter, was not only to gain further knowledge of matter, but to impel the lower kingdoms to come up to where we are. We stand as gods to the lower kingdoms. It is our impulsion that brings them weal or woe. It is our misconception of the aim of life that makes Nature so hard; that causes all the distress and disasters which afflict us in cyclones, tornadoes, diseases, pestilences of every kind. All are our own doing; and why? Because there is a sublimation of mineral, vegetable and animal kingdoms in our bodies, which are lives in themselves. Every cell in our bodies has its birth, youth, manhood, decay and death, and its reincarnation. We are impelling each one of those lives according to whatever thought, will, or feeling we may have, whether for help or injury to others. These lives go out from us for good or evil, back into their kingdoms with good or evil. So by our lack of understanding of our own true natures, without a comprehension of universal brotherhood, we are imperfectly performing our duties on this plane and are imperfectly helping the evolution of the lower kingdoms. We shall realize our responsibility to them only as we see that every being is on his way upward; that all above man have been men at one time; that all below man will some time reach man's estate, when we have gone on further; that all forms, all beings, all individualizations are but aspects of the One Spirit.

Granted, then, that this one unchanging Spirit is in all - the cause of all evolutionary development, the cause of all incarnations - where, we may ask, do we carry the power to see and know from life to life? How is continuity of knowledge, gained by observation and experience, preserved? How is the individual maintained as such?

We should remember that we were self-conscious beings when this planet began; some even were self-conscious when this solar system began; for there is a difference in degree of development among human beings. If the planet or solar system began in a state of primordial substance, or nebulous matter, as Science calls it, then we must have had bodies of that state of substance. In that finest substance are all the possibilities of every grade of matter, and hence it is that within the true body of primordial matter all the changes of courser and courser substance have been brought about; and within that body is all experience. Our birth is within that body. Everything that occurs to us is within that body - a body of a nature which does not change throughout the whole Manvantara. Each one has such a body of finest substance, of the inner nature, which is the real container for the individual. In it he lives and moves and has his being, and yet even the great glory and fineness of that body is not the man; it is merely the highest vesture of the Soul. The Real Man we are is the Man that was, that is, and that ever shall be, for whom the hour will never strike - Man, the thinker; Man, the perceiver - always thinking, continually acting.

Life is one. Spirit is one. Consciousness is one. These three are one - a trinity - and we are that trinity. All the changes of substance and form are brought about by Spirit and Consciousness and expressed in various forms of life. We are that One Spirit, each standing in a vast assemblage of beings in this great universe, seeing and knowing what he can through the instruments he has. We are the Trinity - the Father, the Son, and the Holy Ghost; or, in theosophical parlance, we are *Atma*, *Buddhi*, and *Manas*. *Atma* is the One Spirit, not belonging to anyone, but to all. *Buddhi* is the sublimated experience of all the past. *Manas* is the thinking power, the thinker, the man, the immortal man. There is no man without the Spirit, and no man without that experience of the past; but the mind is the realm of creation, of ideas; and the Spirit itself, with all its power, acts according to the ideas that are in the mind.

The Voice of the Silence says, "Mind is like a mirror. It gathers dust while it reflects." It needs soul-wisdom to brush away the dust. This mind of ours, or that which we call the mind, is merely the reflector, which presents as we train it, different pictures. The Spirit acts in accord with the ideas seen, for good or for evil. Is there evil in the world? It is the power of Spirit that caused it. Is there good in the world? It is the power of Spirit that caused it. For there is only one power. The misdirection of that power brings evil; its right direction brings good.

We must give up the idea that we are poor, weak, miserable creatures who can never do anything for ourselves; for as long as we hold that idea, so long will we never do anything. We must get the other idea - that we are Spirit, that we are immortal - and when we come to realize what that means, the power of it will flow directly in and through us, unrestricted in any direction, save by the instruments which we ourselves caused to be imperfect. So let us get away from the idea that we are this poor, miserable, defective physical body over which we have so little control. We cannot stop a heartbeat; we cannot stop the breath without destroying the body; we cannot stop the constant dissociation of matter that goes on in it, nor prevent its final dissolution. Some people talk of "demonstrating" against death, but we might as well try to demonstrate against the trees shedding their leaves when the winter blasts come. Death will always be, and there is a great advantage in it. If we could not change our bodies, how would there be any chance for advancement? Are we so well pleased with the bodies now ours that we would desire no change? Certainly not. There is only one thing in this life that can be retained permanently, and that is the spiritual nature, and the great divine compassion which we may translate by the word "love."

We are the reincarnating Egos who will continue to incarnate until the great task which we undertook is completed. That task is the raising up of the whole of humanity to the highest possible stage of perfection on an earth of this kind. We incarnate from age to age for the preservation of the just, the destruction of wickedness, and the establishment of righteousness. That is what we are here for, whether we know it or not, and we must come to a recognition of the immortality of our own natures before we shall ever relieve ourselves from the distresses that afflict humanity everywhere. We have to bring ourselves in touch and tune with the whole great purpose of Nature which is the evolution of Soul, and for which alone all the universe exists.

Universal Theosophy
Robert Crosbie

THE SEPTENARY NATURE OF MAN

ENQUIRER. Is it what we call Spirit and Soul, and the man of flesh?

THEOSOPHIST. It is not. That is the old Platonic division. Plato was an Initiate, and therefore could not go into forbidden details; but he who is acquainted with the archaic doctrine finds the seven in Plato's various combinations of Soul and Spirit. He regarded man as constituted of two parts — one eternal, formed of the same essence as the Absoluteness, the other mortal and corruptible, deriving its constituent parts from the *minor* "created" Gods. Man is composed, he shows, of (1) A mortal body, (2) An immortal principle, and (3) A "separate mortal kind of Soul." It is that which we respectively call the physical man, the Spiritual Soul or Spirit, and the animal Soul (the *Nous* and *psuche*). This is the division adopted by Paul, another Initiate, who maintains that there is a psychical body which is sown in the corruptible (astral soul or body), and a *spiritual* body that is raised in incorruptible substance. Even James (iii. 15) corroborates the same by saying that the "wisdom" (of our lower soul) descendeth not from the above, but is terrestrial ("psychical," "demoniacal," *vide* Greek text); while the other is heavenly wisdom. Now so plain is it that Plato and even Pythagoras, while speaking but of three "principles," give them seven separate functions, in their various combinations, that if we contrast our teachings this will become quite plain. Let us take a cursory view of these seven aspects by drawing two tables.

THEOSOPHICAL DIVISION

Lower Quaternary

SANSCRIT TERMS	EXOTERIC MEANING	EXPLANATORY
a. Rupa, or Sthula-Sarira	a. Physical body	a. Is the vehicle of all the other "principles" during life.
b. Prana	b. Life, or Vital principle	b. Necessary only to a, c, d, and the functions of the lower *Manas,* which embrace all

		those limited to the (*physical*) brain.
c. Linga Sharira	c. Astral body	c. The *Double*, the phantom body.
d. Kama rupa	d. The seat of animal desires and passions	d. This is the centre of the animal man, where lies the line of demarcation which separates the mortal man from the immortal entity.

The Upper Imperishable Triad

SANSCRIT TERMS	EXOTERIC MEANING	EXPLANATORY
e. *Manas*—a dual principle in its functions.	e. Mind, Intelligence: which is the higher human mind, whose light, or radiation links the MONAD, for the lifetime, to the mortal man.	e. The future state and the Karmic destiny of man depend on whether *Manas* gravitates more downward to Kama rupa, the seat of the animal passions, or upwards to *Buddhi*, the Spiritual *Ego*. In the latter case, the higher consciousness of the individual Spiritual aspirations of *mind* (*Manas*), assimilating Buddhi, are absorbed by it and form the *Ego*, which goes into Devachanic bliss.[1]

---

[1] In Mr. Sinnett's "*Esoteric Buddhism*" d, e, and f, are respectively called the Animal, the Human, and the Spiritual Souls, which answers as well. Though the principles in *Esoteric Buddhism* are numbered, this is, strictly speaking, useless. The dual *Monad* alone (*Atma-Buddhi*) is susceptible of being thought of as the two highest numbers (the 6th and 7th). As to all

f. Buddhi	f. The Spiritual Soul	f. The vehicle of pure universal spirit. g. One with the Absolute, as its radiation.
g. Atma	g. Spirit	

Now what does Plato teach? He speaks of the *interior* man as constituted of two parts – one immutable and always the same, formed of the same *substance* as Deity, and the other mortal and corruptible. These "two parts" are found in our upper *Triad*, and the lower *Quaternary* (*vide* Table). He explains that when the Soul, *psuche*, "allies herself to the *Nous* (divine spirit or substance)[2], she does everything aright and felicitously"; but the case is otherwise when she attaches herself to *Anoia*, (folly, or the irrational animal Soul). Here, then, we have *Manas* (or the Soul in general) in its two aspects: when attaching itself to *Anoia* (our *Kama rupa*, or the "Animal Soul" in "*Esoteric Buddhism*,") it runs towards entire annihilation, as far as the personal Ego is concerned; when allying itself to the *Nous* (*Atma-Buddhi*) it merges into the immortal, imperishable Ego, and then its spiritual consciousness of the personal that *was*, becomes immortal.

The Distinction Between Soul And Spirit

ENQUIRER. Do you really teach, as you are accused of doing by some Spiritualists and French Spiritists, the annihilation of every personality?

---

others, since *that* "principle" only which is predominant in man has to be considered as the first and foremost, no numeration is possible as a general rule. In some men it is the higher Intelligence (Manas or the 5th) which dominates the rest; in others the Animal Soul (*Kama-rupa*) that reigns supreme, exhibiting the most bestial instincts, etc.

[2] Paul calls Plato's *Nous* "Spirit"; but as this spirit is "substance," then, of course, *Buddhi* and not *Atma* is meant, as the latter cannot philosophically be called "substance" under any circumstance. We include *Atma* among the human "principles" in order not to create additional confusion. In reality it is no "human" but the universal *absolute* principle of which *Buddhi*, the Soul-Spirit, is the carrier.

THEOSOPHIST. We do not. But as this question of the duality – the *individuality* of the Divine Ego, and the *personality* of the human animal—involves that of the possibility of the real immortal Ego appearing in *Seance rooms* as a "materialised spirit," which we deny as already explained, our opponents have started the nonsensical charge.

ENQUIRER. You have just spoken of *psuche* running towards its entire annihilation if it attaches itself to *Anoia*. What did Plato, and do you mean by this?

THEOSOPHIST. The *entire* annihilation of the *personal* consciousness, as an exceptional and rare case, I think. The general and almost invariable rule is the merging of the personal into the individual or immortal consciousness of the Ego, a transformation or a divine transfiguration, and the entire annihilation only of the lower *quaternary* . Would you expect the man of flesh, or the *temporary personality*, his shadow, the "astral," his animal instincts and even physical life, to survive with the "spiritual EGO" and become sempiternal? Naturally all this ceases to exist, either at, or soon after corporeal death. It becomes in time entirely disintegrated and disappears from view, being annihilated as a whole.

ENQUIRER. Then you also reject *resurrection in the flesh?*

THEOSOPHIST. Most decidedly we do! Why should we, who believe in the archaic esoteric philosophy of the Ancients, accept the unphilosophical speculations of the later Christian theology, borrowed from the Egyptian and Greek exoteric Systems of the Gnostics?

ENQUIRER. The Egyptians revered Nature-Spirits, and deified even onions: your Hindus are *idolaters*, to this day; the Zoroastrians worshipped, and do still worship, the Sun; and the best Greek philosophers were either dreamers or materialists — witness Plato and Democritus. How can you compare!

THEOSOPHIST. It may be so in your modern Christian and even Scientific catechism; it is not so for unbiassed minds. The Egyptians revered the "One-Only-One," as *Nout;* and it is from this word that Anaxagoras got his denomination *Nous*, or as he calls it, Νους αυτοκρατες, "the Mind or Spirit Self-potent," the αρχητες κινηδεως, the leading motor, or *primum-mobile* of all. With him the *Nous* was God, and the *logos* was man, his emanation. The *Nous* is the spirit (whether in Kosmos or in man), and the *logos,* whether Universe or astral body, the emanation of the former, the physical body being merely the animal. Our external powers perceive *phenomena*; our *Nous* alone is able to recognise their *noumena*. It is the logos alone, or the *noumenon,* that survives, because it is immortal in its very nature and essence, and the *logos* in man is the Eternal Ego, that which reincarnates and lasts forever. But how can the evanescent or external shadow, the temporary clothing of that divine Emanation which returns to the source whence it proceeded, be that *which is raised in incorruptibility?*

ENQUIRER. Still you can hardly escape the charge of having invented a new division of man's spiritual and psychic constituents; for no philosopher speaks of them, though you believe that Plato does.

THEOSOPHIST. And I support the view. Besides Plato, there is Pythagoras, who also followed the same idea.[3] He described the *Soul* as a self-moving Unit (monad) composed of three elements, the *Nous* (Spirit), the *phren* (mind), and the *thumos* (life, breath or the *Nephesh* of the Kabalists) which three correspond to our "*Atma-Buddhi,*" (higher Spirit-Soul), to *Manas* (the EGO), and to *Kama-rupa* in conjunction with the *lower* reflection of *Manas*. That which the Ancient Greek philosophers termed Soul, in general, we call Spirit, or Spiritual *Soul, Buddhi*, as the vehicle of *Atma* (the *Agathon,* or Plato's Supreme Deity). The fact that Pythagoras and others state that *phren* and *thumos* are shared by us with the brutes, proves that in this case the *lower* Manasic reflection (instinct) and *Kama-rupa* (animal living passions) are meant. And as Socrates and Plato accepted the clue and followed it, if to these five, namely, *Agathon* (Deity or *Atma*), *Psuche* (Soul in its collective sense), *Nous* (Spirit or Mind), *Phren* (physical mind), and *Thumos*

---

[3] "Plato and Pythagoras," says Plutarch, "distribute the soul into two parts, the rational (noetic) and irrational (*agnoia*); that that part of the soul of man which is rational is eternal; for though it be not God, yet it is the product of an eternal deity, but that part of the soul which is divested of reason (*agnoia*) dies." The modern term *Agnostic* comes from *Agnosis,* a cognate word. We wonder why Mr. Huxley, the author of the word, should have connected his great intellect with "the soul divested of reason" which dies? Is it the exaggerated humility of the modern materialist?

(*Kama-rupa* or passions) we add the *eidolon* of the Mysteries, the shadowy *form* or the human double, and the *physical body*, it will be easy to demonstrate that the ideas of both Pythagoras and Plato were identical with ours. Even the Egyptians held to the Septenary division. In its exit, they taught, the Soul (EGO) had to pass through its seven chambers, or principles, those it left behind, and those it took along with itself. The only difference is that, ever bearing in mind the penalty of revealing Mystery-doctrines, which was *death,* they gave out the teaching in a broad outline, while we elaborate it and explain it in its details. But though we do give out to the world as much as is lawful, even in our doctrine more than one important detail is withheld, which those who study the esoteric philosophy and are pledged to silence, *are alone entitled to know.*

The Key to Theosophy, pp. 90-93
H.P. Blavatsky

KARMA

THE child is the father of the man, and none the less true is it:

> My brothers! each man's life
> The outcome of his former living is;
> The bygone wrongs bring forth sorrows and woes
> The bygone right breeds bliss. .
> "This is the doctrine of Karma."

But in what way does this bygone wrong and right affect the present life? Is the stern *nemesis* ever following the weary traveler, with a calm, passionless, remorseless step? Is there no escape from its relentless hand? Does the eternal law of cause and effect, unmoved by sorrow and regret, ever deal out its measure of weal and woe as the consequence of past action? The shadow of the yesterday of sin--must it darken the life of today? Is Karma but another name for fate? Does the child unfold the page of the already written book of life in which each event is recorded without the possibility of escape? What is the relation of Karma to the life of the individual? Is there nothing for man to do but to weave the chequered warp and woof of each earthly existence with the stained and discolored threads of past actions? Good resolves and evil tendencies sweep with resistless tide over the nature of man and we are told:

> "Whatever action he performs, whether good or bad, everything
> done in a former body must necessarily be enjoyed or suffered."
> *Anugita,* Cp. III.

There is good Karma, there is bad Karma, and as the wheel of life moves on, old Karma is exhausted and again fresh Karma is accumulated.

Although at first it may appear that nothing can be more fatalistic than this doctrine, yet a little consideration will show that in reality this is not the case. Karma is twofold, hidden and manifest, Karma is the man that is, Karma is his action. True that each action is a cause from which evolves the countless ramifications of effect in time and space.

"That which ye sow ye reap." In some sphere of action the harvest will be gathered. It is necessary that the man of action should realize this truth. It is equally necessary that the manifestations of this law in the operations of Karma should be clearly apprehended.

Karma, broadly speaking, may be said to be the continuance of the nature of the act, and each act contains within itself the past and future. Every defect which can be realized from an act must be implicit in the act itself or it could never come into existence. Effect is but the nature of the act and cannot exist distinct from its cause. Karma only produces the manifestation of that which already exists; being action it has its operation in time, and Karma may therefore be said to be the same action from another point of time. It must, moreover, be evident that not only is there a relation between the cause and the effect, but there must also be a relation between the cause and the individual who experiences the effect. If it were otherwise, any man would reap the effect of the actions of any other man. We may sometimes appear to reap the effects of the action of others, but this is only apparent. In point of fact it is our own action.

> . . . None else compels
> None other holds you that ye live and die.

It is therefore necessary in order to understand the nature of Karma and its relation to the individual to consider action in all its aspects. Every act proceeds from the mind. Beyond the mind there is no action and therefore no Karma. The basis of every act is desire. The plane of desire or egotism is itself action and the matrix of every act. This plane may be considered as non-manifest, yet having a dual manifestation in what we call cause and effect, that is, the act and its consequences. In reality, both the act and its consequences are the effect, the cause being on the plane of desire. Desire is therefore the basis of action in its first manifestation on the physical plane, and desire determines the continuation of the act in its karmic relation to the individual. For a man to be free from the effects of the Karma of any act he must have passed to a state no longer yielding a basis in which that act can inhere. The ripples in the water caused by the action of the stone will extend to the furthest limit of its expanse, but no further; they are bounded by the shore. Their course is ended when there is no longer a basis or suitable medium in which they can inhere; they expend their force and are not. Karma is, therefore, as dependent upon the present personality for its fulfillment, as it was upon the former for the first initial act. An illustration may be given which will help to explain this.

A seed, say for instance mustard, will produce a mustard tree and nothing else; but in order that it should be produced, it is necessary that the co-operation of soil and culture should be equally present. Without the seed, however much the ground may be tilled and watered, it will not bring forth the plant, but the seed is equally inoperative without the joint action of the soil and culture.

The first great result of Karmic action is the incarnation in physical life. The birth-seeking entity consisting of desires and tendencies, presses forward towards incarnation. It is governed in the selection of its scene of manifestation by the law of economy. Whatever is the ruling tendency, that is to say, whatever group of affinities is strongest, those affinities will lead it to the point of manifestation at which there is the least opposition. It incarnates in those surroundings most in harmony with its Karmic tendencies and all the effects of actions contained in the Karma so manifesting will be experienced by the individual. This governs the station of life, the sex, the conditions of the irresponsible years of childhood, the constitution with the various diseases inherent in it, and in fact all those determining forces of physical existence which are ordinarily classed under the terms, "heredity," and "national characteristics."

It is really the law of economy which is the truth underlying these terms and which explains them. Take for instance a nation with certain special characteristics. These are the plane of expansion for any entity whose greatest number of affinities are in harmony with those characteristics. The incoming entity following the law of least resistance becomes incarnated in that nation, and all Karmic effects following such characteristics will accrue to the individual. This will explain what is the meaning of such expressions as the "Karma of nations," and what is true of the nation will also apply to family and caste.

It must, however, be remembered that there are many tendencies which are not exhausted in the act of incarnation. It may happen that the Karma which caused an entity to incarnate in any particular surrounding, was only strong enough to carry it into physical existence. Being exhausted in that direction, freedom is obtained for the manifestation of other tendencies and their Karmic effects. For instance, Karmic force may cause an entity to incarnate in a humble sphere of life. He may be born as the child of poor parents. The Karma follows the entity, endures for a longer or shorter time, and becomes exhausted. From that point, the child takes a line of life totally different from his surroundings. Other affinities engendered by former action express themselves in their Karmic results. The lingering effect of the past Karma may still manifest itself in the way of obstacles and obstructions which are surmounted with varying degrees of success according to their intensity.

From the standpoint of a special creation for each entity entering the world, there is vast and unaccountable injustice. From the standpoint of Karma, the strange vicissitudes and apparent chances of life can be considered in a different light as the unerring manifestation of cause and sequence. In a family under the same conditions of poverty and ignorance, one child will be separated from the others and thrown into surroundings very dissimilar. He may be adopted by a rich man, or through some freak of fortune receive an education giving him at once a different position. The Karma of incarnation being exhausted, other Karma asserts itself.

A very important question is here presented: Can an individual affect his own Karma, and if so to what degree and in what manner?

It has been said that Karma is the continuance of the act, and for any particular line of Karma to exert itself it is necessary that there should be the basis of the act engendering that Karma in which it can inhere and operate. But action has many planes in which it can inhere. There is the physical plane, the body with its senses and organs; then there is the intellectual plane, memory, which binds the impressions of the senses into a consecutive whole and reason puts in orderly arrangement its storehouse of facts. Beyond the plane of intellect there is the plane of emotion, the plane of preference for one object rather than another: the fourth principle of the man. These three, physical, intellectual, and emotional, deal entirely with objects of sense perception and may be called the great battlefield of Karma. There is also the plane of ethics, the plane of discrimination of the "I ought to do this, I ought not to do that." This plane harmonizes the intellect and the emotions. All these are the planes of Karma or action: what to do, and what not to do. It is the mind as the basis of desire that initiates action on the various planes, and it is only through the mind that the effects of rest and action can be received.

An entity enters incarnation with Karmic energy from past existences, that is to say the action of past lives is awaiting its development as effect. This Karmic energy presses into manifestation in harmony with the basic nature of the act. Physical Karma will manifest in the physical tendencies bringing enjoyment and suffering. The intellectual and the ethical planes are also in the same manner the result of the past Karmic tendencies and the man as he is, with his moral and intellectual faculties, is in unbroken continuity with the past.

The entity at birth has therefore a definite amount of Karmic energy. After incarnation this awaits the period in life at which fresh Karma begins. Up to the time of responsibility it is as we have seen the initial Karma only that manifests. From that time the fresh personality becomes the ruler of his own destiny. It is a great mistake to suppose that an individual is the mere puppet of the past, the helpless victim of fate. The law of Karma is not fatalism, and a little consideration will show that it is possible for an individual to affect his own Karma. If a greater amount of energy be taken up on one plane than on another this will cause the past Karma to unfold itself on that plane. For instance, one who lives entirely on the plane of sense gratification will from the plane beyond draw the energy required for the fulfillment of his desires. Let us illustrate by dividing man into upper and lower nature. By directing the mind and aspirations to the lower plane, a "fire" or centre of attraction, is set up there, and in order to feed and fatten it, the energies of the whole upper plane are drawn down and exhausted in supplying the need of energy which exists below due to the indulgence of sense gratification. On the other hand, the centre of attraction may be fixed in the upper portion, and then all the needed energy goes there to result in increase of spirituality. It must be remembered that Nature is all bountiful and withholds not her hand.

The demand is made, and the supply will come. But at what cost? That energy which should have strengthened the moral nature and fulfilled the aspirations after good, is drawn to the lower desires. By degrees the higher planes are exhausted of vitality and the good and bad Karma of an entity will be absorbed on the physical plane. If on the other hand the interest is detached from the plane of sense gratification, if there is a constant effort to fix the mind on the attainment of the highest ideal, the result will be that the past Karma will find no basis in which to inhere on the physical plane. Karma will therefore be manifested only in harmony with the plane of desire. The sense energy of the physical plane will exhaust itself on a higher plane and thus become transmuted in its effects.

What are the means through which the effects of Karma can be thus changed is also clear. A person can have no attachment for a thing he does not think about, therefore the first step must be to fix the thought on the highest ideal. In this connection one remark may be made on the subject of repentance. Repentance is a form of thought in which the mind is constantly recurring to a sin. It has therefore to be avoided if one would set the mind free from sin and its Karmic results. All sin has its origin in the mind. The more the mind dwells on any course of conduct, whether with pleasure or pain, the less chance is there for it to become detached from such action. The *Manas* (mind) is the knot of the heart, when that is untied from any object, in other words when the mind loses its interest in any object, there will no longer be a link between the Karma connected with that object and the individual.

It is the attitude of the mind which draws the Karmic cords tightly round the soul. It imprisons the aspirations and binds them with chains of difficulty and obstruction. It is desire that causes the past Karma to take form and shape and build the house of clay. It must be through non-attachment that the soul will burst through the walls of pain, it will be only through a change of mind that the Karmic burden will be lifted.

It will appear, therefore, that although absolutely true that action brings its own result, "there is no destruction here of actions good or not good. Coming to one body after another they become ripened in their respective ways." Yet this ripening is the act of the individual.

Free will of man asserts itself and he becomes his own saviour. To the worldly man Karma is a stern *Nemesis,* to the spiritual man Karma unfolds itself in harmony with his highest aspirations. He will look with tranquility alike on past and future, neither dwelling with remorse on past sin nor living in expectation of reward for present action.

Path, December, 1886
W. Q. Judge

EVOLUTION

THE word "evolution" is the best word from a theosophical standpoint to use in treating of the genesis of men and things, as the process which it designates is that which has been always stated in the ancient books from whose perusal the tenets of the wisdom religion can be gathered. In the *Bhagavad Gita* we find Krishna saying that "at the beginning of the day of Brahma all things come forth from the non-developed principle, and at the coming on of Brahma's night they are resolved into it again," and that this process goes on from age to age. This exactly states evolution as it is defined in our dictionaries, where it is said to be a process of coming forth or a development. The "days and nights of Brahma" are immense periods of time during which evolution proceeds, the manifestation of things being the "day" and their periodical resolution into the Absolute the "night."

If, then, everything is evolved, the word creation can only be properly applied to any combination of things already in existence, since the primordial matter or basis cannot be created.

The basis of the theosophical system is evolution, for in Theosophy it is held that all things are already in *esse*, being brought forth or evolved from time to time in conformity to the inherent law of the Absolute. The very next question to be asked is, What is this inherent law of the Absolute? as nearly as can be stated. Although we do not and cannot know the Absolute, we have enough data from which to draw the conclusion that its inherent law is to periodically come forth from subjectivity into objectivity and to return again to the former, and so on without any cessation. In the objective world we have a figure or illustration of this in the rising and setting of the sun, which of all natural objects best shows the influence of the law. It rises, as H. P. Blavatsky says, from the (to us) subjective, and at night returns to the subjective again, remaining in the objective world during the day. If we substitute, as we must when attempting to draw correspondences between the worlds, the word "state" for locality or place, and instead of the sun we call that object "the Absolute," we have a perfect figure, for then we will have the Absolute rising above the horizon of consciousness from the subjective state, and its setting again for that consciousness when the time of night arrives that is, the night of Brahma. This law of periodicity is the same as that of the cycles, which can be seen governing in every department of nature.

But let us assume a point of departure so as to get a rapid survey of evolution theosophically considered. And let it be at the time when this period of manifestation began. What was projected into the objective world at that time must have been life itself, which under the action of the law of differentiation split itself up into a vast number of lives, which we may call individual, the quantity of which it is not possible for us of finite mind to count. In the Hindu system these are called Jivas and Jivatman. Within these lives there is contained the entire plan to be pursued during the whole period of manifestation, since each life is a small copy of the great All from which it came. Here a difficulty arises for studious minds, calling for some attention, for they may ask "What then do you do with that which we call "matter", and by and through which the lives manifest themselves?"

The reply is that the so-called matter is an illusion and is not real matter, but that the latter – sometime known in Europe as primordial matter – cannot be seen by us. The real matter is itself only another form of the life first thrown out, but in a less perfect state of differentiation, and it is on a screen of this real matter that its inner energies project pictures which we call matter, mistaking them for the real. It may then be further asked, "Have we not been led to suppose that that which we supposed was matter but which you now say is an illusion is something absolutely necessary to the soul for acquiring experience of nature?" To this I reply that such is not the case, but that the matter needed for the soul to acquire experience through is the real unseen matter. It is that matter of which psychic bodies are composed, and those other "material" things all the way up to spirit. It is to this that the *Bhagavad Gita* refers where it says that spirit (*purusha*) and matter (*prakriti*) are coeternal and not divisible from each other. That which we and science are accustomed to designate matter is nothing more than our limited and partial cognition of the phenomena of the real or primordial matter. This position is not overturned by pointing to the fact that all men in general have the same cognitions of the same objects, that square objects are always square and that shadows fall in the same line for all normal people, for even in our own experience we see that there is such a thing as a collective change of cognition, and that thus it is quite possible that all normal people are merely on the single plane of consciousness where they are not yet able to cognize anything else. In the case of hypnotizing everything appears to the subject to be different at the will of the operator, which would not be possible if objects had any inherent actuality of their own apart from our consciousness.

In order to justify a discussion of the Theosophical system of evolution, it is necessary to see if there be any radical difference between it and that which is accepted in the world, either in scientific circles or among Theologians. That there is such a distinction can be seen at once, and we will take first that between it and Theology. Here, of course, this is in respect to the genesis of the inner man more especially, although Theology makes some claim to know about race descent. The Church either says that the soul of each man is a special creation in each case or remains silent on the subject, leaving us, as it was once so much the fashion to say, "In the hands of a merciful Providence," who after all says nothing on the matter. But when the question of the race is raised, then the priest points to the *Bible*, saying that we all come from one pair, Adam and Eve. On this point Theology is more sure than science, as the latter has no data yet and does not really know whether we owe our origin to one pair, male and female, or to many. Theosophy, on the other hand, differs from the Church, asserting that *Paramatma* alone is self-existing, single, eternal, immutable, and common to all creatures, high and low alike; hence it never was and never will be created; that the soul of man evolves, is consciousness itself, and is not specially created for each man born on the earth, but assumes through countless incarnations different bodies at different times. Underlying this must be the proposition that, for each *Manvantara* or period of manifestation, there is a definite number of souls or egos who project themselves into the current of evolution which is to prevail for that period or *manvantara*. Of course this subject is limitless, and the consideration of the vast number of systems and worlds where the same process is going on with a definite number of egos in each, staggers the minds of most of those who take the subject up. And of course I do not mean to be understood as saying that there is a definite number of egos in the whole collection of systems in which we may imagine evolution as proceeding, for there could be no such definiteness considered in the mass, as that would be the same as taking the measure of the Absolute. But in viewing any part of the manifestation of the Absolute, it is allowable for us to say that there are to be found such a definite number of egos in that particular system under consideration; this is one of the necessities of our finite consciousness. Following out the line of our own argument we reach the conclusion that, included within the great wave of evolution which relates to the system of which this earth is a part, there are just so many egos either fully developed or in a latent state. These have gone round and round the wheel of rebirth, and will continue to do so until the wave shall meet and be transformed into another. Therefore there could be no such thing as a special creation of souls for the different human beings born on this earth, and for the additional reason that, if there were, then spirit would be made subservient to illusion, to mere human bodies. So that in respect to theology we deny the propositions, *first*, that there is any special creation of souls, *second*, that there is, or was, or could be by any possibility any creation of this world or of any other, and *third*, that the human race descended from one pair.

In taking up the difference existing between our theory and that of science we find the task easy. Upon the question of progress, and how progress or civilization may be attained by man, and whether any progress could be possible if the theories of science be true, our position is that there could be no progress if the law of evolution as taught in the schools is true, even in a material sense. In this particular we are diametrically opposed to science. Its assumption is that the present race on the earth may be supposed to belong to a common stock which in its infancy was rude and barbarous, knowing little more than the animal, living like the animal, and learning all it now knows simply by experience gained in its contest with nature through its development. Hence they give us the paleolithic age, the neolithic age, and so on. In this scheme we find no explanation of how man comes to have innate ideas. Some, however, seeing the necessity for an explanation of this phenomenon, attempt it in various ways; and it is a phenomenon of the greatest importance. It is explained by Theosophy in a way peculiar to itself, and of which more will be said as we go on.

Path, August, 1890
W.Q. Judge

THE COMMON ORIGIN OF MAN

THEOSOPHIST. . . . . selfishness, instead of being eradicated, is daily strengthened and stimulated into a ferocious and irresistible feeling by the present religious education, which tends not only to encourage, but positively to justify it. People's ideas about right and wrong have been entirely perverted by the literal acceptance of the Jewish *Bible*. All the unselfishness of the altruistic teachings of Jesus has become merely a theoretical subject for pulpit oratory; while the precepts of practical selfishness taught in the Mosaic *Bible*, against which Christ so vainly preached, have become ingrained into the innermost life of the Western nations. "An eye for an eye and a tooth for a tooth" has come to be the first maxim of your law. Now, I state openly and fearlessly, that the perversity of this doctrine and of so many others *Theosophy alone* can eradicate.

ENQUIRER. How?

THEOSOPHIST. Simply by demonstrating on logical, philosophical, metaphysical, and even scientific grounds that: (*a*) All men have spiritually and physically the same origin, which is the fundamental teaching of Theosophy. (*b*) As mankind is essentially of one and the same essence, and that essence is one – infinite, uncreate, and eternal, whether we call it God or Nature – nothing, therefore, can affect one nation or one man without affecting all other nations and all other men. This is as certain and as obvious as that a stone thrown into a pond will, sooner or later, set in motion every single drop of water therein.

ENQUIRER. But this is not the teaching of Christ, but rather a pantheistic notion.

THEOSOPHIST. That is where your mistake lies. It is purely *Christian*, although *not* Judaic, and therefore, perhaps, your Biblical nations prefer to ignore it.

ENQUIRER. This is a wholesale and unjust accusation. Where are your proofs for such a statement?

THEOSOPHIST. They are ready at hand. Christ is alleged to have said: "Love each other" and "Love your enemies"; for "if ye love them (only) which love you, what reward (or merit) have ye? Do not even the *publicans*[1] the same? And if you salute your brethren only, what do ye more than others? Do not even publicans so?" These are Christ's words. But *Genesis* ix. 25, says "Cursed be Canaan, a servant of servants shall he be unto his brethren." And, therefore, Christian but Biblical people prefer the law of Moses to Christ's law of love. They base upon the Old Testament, which panders to all their passions, their laws of conquest, annexation, and tyranny over races which they call *inferior.* What crimes have been committed on the strength of this infernal (if taken in its dead letter) passage in *Genesis,* history alone gives us an idea, however inadequate.[2]

---

[1] Publicans – regarded as so many thieves and pickpockets in these days. Among the Jews the name and profession of a publican was the most odious thing in the world. They were not allowed to enter the Temple, and *Matthew* (xviii. 17) speaks of a heathen and a publican as identical. Yet they were only Roman tax-gatherers occupying the same position as the British officials in India and other conquered countries.

[2] "At the close of the Middle Ages slavery, under the power of moral forces, had mainly disappeared from Europe; but two momentous events occurred which overbore the moral power working in European society and let loose a swarm of curses upon the earth such as mankind had scarcely ever known. One of these events was the first voyaging to a populated and barbarous coast where human beings were a familiar article of traffic; and the other the discovery of a new world, where mines of glittering wealth were open, provided labour could be imported to work them. For four hundred years men and women and children were torn from all whom they knew and loved, and were sold on the coast of Africa to foreign traders; they were chained below decks – the dead often with the living – during the horrible 'middle passage,' and, according to Bancroft, an impartial historian, two hundred and fifty thousand out of three and a quarter millions were thrown into the sea on that fatal passage, while the remainder were consigned to nameless misery in the mines, or under the lash in the cane and rice fields. The guilt of this great crime rests on the Christian Church. 'In the name of the most Holy Trinity' the Spanish Government (Roman Catholic) concluded more than ten treaties authorising the sale of five hundred thousand human beings; in 1562 Sir John Hawkins sailed on his diabolical errand of buying slaves in Africa and selling them in the West Indies in a ship which bore the sacred name of Jesus; while Elizabeth, the Protestant Queen, rewarded him for his success in this first adventure of Englishmen in that inhuman traffic by allowing him to wear as his crest 'a demi-

ENQUIRER. I have heard you say that the identity of our physical origin is proved by science, that of our spiritual origin by the Wisdom-Religion. Yet we do not find Darwinists exhibiting great fraternal affection.

THEOSOPHIST. Just so. This is what shows the deficiency of the materialistic systems, and proves that we Theosophists are in the right. The identity of our physical origin makes no appeal to our higher and deeper feelings. Matter, deprived of its soul and spirit, or its divine essence, cannot speak to the human heart. But the identity of the soul and spirit, of real, immortal man, as Theosophy teaches us, once proven and deep-rooted in our hearts, would lead us far on the road of real charity and brotherly goodwill.

ENQUIRER. But how does Theosophy explain the common origin of man?

THEOSOPHIST. By teaching that the *root* of all nature, objective and subjective, and everything else in the universe, visible and invisible, *is*, *was*, and *ever will be* one absolute essence, from which all starts, and into which everything returns. This is Aryan philosophy, fully represented only by the Vedantins, and the Buddhist system. With this object in view, it is the duty of all Theosophists to promote in every practical way, and in all countries, the spread of *non-sectarian* education.

ENQUIRER. What do the written statutes of your Society advise its members to do besides this? On the physical plane, I mean?

THEOSOPHIST. In order to awaken brotherly feeling among nations we have to assist in the international exchange of useful arts and products, by advice, information, and co-operation with all worthy individuals and associations (provided, however, add the statutes, "that no benefit or percentage shall be taken by the Society or the 'Fellows' for its or their corporate services"). For instance, to take a practical illustration. The organization of Society, depicted by Edward Bellamy, in his magnificent work "Looking Backwards," admirably represents the Theosophical idea of what should be the first great step

---

Moor in his proper colour, bound with a cord, or, in other words, a manacled negro slave.' – *Conquests of the Cross* (quoted from the *Agnostic Journal*).

towards the full realization of universal brotherhood. The state of things he depicts falls short of perfection, because selfishness still exists and operates in the hearts of men. But in the main, selfishness and individualism have been overcome by the feeling of solidarity and mutual brotherhood; and the scheme of life there described reduces the causes tending to create and foster selfishness to a minimum.

ENQUIRER. Then as a Theosophist you will take part in an effort to realize such an ideal?

THEOSOPHIST. Certainly; and we have proved it by action. Have not you heard of the Nationalist clubs and party which have sprung up in America since the publication of Bellamy's book? They are now coming prominently to the front, and will do so more and more as time goes on. Well, these clubs and this party were started in the first instance by Theosophists. One of the first, the Nationalist Club of Boston, Mass., has Theosophists for President and Secretary, and the majority of its executive belong to the T. S. In the constitution of all their clubs, and of the party they are forming, the influence of Theosophy and of the Society is plain, for they all take as their basis, their first and fundamental principle, the Brotherhood of Humanity as taught by Theosophy. In their declaration of Principles they state: – "The principle of the Brotherhood of Humanity is one of the eternal truths that govern the world's progress on lines which distinguish human nature from brute nature." What can be more Theosophical than this? But it is not enough. What is also needed is to impress men with the idea that, if the root of mankind is *one,* then there must also be one truth which finds expression in all the various religions – except in the Jewish, as you do not find it *expressed* even in the Kabala.

ENQUIRER. This refers to the common origin of religions, and you may be right there. But how does it apply to practical brotherhood on the physical plane?

THEOSOPHIST. First, because that which is true on the metaphysical plane must be also true on the physical. Secondly, because there is no more fertile source of hatred and strife than religious differences. When one party or another thinks himself the sole possessor of absolute truth, it becomes only natural that he should think his neighbor absolutely in the clutches of Error or the Devil. But once get a man to see that none of them has the *whole* truth, but that they are mutually complementary, that the complete truth can be found only in the combined views of all, after that which is false in each of them has been sifted out – then true brotherhood in religion will be established. The same applies in the physical world.

ENQUIRER. Please explain further.

THEOSOPHIST. Take an instance. A plant consists of a root, a stem, and many shoots and leaves. As humanity, as a whole, is the stem which grows from the spiritual root, so is the stem the unity of the plant. Hurt the stem and it is obvious that every shoot and leaf will suffer. So it is with mankind.

ENQUIRER. Yes, but if you injure a leaf or a shoot, you do not injure the whole plant.

THEOSOPHIST. And therefore you think that by injuring *one* man you do not injure humanity? But how do *you* know? Are you aware that even materialistic science teaches that any injury, however slight, to a plant will affect the whole course of its future growth and development? Therefore, you are mistaken, and the analogy is perfect. If, however, you overlook the fact that a cut in the finger may often make the whole body suffer, and react on the whole nervous system, I must all the more remind you that there may well be other spiritual laws, operating on plants and animals as well as on mankind, although, as you do not recognise their action on plants and animals, you may deny their existence.

ENQUIRER. What laws do you mean?

THEOSOPHIST. We call them Karmic laws; but you will not understand the full meaning of the term unless you study Occultism.

However, my argument did not rest on the assumption of these laws, but really on the analogy of the plant. Expand the idea, carry it out to a universal application, and you will soon find that in true philosophy every physical action has its moral and everlasting effect. Hurt a man by doing him bodily harm; you may think that his pain and suffering cannot spread by any means to his neighbors, least of all to men of other nations. We affirm *that it will, in good time.* Therefore, we say, that unless every man is brought to understand and accept *as an axiomatic truth* that by wronging one man we wrong not only ourselves but the whole of humanity in the long run, no brotherly feelings such as preached by all the great Reformers, pre-eminently by Buddha and Jesus, are possible on earth.

The Key to Theosophy, pp. 41-46
H.P. Blavatsky

THEOSOPHY IN THE CHRISTIAN BIBLE

I have been asked to say a few more words on the subject of Theosophy in the Christian *Bible*; that is, I have been asked to show what Theosophical doctrines can be found in the Christian books.

One of the Theosophical doctrines is the doctrine of Karma; that is, exact justice ruling in the spiritual as well as in the physical; the exact carrying out of effect from cause in the spiritual nature of man, the moral nature as well as in the physical world. That is, that every man is ruled in his life, not by a vengeful and partial God, but by justice. This life is just; whether one is miserable or happy, whether he is poor or rich, it is just. Where is this doctrine found in the Christian Bible, this doctrine that as ye have sown so shall ye reap? That is, having lived before in this world you have made causes which bring about today the life you lead now, which have made the characteristics that you have, which made you what you are now, and have plunged you into a living hell or into a happy heaven today. We say this doctrine has not of late been taught in Christianity; but it is in the books of the Christians and it ought to have been taught, it would have been profitable had it been expounded. Now, where can it be found?

Does not Jesus say, among other things, you should not judge others? Why? Because if you do you will be judged yourself. What you mete out to others will be meted out to you. That is, what men do to others will be done to themselves. Where and when is this to be done? When is the measure to be meted out if not in this life or some other? St. Paul says: "Brethren, be not deceived, God is not mocked, for whatsoever a man soweth that shall he also reap." Do not these quotations prove that in St. Paul and in the words of Jesus can be found this doctrine of Karma: that as you sow so shall you reap? That your circumstances now are the result of your own acts? This is the doctrine which is the most prominent in the Theosophical field. I call it Theosophical, not because the members teach it, nor from its presence in our literature, but because it is found in the religion of every nation; that is why it is Theosophical. But you have been taught that you must be good or you will be punished. In the West you are told you will be rewarded and punished in this life and in the next. But men are not punished in this life. Today thousands of men live lives of luxury, strife, and crime, but they are not punished here, and, according to the teachings of Christianity, they stand a pretty good chance of escaping punishment hereafter if they only believe. We see that many are not rewarded who are good, but are often born into misery.

The doctrine of reincarnation is taught in the Christian *Bible*, that is, that you will be born over and over again in this world according to your destiny, to follow the effects of causes you yourself have put in motion in whatever life. Where is that found? In the mouth of Jesus; and certainly if Jesus, the founder of Christianity, has stated this, has any man or any body of men, has any person any right to say that it is not true? I deny their right, and I say that Christianity has been deprived by theologians of a doctrine which Jesus himself declared, when reincarnation is taken away from it. We say that the doctrine is in the Gospels. One day they brought to Jesus a man who was born blind and asked him why was this man born blind; was it for some sin he had committed or those his parents committed? Now, how could a man be born blind for a sin he had himself committed unless he had lived before that time to commit it? This was a doctrine believed in at that day. The Jews believed it and Jesus was a Jew. He did not deny the doctrine on that occasion. He only said, "Not for that reason." If the doctrine were wrong, certainly Jesus, as the Son of God, would not only have denied it, but he would have said, "The doctrine you enunciate is false." He said nothing of the kind. At another time he himself declared the doctrine, and he asked his disciples, "Whom do men think that I am?", meaning and referring to what was believed at that time, that great sages were born over and over again for the enlightenment of mankind. They call them Avatars in the East. They had an idea great sages and prophets would come back. Will you tell me how such men then could be reborn at all unless under natural law and unless such law governs every man? So Jesus, referring to this idea, said to his disciples: "Whom do men think that I am?" And they said: "Some men think that you are Elias, who was for to come." St. John had been killed just then by the ruler of Judea, and Jesus said to them that Elias had already come back in the person of John and the rulers had killed him, not knowing he was a reincarnation of Elias. So in one case he did not deny and in the other he explicitly asserted the doctrine. And if we take this view we know what he meant when he said to Nicodemus that a man must be born again. He meant not only the regeneration of the soul, but reborn into the body again; that is, that man is a soul who comes into a house to live life after life, and he must go from house to house until he has learned the whole architecture of human life and is able to build a perfect house. In *Revelations*, the last word of all the books, we find the great speaker writing that he heard the voice of God saying to him that him who overcometh the flesh and the devil, the world and sin, "I shall make a pillar in the house of my Father and he shall go out no more." Does not that mean he had gone out before? The old fathers in the early ages of Christianity taught that if we triumphed over the flesh and the devil, the world and sin, God would make each one a pillar in the house of his father and he would not have to go out again. That is the doctrine of reincarnation.

Then if you will look at the history of the Christian Church you find that the doctrine was taught for five hundred years, and not until the Council of Constantinople was it rejected. At that time it was turned out by ignorant monks, and since then it has not been taught by the teachers, but it is in the Christian books, and to these Christian books we appeal. I say these very doctrines are in many other places found there. Another doctrine is that man is not merely a body, but is a composite being of many divisions. St. Paul taught we have a spiritual body as well as a material body, that we are a spiritual body and a physical body and spirit. That will bring in every one of the seven principles of the Theosophical category. So we say, all through the Christian books, in the *Old Testament* and in the *New*, we may find the great doctrines of Theosophy, by which I mean the great universal ideas of unity, of universal brotherhood, of strict justice and no favoritism, of reincarnation, and of the composite nature of man, which permeate every religion as well as the books of the Christians, both old and new.

Parliament of Religions Address
World's Fair, 1893; Chicago, Illinois
W.Q. Judge

PART III:

ON PRACTICAL THEOSOPHY

PRACTICAL THEOSOPHY

The ethics of life propounded by Jesus are not different from those found in Theosophy, but the latter holds in its doctrines a compelling power which is absent from Christianity and from those systems which require a man to be good for virtue's sake alone. It is not easy to practice virtue for the simple reason that we ought to do so, since the desire for reward is inherent in humanity, and is a reflection of the evolutionary law which draws the universe ever upward to higher points of development. A man reads the command of Jesus to turn the other cheek to the smiter, to resist not evil, to forgive without stint, and to take no thought for the morrow, and then - pauses. His next thought is that such a canon is wholly utopian, and would if followed subvert society. In this he is sustained by eminent authority as well as by example, for a great Bishop has declared that no state can exist under such a system.

Theosophic doctrine, however, on either the selfish or spiritual line of life, convinces that the moral law must be obeyed. If we regard only the selfish side, we find when people are convinced that evil done in this life will be met with sure punishment in another reincarnation, they hesitate to continue the old careless life when they lived for themselves alone.

Hence practical Theosophy must enter into every detail of life in our dealings with others and our discipline of ourselves. It reminds us that we should be more critical of ourselves than of others, that we must help all men if we are to be helped ourselves. And herein the Theosophist may escape the accusation of selfishness, for if in desiring to lay up for a future incarnation a store of help from others by giving assistance now himself, he does so in order that he may then be in a still better position to help humanity, there is no selfishness. It is the same as if a man were to desire to acquire this world's goods in order to help those dependent on him, and surely this is not selfish.

The practical Theosophist adds to his charitable deeds upon the material plane the still greater charity of giving to his fellow men a system of thought and life which explains their doubts while it furnishes a logical reason for the practice of virtue. He extinguishes a hell that never could burn, and the terrors of which soon faded from the mind of the sinners; but he lights the lamp of truth and throws its beams upon the mortal's path so that not only the real danger, the real punishment, can be seen, but also the reward and compensation.

The civilized man cannot be guided by fear or superstition, but reason may take hold of him. Theosophy being not only practicable but also reasonable as well as just, its doctrines are destined to be those of the civilized man. They will gradually drive out the time-worn shibboleths of the theologian and the scientist, giving the people of coming centuries a wisdom-religion deeply-based and all-embracing.

Were Theosophical practice universal, we should not see the unjust Judge plotting beforehand with the officials of a railroad company about the decision he should render, nor the venal public officer engaged with the Judge and the officials in arranging the virtuous protest to be offered in court against the foreordained decree, for both would fear to rouse a cause which in their next life might issue in unjust accusation and punishment. Nor would men save their lives, as now they often do, at another's expense, since in succeeding incarnations that person might be the means of depriving them of life twice over. The rich man who now hoards his wealth or spends it on himself alone would not be thus guilty, seeing that, as compensation in another life, his friends would forsake him and nature seem to withdraw subsistence.

The practical Theosophist will do well if he follows the advice of the Masters now many years in print, to spread, explain, and illustrate the laws of Karma and Reincarnation so that they may enter into the lives of the people. Technical occultism and all the allurements of the Astral Light may be left for other times. Men's thoughts must be affected, and this can only be done now by giving them these two great laws. They not only explain many things, but they have also an inherent power due to their truth and their intimate connection with man, to compel attention.

Once heard they are seldom forgotten, and even if rebelled against they have a mysterious power of keeping in the man's mind, until at last, even against his first determination, he is forced to accept them.

The appreciation of justice is common to all, and the exact justice of Karma appeals even to the person who is unfortunate enough to be undergoing heavy punishment: even if, ignoring justice, he does good in order to make good Karma, it is well, for he will be reborn under conditions that may favor the coming out of unselfish motive.

> "Teach, preach, and practice this good law for the benefit of the world, even as all the Buddhas do."

Path, July, 1890
W.Q. Judge

THE FOUR GOLDEN LINKS

ENQUIRER. How, then, should Theosophical principles be applied so that social co-operation may be promoted and true efforts for social amelioration be carried on?

THEOSOPHIST. Let me briefly remind you what these principles are: universal Unity and Causation; Human Solidarity; the Law of Karma; Re-incarnation. These are the four links of the golden chain which should bind humanity into one family, one universal Brotherhood.

ENQUIRER. How?

THEOSOPHIST. In the present state of society, especially in so-called civilized countries, we are continually brought face to face with the fact that large numbers of people are suffering from misery, poverty and disease. Their physical condition is wretched, and their mental and spiritual faculties are often almost dormant. On the other hand, many persons at the opposite end of the social scale are leading lives of careless indifference, material luxury, and selfish indulgence. Neither of these forms of existence is mere chance. Both are the effects of the conditions which surround those who are subject to them, and the neglect of social duty on the one side is most closely connected with the stunted and arrested development on the other. In sociology, as in all branches of true science, the law of universal causation holds good. But this causation necessarily implies, as its logical outcome, that human solidarity on which Theosophy so strongly insists. If the action of one reacts on the lives of all, and this is the true scientific idea, then it is only by all men becoming brothers and all women sisters, and by all practising in their daily lives true brotherhood and true sisterhood, that the real human solidarity, which lies at the root of the elevation of the race, can ever be attained. It is this action and interaction, this true brotherhood and sisterhood, in which each shall live for all and all for each, which is one of the fundamental Theosophical principles that every Theosophist should be bound, not only to teach, but to carry out in his or her individual life.

ENQUIRER. All this is very well as a general principle, but how would you apply it in a concrete way?

THEOSOPHIST.   Look for a moment at what you would call the concrete facts of human society. Contrast the lives not only of the masses of the people, but of many of those who are called the middle and upper classes, with what they might be under healthier and nobler conditions, where justice, kindness, and love were paramount, instead of the selfishness, indifference, and brutality which now too often seem to reign supreme. All good and evil things in humanity have their roots in human character, and this character is, and has been, conditioned by the endless chain of cause and effect. But this conditioning applies to the future as well as to the present and the past. Selfishness, indifference, and brutality can never be the normal state of the race – to believe so would be to despair of humanity – and that no Theosophist can do. Progress can be attained, and only attained, by the development of the nobler qualities. Now, true evolution teaches us that by altering the surroundings of the organism we can alter and improve the organism; and in the strictest sense this is true with regard to man. Every Theosophist, therefore, is bound to do his utmost to help on, by all the means in his power, every wise and well-considered social effort which has for its object the amelioration of the condition of the poor. Such efforts should be made with a view to their ultimate social emancipation, or the development of the sense of duty in those who now so often neglect it in nearly every relation of life.

ENQUIRER. Agreed. But who is to decide whether social efforts are wise or unwise?

THEOSOPHIST.   No one person and no society can lay down a hard-and-fast rule in this respect. Much must necessarily be left to the individual judgment. One general test may, however, be given. Will the proposed action tend to promote that true brotherhood which it is the aim of Theosophy to bring about? No real Theosophist will have much difficulty in applying such a test; once he is satisfied of this, his duty will lie in the direction of forming public opinion. And this can be attained only by inculcating those higher and nobler conceptions of public and private duties which lie at the root of all spiritual and material improvement. In every conceivable case he himself must be a centre of spiritual action, and from him and his own daily individual life must radiate those higher spiritual forces which alone can regenerate his fellow-men.

ENQUIRER. But why should he do this? Are not he and all, as you teach, conditioned by their Karma, and must not Karma necessarily work itself out on certain lines?

THEOSOPHIST. It is this very law of Karma which gives strength to all that I have said. The individual cannot separate himself from the race, nor the race from the individual. The law of Karma applies equally to all, although all are not equally developed. In helping on the development of others, the Theosophist believes that he is not only helping them to fulfil their Karma, but that he is also, in the strictest sense, fulfilling his own. It is the development of humanity, of which both he and they are integral parts, that he has always in view, and he knows that any failure on his part to respond to the highest within him retards not only himself but all, in their progressive march. By his actions, he can make it either more difficult or more easy for humanity to attain the next higher plane of being.

ENQUIRER. How does this bear on the fourth of the principles you mentioned, viz., Re-incarnation?

THEOSOPHIST. The connection is most intimate. If our present lives depend upon the development of certain principles which are a growth from the germs left by a previous existence, the law holds good as regards the future. Once grasp the idea that universal causation is not merely present, but past, present and future, and every action on our present plane falls naturally and easily into its true place, and is seen in its true relation to ourselves and to others. Every mean and selfish action sends us backward and not forward, while every noble thought and every unselfish deed are steppingstones to the higher and more glorious planes of being. If this life were all, then in many respects it would indeed be poor and mean; but regarded as a preparation for the next sphere of existence, it may be used as the golden gate through which we may pass, not selfishly and alone, but in company with our fellows, to the palaces which lie beyond.

The Key to Theosophy, pp 231-237
H.P. Blavatsky

THEOSOPHY IN DAILY LIFE

Many people think that religion means a preparation for death or the states of the future. Religion really means a preparation for and a knowledge of life – a living of our life as it should be lived. That which prepares for death is life, and ever living. Formal religions do not even answer the question, why is death – nor any of the other burning questions in daily life. Why do we have suffering and sorrow? Why are we here? What was the origin of man? Why so many different conditions among mankind; why are some born to sorrow, and others to joy; why some in lowly places, some in high; why some with great faculties and others with very few and poor ones? Justice demands an answer which is not furnished by religion, with its "Creator"—for if man is the creature of a creator he cannot help himself and is absolutely irresponsible. Any being, if "perfect," would maintain justice; yet there are injustices among men. The caprice or whim of a creator does not explain the difficulty. Any being, however great or high, must of necessity be limited, finite, and imperfect – something outside us, something which does not contain the universe but is contained by it.

We have to go behind any idea of a Being, to the source of all being – to a basis common to the highest and to the lowest being. That basis and source is not to be found by looking outward at all, but is the very power to perceive, wherever there is life. Spirit, Life, Consciousness are the same in every being – undivided, however many and varied the perceptions. Evolution is not a compelling force from without, but the impelling force of Spirit from within, urging on to better and better expression. All advancement is from within. All the knowledge that we gain, all the experience that we obtain, is obtained and held within. Each one, then, is the Seer; all the rest are seen. So, the knowledge that we have to obtain is not information from without, not the thoughts of other men, but an understanding of our own essential nature, which represents every element in the great universe, from the basis of all life to every outward expression, and every possibility of further expression – just as each drop of water contains in itself everything existing in the great ocean from which it came. Nor does Law exist outside of us. Law is always inherent in Spirit; it is the action which brings re-action in every individual case, and to the collective mass of humanity. We are here under law and under justice. There is no such thing as injustice in the universe.

Knowing something as to our essential nature, knowing something of the purpose of life, and that life is all made up of learning, knowing that the universe is all alive, and that there is in reality no injustice save that which we inflict upon ourselves by re-action, we would take an entirely different view of life and put these ideas into daily practice. We would take the position which most of all we need to take – that of our own responsibility, which religions have taught us to shift on to some God or devil. Recognizing that each one of us is from the same Source and going towards the same goal, though the path will vary with the pilgrim, we will act toward each one as if he were a part of ourselves. Like us, each one is moving onward – perhaps below us, possibly above. From the one above, we can obtain help. To the one below, we can give help. Such is the interdependence which should exist between all conscious beings; and under such a conception our civilization would not be as it is now. We should not find every man's hand raised against every other man. We should not see those in poor case finding fault with the wrong conditions, but finding fault rather with their own wrong relations to others at some time when they abused the power they had. We should see each one trying to discipline himself, trying to bring himself into proper relation with all the rest – not so much outwardly, perhaps, as inwardly; for we may be sure that if we make clean the inside of the bowl, the outside will take care of itself. We have no greater duty to perform than to make clear and clean our natures – to make them true, to make them in accord with the great object of all life, the evolution of soul.

We cannot wait to make our start in this direction until the nation wakes up to Theosophy; for the nation will itself awake only when each individual wakes up to that which is in himself and by his thought and action instills a similar thought and action in other human beings. Supposing each one determined to do all he could for every other one wherever he could, do you think that anybody would suffer? Not one! There would be more to help than those to suffer. But we are afraid that if we so act, the other man will not. So we do not move at all along that line. The majority of people are thinking about quite other things. They are busy at the shrine of their gods of comfort, seeking to get the best of everything in life at the expense of someone else. Or they are seeking to acquire "the power of will," so that they can get something for nothing from someone else. That is the kind of "will" which is generally desired, its object being the getting of exactly what one pleases. Is not this psychic banditry? Anything gotten that way is taken from another, and we shall have to pay it back to the uttermost farthing – if not in this life, then in some other, for the scales of justice are unerring.

Do we not see that we can trust a universe that moves along unerringly under the law of perfect justice? 'We certainly can. We can go forward with an absolute reliance on the law of our own spiritual being, knowing whatever conditions come are necessary for us, knowing that those very things we feel so hardly are object lessons for us because they indicate a wrong tendency or defect in us which this present distress affords us an opportunity to overcome, to strengthen our true character. That is all we have at the end of life, whatever of character – good, bad, or indifferent – we have acquired. Men spend their lives trying to avoid what they do not like, and trying to get what they like – what they can and while they can. Yet if they got all the wealth of the world, every possession and every possible desire, what good would it do them? At death everything would be left where they got it, because nothing adheres to Spirit. The idea of getting for themselves is one of the false notions which prevent men from understanding themselves as spiritual beings and using the power which belongs to them – for all powers of every kind – electrical, dynamic or explosive – come from the One Universal Spirit, and each man has latent in him all the powers in the universe. Physical life is not necessarily a vale of sorrow. The time must come when we shall have made man's life on earth what it ought to be, when we shall have no fear of anything, when we shall not be afraid of our fellowmen. It was said of Daniel, when he entered the lions' den, the beasts of prey did not touch him at all. Why? Because his heart was pure. He had no harm in it for anyone. He trusted to the spiritual law of his own being, and all nature makes obeisance to that. We could go out calmly, courageously, happily, relying on the laws of our own natures. If we did so, we would bring our daily lives in line with that nature; for there is nothing of our action which does not come from the mind, and back of the mind is the 'motive we have in acting. Motive is what makes our actions really "good" or "bad." If we are righteous in ourselves and desirous of doing right, then all that we do will flow rightly from us and every function will be a righteous function. All action springs from and is colored by the motive held in performing it.

Theosophy is the only philosophy that can be used in every direction in daily life. It can be used in all directions, high or low, because that use comes from an understanding of the Spirit itself, from acting for that Self and as that Self – for the Self acts only through the creatures. Acting for and as that Self in every direction, all else flows into line. All the destruction that is around us, all the misery that we see, has been brought about through our denial of the Holy Ghost – our denial of the Spirit within us. We deny it when we act as if we are our bodies, or our minds. THAT will not be denied. So man, meeting all the results of that denial and seeing them to be evil, learns that this is not the way. Then he seeks for Truth, and finding the truth, obtains all that he can desire – hope, happiness and a better understanding of his and all existence. It was to give to men all they could take in regard to the nature of the soul – that they might come out from this vale of sorrow – that those Beings known as Divine Incarnations have descended here of Their own will. They have carried forward from age to age this knowledge of nature and of man and of the purpose of life, learned through many civilizations of mankind. It is this knowledge which makes Them as gods to us in Their glory and power.

Universal Theosophy
Robert Crosbie

THE HERMETIC METHOD

Are we the creators of our destiny, or are we the agents, unknowing, unwilling, or unwitting of a cosmic plan? To ask this is to attempt to understand the relations between the conscious the unconscious, and the self-conscious in all of us. To achieve universal self-consciousness is to dispel all illusions and to know no difference between oneself and the whole of nature. It is to make the plan of nature the very framework of one's being and the deliberate basis of one's destiny. It is like floating on the ocean of life. That is difficult enough on the physical plane, but in relation to the whole of cosmic life it is extremely difficult for us to grasp. Because we are only partly conscious, we are also partly unconscious, and therefore liable to self-deception. In another way, we face the problem of protective illusions. No man could live if he did not have some protective illusion. Each must attach a somewhat exaggerated reality to something in order to live at all. To the extent that we have to do this, we are used by the plan, because the exaggeration is eventually going to be cut down. Growing up means the removal of the protection.

Ordinarily, men replace one kind of protective illusion by another kind of protective illusion, which means they are part of the process and cannot stand outside it. To that extent free will is an illusion. If the universe is mathematically just, there is an incredible intricacy to its complex systems dynamics and, in the sense which Spinoza understood, no man is free. As long as you are a particular being, mentally separate from the whole, you are not free. What you think is freedom amounts to being determined by likes, dislikes and impulses which you do not fully choose. This is true of all of us, but to the extent to which, unlike the kingdoms below man, we can adapt ourselves to the environment and also adapt the environment to us, we are Prometheans, we are gods, we are self-determining agents.

For millennia we have been brought up in the terrible habit of dichotomous thinking, assuming that everything must be one thing or its opposite. Pythagoras actually discouraged people from even thinking in terms of the number 2. So much did the Sophists encourage it that Plato said the very method should be abandoned. In other words, when we ask whether we are creative or passive in relation to our own destiny, we should start by saying, "Yes, we are both," but then ask what it means to say we are either. What does it mean effectively for us - philosophically, or impersonally; psychologically, in the realm where we can relate it to our life; ethically, in relation to our problems; and also socially or collectively? Look at the men who make plans. As Robert Burns said:

> The best laid schemes o' mice an' men
> Gang aft a-gley.

In Tolstoy's *War and Peace* the most powerful men of history are still instruments. On the other hand, each of us should ask what it means to say that we create and choose, because we do take decisions which can make a tremendous difference. We have to understand to what extent we are beings who have got our heads above the waters of life and to what extent we are immersed in the process.

Even this measure is not constant or static. It is ever-changing, and hence there is growth. There is a danger of being drowned, but it is also possible for a person to come right out. This is a matter of degrees, however, and when we consider degrees of self-awareness in the highest sense, we are confronting something way beyond simple delusions and phenomenal relativities. We have to come clean and be confident enough to impose no petty prejudices or minor obsessions, to which the fullness of the universe is irrelevant, on our pathway. We have to do a preliminary therapy and cleanse ourselves before we are ready to accept the universe and before we are ready to enter the first portal.

But this, of course, recurs at a later level as well. The unavoidable trouble with so many paradigms of the Path is that they seem to suggest that the process is a linear movement. Even the analogy of climbing one mountain can be misleading. We have got to imagine a tremendous mountain range. We climb, we come down, we climb again. In other words, it is like a spiral. The problem will keep recurring. At any level, in attempting to maintain awareness, you run the risk of either seeing so much of the huge perspective that you don't notice particular things, or of so concentrating on the particular that you forget the whole perspective.

A beautiful example of this can be found in Japanese landscape paintings. It takes time to realize that the most important thing in the paintings is blank space and its relation to the mobile trees and blades of grass. But even more, the blank space is not only the blank space in the painting. It involves the relationship to the space in the room where the painting is hanging. When you really appreciate these incredible paintings, you can appreciate pure empty space. In other words, you can begin to understand perspectives on that of which you are aware. You can be aware, at one level, of the objects in the painting, or you can move to a distance and be aware only of relations, not of forms. If you come close, then you are aware of nothing. Or, you may move to another point where you become aware of empty space. The important thing, then, is mobility in awareness.

What is true of space is also true of time. To adapt Heraclitus to a contemporary example: you are not sitting for two successive moments in the same room. The moment you come in, you come into one kind of place, and an instant later it is a different kind of place. Where the universe is ever-changing, we are never for two moments in the same point, either in a spatial or a temporal sense. From this perspective there can be no recurrence. There is only flux because nothing is ever like anything else. But from another standpoint you could take the opposite point of view, for example that of Parmenides and the Vedanta. You could say that all of these changes have no meaning. There is always a one changeless reality. But then, if you merely want to say, dogmatically, that there is one changeless reality, you cannot understand process. The problem is how can you see both - that everything is ever changeless and that everything is so constantly changing that there are no two similars.

Plato called this the problem of the "same and the other." H.P.

Blavatsky says that what Plato taught is what the Wisdom-Religion teaches, terming it objective idealism. It is no subjective idealism, which says the One is the Real, and it is not that kind of materialism or realism or atomism which says the Many are Real. Nor is it any fixed relation between the One and the Many. It is a dynamic participation, but involving degrees of participation of the One in the Many and the Many in the One. As examples in our everyday life, take eating for a person who is a gourmet, or the act of love for two people who are extraordinarily proud of each other. In either case you will see there is one sense in which each instance is unique, inimitable and irreproducible. There can be no recurrence. But in another sense, there is recurrence. In effect, we have to say that at the level of particulars there can never be recurrence except in principle, and not a recurrence in a literal way. But equally, in terms of ideas or matrices there is constancy, but a constancy that is relative. What is constant in one long period of time will itself change over a longer period of time. This becomes a problem of periods of manifestation. This, then, is why all questions about human destiny and choice merely show that in the end we have to learn the dialectic, the method of analogy and correspondence. However much the term dialectic, like every sacred word, is tortured and abused, it remains the sovereign method of maintaining a mobile relationship in reference to degrees of reality, knowledge, and truth.

Students of Theosophy are helped to do this and are thus prepared for true meditation by study of *The Secret Doctrine*. This study is literally what it says, a study of the *Secret* Doctrine, not merely of a book. The Secret Doctrine is in nature and it is in every one of us. Concerning the book *The Secret Doctrine*, unlike almost any other book of the modern age, one could assume that every word has been chosen with great care. It is also wise to assume that there are a lot of blinds and also a lot of aids. It is meant to speak authentically to the widest possible audience, but in that code language where each one determines what he can receive. In Shelley's words, "It talks according to the wit of its companions; and no more is heard than has been felt before..."

It uses many conceptual languages and speaks in terms of many myths. No one finds all of these immediately meaningful. There is also a catechism and a hidden mathematical logic to the book, but grasping them involves the reflection of *Buddhi*, or intuition, in *Manas*, the focus of ideation.

What this means for us, first of all, is not to read the book except when in a state of calm; secondly, not to read the book with any anxiety. Put as a paradox, we give it its importance by treating it casually. We can become familiar and friendly with the book and put ourselves in the position of the writer in trying to see why there is a certain framework. We can read the contents of both volumes and try to see not the details of the framework, but the method which is in the contents. It is the Hermetic method of coming from above below, the method of analogy and correspondence, of the same and the other. It is not taught in the modern age in schools, in universities, or in our society. It includes what we call deductive reasoning and has a place for experience, but excludes induction. It really goes beyond all such divisions. It is what used to be called in the East the archetypal dialectic, *Buddhi Yoga*, and was also taught by Pythagoras and Plato.

The Secret Doctrine, then, involves planes of consciousness, degrees of knowledge, stairways of reality, a series of superimpositions of pictures - like pictures created with certain photographic techniques where different forms and shapes assumed by the same object are simultaneously represented. One might say of the book, and this is a paradox, that, like everything cosmic, the more we study it, the more we learn how to study it. The more we read it, but with love, the more that is worthwhile will emerge. Particularly to be enjoyed are those statements in the book which are combinations of sounds that are mathematically precise. One day there will be men who will pronounce the Stanzas and perform magic. But that will be a very different kind of humanity. Today there are men who can enter into the deeper realm of the book, even though they don't know where they are in terms of ordinary conceptions of growth and progress. In other words, *The Secret Doctrine* is a book to take up again and again. We should read it up to that point where the mind is calm and not exhausted. Put it away, and preferably sleep, after one has read it. Let things happen.

Whichever method one chooses, one should not cling to it, because another method may be found that will seem more appropriate later on. This is why a simple chronological way of reading the book may not be suitable. On the other hand, too awe-inspired a reception of the Stanzas may not be appropriate either. Certainly the lower *Manas* cannot understand the book, and trying to "fit it together" with other things for the sake of fitting is a waste of time.

A broad and simple statement of how to approach the book is to approach the mind of the author and to see that mind in relation to *Mahat*, the collective mind of nature, and to see that in oneself. Put in concrete terms, a point comes in any important book where you want to ask not "Do I understand?" - which is to start off too apologetically - but "If I were this man, why would I want to be saying this?" This may sound presumptuous, but it is a legitimate way of becoming one with the author. So one says, "If what is said in the Preface is true, and if these things happened to anyone in the particular kind of instruction to which H. P. Blavatsky refers in the Proem and the Preface, then what would be the point of doing this and that?" This is a means to unite or yoke through yoga one's mind with the mind of the author. The most important clue which gives away the code language of *The Secret Doctrine* is in the very first words. The book begins by saying "The author - the writer, rather." Right away the book tells you that its author is not any one person. It is a very enigmatic book.

In the practice of meditation for which *The Secret Doctrine* prepares us, we can see the method of the dialectic in the relationship between meditation with a seed and meditation without a seed. According to Patanjali, the oldest text on meditation, whichever seed you take, you must dissolve it. To take a simple example, in the ideal school of the future, children would start very early on to take a slate, make diagrams, and wipe them out; then make different diagrams and wipe them out as well. There should be a tremendous freedom in relation to the seed that one takes and a recognition that whichever seed is taken, it is for the purpose of obliterating the seed. It is attempting to go from form to the formless, but in the formless not to be reacting against a particular form. It is a matter of repeated and various modes, and what works for one person will not work for another. Probably it is better to choose as a seed that which makes you less emotional rather than more, and this each one has to decide individually. To the extent to which it does make one emotional and involves exaggeration or protective illusions, better that the emotions are positive rather than negative. As the Buddhist meditations teach, we can make corrections for our own particular needs, and we can do this empirically within the context of our prevailing understanding of our unfolding and evolving destiny.

Toronto
October 9, 1971

Hermes, April 1976
Raghavan Iyer

WHAT IS PRACTICAL THEOSOPHY?

On Duty

ENQUIRER. Why, then, the need for re-births, since all alike fail to secure a permanent peace?

THEOSOPHIST. Because the final goal cannot be reached in any way but through life experiences, and because the bulk of these consist in pain and suffering. It is only through the latter that we can learn. Joys and pleasures teach us nothing; they are evanescent, and can only bring in the long run satiety. Moreover, our constant failure to find any permanent satisfaction in life which would meet the wants of our higher nature, shows us plainly that those wants can be met only on their own plane, to wit — the spiritual.

ENQUIRER. Is the natural result of this a desire to quit life by one means or another?

THEOSOPHIST. If you mean by such desire "suicide," then I say, most decidedly not. Such a result can never be a "natural" one, but is ever due to a morbid brain disease, or to most decided and strong materialistic views. It is the worst of crimes and dire in its results. But if by desire, you mean simply aspiration to reach spiritual existence, not a wish to quit the earth, then I would call it a very natural desire indeed. Otherwise voluntary death would be an abandonment of our present post and of the duties incumbent on us, as well as an attempt to shirk Karmic responsibilities, and thus involve the creation of new Karma.

ENQUIRER. But if actions on the material plane are unsatisfying, why should duties, which are such actions, be imperative?

THEOSOPHIST. First of all, because our philosophy teaches us that the object of doing our duties to all men and to ourselves the last, is not the attainment of personal happiness, but of the happiness of others; the fulfilment of right for the sake of right, not for what it may bring us. Happiness, or rather contentment, may indeed follow the performance of duty, but is not and must not be the motive for it.

ENQUIRER. What do you understand precisely by "duty" in Theosophy? It cannot be the Christian duties preached by Jesus and his Apostles, since you recognise neither?

THEOSOPHIST. You are once more mistaken. What you call "Christian duties" were inculcated by every great moral and religious Reformer ages before the Christian era. All that was great, generous, heroic, was, in days of old, not only talked about and preached from pulpits as in our own time, but *acted upon* sometimes by whole nations. The history of the Buddhist reform is full of the most noble and most heroically unselfish acts. "Be ye all of one mind, having compassion one of another; love as brethren, be pitiful, be courteous; not rendering evil for evil, or railing for railing; but contrariwise, blessing" was practically carried out by the followers of Buddha, several centuries before Peter. The Ethics of Christianity are grand, no doubt; but as undeniably they are not new, and have originated as "Pagan" duties.

ENQUIRER. And how would you define these duties, or "duty," in general, as you understand the term?

THEOSOPHIST. Duty is that which *is due* to Humanity, to our fellow-men, neighbours, family, and especially that which we owe to all those who are poorer and more helpless than we are ourselves. This is a debt which, if left unpaid during life, leaves us spiritually insolvent and moral bankrupts in our next incarnation. Theosophy is the quintessence of *duty*.

ENQUIRER. So is Christianity when rightly understood and carried out.

THEOSOPHIST. No doubt it is; but then, were it not a *lip-religion* in practice, Theosophy would have little to do amidst Christians. Unfortunately it is but such lip-ethics. Those who practise their duty towards all, and for duty's own sake, are few; and fewer still are those who perform that duty, remaining content with the satisfaction of their own secret consciousness. It is –

> ". . . . . . the public voice
> Of praise that honours virtue and rewards it,"

which is ever uppermost in the minds of the "world renowned" philanthropists. Modern ethics are beautiful to read about and hear discussed; but what are words unless converted into actions? Finally: if you ask me how we understand Theosophical duty practically and in view of Karma, I may answer you that our duty is to drink without a murmur to the last drop, whatever contents the cup of life may have in store for us, to pluck the roses of life only for the fragrance they may shed on *others,* and to be ourselves content but with the thorns, if that fragrance cannot be enjoyed without depriving someone else of it.

ENQUIRER. All this is very vague. What do you do more than Christians do?

THEOSOPHIST. It is not what we members of the Theosophical Society do – though some of us try our best – but how much farther Theosophy leads to good than modern Christianity does. I say – *action,* enforced action, instead of mere intention and talk. A man may be what he likes, the most worldly, selfish and hard-hearted of men, even a deep-dyed rascal, and it will not prevent him from calling himself a Christian, or others from so regarding him. But no Theosophist has the right to this name, unless he is thoroughly imbued with the correctness of Carlyle's truism: "The end of man is an *action* and not a *thought,* though it were the noblest" – and unless he sets and models his daily life upon this truth. The profession of a truth is not yet the enactment of it; and the more beautiful and grand it sounds, the more loudly virtue or duty is talked about instead of being acted upon, the more forcibly it will always remind one of the Dead Sea fruit. *Cant* is the most loathsome of all vices; and *cant* is the most prominent feature of the greatest Protestant country of this century – England.

ENQUIRER. What do you consider as due to humanity at large?

THEOSOPHIST. Full recognition of equal rights and privileges for all, and without distinction of race, colour, social position, or birth.

ENQUIRER. When would you consider such due not given?

THEOSOPHIST. When there is the slightest invasion of another's right — be that other a man or a nation; when there is any failure to show him the same justice, kindness, consideration or mercy which we desire for ourselves. The whole present system of politics is built on the oblivion of such rights, and the most fierce assertion of national selfishness. The French say: "Like master, like man"; they ought to add, "Like national policy, like citizen."

ENQUIRER. Do you take any part in politics?

THEOSOPHIST. As a Society, we carefully avoid them, for the reasons given below. To seek to achieve political reforms before we have effected a reform in *human nature, is like putting new wine into old bottles.* Make men feel and recognise in their innermost hearts what is their real, true duty to all men, and every old abuse of power, every iniquitous law in the national policy, based on human, social or political selfishness, will disappear of itself. Foolish is the gardener who seeks to weed his flower-bed of poisonous plants by cutting them off from the surface of the soil, instead of tearing them out by the roots. No lasting political reform can be ever achieved with the same selfish men at the head of affairs as of old.

The Key to Theosophy, pp. 227-231
H.P. Blavatsky

WHAT IS PRACTICAL THEOSOPHY?

On Self-Sacrifice

ENQUIRER. Is equal justice to all and love to every creature the highest standard of Theosophy?

THEOSOPHIST. No; there is an even far higher one.

ENQUIRER. What can it be?

THEOSOPHIST. The giving to others *more* than to oneself – *self-sacrifice*. Such was the standard and abounding measure which marked so pre-eminently the greatest Teachers and Masters of Humanity – *e. g.*, Gautama Buddha in History, and Jesus of Nazareth as in the Gospels. This trait alone was enough to secure to them the perpetual reverence and gratitude of the generations of men that come after them. We say, however, that self-sacrifice has to be performed with discrimination; and such a self-abandonment, if made without justice, or blindly, regardless of subsequent results, may often prove not only made in vain, but harmful. One of the fundamental rules of Theosophy is, justice to oneself – viewed as a unit of collective humanity, not as a personal self-justice, not more but not less than to others; unless, indeed, by the sacrifice of the *one*self we can benefit the many.

ENQUIRER. Could you make your idea clearer by giving an instance?

THEOSOPHIST. There are many instances to illustrate it in history. Self-sacrifice for practical good to save many, or several people, Theosophy holds as far higher than self-abnegation for a sectarian idea, such as that of "saving the heathen from *damnation*," for instance. In our opinion, Father Damien, the young man of thirty who offered his whole life in sacrifice for the benefit and alleviation of the sufferings of the lepers at Molokai, and who went to live for eighteen years alone with them, to finally catch the loathsome disease and die, *has not died in vain*. He has given relief and relative happiness to thousands of miserable wretches. He has brought to them consolation, mental and physical. He threw a streak of light into the black and dreary night of an existence, the hopelessness of which is unparalleled in the records of human suffering. He was a *true Theosophist,* and his memory will live for ever in our annals. In our sight this poor Belgian priest stands immeasurably higher than – for instance – all those sincere but vain-glorious fools, the Missionaries who have sacrificed their lives in the South Sea Islands or China. What good have they done? They went in one case to those who are not yet ripe for any truth; and in the other to a nation whose systems of religious philosophy are as grand as any, if only the men who have them would live up to the standard of Confucius and their other sages. And they died victims of irresponsible cannibals and savages, and of popular fanaticism and hatred. Whereas, by going to the slums of Whitechapel or some other such locality of those that stagnate right under the blazing sun of our civilization, full of Christian savages and mental leprosy, they might have done real good, and preserved their lives for a better and worthier cause.

ENQUIRER. But the Christians do not think so?

THEOSOPHIST. Of course not, because they act on an erroneous belief. They think that by baptising the body of an irresponsible savage they save his soul from damnation. One church forgets her martyrs, the other beatifies and raises statues to such men as Labro, who sacrificed his body for forty years only to benefit the vermin which it bred. Had we the means to do so, we would raise a statue to Father Damien, the true, practical saint, and perpetuate his memory for ever as a living exemplar of Theosophical heroism and of Buddha- and Christ-like mercy and self-sacrifice.

ENQUIRER. Then you regard self-sacrifice as a duty?

THEOSOPHIST. We do; and explain it by showing that altruism is an integral part of self-development. But we have to discriminate. A man has no right to starve himself *to death* that another man may have food, unless the life of that man is obviously more useful to the many than is his own life. But it is his duty to sacrifice his own comfort, and to work for others if they are unable to work for themselves. It is his duty to give all that which is wholly his own and can benefit no one but himself if he selfishly keeps it from others. Theosophy teaches self-abnegation, but does not teach rash and useless self-sacrifice, nor does it justify fanaticism.

ENQUIRER. But how are we to reach such an elevated status?

THEOSOPHIST. By the enlightened application of our precepts to practice. By the use of our higher reason, spiritual intuition and moral sense, and by following the dictates of what we call "the still small voice" of our conscience, which is that of our EGO, and which speaks louder in us than the earthquakes and the thunders of Jehovah, wherein "the Lord is not."

ENQUIRER. If such are our duties to humanity at large, what do you understand by our duties to our immediate surroundings?

THEOSOPHIST. Just the same, *plus* those that arise from special obligations with regard to family ties.

ENQUIRER. Then it is not true, as it is said, that no sooner does a man enter into the Theosophical Society than he begins to be gradually severed from his wife, children, and family duties?

THEOSOPHIST. It is a groundless calumny, like so many others. The first of the Theosophical duties is to do one's duty by *all* men, and especially by those to whom one's *specific* responsibilities are due, because one has either voluntarily undertaken them, such as marriage ties, or because one's destiny has allied one to them; I mean those we owe to parents or next of kin.

ENQUIRER. And what may be the duty of a Theosophist to himself?

THEOSOPHIST. To control and conquer, *through the Higher, the lower self.* To purify himself inwardly and morally; to fear no one, and nought, save the tribunal of his own conscience. Never to do a thing by halves; *i. e.,* if he thinks it the right thing to do, let him do it openly and boldly, and if wrong, never touch it at all. It is the duty of a Theosophist to lighten his burden by thinking of the wise aphorism of Epictetus, who says: "Be not diverted from your duty *by any idle reflection the silly world may make upon you,* for their censures are not in your power, and consequently should not be any part of your concern."

ENQUIRER. But suppose a member of your Society should plead inability to practise altruism by other people, on the ground that "charity begins at home"; urging that he is too busy, or too poor, to benefit mankind or even any of its units – what are your rules in such a case?

THEOSOPHIST. No man has a right to say that he can do nothing for others, on any pretext whatever. "By doing the proper duty in the proper place, a man may make the world his debtor," says an English writer. A cup of cold water given in time to a thirsty wayfarer is a nobler duty and more worth, than a dozen of dinners given away, out of season, to men who can afford to pay for them. No man who has not got it in him will ever become a *Theosophist;* but he may remain a member of our Society all the same. We have no rules by which we could force any man to become a practical Theosophist, if he does not desire to be one.

ENQUIRER. Then why does he enter the Society at all?

THEOSOPHIST. That is best known to him who does so. For, here again, we have no right to pre-judge a person, not even if the voice of a whole community should be against him, and I may tell you why. In our day, *vox populi* (so far as regards the voice of the educated, at any rate) is no longer *vox dei,* but ever that of prejudice, of selfish motives, and often simply that of unpopularity. Our duty is to sow seeds broadcast for the future, and see they are good; not to stop to enquire *why* we should do so, and how and wherefore we are obliged to lose our time, since those who will reap the harvest in days to come will never be ourselves.

The Key to Theosophy, pp. 237-242
H.P. Blavatsky

WHAT IS PRACTICAL THEOSOPHY?

On Charity

ENQUIRER. How do you Theosophists regard the Christian duty of charity?

THEOSOPHIST. What charity do you mean? Charity of mind, or practical charity in the physical plane?

ENQUIRER. I mean practical charity, as your idea of Universal brotherhood would include, of course, charity of mind.

THEOSOPHIST. Then you have in your mind the practical carrying out of the commandments given by Jesus in the Sermon on the Mount?

ENQUIRER. Precisely so.

THEOSOPHIST. Then why call them "Christian"? Because, although your Saviour preached and practised them, the last thing the Christians of to-day think of is to carry them out in their lives.

ENQUIRER. And yet many are those who pass their lives in dispensing charity?

THEOSOPHIST. Yes, out of the surplus of their great fortunes. But point out to me that Christian, among the most philanthropic, who would give to the shivering and starving thief, who would steal his coat, his cloak also; or offer his right cheek to him who smote him on the left, and never think of resenting it?

ENQUIRER. Ah, but you must remember that these precepts have not to be taken literally. Times and circumstances have changed since Christ's day. Moreover, He spoke in Parables.

THEOSOPHIST. Then why don't your Churches teach that the doctrine of damnation and hell-fire is to be understood as a *parable* too? Why do some of your most popular preachers, while virtually allowing these "parables" to be understood as you take them, insist on the literal meaning of the fires of Hell and the *physical* tortures of an "Asbestos-like" soul? If one is a "parable," then the other is. If Hell-fire is a literal truth, then Christ's commandments in the Sermon on the Mount have to be obeyed to the very letter. And I tell you that many who do not believe in the Divinity of Christ — like Count Leo Tolstoi and more than one Theosophist — do carry out these noble, because universal, precepts literally; and many more good men and women would do so, were they not more than certain that such a walk in life would very probably land them in a lunatic asylum — so *Christian are your laws!*

ENQUIRER. But surely everyone knows that millions and millions are spent annually on private and public charities?

THEOSOPHIST. Oh, yes; half of which sticks to the hands it passes through before getting to the needy; while a good portion or remainder gets into the hands of professional beggars, those who are too lazy to work, thus doing no good whatever to those who are really in misery and suffering. Haven't you heard that the first result of the great outflow of charity towards the East-end of London was to raise the rents in *Whitechapel* by some 20 per cent.?

ENQUIRER. What would you do, then?

THEOSOPHIST. Act individually and not collectively; follow the Northern Buddhist precepts: "Never put food into the mouth of the hungry by the hand of another"; "Never let the shadow of thy neighbour (*a third person*) come between thyself and the object of thy bounty"; "Never give to the Sun time to dry a tear before thou hast wiped it." Again "Never give money to the needy, or food to the priest, who begs at thy door, *through thy servants*, lest thy money should diminish gratitude, and thy food turn to gall."

ENQUIRER. But how can this be applied practically?

THEOSOPHIST. The Theosophical ideas of charity mean *personal* exertion for others; *personal* mercy and kindness; *personal* interest in the welfare of those who suffer; *personal* sympathy, forethought and assistance in their troubles or needs. We Theosophists do not believe in giving money (N. B., if we had it) through other people's hands or organizations. We believe in giving to the money a thousand-fold greater power and effectiveness by our personal contact and sympathy with those who need it. We believe in relieving the starvation of the soul, as much if not more than the emptiness of the stomach; for gratitude does more good to the man who feels it, than to him for whom it is felt. Where's the gratitude which your "millions of pounds" should have called forth, or the good feelings provoked by them? Is it shown in the hatred of the East-End poor for the rich? in the growth of the party of anarchy and disorder? or by those thousands of unfortunate working girls, victims to the "sweating" system, driven daily to eke out a living by going on the streets? Do your helpless old men and women thank you for the workhouses; or your poor for the poisonously unhealthy dwellings in which they are allowed to breed new generations of diseased, scrofulous and rickety children, only to put money into the pockets of the insatiable Shylocks who own houses? Therefore it is that every sovereign of all those "millions," contributed by good and would-be charitable people, falls like a burning curse instead of a blessing on the poor whom it should relieve. We call this *generating national Karma,* and terrible will be its results on the day of reckoning.

The Key to Theosophy, pp. 242-245
H.P. Blavatsky

THE LODGE AND THE SANGHA

The only object to be striven for is the amelioration of the condition of MAN by the spread of truth suited to the various stages of his development and that of the country he inhabits and belongs to. TRUTH has no ear-mark and does not suffer from the name under which it is promulgated – if the said object is attained.

Mahatma K. H.

Theosophy teaches mutual-culture before self-culture to begin with. Union is strength. . . . For real moral advancement – there "where two or three are gathered" in the name of the SPIRIT OF TRUTH – there that Spirit or Theosophy will be in the midst of them.

H. P. Blavatsky

Every individual and every association, if they are to serve an enduring aim and purpose, must strive to secure a balance between uniqueness and universality, and to seek some abiding basis of union beyond the differences that pertain to finite and transient particulars. In the cosmos, every particle of matter is a manifestation of the spirit that is, by definition, unique in reference to the spatio-temporal context in which it finds itself. In an ever-changing universe, every particle changes continually in a ceaselessly changing spatio-temporal context, through the power of Eternal Motion or Universal Consciousness, the One Life. The continuity that underlies a series of shifting positions of uniqueness represents the universality of consciousness that ensouls every particle of matter. This truth about continuity and change is expressed in the maxim that duality characterizes all manifestation, the result of the coexistence and cooperation of ideation and image, force and form, spirit and matter, intention and result. Without a universal basis, uniqueness of expression would be impossible to attain; without the latter, the former would be abstract and unrealized.

In human society, which is at present a chaos rather than a cosmos, the affirmations of uniqueness and of universality are alike artificial. Cooperation and conscious interdependence can only be found by formulating a basis of union that can bind seemingly independent, imperfectly unique, entities in a manner that makes concrete the universality that ultimately underlies all of them, as a fact of nature rather than as a result of artifice. We clearly cannot dispense with associations in human society, whatever our aims and purposes. Most associations, however, are at best partial brotherhoods, fraternal in name rather than in fact, held together precariously by limited and temporary loyalties. Unique claims may be made for their members merely by virtue of their formal allegiance, but these exclusive and extravagant claims generate counteracting currents of opposition and even hostility from other associations and sects. This familiar phenomenon, competitive and conflict-creating, is elevated in sectarian religion to the status of righteous-seeming rivalry, and in partisan politics, to the level of legitimacy that is regarded as essential to the political dialogue of a liberal democracy, which in practice is no more than a demagogic oligarchy. The sun of Truth is thus obscured by the mists of so-called revelations or the clouds of nebulous ideologies.

The Declaration of the United Lodge of Theosophists points to a method of association which is based upon adherence to definite principles, which is genuinely universal in scope, which is capable of respecting and preserving the uniqueness of every one of its Associates, with their many differences of perspective and of personality. The basis of union is triple and is closely similar to the ancient submission, affirmed in early Buddhist monasticism, to the *Dhamma*, the *Sangha* and the *Buddhas*. The Buddhist contribution to India was not merely the shift of emphasis from *Moksha* to *Dhamma* and from God to Law, but also the stress on the *Sangha* and the monastic ideal in the midst of society. The *Sangha* was set up to teach mankind the discipline of self-culture through study and meditation, sacrifice and mutual aid, and the continuous service of all men. The very existence, and certainly the effectiveness, of the *Sangha* depended upon the observance of *Vinaya* and concentration on the *Sutta*. The *Vinaya* constituted the practical *Dhamma* or the code of discipline governing the conduct of the *Sangha*, while the *Sutta* constituted the theoretical side of the *Dhamma*, meant for regulating the inner life and thought of the *Bhikkhus*. Further, *Vinaya* had two aspects, *Shila* and *Achara*. The purity of the individual members of the *Sangha* depended on the practice of the *Shila-Vinaya* and the solidarity of the *Sangha* on the observance of the *Achara-Vinaya*. The former, embodying the *Patimokkha* rules, was laid down from the start of the *Sangha* and remained constant, while the latter was adapted to different climes and the varying modes of living of different peoples.

The United Lodge of Theosophists that emerged seven years after the Aquarian age began sought to do quietly what the *Sangha* afforded for both monks and laity in the early period after the passing away of the Buddha. The *Sutta* of the Lodge had been recorded in the writings of H.P. Blavatsky and W.Q. Judge. The *Vinaya* was transmitted by Robert Crosbie through the Declaration of the Lodge, which lays equal stress on both *Shila* and *Achara* as the means to purity and solidarity. Its policy is independent devotion to the *Dhamma* and it is loyal to the great founders of the original *Sangha* and the great Lodge of Buddhas that was behind them. The *Shila-Vinaya* of the United Lodge of Theosophists stresses the truer realization of the SELF and a profounder conviction of Universal Brotherhood. The *Achara-Vinaya* of the United Lodge of Theosophists is embodied in the phrase, "*similarity of aim, purpose and teaching.*"

Similarity of teaching is clearly crucial to any association which is spiritual and not mundane, which seeks to become a *Sangha* of co-disciples and not merely a club or a coterie, a forum or a Tower of Babel. In the Lodge the teaching is both transcendental and embodied, both *THEOSOPHIA* or the Wisdom-Religion in its entirety and the Theosophy taught by H.P. Blavatsky. *THEOSOPHIA* cannot be wholly contained or properly preserved in any single text or scripture or in any particular form of words in any known language. Theosophy was, however, embodied in the recorded teachings of H.P. Blavatsky and W.Q. Judge for the centenary cycle and beyond; this embodiment is inevitably partial and need not be taken as wholly perfect, but it has been declared and may be shown to be the completest and the best available. A person cannot need the *Sangha* of the Lodge if he claims private and direct access to the pure *Dhamma*. Equally, those who are concerned to concentrate on the *Sutta* cannot find any basis for collaboration (as distinct from good-will) with those who wish to pick and choose among H.P. Blavatsky's writings and alter them, or to ignore the contribution of W.Q. Judge to the formulation, exemplification and preservation of the *Sutta*.

Similarity of aim is what distinguishes the *Sangha* from passive and ineffective sects which cling to a common teaching as to a crutch and are thus reduced to mere cults. If the Lodge is not to go the fanciful way of the various religious factions that rely blindly on a literal and final revelation, its Associates must concentrate their collective efforts on a single target and work steadily with a unity of wills in the direction of their constant aim. The word "aim" signifies a mark or a butt, the reaching of which requires that we calculate and direct our course and endeavour earnestly in the desired direction with continuous concentration and one-pointedness, without any wavering or deviation. The Lodge is a training-ground and a vehicle for the art of spiritual archery, about which Mr. Judge has written in his article, "*Hit the Mark*" (*Hermes,* January 1975). The aim is clearly the study, application and dissemination of the truths of the Eternal Religion or *Sanatana Dharma* – THEOSOPHIA. Every Associate is expected, but cannot be constrained, to contemplate the universal conceptions of Theosophy, to apply them with imagination and true originality to the problems of daily life, to develop impersonal and pure feelings, and to make the impact of Theosophy felt by the collective mind and heart of humanity, leaving the fruits entirely to Karmic Law. The *Sangha* derives its strength and inspiration from the *Dhamma* and it becomes and remains a living power in the world to the extent that its members embody in their lives and spread the light and life-giving quality of the *Dhamma.*

This great work requires continuous and silent preparation, active and sincere cooperation that is the result of a communion of minds and hearts, and the healing touch of true conviction and altruism in precept and by example. Each man is a potency in himself and could be a lever that moves others and brings about concrete, if unknown, results. No one is converted to Theosophy except in so far as he sees for himself that it is a logical extension of his own earlier beliefs, based upon his own experiences which are indeed unique for him. This is what Blake and Yeats meant when they said that Christ reveals himself uniquely to each human soul. If the United Lodge of Theosophists is to help in this process of soul-evolution, its Associates must take a firm position, concentrate their minds and hearts, eyes and hands, on the fixed target, improve the texture and the tension of their common bow, allow for the trajectory that is determined by their common limitations, and repeatedly release arrows of intention and effort in a smooth and steady manner at the moment of full draw, until they hit the mark and significantly affect the receptive souls that they are able to attract through the purity and strength of their devotion. This is a mighty undertaking, involving the operation of laws beyond our ken. Every Associate would do well to take seriously to heart Mr. Judge's advice: "Make up your mind to follow a certain line of theosophical work, for concentrated endeavour in one direction will sooner bring results than a miscellaneous, wandering and spasmodic effort."

Similarity of purpose is required if the *Sangha*, rooted in *Dhamma*, united in the study and the spread of the *Dhamma*, is to remain in accord with the profoundly potent resolve and constant ideation and sacrifice of the Buddhas who are the greatest masters of nature and servants of mankind that the world has ever known. Motive is more important than method; the art of sacrifice is even more difficult to grasp or to attain than the art of archery. The single purpose of the Lodge, in the pursuit of its single aim, is the spiritual elevation of the *Manas* and the *Buddhi* of our race and the constant alleviation of the sufferings of myriads of human souls, lost and storm-tossed in their frail barks on the sea of *Samsara*. The archetypal model and paradigm for the Lodge is the Great Sacrifice, the wondrous Being whom *The Secret Doctrine* depicts, the Teacher of Teachers who cannot rest until every human soul is saved. The Lodge is an imperfect but invaluable instrument for training those who are willing to become ready to participate, in however meagre a manner, in the constant sacrifices of the trans-Himalayan Brotherhood of Adepts, which assists in the cosmic undertaking of the Great Sacrifice. The power of resolve must be pondered upon by every Associate of the Lodge who wishes to study the art of sacrifice taught and exemplified by the Founders of the Theosophical Movement. The word "purpose" refers to the intention and the determination to act with conscious design. The power of a vow is tremendous, but it is derived not merely from an initial resolve, however lofty, but from the continual practice of devotion and of fidelity. We have been told: "Broaden instead of narrowing your sympathies, try to identify yourself with your fellows, rather than to contract your circle of affinity." Far from remaining an exclusive, self-sufficient, self-centred fraternity, the Lodge is a living force for good only to the extent that its members are drawn through its efforts to an increasingly wider circle of affinities with our suffering fellow men. Its Associates must become better and more effective philanthropists if the Lodge is to remain in touch with the spirit of the Original Programme of the Theosophical Movement, and serve as a suitable instrument for the 1975 cycle.

In conclusion, everyone would do well to reflect upon the following three extracts from H.P. Blavatsky's important article on "*The Original Programme,*" written in 1886:

> The Founders had to exercise all their influence *to oppose selfishness of any kind,* by insisting upon sincere, fraternal feelings among the Members – at least outwardly; working for it to bring about a spirit of unity and harmony, the great diversity of creeds notwithstanding; expecting and demanding from the Fellows a great mutual toleration and charity for each other's shortcomings; mutual help in the research of truths in every domain – moral or physical – and even in daily life.

> It is by gathering many Theosophists of the same way of thinking into one or more groups, and making them closely united by the same magnetic bond of fraternal unity and sympathy that the objects of *mutual* development and progress in Theosophical thought may be best achieved.

> That which was generated through and founded by the "High Masters" and under their authority if not their instruction – MUST AND WILL LIVE.

Hermes, June 1975
Raghavan Iyer

OF STUDYING THEOSOPHY

It is often asked: How should I or my friend study Theosophy?

In beginning this study a series of "don'ts" should first engage the student's attention. Don't imagine that you know everything, or that any man in scientific circles has uttered the last word on any subject; don't suppose that the present day is the best, or that the ancients were superstitious, with no knowledge of natural laws. Don't forget that arts, sciences, and metaphysics did not have their rise with European civilization; and don't forget that the influence of Socrates, Plato, and Aristotle of ancient Greece is still imposed upon the modern mind. Don't think that our astronomers would have made anything but a mess of the zodiac if the old Chaldeans had not left us the one we use. Don't forget that it is easy to prove that civilization of the highest order has periodically rolled around this globe and left traces great and small behind. Don't confuse Buddhism with Brahmanism, or imagine that the Hindus are Buddhists; and don't take the word of English or German Sanscrit scholars in explanation of the writings and scriptures of eastern nations whose thoughts are as foreign in their form to ours as our countries are. One should first be prepared to examine with a clear and unbiased mind.

But suppose the enquirer is disposed at the outset to take the word of theosophical writers, then caution is just as necessary, for theosophical literature does not bear the stamp of authority. We should all be able to give a reason for the hope that is within us, and we cannot do that if we have swallowed without study the words of others.

But what is study? It is not the mere reading of books, but rather long, earnest, careful thought upon that which we have taken up. If a student accepts reincarnation and karma as true doctrines, the work is but begun. Many Theosophists accept doctrines of that name, but are not able to say what it is they have accepted. They do not pause to find out what reincarnates, or how, when, or why karma has its effects, and often do not know what the word means. Some at first think that when they die they will reincarnate, without reflecting that it is the lower personal I they mean, which cannot be born again in a body. Others think that karma is - well, karma, with no clear idea of classes of karma, or whether of not it is punishment or reward or both. Hence a careful learning from one or two books of the statement of the doctrines, and then a more careful study of them, are absolutely necessary.

There is too little of such right study among Theosophists, and too much reading of new books. No student can tell whether Mr. Sinnett in *Esoteric Buddhism* writes reasonably unless his book is learned and not merely skimmed. Although his style is clear, the matter treated is difficult, needing firm lodgment in the mind, followed by careful thought. A proper use of his book, *The Secret Doctrine, The Key to Theosophy,* and all other matter written upon the constitution of man, leads to an acquaintance with the doctrines as to the being most concerned, and only when that acquaintance is obtained is one fitted to understand the rest.

Another branch of study is that pursued by natural devotees, those who desire to enter into the work itself for the good of humanity. Those should study all branches of Theosophical literature all the harder, in order to be able to clearly explain it to others, for a weak reasoner or an apparently credulous believer has not much weight with others.

Western Theosophists need patience, determination, discrimination, and memory, if they ever intend to seize and hold the attention of the world for the doctrines they disseminate.

Path, January, 1890
W.Q. Judge

THE AQUARIAN TIDE

Let us prepare, and let us study Truth in all its aspects, trying not to ignore any of them, if we do not wish, when the hour will have struck, to fall into the abyss of the unknown. It is useless to rely on chance, and to await the approaching intellectual and psychic crisis with indifference if not with total incredulity, saying to oneself that if worse comes to worst, the tide will carry us quite naturally to the shore; for there is a strong likelihood of the tide stranding but a corpse! The battle will be fierce, in any case, between brutal materialism and blind fanaticism on the one hand, and on the other philosophy and mysticism – that more or less thick veil of the Eternal Truth.

It is not materialism that will have the upper hand.

La Revue Theosophique, March 1889
H. P. Blavatsky

According to the enigmatic maxim of Protagoras, "Man is the measure of all things; of things that are, that they are; of things that are not, that they are not." However interpreted, this evidently implies that every individual and collective crisis is a crisis of self-concept, self-reference and identity. It further implies that every response to a crisis is shaped and prefigured by factors within human nature. At root, one's ontological estimate of humanity and one's cosmological calculation of the position of man relative to Nature will determine one's capacity to respond creatively in any situation. It should be common sense that the expression of wisdom in human life cannot exceed the sum-total allotted to man by Nature. Nonetheless, the measure of human wisdom postulated by any human being or culture may be seriously defective or needlessly self-constrained. As practical self-knowledge inevitably involves self-reference, the human being who gives short measure to humanity will not be able to draw upon the full potential of human nature. The individual who seeks to integrate the Logoic principle of cosmos with the essential being of man in Nature can remain inwardly open to the whole measure of wisdom attainable by man. It is a paradox of human self-consciousness that Nature will always negate vanity, though it cannot negate despair without human assistance.

This asymmetry in human consciousness, with its awesome implications for pessimism and optimism, arises out of the basic distinction between the evolutionary and involutionary arcs of manifestation. The upward progress of humanity along the evolutionary arc ascending towards self-conscious realization of Spirit depends decisively upon human initiative. It is part of the tragedy of the modern age that, offered the Promethean fire of wisdom, it has chosen instead to bind itself into servitude to Zeus with the gilded chains of kamamanasic desire. Offered the call of the Christos, capable of resurrecting Lazarus from the dead, the western world adopted instead the self-mutilating worship of the cross of matter. Like Procrustes caught in his own clumsy contrivance, for nearly two millennia the West has suffered spiritual deprivation under its self-imposed idolatry of psychic materialism. Since the fourteenth century, the Great Lodge of *Mahatmas* has sustained a cyclic effort to ameliorate this anguished condition. The culmination of this effort, adjusting the entire range of human principles, was planned to coincide with the Avataric impulse accompanying the Aquarian Age and profoundly affecting the future races of humanity.

Thirteen years before the beginning of the Aquarian Age, in an essay entitled "The New Cycle", addressed in French to a European audience, H.P. Blavatsky powerfully spelt out the choices open to the West. By the latter decades of the nineteenth century, certain divisions of society and thought had already become acute. Millions were caught up either in the spiritual materialism of orthodox religion, or the soulless materialism of mechanistic science. Throughout the seventies and eighties of the Victorian era, a tremendous debate had blown up around human evolution, with science and religion drawing up lines on opposite sides. Going beyond the closed terms of this dilettantish debate, H.P. Blavatsky drew attention to what had already been noticed by a variety of writers, especially in Russia; namely, what she called the death-struggle between brutal materialism and blind fanaticism on the one side, and philosophy and mysticism on the other. This fierce battle, she affirmed, would be the crucial issue of the twentieth century, and, she prophesied:

Everyone fanatically clinging to an idea isolating him from the universal axiom – "There is no Religion higher than Truth" – will find himself separated like a rotten plank from the new ark called Humanity. Tossed by the waves, chased by the winds, buffeted by this element so terrible because unknown, he will soon find himself swallowed up.

Ibid.

H.P. Blavatsky was actually sounding a grave and compassionate warning that those souls unable to enter the current of the future would be discarded by Nature. In the 1890's, and increasingly throughout the twentieth century, the growing perception of this fateful choice has instilled a tremendous fear in a despairing element within the human race. Instead of discovering brave and powerful responses to the challenge of the future, that minuscule percentage of the human race which is terrified, for karmic reasons, that it has no future, has developed nihilistic literature and thought, a full-blown psychology of doom. Through the power of the printed word, and later the electronic media, and with the aid of pathological art and pessimistic fiction, this vociferous minority managed to transfer its psychological ailments to vast numbers of human beings. Entire societies have become caught up in this pathology – in Vienna before the First World War, and even more acutely after the war; in France before the Second World War, and especially during the war and after; and in pre-Nazi Germany. The pathology converged in England during the late 1930's in a literature of bitter disenchantment. It appeared in Russia, particularly during the early days of the Stalinist era, in pessimistic poems and novels, to be somewhat eclipsed by a more heroic stance in the later 1940's and 1950's. It has reappeared in England in recent decades, and it has been a constant problem in post-war America. Like the deadly emanations of the *upas* tree, it spreads its contagion wherever hapless individuals are neither self-innoculated through spiritual resolve nor actually immune through the protection of vital ethical traditions.

Through many forms of scholarship and literature, and a system of semi-institutionalized opinions and manipulated media, a modern system of negative thought-control fosters and diffuses a sense of hopelessness and helplessness. This entire phenomenon in fact represents the death-throes of those elaborate structures of psychology and philosophy rooted in the ideas of ontological scarcity and bourgeois materialism. The present manifestation is a long shadow cast by the seventeenth century where the power of the Catholic Church, particularly on the Continent, cramped those philosophers who sought to celebrate the human spirit. In trying to comprehend human nature, thinkers of the seventeenth century were unable to remove themselves from an obsession with original sin. As this notion became secularized and disguised through sociology and psychology, it came to pervade the intellectual life of the nineteenth century. And as an unsolicited and unsuspected term of debate, it crept into the twentieth century in every field of thought affected by theories of behavioural conditioning. In every case, it shrinks the conception of Nature and of human nature. But, ultimately, all such stultifying and self-crippling conceptions of man are doomed. Parasitic and vampiric, their borrowed and vicarious life may continue for a while, but they will become increasingly irrelevant to the human condition.

Already, millions are tired of nihilists and misanthropes and are stimulated instead by the positive urges of their own sporadic intuitions of the Divine. This is especially true in America, where mass belief is rarely registered by the media, which bases its claims upon limited surveys and the pronouncements of self-appointed experts who speak gibberish while presuming to represent the American spirit. Indeed, throughout the world, human beings refuse to be trapped within negativism. H.P. Blavatsky spoke of the time "when the flame of modern materialism, artificial and cold, will be extinguished for lack of fuel". The evidence of this can be seen in the decaying heart of the cities which were once the centres of civilization. In Paris and London, New York and Los Angeles, materialistic entrepreneurs and purveyors of the doctrine of inescapable selfishness are finding it difficult to find living human fuel to sustain the structures of human confinement. Their children simply will not go along. They would rather do almost anything else. Like Ahab bound to the sounding whale, the materialist is fast becoming lonely and hopeless, though at times angry and desperate.

It is not easy for the human soul to shake off the yoke of materialism, for even with a strong conviction in the immortal soul, one may unknowingly retain mental habits that are materialistic. Any concern for spiritual progress for oneself must, therefore, be rooted out and dispelled as a pernicious form of spiritual materialism. Any tendency to identify with the physical body, or act for the sake of oneself as a separative entity in order to gain spiritual gifts and advantages, is incompatible with conscious life in spirit, as opposed to matter. To conceive truly of the *Atman* and the *Atma-Buddhi*, the light of the Universal Spirit and the Divine Self, one must shun all separative thinking. It is to this contrast of the living and the dead within human nature that H.P. Blavatsky referred when she wrote:

> The Spirit of Truth is at this moment moving upon the face of these black waters, and, separating them, forces them to yield their spiritual treasures. This spirit is a force that cannot be either checked or stopped. Those who recognize it and feel that this is the supreme moment of their salvation, will be carried by it beyond the illusions of the great astral serpent.

> *Ibid.*

Those who are vitalized by the vigorous current of spiritual energy can enjoy states of consciousness and peak experiences that transcend the personality. Freed from the thraldom and tension of self-concern, they will become happy that other human beings exist, thrilled that there are babies on earth, and convinced that where there is a larger view, there is always hope.

Owing to the relentless pressure of the age, it is more and more necessary to abjure separative thinking and join the larger perspective of the majority of mankind. The intensity of the struggle happily compels individuals to choose. Those who pretend to remain indifferent to the prospects of the future only doom themselves to the "arid wastes of matter...to vegetate there through a long series of lives, content henceforth with feverish hallucinations instead of spiritual perceptions, with passions instead of love, with the rind instead of the fruit". Unless they scorn selfish assumptions, they will come to resemble the squirrel on its ceaselessly revolving wheel, whirling round and round chewing the nut of nihilism. But once spiritual starvation and material satiety move them to forget self, they will recognize the necessity of an intellectual and moral reform. The privilege of beginning this fundamental reform within oneself, and working for its fulfilment on behalf of other human beings, is extended by the Brotherhood of *Bodhisattvas* to every true friend of the human race.

> This reform cannot be accomplished except through Theosophy, and, let us say it, Occultism, or the Wisdom of the East. Many are the paths leading to it, but Wisdom is forever one. Artists foresee it, those who suffer dream of it, the pure in spirit know it. Those who work for others cannot remain blind before its reality even though they do not always know it by name. It is only the light-headed and empty-minded, the selfish and vain drones deafened by the sound of their own buzzing who can ignore this high ideal.
>
> *Ibid.*

Whilst many have dreamt of ideal wisdom, some actually know it. They know it in their bones and in their blood; they have tested and tasted it; they have found that it works, and made it the basis of their thought and their lives. In the best cases, they have made it the basis of their unlimited devotion to the interests of others, and in the unselfishness of their service they have become invulnerable and indifferent towards the world and its evanescent opinions.

This is a very high state indeed. But in contemplating it, one should not fall prey to self-recrimination and recurring doubt. To do so would only reaffirm the contagious materialism that one wishes to leave behind. It does not matter at what level a human being approaches Divine Wisdom. Even if one can embody only one percent of the ideal, one must hold fast to the conviction that what is real in oneself and can be realized in practice is the only element that truly counts. This alone must be taken as the focus of one's concentration. Whilst it is always possible at any given time to say that one can only do so much, and no more, it is also always possible to enjoy and contemplate the ideal in meditation. The ideal can, and must, be separated from the limitations of incarnated existence. Thus, two different types of development emerge. First of all, one is intensifying through devotion to the ideal the architectonics of one's thought with regard to the ideal. This will be elaborated in *devachan* after death in the celestial condition of dreams of goodwill and creativity which can cut grooves in the *karana sharira*, the causal body, and affect lives to come. At the same time, one may recognize in other aspects of the vestures, particularly in the *linga sharira* or astral form, that one is unfortunately enslaved by many habits.

Under the karmic curve of the present life, one cannot enormously increase one's power of concentration however much one tries, because one lacks the strength to resist negative forces. Therefore, whilst maximizing development within the present lifetime, individuals must also recognize how little they can do and consequently how modest and honest they must be in the day to day walk of life. By understanding this dual process affecting both the present life and future lives, one can awaken a balanced courage and a spirit of unconditionality in one's commitment to an ideal.

> To take the first step on this ideal path requires a perfectly pure motive; no frivolous thought must be allowed to divert our eyes from the goal; no hesitation, no doubt must fetter our feet. Yet, there are men and women perfectly capable of all this, and whose only desire is to live under the aegis of their Divine Nature. Let these, at least, have the courage to live this life and not to hide it from the sight of others! No one's opinion could ever be above the rulings of our own conscience, so, let that conscience, arrived at its highest development, be our guide in all our common daily tasks. As to our inner life, let us concentrate all our attention on our chosen Ideal, and let us ever look *beyond* without ever casting a glance at the mud at our feet.
>
> *Ibid.*

It may be natural enough and even nutritionally sound for children to eat a little dirt, but it is unnatural and unhealthy for adults to savour the mentally negative or psychically muddy. They must rather train themselves always to look beyond, towards the stars and towards the future. By gazing towards the radiant though distant summit of enlightenment, they can keep their heads above the waters of chaos. By learning to float, by learning to tread water, they can begin to swim, and even to deal with the shifting tides of the psychic nature. Under karma, these forces work differently for different people. Some can concentrate on that which is universal and impersonal for long periods of time; others find that they cannot do so for more than a few minutes at a time. Again, the length of meaningful meditation is less important than the authenticity of the attempt. The more one can calmly accept the limits of one's abilities, the more those limits will expand. Here as everywhere, the greater one's application, the greater one's results. And like many physical habits, these mental exercises must be established at an early age. What is easy for the young is not so easy for the old. If one acquires healthy mental habits whilst young, one should be grateful for the auspicious karma. If one does not recognize the need for a mental reform until later in life, again, one should be grateful for the recognition itself, as for the counsel required to carry out the reform. One must desire reform, and having embarked upon it, persevere with courage. One must become a true friend of oneself and strive without guilt, enjoying progress, without falling into the anxious traps that began with "original sin". Like Job, one must learn that one's burden is neither greater nor less than one can bear, and thus become receptive to every form of good.

As Pythagoras taught, spiritual courage arises out of the conviction that the race of men is immortal. From the soil of its lunar beginnings to its ultimate dwelling-place beyond the stars, humanity follows the cyclic path of transformation wherein each element of human nature is transmuted into a self-conscious aspect of Divine Wisdom. The acquisition and unfoldment of knowledge of these elements in man and in Nature is an essential component of the collective spiritual progress of the race. The vivifying ideal of wisdom itself is inconceivable apart from the practical acquisition of knowledge, and the perfection of human nature is thus impossible where the mind-principle is either degraded or defamed. It is the peculiar demerit of materialism enforced through the dogma of original sin that it attempts to accomplish both these negative ends at once. Thus in the last century, H.P. Blavatsky had to oppose materialism in both religion and science. Owing to concretized conceptions of progress, connected with a unilinear view of history and a short-sighted enthusiasm about technological change, it was very difficult in the latter part of the nineteenth century to challenge a prevailing blind faith in science. Nonetheless, H.P. Blavatsky prophetically anticipated the demise of this faith, which would take place in Europe because of the First World War. She also anticipated and stimulated a series of revolutionary scientific changes in the early decades of the Aquarian Age. Since then, even at a popular level, people have begun to assimilate something of quantum theory and theories of light, much that was implicit in the work of Einstein, Eddington and the early biologists. They have come to see that most of the nineteenth century categories of science are obsolete and irrelevant. This perception was already common in Europe in the 1920's and 1930's, but was considerably slower in coming to America, which is perhaps the last colonial country left on earth and usually moves about thirty years behind Europe in acknowledging significant shifts in thought.

After the Second World War, America tended to nurture an adolescent glorification of technology, but even this was challenged in the 1960's, and most thinking individuals discovered that they could not return to their earlier blind faith in technology. Unfortunately, this has produced an actual obstacle to understanding how the fruits of contemporary science and technology, for example micro-electronics, can be used to extend the effectiveness of human potential. Attitudes in America, unlike those in Sweden or Japan, are often polarized by mass society. Science and technology are met with a sluggish indifference or an incapacity to understand how they may be put to constructive use. Through the powerful blandishments of economics, however, there has recently been an enormous increase in the numbers of people seeking training in the use of computers, so much so that the facilities of educational institutions have been sorely taxed.

What is important and unusual in these developments is that people have set aside their former blind faith and begun to learn whatever skills are needed to put science and technology to use. Instead of reinforcing and reinvigorating outmoded conceptions of science, many have now learnt how to use the media to acquire information about cosmology and astronomy, about the earth and the oceans, about the body and the brain. Suddenly Americans, like Russians over the past thirty or forty years, have become more aware of the spiritual implications of science. They have begun to understand that the best science forces a rethinking of one's view of human nature, human potential, and the place of man in the cosmos. Once the spirituality of advanced science is recognized, there can be no return to a merely materialistic interest in technology. Men and women are now concerned with the creative noetic uses of scientific knowledge, and also with the raising of scientific questions that go to the heart of human existence. The largest questions in science always prompt honest disagreement and ultimately a ready recognition of ignorance.

Today, as was not true of the nineteenth century, enough is known in every field of science to recognize that what is known is a minute fragment of what is possible to know; leading scientists distinguish themselves in their fields only by admitting that they know next to nothing about fundamentals. Physiologists cannot penetrate all the miracles of the human brain. The finest physicists admit that almost nothing is known about the ultimate nature of matter. The best astronomers readily allow that they know little of the depths of outer space. The foremost biologists remain modestly silent before the mysteries of embryology. All of this is consonant with the vital keynote of the Aquarian Age, and extremely hopeful for the future of humanity. It is to this keynote that H.P. Blavatsky made reference when she declared:

> ...you Occultists, Kabalists, and Theosophists, you know well that a word as old as the world, though new to you, has been sounded at the beginning of this cycle...you know that a note, never before heard by the men of the present era, has just been sounded, and that a new kind of thought has arisen, fostered by the evolutionary forces. This thought differs from all that has ever been produced in the 19th Century; yet it is identical with what was the keynote and the keystone of every century, especially the last one: "Absolute Freedom of Human Thought."

Ibid.

As more and more people become aware of what the best minds of every age have always known – that they have hardly touched the threshold of the unknown – they will, paradoxically, be thrown back upon themselves. The willingness of people to become self-dependent is an important sign of the inception of the Aquarian Age. It is becoming progressively more difficult to convince people through statistical polls that what several million people think is necessarily true. Many individuals now prefer to think for themselves. As the antiquated machinery of thought-control breaks down, individuals are now discovering within themselves a willingness to exercise their own faculties. As they discover the challenge of true self-reliance, they become less blindly acquiescent to narrow scientific or religious dogmatism. With every increment of mental, moral and spiritual freedom gained, grand vistas of human possibility are opened before them. Even though the average human being uses much less than ten percent of the brain's potential, and even less of the heart's, the tide has begun to turn. Even though many still live like spiritual paupers, well below their potential means, they have begun to recognize their possibilities and the need for initiative in improving the human condition.

Relinquishing the mummeries of the past, they have begun to understand that only through developing the natural powers of concentration and spiritual attention can they enrich their collective future. Through the joy and the beauty, the dignity and the self-respect, that come from self-discipline, they can alchemically quicken their creative faculties and thereby tap the potential energies of the higher mind and heart. Thus, following the small old path depicted in every true philosophy and intimated in every authentic myth, each good and true human soul may discern the spiritual possibilities of the Aquarian Age and stay abreast of the vanguard of humanity.

Hermes, January 1983
by Raghavan Iyer

FRIENDS OR ENEMIES IN THE FUTURE

THE fundamental doctrines of Theosophy are of no value unless they are applied to daily life. To the extent to which this application goes they become living truths, quite different from intellectual expressions of doctrine. The mere intellectual grasp may result in spiritual pride, while the living doctrine becomes an entity through the mystic power of the human soul. Many great minds have dwelt on this. Saint Paul wrote:

> Though I speak with the tongues of men and of angels and have not charity, I am become as sounding brass or a tinkling cymbal. And though I have the gift of prophecy and understand all mysteries and all knowledge, and though I have all faith so that I could remove mountains, and have not charity, I am nothing. And though I bestow all my goods to feed the poor, and though I give my body to be burned, and have not charity, it profiteth me nothing.

The Voice of the Silence, expressing the views of the highest schools of occultism, asks us to step out of the sunlight into the shade so as to make more room for others, and declares that those whom we help in this life will help us in our next one.

Buttresses to these are the doctrines of Karma and Reincarnation. The first shows that we must reap what we sow, and the second that we come back in the company of those with whom we lived and acted in other lives. St. Paul was in complete accord with all other occultists, and his expressions above given must be viewed in the light Theosophy throws on all similar writings. Contrasted with charity, which is love of our fellows, are all the possible virtues and acquirements. These are all nothing if charity be absent. Why? Because they die with the death of the uncharitable person; their value is naught, and that being is reborn without friend and without capacity.

This is of the highest importance to the earnest Theosophist, who may be making the mistake of obtaining intellectual benefits, but remains uncharitable. The fact that we are now working in the Theosophical movement means that we did so in other lives, must do so again, and, still more important, that those who are now with us will be reincarnated in our company on our next rebirth.

Shall those whom we now know or whom we are destined to know before this life ends be our friends or enemies, our aiders or obstructors in that coming life? And what will make them hostile or friendly to us then? Not what we shall say or do to and for them in the future life. For no man becomes your friend in a present life by reason of present acts alone. He was your friend, or you his, before in a previous life. Your present acts but revive the old friendship, renew the ancient obligation.

Was he your enemy before, he will be now even though you do him service now, for these tendencies last always more than three lives. They will be more and still more our aids if we increase the bond of friendship of today by charity. Their tendency to enmity will be one-third lessened in every life if we persist in kindness, in love, in charity now. And that charity is not a gift of money, but charitable thought for every weakness, to every failure.

Our future friends or enemies, then, are those who are with us and to be with us in the present. If they are those who now seem inimical, we make a grave mistake and only put off the day of reconciliation three more lives if we allow ourselves today to be deficient in charity for them. We are annoyed and hindered by those who actively oppose as well as others whose mere looks, temperament, and unconscious action fret and disturb us. Our code of justice to ourselves, often but petty personality, incites us to rebuke them, to criticise, to attack. It is a mistake for us to so act. Could we but glance ahead to next life, we would see these for whom we now have but scant charity crossing the plain of that life with ourselves and ever in our way, always hiding the light from us. But change our present attitude, and that new life to come would show these bores and partial enemies and obstructors helping us, aiding our every effort. For Karma may give them then greater opportunities than ourselves and better capacity.

Is any Theosophist, who reflects on this, so foolish as to continue now, if he has the power to alter himself, a course that will breed a crop of thorns for his next life's reaping? We should continue our charity and kindness to our friends whom it is easy to wish to help, but for those whom we naturally dislike, who are our bores now, we ought to take especial pains to aid and carefully toward them cultivate a feeling of love and charity. This adds interest to our Karmic investment. The opposite course, as surely as sun rises and water runs downhill, strikes interest from the account and enters a heavy item on the wrong side of life's ledger.

And especially should the whole Theosophical organization act on the lines laid down by St. Paul and *The Voice of the Silence*. For Karmic tendency is an unswerving law. It compels us to go on in this movement of thought and doctrine; it will bring back to reincarnation all in it now. Sentiment cannot move the law one inch; and though that emotion might seek to rid us of the presence of these men and women we presently do not fancy or approve – and there are many such in our ranks for every one – the law will place us again in company with friendly tendency increased or hostile feeling diminished, just as we now create the one or prevent the other. It was the aim of the founders of the Society to arouse tendency to future friendship; it ought to be the object of all our members.

What will you have? In the future life, enemies or friends?

Path, January, 1893
W.Q. Judge

HOW SHOULD WE TREAT OTHERS?

THE subject relates to our conduct toward and treatment of our fellows, including in that term all people with whom we have any dealings. No particular mode of treatment is given by Theosophy. It simply lays down the law that governs us in all our acts, and declares the consequences of those acts. It is for us to follow the line of action which shall result first in harmony now and forever, and second, in the reduction of the general sum of hate and opposition in thought or act which now darkens the world.

The great law which Theosophy first speaks of is the law of karma, and this is the one which must be held in view in considering the question. Karma is called by some the "law of ethical causation," but it is also the law of action and reaction; and in all departments of nature the reaction is equal to the action, and sometimes the reaction from the unseen but permanent world seems to be much greater than the physical act or word would appear to warrant on the physical plane. This is because the hidden force on the unseen plane was just as strong and powerful as the reaction is seen by us to be. The ordinary view takes in but half of the facts in any such case and judges wholly by superficial observation.

If we look at the subject only from the point of view of the person who knows not of Theosophy and of the nature of man, nor of the forces Theosophy knows to be operating all the time, then the reply to the question will be just the same as the everyday man makes. That is, that he has certain rights he must and will and ought to protect; that he has property he will and may keep and use any way he pleases; and if a man injure him he ought to and will resent it; that if he is insulted by word or deed he will at once fly not only to administer punishment on the offender, but also try to reform, to admonish, and very often to give that offender up to the arm of the law; that if he knows of a criminal he will denounce him to the police and see that he has meted out to him the punishment provided by the law of man. Thus in everything he will proceed as is the custom and as is thought to be the right way by those who live under the Mosaic retaliatory law.

But if we are to inquire not the subject as Theosophists, and as Theosophists who know certain laws and who insist on the absolute sway of karma, and as people who know what the real constitution of man is, then the whole matter takes on, or ought to take on, a wholly different aspect.

The untheosophical view is based on separation, the Theosophical upon unity absolute and actual. Of course if Theosophists talk of unity but as a dream or a mere metaphysical thing, then they will cease to be Theosophists, and be mere professors, as the Christian world is today, of a code not followed. If we are separate one from the other the world is right and resistance is a duty, and the failure to condemn those who offend is a distinct breach of propriety, of law, and of duty. But if we are all united as a physical and psychical fact, then the act of condemning, the fact of resistance, the insistance upon rights on all occasions – all of which means the entire lack of charity and mercy – will bring consequences as certain as the rising of the sun tomorrow.

What are those consequences, and why are they?

They are simply this, that the real man, the entity, the thinker, will react back on you just exactly in proportion to the way you act to him, and this reaction will be in another life, if not now, and even if now felt will still return in the next life.

The fact that the person whom you condemn, or oppose, or judge seems now in this life to deserve it for his acts in this life, does not alter the other fact that his nature will react against you when the time comes. The reaction is a law not subject to nor altered by any sentiment on your part. He may have, truly, offended you and even hurt you, and done that which in the eye of man is blameworthy, but all this does not have anything to do with the dynamic fact that if you arouse his enmity by your condemnation or judgment there will be a reaction on you, and consequently on the whole of society in any century when the reaction takes place. This is the law and the fact as given by the

Adepts, as told by all sages, as reported by those who have seen the inner side of nature, as taught by our philosophy and easily provable by anyone who will take the trouble to examine carefully. Logic and small facts of one day or one life, or arguments on lines laid down by men of the world who do not know the real power and place of thought nor the real nature of man cannot sweep this away. After all argument and logic it will remain. The logic used against it is always lacking in certain premises based on facts, and while seeming to be good logic, because the missing facts are unknown to the logician, it is false logic. Hence an appeal to logic that ignores facts which we know are certain is of no use in this inquiry. And the ordinary argument always uses a number of assumptions which are destroyed by the actual inner facts about thought, about karma, about the reaction by the inner man.

The Master "K. H.", once writing to Mr. Sinnett in the *Occult World*, and speaking for his whole order and not for himself only, distinctly wrote that the man who goes to denounce a criminal or an offender works not with nature and harmony but against both, and that such act tends to destruction instead of construction. Whether the act be large or small, whether it be the denunciation of a criminal, or only your own insistence on rules or laws or rights, does not alter the matter or take it out of the rule laid down by that Adept. For the only difference between the acts mentioned is a difference of degree alone; the act is the same in kind as the violent denunciation of a criminal. Either this Adept was right or wrong. If wrong, why do we follow the philosophy laid down by him and his messenger, and concurred in by all the sages and teachers of the past? If right, why this swimming in an adverse current, as he said himself, why this attempt to show that we can set aside karma and act as we please without consequences following us to the end of time? I know not. I prefer to follow the Adept, and especially so when I see that what he says is in line with facts in nature and is a certain conclusion from the system of philosophy I have found in Theosophy.

I have never found an insistence on my so-called rights at all necessary. They preserve themselves, and it must be true if the law of karma is the truth that no man offends against me unless I in the past have offended against him.

In respect to man, karma has no existence without two or more persons being considered. You act, another person is affected, karma follows. It follows on the thought of each and not on the act, for the other person is moved to thought by your act. Here are two sorts of karma, yours and his, and both are intermixed. There is the karma or effect on you of your own thought and act, the result on you of the other person's thought; and there is the karma on or with the other person consisting of the direct result of your act and his thoughts engendered by your act and thought. This is all permanent. As affecting you there may be various effects. If you have condemned, for instance, we may mention some: (*a*) the increased tendency in yourself to indulge in condemnation, which will remain and increase from life to life; (*b*) this will at last in you change into violence and all that anger and condemnation may naturally lead to; (*c*) an opposition to you is set up in the other person, which will remain forever until one day both suffer for it, and this may be in a tendency in the other person in any subsequent life to do you harm and hurt you in the million ways possible in life, and often also unconsciously. Thus it may all widen out and affect the whole body of society. Hence no matter how justifiable it may seem to you to condemn or denounce or punish another, you set up cause for sorrow in the whole race that must work out some day. And you must feel it.

The opposite conduct, that is, entire charity, constant forgiveness, wipes out the opposition from others, expends the old enmity and at the same time makes no new similar causes. Any other sort of thought or conduct is sure to increase the sum of hate in the world, to make cause for sorrow, to continually keep up the crime and misery in the world. Each man can for himself decide which of the two ways is the right one to adopt.

Self-love and what people call self-respect may shrink from following the Adept's view I give above, but the Theosophist who wishes to follow the law and reduce the general sum of hate will know how to act and to think, for he will follow the words of the Master of H.P.B. who said: "Do not be ever thinking of yourself and forgetting that there are others; for you have no karma of your own, but the karma of each one is the karma of all." And these words were sent by H.P.B. to the American Section and called by her words of wisdom, as they seem also to me to be, for they accord with law. They hurt the *personality* of the nineteenth century, but the personality is for a day, and soon it will be changed if Theosophists try to follow the law of charity as enforced by the inexorable law of karma. We should all constantly remember that if we believe in the Masters we should at least try to imitate them in the charity they show for our weakness and faults. In no other way can we hope to reach their high estate, for by beginning thus we set up a tendency which will one day perhaps bring us near to their development; by not beginning we put off the day forever.

Path, February, 1896
W.Q. Judge

TRUE MORALITY

TRUE morality is not a thing of words or phrases or modes of action of any kind, nor is its basis to be found in the many kinds of ideas of morality in the world, which vary as to time and place. What is "moral" at one time is "immoral" at another. There is no basis whatever in this changing attitude towards actions, changing classifications of good and evil, in a changing "division of the universe."

Intolerance is their sure resultant; for those who pride themselves upon their own special brands of "morality" are always intolerant of others who do not accept that brand. True morality rests in an understanding and in a realization of man's own spiritual nature, and must of necessity flow from it, irrespective of all kinds of conventions. We need to know our own inner natures in order to know what is, in truth, morality.

The conventions of external life are established merely by a consensus of opinion of the beings living at any one time and in any one place. They are not necessarily based on truth, and certainly not on a perception of the whole of truth. As we may see, the best interests of all are not served by the ideas that are generally held. The world is in a tremendously evil and selfish state. With all our prevailing ideas of progress, of morality and of religion, it is not anywhere nearly so happy a place as it was perhaps a century or two ago; it is not nearly so good a place for human beings to live in as it was in the more innocent and less complex civilizations of the older nations. There is evidently something wrong with the ideas that we hold, if we find it impossible to deny the fact that instead of the world getting better and instead of life becoming more simple, the world is growing worse and life is becoming more and more complex. We should not find ourselves in the present condition if our ideas, religious and moral, flowed from the underlying basic ideas of all religions, philosophies, and systems of thought.

The basis of understanding of life accepted by the majority of

Western peoples has been a revealed religion, and a personal God who revealed that religion. From this basis have sprung all our wrong conceptions. Hence the great stress laid on physical existence. in fact, one might say that the generality of human thinking is centered entirely on physical existence. The question has not even been asked, "How is it that I am born at this time, under such conditions, in this people, and not at some previous or future time, when the world might be better?" The question has not been asked, "Why are we here at all?" Nor have we asked, "What is the pre-existing cause that brought us into this relation? Was it at the whim or caprice a special Being, or was it under the operation of an indwelling, inherent law within ourselves?" If we are here with our present qualities, surrounded with difficulties, not because of anything we ourselves have done, but because of the whim or caprice of some Being, then we must regard ourselves as absolutely irresponsible for anything whatever. If we were so created, there is nothing that can undo that creation and we must suffer the consequences, the causes for which we did not set in motion!

The true ideas of the ancient philosophy relieve us of two misconceptions: one, the idea that there is a revengeful God who punishes us for those things that we are unable to prevent ourselves from doing; and second, the idea of a Devil to whom we are consigned if we do not follow the lines that some people have laid down for us. A knowledge of Theosophy enables us to understand that there never was any "creation," in the sense of making something out of nothing; but that everything – every being of every kind – has evolved, and is still evolving. The beings below us are evolving to our estate, where the beings, now evolved so far beyond us, sometime in the distant past went through a similar stage. All beings are what they are through evolution from within outwards, that evolution proceeding under Law.

Law is operative everywhere and upon every being, because the Law is not something separate from him; it is not separate from the inner spiritual man. Law is the law of man's own action. So, as we act along those lines that affect others for good or for evil, we necessarily receive the return from those good or evil effects which we cause others to experience. Each individual is the operator of the Law; according to his actions he gets the re-actions; according to his sowing, does he reap. In place, then, of the idea of a revengeful God, we have the ideas of absolute Justice and individual responsibility.

If, from the point of view of Law, we ask ourselves what pre-existing causes brought us into these relations, we can see that what now is must have been brought about by ourselves, and what now is is similar to what was. At once the idea is presented to our minds that this is not the first time, by many times, we have been in a body; that re-incarnation is the process by which human beings reach greater and greater heights; that there is no other way or means to learn all the lessons to be gained in physical life among our fellow-men, except through repeated incarnations.

We come, then, to another phase of our being – for we see there is in us something that is continuous in its operation, something which was never born and never dies. If it continues from one life to another, through many lives, and for many lives, there must be a permanency in us which no change of condition or body or circumstance can alter for a single instant. As we thus think in terms of ages rather than in the days of one short life, we begin to get a glimpse of that Reality which lies within us; we open the door so that those internal, real, more permanent perceptions can find operation in our daily waking thoughts – for every single human being has sprung from the One Great Source, is animated by That, is, in fact, That at the very root of his being; in That is his power of perception and of action, which is spiritual and permanent. The power of perception and of action exists in everyone; the direction of that perception and action rests in each one. Each has the power to take the course which to him seems best; but, in taking the course, he sows, and must also reap as was the nature of his sowing. Every being in this universe of Law is experiencing as he is because of his own thoughts, words, and deeds; every circumstance, every misshapen day, every evil that comes to us as well as every good, is due to thought, word of deed of ours in the past. In each incarnation we find friends as well as enemies. So our minds may be set at rest with regard to either God or Devil. Each one of us represents both the Spirit – the highest divine nature – and also, the very lowest – the infernal nature. Man is spiritual, in fact, but, thinking himself material and separate, and acting in accordance with his thinking, he brings about the battle between the two natures in him.

The great mistake of religionists in our age has been the classification of good and evil. There is nothing good in itself. There is nothing evil in itself. It is the use to which anything is put that makes it good or makes it evil. How can we draw a fine line between good and bad in every case? Good and evil are judged by the effects that flow from the action done, but what might seem bad in one case might be in fact the highest good, and what might seem good in another case might, in fact, lead to the greatest evil. Just a hair's line divides the Divine from the Satanic. And that hair's line consists, not in this nor in that mode of conduct, but in the clearly presented motive or intention of the one who acts. A good motive can never produce altogether evil results, and yet a good motive is not enough. We may have the best motive in the world, but if we have not also knowledge and wisdom, we may unintentionally do a wrong thing when we intended to do good; and sometimes we may do a good thing when we intended to do evil. Thus true morality may be seen to lie not in the act itself, but in the motive; it depends on the knowledge and intelligence of the being acting.

The lines of true morality may go anywhere, but by this is not meant that we do evil that good may come! How could we do evil if our perception is good, if our knowledge is clear, if our motive is unquestioned and without self-interest? No imaginable evil could flow under such conditions, which are of the nature of the Spirit. The widest range of intelligence and wisdom are required to make it possible for no evil effects to flow even if good is intended. Wisdom is always required, because the very nature and essence of our being is wisdom itself, the object of wisdom, and that which is to be obtained by wisdom. There is nothing higher than that essence of our being, and we may consciously gain it by first setting aside all those ideas that conflict with it, and then, acting from the basis of our spiritual nature, from the basis of absolute, unerring Law. Once these ideas are held in mind to the exclusion of all other separative ideas, unity of Spirit, unity of thought and unity of action take place.

This great philosophy of Theosophy, then, presents a basis from which the truest kind of morality can be perceived. True morality does not depend upon words, phrases, or conventions, but upon a universal perception of all things, whereby everything is done for good, every thought and feeling expended for the benefit of others rather than for one's self. A clear perception of one's own spiritual nature, and the motive to benefit mankind in every direction and in every case, without self-interest, are the two essentials for true morality. True morality is, in fact, a universal existence, and the beginning of it is in the desire to live to benefit mankind without self-interest or hope of any reward whatever; then, to practice and to help those who know still less than we do.

This is quite the reverse of prevailing religious ideas of personal salvation, yet this universal existence is our salvation. At once, when these universal ideas are seen and to some extent realized, one loses all fears. Neither change nor death, nor things present or to come, can have any effect upon that one. He meets conditions as they come, does what he can, and lets other conditions succeed them. He moves through life, far from an unhappy being, quite capable of taking all the joy and pleasure that exist in the world – all that upon which his fellow-men only subsist or hope to subsist. He moves among his fellow-men, understanding everything that they are going through, enjoying with their joy and sorrowing when they sorrow, yet himself free from either joy or sorrow. When we arrive at that condition, our sense of morality will be based on the nature of man. We shall then look on each and every being as of the same kind as ourselves, differing only in degree of understanding. There cannot be in us anything but tolerance and mercy, for we shall know we cannot judge others in their struggles; we cannot say that there is good in this case, bad in that; we shall understand that goodness and badness are entirely relative in men, while they perceive the Reality not at all; we shall see that the best thing we can do for anyone is to assist him to understand himself, so that he may reach that point of perception and knowledge and power which is, in reality, his own and which he has but to realize.

Man's false conceptions of life are what prevent him from knowing the truth, and it is evident that the first step towards true perception lies in throwing aside the prejudices and predilections he has lived by. And there is always help. Never have we been left alone. Always there are beings greater in evolution than we, who return to this field of physical existence to help us, to wake us up to a perception of our natures. Such has been the mission of all Divine Incarnations down the ages. Those beings have come and lived among us, have become "in all things like unto us," as was said of Jesus, in order that the human words They spoke should be words we would understand. They meet us on the basis of our ideas and try to clarify them and set them in a true course. They can do nothing to stop what we have done and what we want to do; They cannot interfere; but They can help us to see the right direction, if we are so willed; They can give help when we turn to that direction which They indicate – that Path which They themselves followed so many ages ago. Always They try to help us, even when we are proceeding along wrong lines and bringing upon ourselves the suffering such wrong lines entail – even then They try to direct the results into a better channel. They hold back the awful Karma that would shake the world, and let the effects come so gradually that we can stand and bear them. That is part of the protective power of the spiritual nature, and it operates in every direction.

It is for us, then, to say which way we shall go. We are not creatures of circumstance. We are not the creatures of environment. We are their creators. It is for us to see that we think right, that we build right, that we build upon the strong foundation of the eternal verities, and that we keep our eyes upon that Path which the great Masters of Wisdom have sought to open before us. So in our turn we shall point out the Way among the hosts who are moving in delusion and ignorance, and as we help each one, we help ourselves. As we help ourselves by helping others, we raise all.

Universal Theosophy
Robert Crosbie

THEOSOPHICAL GLOSSARY

A

Absoluteness. When predicated of the UNIVERSAL PRINCIPLE, it denotes an abstract noun, which is more correct and logical than to apply the adjective "absolute " to that which has neither attributes nor limitations, nor can IT have any.

Adam (Heb.). In the *Kabalah* Adam is the "only-begotten", and means also "red earth". (See "Adam-Adami" in the *S.D.* II p. 452.) It is almost identical with *Athamas* or *Thomas*, and is rendered into Greek by *Didumos*, the "twin"– Adam, "the first", in chap. 1 of *Genesis,* being shown, "male-female."

Adam Kadmon *(Heb)*. Archetypal Man; Humanity. The "Heavenly Man" not fallen into sin; Kabalists refer it to the Ten Sephiroth on the plane of human perception. [w.w.w.]

In the *Kabalah* Adam Kadmon is the manifested Logos corresponding to our *Third* Logos; the Unmanifested being the first paradigmic ideal Man, and symbolizing the Universe in *abscondito*, or in its "privation" in the Aristotelean sense. The First Logos is the "Light of the World", the Second and the Third – its gradually deepening shadows.

Adept (*Lat.*). *Adeptus*, "He who has obtained." In Occultism one who has reached the stage of Initiation, and become a Master in the science of Esoteric philosophy.

Âditi (*Sk.*). The Vedic name for the *Mûlaprakriti* of the Vedantists; the abstract aspect of Parabrahman, though both unmanifested and unknowable. In the *Vedas* Âditi is the "Mother-Goddess", her terrestrial symbol being infinite and shoreless space.

Adwaita (*Sk.*). A Vedânta sect. The non-dualistic (A-dwaita) school of Vedântic philosophy founded by Sankarâchârya, the greatest of the historical Brahmin sages. The two other schools are the Dwaita (dualistic) and the Visishtadwaita; all the three call themselves Vedântic.

Adwaitin (*Sk.*). A follower of the said school.

Æther (*Gr.*). With the ancients the divine luminiferous substance which pervades the whole universe, the "garment" of the Supreme Deity, Zeus, or Jupiter. With the moderns, Ether, for the meaning of which in physics and chemistry see Webster's *Dictionary* or any other. In esotericism Æther is the third principle of the Kosmic Septenary; the Earth being the lowest, then the Astral light, Ether and *Âkâsa* (phonetically *Âkâsha*) the highest.

Agathodæmon (*Gr.*). The beneficent, good Spirit as contrasted with the bad one, Kakodæmon. The "Brazen Serpent" of the Bible is the former; the flying serpents of fire are an aspect of Kakodæmon. The Ophites called Agathodæmon the Logos and Divine Wisdom, which in the Bacchanalian Mysteries was represented by a serpent erect on a pole.

Agathon (*Gr.*). Plato's Supreme Deity. Lit., "The Good", our ALAYA, or "Universal Soul".

Agni (*Sk.*). The God of Fire in the Veda; the oldest and the most revered of Gods in India. He is one of the three great deities: Agni, Vâyu and Sûrya, and also all the three, as he is the triple aspect of fire; in heaven as the Sun; in the atmosphere or air (Vâyu), as Lightning; on. earth, as ordinary Fire. Agni belonged to the earlier Vedic *Trimûrti* before Vishnu was given a place of honour and before Brahmâ and Siva were invented.

Agnishwattas (*Sk.*). A class of Pitris, the creators of the first ethereal race of men. Our solar ancestors as contrasted with the *Barhishads,* the "lunar" Pitris or ancestors, though otherwise explained in the *Purânas.*

Aham (*Sk.*). "I" – the basis of *Ahankâra*, Self-hood.

Ahankâra (*Sk.*). The conception of "I", Self-consciousness or Self- identity; the "I", the egotistical and *mâyâvic* principle in man, due to our ignorance which separates our "I" from the Universal ONE-SELF Personality, Egoism.

Ain Soph (*Heb.*). The "Boundless" or Limitless; Deity emanating and extending. [w.w.w.]

Ain Soph is also written *En Soph* and *Ain Suph*, no one, not even Rabbis, being sure of their vowels. In the religious metaphysics of the old Hebrew philosophers, the ONE Principle was an abstraction, like Parabrahmam, though modern Kabbalists have succeeded now, by dint of mere sophistry and paradoxes, in making a "Supreme God" of it and nothing higher. But with the early Chaldean Kabbalists Ain Soph is "without form or being", having "no likeness with anything else" (Franck, *Die Kabbala,* p. 126). That Ain Soph has never been considered as the "Creator" is proved by even such an orthodox Jew as Philo calling the "Creator" the *Logos*, who stands next the "Limitless One", and the "Second God". "The Second God is its (Ain Soph's) wisdom", says Philo *(Quaest. et Solut.)*. Deity is NO-THING; it is nameless, and therefore called Ain Soph; the word *Ain* meaning NOTHING. (See Franck's *Kabbala*, p. 153 ff.)

Aitareya *(Sk.).* The name of an Aranyaka (Brâhmana) and a Upanishad of the *Rig Veda.* Some of its portions are purely Vedântic.

Akâsa *(Sk.).* The subtle, supersensuous spiritual essence which pervades all space; the primordial substance erroneously identified with Ether. But it is to Ether what Spirit is to Matter, or *Âtmâ* to *Kâma-rûpa.* It is, in fact, the Universal Space in which lies inherent the eternal Ideation of the Universe in its ever-changing aspects on the planes of matter and objectivity, and from which radiates the *First Logos*, or expressed thought. This is why it is stated in the *Purânas* that Âkâsa has but one attribute, namely sound, for sound is but the translated symbol of Logos – "Speech" in its mystic sense. In the same sacrifice (*the Jyotishtoma Agnishtoma*) it is called the "God Âkâsa". In these sacrificial mysteries Âkâsa is the all-directing 'and omnipotent Deva who plays the part of Sadasya, the superintendent over the magical effects of the religious performance, and it had its own appointed Hotri (priest) in days of old, who took its name. The Âkâsa is the indispensable agent of every *Krityâ* (magical performance) religious or profane. The expression "to stir up the Brahmâ", means to stir up the power which lies latent at the bottom of every magical operation, Vedic sacrifices being in fact nothing if not ceremonial magic. This power is the Âkâsa – in another aspect, *Kundalini* – occult electricity, the alkahest of the alchemists in one sense, or the universal solvent, the same *anima mundi* on the higher plane as the *astral light* is on the lower. "At the moment of the sacrifice the priest becomes imbued with the spirit of Brahmâ, is, for the time being, Brahmâ himself". *(Isis Unveiled).*

Alaya *(Sk.).* The Universal Soul (See *Secret Doctrine* Vol. I. pp. 47 *et seq.*). The name belongs to the Tibetan system of the contemplative *Mahâyâna* School. Identical with *Âkâsa* in its mystic sense, and with *Mulâprâkriti,* in its essence, as it is the basis or root of all things.

Amânasa *(Sk.).* The " Mindless", the early races of this planet; also certain Hindu gods.

Ambhâmsi *(Sk.)*. A name of the chief of the Kumâras Sanat-Sujâta, signifying the "waters". This epithet will become more comprehensible when we remember that the later type of Sanat-Sujâta was Michael, the Archangel, who is called in the Talmud "the Prince of *Waters*", and in the Roman Catholic Church is regarded as the patron of gulfs and promontories. Sanat-Sujâta is the immaculate son of the immaculate mother (Ambâ or Aditi, chaos and space) or the "waters" of limitless space. (See *Secret Doctrine-*, Vol. I., p. 460.)

Androgyne Ray *(Esot.)*. The first differentiated ray; the Second Logos; Adam Kadmon in the *Kabalah;* the "male and female created he them", of the first chapter of *Genesis.*

Anima Mundi *(Lat.)*. The"Soul of the World", the same as the *Alaya* of the Northern Buddhists; the divine essence which permeates, animates and informs all, from the smallest atom of matter to man and god. It is in a sense the "seven-skinned mother" of the stanzas in the *Secret Doctrine*, the essence of seven planes of sentience, consciousness and differentiation, moral and physical. In its highest aspect it is *Nirvâna*, in its lowest Astral Light. It was feminine with the Gnostics, the early Christians and the Nazarenes; bisexual with other sects, who considered it only in its four lower planes. Of igneous, ethereal nature in the objective world of form (and then ether), and divine and spiritual in its three higher planes. When it is said that every human soul was born by detaching itself from the *Anima Mundi*, it means, esoterically, that our higher Egos are of an essence identical with **It,** which is a radiation of the ever unknown Universal ABSOLUTE.

Annamaya Kosha *(Sk.)*. A Vedantic term. The same as *Sthûla Sharîra* or the physical body. It is the first "sheath" of the *five* sheaths accepted by the Vedantins, a sheath being the same as that which is called "principle" in Theosophy.

Anoia *(Gr.)*. "Want of understanding", "folly". *Anoia* is the name given by Plato and others to the lower *Manas* when too closely allied with Kâma, which is irrational *(agnoia)*. The Greek word agnoia is evidently a derivation from and cognate to the Sanskrit word *ajnâna* (phonetically, *agnyana*) or ignorance, irrationality, absence of knowledge. (See "Agnoia" and "Agnostic".)

Antahkarana *(Sk.)*., or Antaskarana. The term has various meanings, which differ with every school of philosophy and sect. Thus

Sankârachârya renders the word as "understanding"; others, as "the internal instrument, the Soul, formed by the thinking principle and egoism"; whereas the Occultists explain it as the *path* or bridge between the Higher and the Lower *Manas,* the divine *Ego,* and the *personal* Soul of man. It serves as a medium of communication between the two, and conveys from the Lower to the Higher Ego all those personal impressions and thoughts of men which can, by their nature, be assimilated and stored by the undying Entity, and be thus made immortal with it, these being the only elements of the evanescent *Personality* that survive death and time. It thus stands to reason that only that which is noble, spiritual and divine in man can testify in Eternity to his having lived.

Anthropomorphism (*Gr.*). From "anthropos" meaning man. The act of endowing god or gods with a human form and human attributes or qualities.

Anugîtâ (*Sk.*). One of the *Upanishads.* A very occult treatise. (*See The sacred Books of the East.*)

Anupâdaka (*Sk.*). Anupapâdaka, also Aupapâduka; means parentless", "self-existing", born without any parents or progenitors. A term applied to certain self-created gods, and the Dhyâni Buddhas.

Arjuna (*Sk.*) Lit., the "white". The third of the five Brothers Pandu or the reputed Sons of Indra (esoterically the same as Orpheus). A disciple of Krishna, who visited him and married Su-bhadrâ, his sister, besides many other wives, according to the allegory. During the fratricidal war between the *Kauravas* and the *Pândavas,* Krishna instructed him in the highest philosophy, while serving as his charioteer. (*See Bhagavad Gîtâ.*)

Arûpa (*Sk.*). "Bodiless", formless, as opposed to *rûpa,* "body", or form.

Arvâksrotas (*Sk.*). The *seventh* creation, that of man, in the *Vishnu Purâna.*

Âryasangha (*Sk.*) The Founder of the *first* Yogâchârya School. This Arhat, a direct disciple of Gautama, the Buddha, is most unaccountably mixed up and confounded with a personage of the same name, who is said to have lived in Ayôdhya (Oude) about the fifth or sixth century of our era, and taught Tântrika worship in addition to the Yogâchârya system. Those who sought to make it popular, claimed that he was the same Âryasangha, that had been a follower of Sâkyamuni, and that he was 1,000 years old. Internal evidence alone is sufficient to show that the works written by him and translated about the year 600 of our era, works full of Tantra worship, ritualism, and tenets followed now considerably by the "red-cap" sects in Sikhim, Bhutan, and Little Tibet, cannot be the same as the lofty system of the early Yogâcharya school of pure Buddhism, which is neither northern nor southern, but absolutely esoteric. Though none of the genuine Yogâchârya books (the *Narjol chodpa*) have ever been made public or marketable, yet one finds in the *Yogâchârya Bhûmi Shâstra* of the *pseudo-Âryasangha* a great deal from the older system, into the tenets of which he may have been initiated. It is, however, so mixed up with Sivaism and Tantrika magic and superstitions, that the work defeats its own end, notwithstanding its remarkable dialectical subtilty. (See the *Theosophical Glossary*)

Asakrit Samâdhi (Sk.). A certain degree of ecstatic contemplation. A stage in *Samâdhi.*

Âsana *(Sk.).* The third stage of *Hatha Yoga,* one of the prescribed postures of meditation.

Ashta Siddhis *(Sk.).* The eight consummations in the practice of Hatha Yoga.

Astral Body, or Astral "Double". The ethereal counterpart or shadow of man or animal. The ***Linga Sharira,*** the "Doppelgäinger". The reader must not confuse it with the ASTRAL SOUL, another name for the lower *Manas,* or Kama-*Manas* so-called, the reflection of the HIGHER EGO.

Astral Light *(Occult)* The invisible region that surrounds our globe, as it does every other, and corresponding as the second Principle of Kosmos (the third being Life, of which it is the vehicle) to the *Linga Sharira* or the Astral Double in man. A subtle Essence visible only to a clairvoyant eye, and the lowest but one (*viz.,* the earth), of the Seven Akâsic or Kosmic Principles. Eliphas Levi calls it the great Serpent and the Dragon from which radiates on Humanity every evil influence. This is so; but why not add that the Astral Light gives out nothing but what it has received; that it is the great terrestrial crucible, in which the vile emanations of the earth (moral and physical) upon which the Astral Light is fed, are all converted into their subtlest essence, and radiated back intensified, thus becoming epidemics – moral, psychic and physical. Finally, the Astral Light is the same as the *Sidereal Light* of Paracelsus and other Hermetic philosophers. "Physically, it is the ether of modern science. Metaphysically, and in its spiritual, or occult sense, ether is a great deal more than is often imagined. In occult physics, and alchemy, it is well demonstrated to enclose within its shoreless waves not only Mr. Tyndall's *'promise* and potency of every quality of life', but also the *realization* of the potency of every quality of spirit. Alchemists and Hermetists believe that their *astral*, or sidereal ether, besides the above properties of sulphur, and white and red magnesia, or *magnes*, is the *anima mundi,* the workshop of Nature and of all the Kosmos, spiritually, as well as physically. The 'grand magisterium' asserts itself in the phenomenon of mesmerism, in the 'levitation' of human and inert objects; and may be called the ether from its spiritual aspect. The designation *astral* is ancient, and was used by some of the Neo-platonists, although it is claimed by some that the word was coined by the Martinists. Porphyry describes the celestial body which is always joined with the soul as 'immortal, luminous, and star-like'. The root of this word may be found, perhaps, in the Scythic *Aist-aer* – which means star, or the Assyrian *Istar,* which, according to Burnouf has the same sense." *(Isis Unveiled.)*

Asuras *(Sk.)*. Exoterically, elementals and evil, gods – considered maleficent; demons, and *no* gods. But esoterically – the reverse. For in the most ancient portions of the *Rig Veda,* the term is used for the Supreme Spirit, and therefore the Asuras are spiritual and divine It is only in the last book of the *Rig Veda*, its latest part, and in the *Atharva Veda,* and the *BrâhManas,* that the epithet, which had been given to Agni, the greatest Vedic Deity, to Indra and Varuna, has come to signify the reverse of gods. *Asu* means breath, and it is with his breath that Prajâpati (Brahmâ) creates the Asuras. When ritualism and dogma got the better of the Wisdom religion, the initial letter **a** was adopted as a negative prefix, and the term ended by signifying "not a god", and Sura only a deity. But in the Vedas the Suras have ever been connected with *Surya,* the sun, and regarded as *inferior* deities, devas.

Aswattha *(Sk.)* The **Bo-tree**, the tree of knowledge, *ficus religiosa.*

Atmâ (or **Atman**) *(Sk.)*. The Universal Spirit, the divine Monad, the 7th Principle, so-called, in the septenary constitution of man. The Supreme Soul.

Atma-bhu *(Sk.)*. Soul-existence, or existing as soul. (See "*Alaya*".)

Atmabodha *(Sk.)*. Lit., "Self-knowledge"; the title of a Vedantic treatise by Sankârachârya.

Atma-jnâni *(Sk.)* The Knower of the World-Soul, or Soul in general.

Atma Vidyâ *(Sk.)*. The highest form of spiritual knowledge; lit., "Soul-knowledge".

Atri, Sons of (*Sk.*). A class of Pitris, the "ancestors of man", or the so-called Prâjapâti, "progenitors"; one of the seven Rishis who form the constellation of the Great Bear.

Attavada (*Pali*). The sin of personality.

Aum (*Sk.*). The sacred syllable; the triple-lettered unit; hence the trinity in One.

Avalokiteswara (*Sk.*) "The on-looking Lord" In the exoteric interpretation, he is Padmapâni (the lotus bearer and the lotus-born) in Tibet, the first divine ancestor of the Tibetans, the complete incarnation or Avatar of Avalokiteswara; but in esoteric philosophy Avaloki, the "on-looker", is the Higher Self, while Padmapâni is the Higher Ego or *Manas*. The mystic formula "Om mani padme hum" is specially used to invoke their joint help. While popular fancy claims for Avalokiteswara many incarnations on earth, and sees in him, not very wrongly, the spiritual guide of every believer, the esoteric interpretation sees in him the Logos, both celestial and human. Therefore, when the Yogâchârya School has declared Avalokiteswara as Padmâpani "to be the Dhyâni Bodhisattva of Amitâbha Buddha", it is indeed, because the former is *the spiritual reflex in the world of forms* of the latter, both being one – one in heaven, the other on earth.

Avatâra (*Sk.*) Divine incarnation. The descent of a god or some exalted Being, who has progressed beyond the necessity of Rebirths, into the body of a simple mortal. Krishna was an avatar of Vishnu. The Dalai Lama is regarded as an avatar of Avalokiteswara, and the Teschu Lama as one of Tson-kha-pa, or Amitâbha. There are two kinds of avatars: those born from woman, and the parentless, the *anupapâdaka*.

Avidyâ (*Sk.*). Opposed to *Vidyâ*, Knowledge. Ignorance which proceeds from, and is produced by the illusion of the Senses or *Viparyaya*.

B.

Barhishad (*Sk.*). A class of the "lunar" Pitris or "Ancestors", Fathers, who are believed in popular superstition to have kept up in their past incarnations the household sacred flame and made fire-offerings. Esoterically the Pitris who evolved their shadows or *chhayas* to make there-with the first man. (See *Secret Doctrine*, Vol. II.)

Bhagavad-Gita (*Sk.*). Lit., "the Lord's Song". A portion of the Mahabharata, the great epic poem of India. It contains a dialogue wherein Krishna—the "Charioteer"—and Arjuna, his Chela, have a discussion upon the highest spiritual philosophy. The work is pre-eminently occult or esoteric.

Bhagavat (*Sk.*). A title of the Buddha and of Krishna. "The Lord" literally.

Bhâshya (*Sk*) A commentary.

Bodhisattva (*Sk*). Lit., "he, whose essence (*sattva*) has become intelligence (*bodhi*)"; those who need but one more incarnation to become perfect Buddhas, i.e., to be entitled to Nirvâna. This, as applied to *Manushi* (terrestrial) Buddhas. In the metaphysical sense, *Bodhisattva* is a title given to the sons of the celestial *Dhyâni* Buddhas.

Brahma (*Sk.*). The student must distinguish between Brahma the neuter, and Brahmâ, the male creator of the Indian Pantheon. The former, Brahma or Brahman, is the impersonal, supreme and uncognizable Principle of the Universe from the essence of which all emanates, and into which all returns, which is incorporeal, immaterial, unborn, eternal, beginningless and endless. It is all-pervading, animating the highest god as well as the smallest mineral atom. Brahmâ on the other hand, the male and the alleged Creator, exists periodically in his manifestation only, and then again goes into pralaya, i.e., disappears and is annihilated.

Brahmâ's Day. A period of 2,160,000,000 years during which Brahmâ having emerged out of his golden egg (*Hiranyagarbha*), creates and fashions the material world (being simply the fertilizing and creative force in Nature). After this period, the worlds being destroyed in turn, by fire and water, he vanishes with objective nature, and then comes Brahmâ's Night.

Brahmâ's Night. A period of equal duration, during which Brahmâ. is said to be asleep. Upon awakening he recommences the process, and this goes on for an AGE of Brahmâ composed of alternate "Days", and "Nights", and lasting 100 years (of 2,160,000,000 years each). It requires fifteen figures to express the duration of such an age; after the expiration of which the *Mahapralaya* or the Great Dissolution sets in, and lasts in its turn for the same space of fifteen figures.

Brahmâ Vâch (*Sk*) Male and female Brahmâ. Vâch is also some-times called the female logos; for Vâch means Speech, literally. (See *Manu* Book I., and *Vishnu Purâna*.)

Brahma Vidyâ (*Sk*) The knowledge, the esoteric science, about the two Brahmas and their true nature.

Brahmâ Virâj (*Sk.*) The same: Brahmâ separating his body into two halves, male and female, creates in them Vâch and Virâj. In plainer terms and *esotericlly* Brahmâ the Universe, differentiating, produced thereby material nature, Virâj, and spiritual intelligent Nature, Vâch – which is the *Logos* of Deity or the manifested expression of the eternal divine Ideation.

Brâhman (*Sk.*) The highest of the four castes in India, one supposed or rather fancying himself, as high among men, as Brahman, the ABSOLUTE of the Vedantins, is high among, or above the gods.

Brahmâputrâs (*Sk.*) The Sons of Brahmâ.

Buddha (*Sk.*). Lit., "The Enlightened". The highest degree of knowledge. To become a Buddha one has to break through the bondage of sense and personality; to acquire a complete perception of the REAL SELF and learn not to separate it from all otherselves; to learn by experience the utter unreality of all phenomena of the visible Kosmos foremost of all; to reach a complete detachment from all that is evanescent and finite, and live while yet on Earth in the immortal and the everlasting alone, in a supreme state of holiness.

Buddhi (*Sk.*). Universal Soul or Mind. *Mahâbuddhi* is a name of *Mahat* (see "Alaya"); also the spiritual Soul in man (the sixth principle), the vehicle of Atmâ exoterically the seventh.

Buddhism. Buddhism is now split into two distinct Churches : the Southern and the Northern Church. The former is said to be the purer form, as having preserved more religiously the original teachings of the Lord Buddha. It is the religion of Ceylon, Siam, Burmah and other places, while Northern Buddhism is confined to Tibet, China and Nepaul. Such a distinction, however, is incorrect. If the Southern Church is nearer, in that it has not departed, except perhaps in some trifling dogmas due to the many councils held after the death of the Master, from the public or *exoteric* teachings of Sâkyamuni – the Northern Church is the outcome of Siddhârta Buddha's esoteric teachings which he confined to his elect Bhikshus and Arhats. In fact, Buddhism in the present age, cannot he justly judged either by one or the other of its exoteric popular forms. Real Buddhism can be appreciated only by blending the philosophy of the Southern Church and the metaphysics of the Northern Schools. If one seems too iconoclastic and stero:, and the other too metaphysical and transcendental, even to being overgrown with the weeds of Indian exotericism – many of the gods of its Pantheon having been transplanted under new names to Tibetan soil – it is entirely due to the popular expression of Buddhism in both Churches. Correspondentially they stand in their relation to each other as Protestantism to Roman Catholicism. Both err by an excess of zeal and erroneous interpretations, though neither the Southern nor the Northern Buddhist clergy have ever departed from truth consciously, still less have they acted under the dictates of *priestocracy*, ambition, or with an eye to personal gain and power, as the two Christian Churches have.

C

Causal Body. This "body", which is no body either objective or subjective, but *Buddhi,* the Spiritual Soul, is so called because it is the direct cause of the Sushupti condition, leading to the *Turya* state, the highest state of *Samadhi*. It is called *Karanopadhi*, "the basis of the Cause", by the Târaka Raja Yogis; and in the Vedânta system it corresponds to both the *Vignânamaya* and *Anandamaya Kosha*, the latter coming next to Atma, and therefore being the vehicle of the universal Spirit. Buddhi alone could not be called a "Causal Body ", but becomes so in conjunction with *Manas*, the incarnating Entity or EGO.

Chakra (*Sk.*) A wheel, a disk, or the circle of Vishnu generally. Used also of a cycle of time, and with other meanings.

Chaldeans, or *Kasdim.* At first a tribe, then a caste of learned Kabbalists. They were the *savants,* the magians of Babylonia, astrologers and diviners. The famous Hillel, the precursor of Jesus in philosophy and in ethics, was a Chaldean. Franck in his *Kabbala* points to the close resemblance of the "secret doctrine" found in the *Avesta* and the religious metaphysics of the Chaldees.

Chelâ (*Sk.*) A disciple, the pupil of a Guru or Sage, the follower of some adept of a school of philosophy (*lit.*, child).

Chhâyâ (*Sk.*) "Shade" or " Shadow". The name of a creature produced by Sanjnâ, the wife of Surya, from herself (astral body). Unable to endure the ardour of her husband, Sanjnâ left Chhâyâ in her place as a wife, going herself away to perform austerities. Chhâyâ is the astral image of a person in esoteric philosophy.

Chhaya loka (*Sk.*) The world of Shades; like Hades, the world of the *Eidola* and *Umbræ*. We call it *Kâmaloka*.

Chidâkâsam (Sk); The field, or basis of consciousness.

Chohan (*Tib.*) "Lord" or "Master" ; a chief; thus **Dhyan-Chohan** would answer to "Chief of the Dhyanis", or celestial Lights – which in English would be translated Archangels.

Chréstos (*Gr.*) The early Gnostic form of Christ. It was used in the fifth century B.C. by Æschylus, Herodotus, and others. The *Manteumata pythochresta,* or the "oracles delivered by a Pythian god" "through a pythoness, are mentioned by the former (*Choeph.*901). *Chréstian* is not only "the seat of an oracle", but an offering to, or for, the oracle.

Chréstés is one who explains oracles, "a prophet and soothsayer", and Chrésterios one who serves an oracle or a god. The earliest Christian writer, Justin Martyr, in his first *Apology* calls his co-religionists Chréstians. It is only through ignorance that men call themselves Christians instead of Chréstians," says Lactantius (lib. iv., cap. vii.). The terms Christ and Christians, spelt originally Chrést and Chréstians, were borrowed from the Temple vocabulary of the Pagans. Chréstos meant in that vocabulary a disciple on probation, a candidate for hierophantship. When he had attained to this through initiation, long trials, and suffering, and had been *"anointed"* (i.e., "rubbed with oil", as were Initiates and even idols of the gods, as the last touch of ritualistic observance), his name was changed into Christos, the "purified", in esoteric or mystery language. In mystic symbology, indeed, *Christés*, or *Christos,* meant that the "Way", the Path, was already trodden and the goal reached ; when the fruits of the arduous labour, uniting the personality of evanescent clay with the indestructible INDIVIDUALITY, transformed it thereby into the immortal EGO. "At the end of the Way stands the *Chréstes*", the *Purifier,* and the union once accomplished, the *Chrestos,* the "man of sorrow", became *Christos* himself. Paul, the Initiate, knew this, and meant this precisely, when he is made to say, in bad translation : "I travail in birth again until Christ be formed in you" (Gal. iv.19), the true rendering of which is . . . "until ye form the Christos within yourselves" But the profane who knew only that Chréstés was in some way connected with priest and prophet, and knew nothing about the hidden meaning of Christos, insisted, as did Lactantius and Justin Martyr, on being called *Chréstians* instead of Christians. Every good individual, therefore, may find Christ in his "inner man" as Paul expresses it (Ephes. iii. 16,17), whether he be Jew, Mussulman, Hindu, or Christian. Kenneth Mackenzie seemed to think that the word *Chréstos* was a synonym of Soter, "an appellation assigned to deities, great kings and heroes," indicating "Saviour," – and he was right. For, as he adds:"It has been applied redundantly to Jesus Christ, whose name Jesus or Joshua bears the same interpretation. The name Jesus, in fact, is rather a title of honour than a name – the true name of the Soter of Christianity being Emmanuel, or God with us (*Matt*.i, 23.).Great divinities among all nations, who are represented as expiatory or self-sacrificing, have been designated by the same title." *(R. M. Cyclop*.) The Asklepios (or Æsculapius) of the Greeks had the title of *Soter*.

Cosmic Gods. Inferior gods, those connected with the formation of matter.

Cosmic ideation (*Occult*.) Eternal thought, impressed on substance or spirit-matter, in the eternity ; thought which becomes active at the beginning of every new life-cycle.

Cycle. From the Greek *Kuklos*. The ancients divided time into end less cycles, wheels within wheels, all such periods being of various durations, and each marking the beginning or the end of some event either cosmic, mundane, physical or metaphysical. There were cycles of only a few years, and cycles of immense duration, the great Orphic cycle, referring to the ethnological change of races, lasting 120,000 years, and the cycle of Cassandrus of 136,000, which brought about a complete change in planetary influences and their correlations between men and gods – a fact entirely lost sight of by modern astrologers.

D

Dæmon (*Gr*.) In the original Hermetic works and ancient classics it has a meaning identical with that of "god", "angel" or "genius". The Dæmon of Socrates is the incorruptible part of the man, or rather the real inner man which we call Nous or the rational divine Ego. At all events the Dæmon (or Daimon of the great Sage was surely not the demon of the Christian Hell or of Christian orthodox theology. The name was given by ancient peoples, and especially the philosophers of the Alexandrian school, to all kinds of spirits, whether good or bad, human or otherwise. The appellation is often synonymous with that of gods or angels. But some philosophers tried, with good reason, to make a just distinction between the many classes.

Daitya Guru (*Sk*.) The instructor of the giants, called *Daityas (q.v.)* Allegorically, it is the title given to the planet Venus-Lucifer, or rather to its indwelling Ruler, *Sukra,* a male deity (See *Sec. Doct.*. ii. p. 30).

Daityas (*Sk.*) Giants, Titans, and exoterically demons, but in truth identical with certain Asuras, the intellectual gods, the opponents of the useless gods of ritualism and the enemies of *puja* sacrifices.

Daksha (*Sk.*) A form of Brahmâ and his son in the Purânas But the *Rig Veda* states that "Daksha sprang from Aditi, and Aditi from Daksha", which proves him to be a personified correlating Creative Force acting on *all the planes.* The Orientalists seem very much perplexed what to make of him; but Roth is nearer the truth than any, when saying that Daksha is the spiritual power, and at the same time the male energy that generates the gods in eternity, which is represented by Aditi. The Purânas as a matter of course, anthropomorphize the idea, and show Daksha instituting "sexual intercourse on this earth", after trying every other means of procreation. The generative Force, spiritual at the commencement, becomes of course at the most material end of its evolution a procreative Force on the physical plane ; and so far the Purânic allegory is correct, as the Secret Science teaches that our present mode of procreation began towards the end of the third Root-Race.

Dangma (*Sk.*) In Esotericism a purified Soul. A Seer and an Initiate; one who has attained full wisdom.

Darsanas (*Sk.*) The Schools of Indian philosophy, of which there are six; *Shad-darsanas* or six demonstrations.

Day of Brahmâ. See "Brahmâ's Day" etc.

Demiurgic Mind. The same as "Universal Mind". *Mahat*, the first "product" of Brahmâ, or himself.

Demiurgos (*Gr*) The Demiurge or Artificer; the Supernal Power which built the universe. Freemasons derive from this word their phrase of "Supreme Architect ". With the Occultists it is the third manifested Logos, or Plato's "second god", the second logos being represented by him as the "Father", the only Deity that he dared mention as an Initiate into the Mysteries.

Demons. According to the Kabbalah, the demons dwell in the world of Assiah, the world of matter and of the "shells'" of the dead. They are the Klippoth. There are Seven Hells, whose demon dwellers represent the vices personified. Their prince is Samael, his female companion is Isheth Zenunim – the woman of prostitution: united in aspect, they are named "The Beast", Chiva. [w.w.w.]

Demon est Deus inversus (*Lat*) A Kabbalistic axiom; lit., "the devil is god reversed"; which means that there is neither evil nor good, but that the forces which create the one create the other, according to the nature of the materials they find to work upon.

Deva (*Sk.*). A god, a "resplendent" deity. Deva-Deus, from the root *div* "to shine". A Deva is a celestial being – whether good, bad, or indifferent. Devas inhabit "the three worlds", which are the *three planes* above us. There are 33 groups or 330 millions of them.

Deva Sarga (*Sk.*). Creation: the origin of the principles, said to be Intelligence born of the qualities or the attributes of nature.

Devachan (*Sk.*). The "dwelling of the gods". A state intermediate between two earth-lives, into which the EGO (Atmâ-Buddhi-*Manas*, or the Trinity made One) enters, after its separation from Kâma Rupa, and the disintegration of the lower principles on earth.

Devajnânas (*Sk.*). or *Daivajna*. The higher classes of celestial beings, those who possess divine knowledge.

Deva-lôkas (*Sk.*). The abodes of the Gods or Devas in superior spheres. The seven celestial worlds above Meru.

Devamâtri (*Sk.*). Lit., "the mother of the gods". A title of Aditi, Mystic Space.

Dhârana (*Sk*). That state in Yoga practice when the mind has to be fixed unflinchingly on some object of meditation.

Dhâranî (*Sk.*). In Buddhism—both Southern and Northern—and also in Hinduism, it means simply a *mantra* or *mantras*—sacred verses from the *Rig Veda*. In days of old these mantras or Dhâranî were all considered mystical and practically efficacious in their use. At present, however, it is the Yogâchârya school alone which proves the claim in practice. When chanted according to given instructions a **Dhâranî** produces wonderful effects. Its occult power, however, does not reside in the *words* but in the inflexion or accent given and the resulting sound originated thereby. (See "Mantra" and "Akasa").

Dharma (*Sk.*). The sacred Law; the Buddhist Canon.

Dharmachakra (*Sk.*). Lit., The turning of the "wheel of the Law". The emblem of Buddhism as a system of cycles and rebirths or reincarnations.

Dharmakâya (*Sk*). Lit., "the glorified spiritual body" called the "Vesture of

Bliss". The third, or highest of the *Trikâya* (Three Bodies), the attribute developed by every "Buddha", i.e., every initiate who has crossed or reached the end of what is called the "fourth Path" (in esotericism the sixth "portal" prior to his entry on the seventh). The highest of the *Trikâya,* it is the *fourth* of the *Buddhakchêtra,* or Buddhic planes of consciousness, represented figuratively in Buddhist asceticism as a robe or vesture of luminous Spirituality. In popular Northern Buddhism these vestures or robes are: (1) Nirmanakâya (2) Sambhogakâya (3) and Dharmakâya the last being the highest and most sublimated of all, as it places the ascetic on the threshold of Nirvâna. (See, however, the *Voice of the Silence,* page 96, *Glossary,* for the true *esoteric* meaning.)

Dhyan Chohans (*Sk*). Lit., "The Lords of Light". The highest gods, answering to the Roman Catholic Archangels. The divine Intelligences charged with the supervision of Kosmos.

Dhyâna (*Sk.*). In Buddhism one of the six Paramitas of perfection, a state of abstraction which carries the ascetic practising it far above this plane of sensuous   perception   and   out   of   the   world   of   matter. Lit., "contemplation". The six stages of Dhyan differ only in the degrees of abstraction of the personal Ego from sensuous life.

Dhyani Bodhisattyas (*Sk.*). In Buddhism, the five sons of the Dhyani-Buddhas. They have a mystic meaning in Esoteric Philosophy.

Dhyani Buddhas (*Sk.*). They "of the Merciful Heart"; worshipped especially in Nepaul. These have again a secret meaning.

Dianoia (*Gr.*). The same as the Logos. The eternal source of thought, "divine ideation", which is the root of all thought. (See "Ennoia.")

Djnâna (*Sk*), or *Jnâna.* Lit., Knowledge; esoterically, "supernal or divine knowledge acquired by Yoga". Written also *Gnyana.*

Drakôn (*Gr.*) or Dragon. Now considered a "mythical" monster, perpetuated in the West only on seals,. &c., as a heraldic griffin, and the Devil slain by St. George, &c. In fact an extinct antediluvian monster In Babylonian antiquities it is referred to as the "scaly one" and connected on many gems with Tiamat the sea. "The Dragon of the Sea" is repeatedly mentioned. In Egypt, it is the star of the Dragon (then the North Pole Star), the origin of the connection of almost all the gods with the Dragon. Bel and the Dragon, Apollo and Python, Osiris and Typhon, Sigur and Fafnir, and finally St. George and the Dragon, are the same. They were all solar gods, and wherever we find the Sun there also is the Dragon, the symbol of Wisdom—Thoth-Hermes. The Hierophants of Egypt and of Babylon styled themselves "Sons of the Serpent-God" and "Sons of the Dragon". "I am a Serpent, I am a Druid", said the Druid of the Celto-Britannic regions, for the Serpent and the Dragon were both types of Wisdom, Immortality and Rebirth. As the serpent casts its old skin only to reappear in a new one, so does the immortal Ego cast off one personality but to assume another.

Dwapara Yuga (*Sk.*). The third of the "Four Ages" in Hindu Philosophy; or the second age counted from below.

Dynasties. In India there are two, the Lunar and the Solar, or the *Somavansa* and the *Suryavansa*. In Chaldea and Egypt there were also two distinct kinds of dynasties, the *divine* and the *human*. In both countries people were ruled in the beginning of time by Dynasties of Gods. In Chaldea they reigned one hundred and twenty Sari, or in all 432,000 years; which amounts to the same figures as a Hindu Mahayuga 4,320,000 years. The chronology prefacing the *Book of Genesis* (English translation) is given "Before Christ, 4004". But the figures are a rendering by solar years. In the original Hebrew, which preserved a lunar calculation, the figures are 4,320 years. This "coincidence" is well explained in Occultism.

Dzyan or Dzyn (*Tib.*). Written also *Dzen*. A corruption of the Sanskrit Dhyan and *jnâna* (or *gnyâna* phonetically) – Wisdom, divine knowledge. In Tibetan, learning is called *dzin*.

E

Ego (*Lat.*). " Self" ; the consciousness in man "I am I" – or the feeling of "I-am-ship". Esoteric philosophy teaches the existence of two Egos in man, the mortal or personal, and the Higher, the Divine and the Impersonal, calling the former "personality" and the latter "Individuality Egoity. From the word "Ego". Egoity means "individuality", never "personality", and is the opposite of egoism or "selfishness", the characteristic par excellence of the latter.

Elementals. Spirits of the Elements. The creatures evolved in the four Kingdoms or Elements – earth, air, fire, and water. They are called by the Kabbalists, Gnomes (of the earth), Sylphs (of the air), Salamanders (of the fire), and Undines (of the water). Except a few of the higher kinds, and their rulers, they are rather forces of nature than ethereal men and women. These forces, as the servile agents of the Occultists, may produce various effects; but if employed by" Elementaries" *(q.v.)*_in which case they enslave the mediums – they will deceive the credulous. All the lower invisible beings generated on the 5th 6th, and 7th planes of our terrestrial atmosphere, are called Elementals Peris, Devs, Djins, Sylvans, Satyrs, Fauns, Elves, Dwarfs, Trolls, Kobolds, Brownies, Nixies, Goblins, Pinkies, Banshees, Moss People, White Ladies, Spooks, Fairies, etc., etc., etc.

Elementaries. Properly, the disembodied souls of the depraved; these souls having at some time prior to death separated from themselves their divine spirits, and so lost their chance for immortality; but at the present stage of learning it has been thought best to apply the term to the spooks or phantoms of disembodied persons, in general, to those whose temporary habitation is the Kâma Loka. Eliphas Lévi and some other Kabbalists make little distinction between elementary spirits who have been men, and those beings which people the elements, and are the blind forces of nature. Once divorced from their higher triads and their bodies, these souls remain in their *Kâma-rupic* envelopes, and are irresistibly drawn to the earth amid elements congenial to their gross natures. Their stay in the Kâma Loka varies as to its duration; but ends invariably in disintegration, dissolving like a column of mist, atom by atom, in the surrounding elements.

Elohîm *(Heb.).* Also *Alhim,* the word being variously spelled. Godfrey Higgins, who has written much upon its meaning, always spells it *Aleim.* The Hebrew letters are *aleph, lamed, hé,yod, mem,* and are numerically 1, 30, 5, 10, 40 = 86. It seems to be the plural of the feminine noun *Eloah,* ALH, formed by adding the common plural form IM, a masculine ending; and hence the whole seems to imply the emitted active and passive essences. As a title it is referred to "Binah" the Supernal Mother, as is also the fuller title IHVH ALHIM, Jehovah Elohim. As Binah leads on to seven succeedent Emanations, so " Elohim" has been said to represent a sevenfold power of godhead. [w.w. w.]

Emanation *the Doctrine of.* In its metaphysical meaning, it is opposed to Evolution, yet one with it. Science teaches that evolution is physiologically a mode of generation in which the germ that develops the foetus pre-exists already in the parent, the development and final form and characteristics of that germ being accomplished in nature; and that in cosmology the process takes place blindly through the correlation of the elements, and their various compounds. Occultism answers that this is only the ***apparent*** mode, the real process being Emanation, guided by intelligent Forces under an immutable LAW. Therefore, while the Occultists and Theosophists believe thoroughly in the doctrine of Evolution as given out by Kapila and Manu, they are *Emanationists* rather than *Evolutionists.* The doctrine of Emanation was at one time universal. It was taught by the Alexandrian as well as by the Indian philosophers, by the Egyptian, the Chaldean and Hellenic Hierophants, and also by the Hebrews (in their Kabbala, and even in *Genesis)*. For it is only owing to deliberate mistranslation that the Hebrew word asdt has been translated "angels" from the Septuagint, when it means *Emanations, Æons*, precisely as with the Gnostics. Indeed, in Deuteronomy (xxxiii., 2) the word *asdt* or *ashdt* is translated as" fiery law", whilst the correct rendering of the passage should be "from his right hand went [not a fiery law, but a fire according to law "; viz., that the fire of one flame is imparted to, and caught up by another like as in a trail of inflammable substance. This is precisely emanation. As shown in Isis Unveiled : "In Evolution, as it is now beginning to he understood, there is supposed to be in all matter an impulse to take on a higher form – a supposition clearly expressed by Manu and other Hindu philosophers of the highest antiquity. The philosopher's tree illustrates it in the case of the zinc solution. The controversy between the followers of this school and the Emanationists may he briefly stated thus The Evolutionist stops all inquiry at the borders of ' the Unknowable "; the Emanationist believes that nothing can be evolved – or, as the word means, unwombed or born – except it has first been involved, thus indicating that life is from a spiritual potency above the whole."

En (or **Ain**) **Soph** (*Heb.*). The endless, limitless and boundless. The absolute deific Principle, impersonal and unknowable. It means literally "no-thing" i.e., nothing that could be classed with anything else. The word and ideas are equivalent to the Vedantic conceptions of Parabrahmn. [w.w.w.]

Some Western Kabbalists, however, contrive to make of IT, a personal "He", a male deity instead of an impersonal deity.

Epimetheus (*Gr.*). Lit., "He who takes counsel *after*" the event. A brother of Prometheus in Greek Mythology.

Epinoia (*Gr.*). Thought, invention, design. A name adopted by the Gnostics for the first passive Æon.

Eros (*Gr.*). Hesiod makes of the god Eros the third personage of the

Hellenic primordial Trinity composed of Ouranos, Gæa and Eros. It is the personified procreative Force in nature in its abstract sense, the propeller to "creation" and procreation. Exoterically, mythology makes of Eros the god of lustful, animal desire, whence the term *erotic* esoterically, it is different. (See " Kâma".)

Esoteric (*Gr.*). Hidden, secret. From the Greek *esotericos*, "inner" concealed.

Esoteric Bodhism. Secret wisdom or intelligence from the Greek *esotericos* "inner", and the Sanskrit *Bodhi*, "knowledge", intelligence – in contradistinction to *Buddhi*, "the *faculty* of knowledge or intelligence" and *Buddhism*, the philosophy or Law of Buddha (the Enlightened). Also written " Budhism", from *Budha* (Intelligence and Wisdom) the Son of Soma.

Ether. Students are but too apt to confuse this with Akâsa and with Astral Light. It is neither, in the sense in which ether is described by physical Science. Ether is a material agent, though hitherto undetected by any physical apparatus; whereas Akâsa is a distinctly spiritual agent, identical, in one sense, with the Anima Mundi, while the Astral Light is only the seventh and highest principle of the terrestrial atmosphere, as undetectable as Akâsa and real Ether, because it is something quite on another plane. The seventh principle of the earth's atmosphere, as said, the Astral Light, is only the second on the Cosmic scale. The scale of Cosmic Forces, Principles and Planes, of Emanations – on the metaphysical – and Evolutions – on the physical plane – is the Cosmic Serpent biting its own tail, the Serpent reflecting the Higher, and reflected in its turn by the lower Serpent. The Caduceus explains the mystery, and the four-fold Dodecahedron on the model of which the universe is said by Plato to have been built by the manifested Logos – synthesized by the unmanifested First-Born – yields geometrically the key to Cosmogony and its microcosmic reflection – our Earth.

Evolution. The development of higher orders of animals from lower. As said in *Isis Unveiled:* "Modern Science holds but to a one-sided physical evolution, prudently avoiding and ignoring the higher or spiritual evolution, which would force our contemporaries to confess the superiority of the ancient philosophers and psychologists over themselves. The ancient sages, ascending to the UNKNOWABLE, made their starting-point from the first manifestation of the unseen, the unavoidable, and, from a strictly logical reasoning, the absolutely necessary creative Being, the Demiurgos of the universe. Evolution began with them from pure spirit, which descending lower and lower down, assumed at last a visible and comprehensible form, and became matter. Arrived at this point, they speculated in the Darwinian method, but on a far more large and comprehensive basis." (See "Emanation".)

Exoteric. Outward, public; the opposite of esoteric or hidden.

F

First Point. Metaphysically the first point of manifestation, the germ of primeval differentiation, or the point in the infinite Circle "whose centre is everywhere, and circumference nowhere". The Point is the Logos.

Fire (*Living*). A figure of speech to denote deity, the "One" life. A theurgic term, used later by the Rosicrucians. The symbol of the *living fire* is the sun, *certain of whose rays develope the fire of life in a diseased body, impart the knowledge of the future* to the sluggish mind, and stimulate to active function a certain psychic and generally dormant faculty in man. The meaning is very occult.

Fohat (*Tib.*). A term used to represent the active (male) potency of the Sakti (female reproductive power) in nature. The essence of cosmic electricity. An occult Tibetan term for *Daiviprakriti* primordial light: and in the universe of manifestation the ever-present electrical energy and ceaseless destructive and formative power. Esoterically, it is the same, Fohat being the universal propelling Vital Force, at once the propeller and the resultant.

G

Gautama (*Sk.*) The Prince of Kapilavastu, son of Sudhôdana, the Sâkya king of a small realm on the borders of Nepaul, born in the seventh century B.c., now called the "Saviour of the World". Gautama or Gôtama was the sacerdotal name of the Sâkya family, and Sidhârtha was Buddha's name before he became a Buddha. Sâkya Muni, means the Saint of the Sâkya family. Born a simple mortal he rose to Buddhaship through his own personal and unaided merit. A man—verily greater than any god!

Gayâtri (*Sk.*) also *Sâvitri*. A most sacred verse, addressed to the Sun, in the Rig -Veda, which the Brahmans have to repeat mentally every morn and eve during their devotions.

Genii (*Lat.*) A name for Æons, or angels, with the Gnostics. The names of their hierarchies and classes are simply legion.

Gnâna (*Sk.*) Knowledge as applied to the esoteric sciences.

Gnân Devas (*Sk.*) Lit., "the gods of knowledge". The higher classes of gods or devas; the "mind-born" sons of Brahmâ, and others including the *Manasa*-putras (the Sons of Intellect). Esoterically, our reincarnating Egos.

Gnânasakti (Sk.) The power of true knowledge, one of the seven great forces in Nature (*six*, exoterically).

Gnôsis (*Gr.*) Lit., "knowledge". The technical term used by the schools of religious philosophy, both before and during the first centuries of so-called Christianity, to denote the object of their enquiry. This Spiritual and Sacred Knowledge, the *Gupta Vidya* of the Hindus, could only be obtained by Initiation into Spiritual Mysteries of which the ceremonial "Mysteries" were a type.

Gnostics (*Gr.*) The philosophers who formulated and taught the Gnôsis or Knowledge (*q.v.*). They flourished in the first three centuries of the Christian era: the following were eminent, Valentinus, Basilides, Marcion, Simon Magus, etc. [w.w. w.]

Golden Age. The ancients divided the life cycle into the Golden, Silver, Bronze and Iron Ages. The Golden was an age of primeval purity, simplicity and general happiness.

Great Age. There were several "great ages" mentioned by the ancients. In India it embraced the whole Maha-manvantara, the "age of Brahmâ", each "Day" of which represents the life cycle of a chain – i.e. it embraces a period of seven Rounds. (See *Esoteric Buddhism,* by A. P. Sinnett.) Thus while a "Day" and a "Night" represent, as Manvantara and Pralaya, 8,640,000,000 years, an "age" lasts through a period of 311,040,000,000,000 years; after which the Pralaya, or dissolution of the universe, becomes universal. With the Egyptians and Greeks the "great age" referred only to the tropical or sidereal year, the duration of which is 25,868 solar years. Of the complete age – that of the gods – they say nothing, as it was a matter to he discussed and divulged only in the Mysteries, during the initiating ceremonies. The "great age" of the Chaldees was the same in figures as that of the Hindus.

Grihastha (*Sk.*) Lit., "a householder", "one who lives in a house with his family". A Brahman " family priest" in popular rendering, and the sarcerdotal hierarchy of the Hindus.

Guardian Wall. A suggestive name given to the host of translated adepts

(Narjols) or the Saints collectively, who are supposed to watch over, help and protect Humanity. This is the so-called "Nirmanâkâya" doctrine in Northern mystic Buddhism. (See *Voice of the Silence*, Part III.)

Guhya Vidyâ(*Sk.*) The secret knowledge of mystic Mantras.

Gunas (*Sk*) Qualities, attributes (See" Triguna") ; a thread, also a cord.

Gupta Vidyâ (*Sk.*) The same as Guhya Vidyâ; Esoteric or Secret Science; knowledge.

Guru (*Sk.*) Spiritual Teacher; a master in metaphysical and ethical doctrines; used also for a teacher of any science.

Guru Deva (*Sk.*) Lit., "divine Master".

H

Hatha Yoga (*Sk.*) The lower form of Yoga practice; one which uses physical means for purposes of spiritual self-development The opposite of *Râja Yoga.*

Hermaphrodite (*Gr.*). Dual-sexed; a male and female Being, whether man or animal.

Hermes Trismegistus (*Gr.*). The "thrice great Hermes", the Egyptian. The mythical personage after whom the Hermetic philosophy was named. In Egypt the God Thoth or Thot. A generic name of many ancient Greek writers on philosophy and Alchemy. Hermes Trismegistus is the name of Hermes or Thoth in his human aspect, as a god he is far more than this. As *Hermes-Thoth-Aah*, he is Thoth, the moon, i.e., his symbol is the bright side of the moon, supposed to contain the essence of creative Wisdom, "the elixir of Hermes ". As such he is associated with the Cynocephalus, the dog-headed monkey, for the same reason as was Anubis, one of the aspects of Thoth. (See " Hermanubis".) The same idea underlies the form of the Hindu God of Wisdom, the elephant-headed Ganesa, or Ganpat, the son of Parvati and Siva. (See "Ganesa".) When he has the head of an *ibis,* he is the sacred scribe of the gods; but even then he wears the crown *atef* and the lunar disk. He is the most mysterious of gods. As a serpent, Hermes Thoth is the divine creative 'Wisdom. The Church Fathers speak at length of Thoth-Hermes. (See "Hermetic".)

Hermetic. Any doctrine or writing connected with the esoteric teachings of Hermes, who, whether as the Egyptian Thoth or the Greek Hermes, was the God of Wisdom with the Ancients, and, according to Plato, "discovered numbers, geometry, astronomy and letters". Though mostly considered as spurious, nevertheless the Hermetic writings were highly prized by St. Augustine, Lactantius, Cyril and others. In the words of Mr. J. Bonwick, " They are more or less touched up by the Platonic philosophers among the early Christians (such as Origen and Clemens Alexandrinus) who sought to substantiate their Christian arguments by appeals to these heathen and revered writings, though they could not resist the temptation of making them say a little too much. Though represented by some clever and interested writers as teaching pure monotheism, the Hermetic or Trismegistic books are, nevertheless, purely pantheistic. The Deity referred to in them is defined by Paul as that in *which* "we live, and move and have our being" – notwithstanding the "in Him" of the translators.

Hierophant. From the Greek "Hierophantes"; literally, "One who explains sacred things ". The discloser of sacred learning and the Chief of the Initiates. A title belonging to the highest Adepts in the temples of antiquity, who were the teachers and expounders of the Mysteries and the Initiators into the final great Mysteries. The Hierophant represented the Demiurge, and explained to the postulants for Initiation the various phenomena of Creation that were produced for their tuition. " He was the sole expounder of the esoteric secrets and doctrines. It was forbidden even to pronounce his name before an uninitiated person. He sat in the East, and wore as a symbol of authority a golden globe suspended from the neck. He was also called *Mystagogus*" (Kenneth R. H. Mackenzie, ix., F.T.S., in *The Royal Masonic cyclopædia*). In Hebrew and Chaldaic the term was *Peter*, the opener, discloser; hence the Pope as the successor of the hierophant of the ancient Mysteries, sits in the Pagan chair of St. Peter.

Higher Self. The Supreme Divine Spirit overshadowing man. The crown of the upper spiritual Triad in man – Atmân.

Hochmah (*Heb.*). See "Chochmah".

Hotri (*Sk.*). A priest who recites the hymns from the *Rig Veda*, and makes oblations to the fire.

Hotris (*Sk*). A symbolical name for the *seven* senses called, in the *Anugita* "the Seven Priests". "The senses supply the fire of mind (i.e., desire) with the oblations of external pleasures." An occult term used metaphysically.

Humanity. Occultly and Kabbalistically, the whole of mankind is symbolised, by Manu in India; by Vajrasattva or Dorjesempa, the head of the Seven Dhyani, in Northern Buddhism; and by Adam Kadmon in the Kabbala. All these represent the totality of mankind whose beginning is in this androgynic protoplast, and whose end is in the Absolute, beyond all these symbols and myths of human origin. Humanity is a great Brotherhood by virtue of the sameness of the material from which it is formed physically and morally. Unless, however, it becomes a Brotherhood also intellectually, it is no better than a superior genus of animals.

I

Ichchha (*Sk.*). Will, or will-power.

Ichchha Sakti (*Sk.*). Will-power; force of desire; one of the occult Forces of nature. That power of the will which, exercised in occult practices, generates the nerve-currents necessary to set certain muscles in motion and to paralyze certain others.

Illusion. In Occultism everything finite (like the universe and all in it) is called illusion or *maya.*

Illuminati (*Lat.*). The "Enlightened", the initiated adepts.

Image. Occultism permits no other image than that of the living image of divine man (the symbol of Humanity) on earth. The *Kabbala* teaches that this divine Image, the copy of the *sublime and holy upper Image* (the Elohim) has now changed into *another similitude*, owing to the development of men's sinful nature. It is only the *upper divine Image* (the Ego) which is the same; the lower (personality) has changed, and man, now fearing the wild beasts, has grown to bear on his face the similitude of many of them. (*Zohar* I. fol. 71a.) In the early period of Egypt there were no images; but later, as Lenormand says, "In the sanctuaries of Egypt they divided the properties of nature and consequently of Divinity (the Elohim, or the Egos), into seven abstract qualities, characterised each by an emblem, which are matter, cohesion, fluxion, coagulation, accumulation, station and division ". These were all attributes symbolized in various images.

Incarnations (*Divine*) or *Avatars*. The Immaculate Conception is as pre-eminently Egyptian as it is Indian. As the author of *Egyptian Belief* has it: "It is not the vulgar, coarse and sensual story as in Greek mythology, but refined, moral and spiritual "; and again the incarnation idea was found revealed on the wall of a Theban temple by Samuel Sharpe, who thus analyzes it: "First the god Thoth . . . as the messenger of the gods, like the Mercury of the Greeks (or the Gabriel of the first Gospel), tells the *maiden* queen Mautmes, that she is to give birth to a son, who is to be king Amunotaph III. Secondly, the god Kneph, the Spirit . . . . and the goddess Hathor (Nature) both take hold of the queen by the hands and put into her mouth the character for life, a cross, which is to be the life of the coming child", etc., etc. Truly divine incarnation, or the *avatar* doctrine, constituted the grandest mystery of every old religious system!

Individuality. One of the names given in Theosophy and Occultism to the Human Higher EGO. We make a distinction between the immortal and divine Ego, and the mortal human Ego which perishes. The latter, or "personality" (personal Ego) survives the dead body only for a time in the Kama Loka; the Individuality prevails forever.

Initiate. From the Latin *Initiatus*. The designation of anyone who was received into and had revealed to him the mysteries and secrets of either Masonry or Occultism. In times of antiquity, those who had been initiated into the arcane knowledge taught by the Hierophants of the Mysteries; and in our modern days those who have been initiated by the adepts of mystic lore into the mysterious knowledge, which, notwithstanding the lapse of ages, has yet a few real votaries on earth.

Initiation. From the same root as the Latin *initia,* which means the basic or first principles of any Science. The practice of initiation or admission into the sacred Mysteries, taught by the Hierophants and learned priests of the Temples, is one of the most ancient customs. This was practised in every old national religion. In Europe it was abolished with the fall of the last pagan temple. There exists at present but one kind of initiation known to the public, namely that into the Masonic rites. Masonry, however, has no more secrets to give out or conceal. In the palmy days of old, the Mysteries, according to the greatest Greek and Roman philosophers, were the most sacred of all solemnities as well as the most beneficent, and greatly promoted virtue. The Mysteries represented the passage from mortal life into finite death, and the experiences of the disembodied Spirit and Soul in the world of subjectivity. In our own day, as the secret is lost, the candidate passes through sundry meaningless ceremonies and is initiated into the solar allegory of Hiram Abiff, the "Widow's Son".

Inner Man. An occult term, used to designate the true and immortal Entity in us, not the outward and mortal form of clay that we call our body. The term applies, strictly speaking, only to the Higher Ego, the "astral man" being the appellation of the Double and of Kâma Rupa (*q.v.*) or the surviving *eidolon*.

Intercosmic gods. The Planetary Spirits, Dhyan-Chohans, Devas of various degrees of spirituality, and "Archangels" in general.

Isis. In Egyptian *Issa,* the goddess Virgin-Mother; personified nature. In Egyptian or Koptic *Uasari,* the female reflection of *Uasar* or Osiris. She is the "woman clothed with the sun" of the land of Chemi. Isis Latona is the Roman Isis.

Iswara (*Sk.*). The "Lord" or the personal god – *divine Spirit in man. Lit.,* sovereign (independent) existence. A title given to Siva and other gods in India. Siva is also called Iswaradeva, or sovereign deva.

J

Jhâna (*Sk.*) or *Jnana.* Knowledge; Occult Wisdom.

Jiva *(Sk.).* Life, as the Absolute; the Monad also or "Atma-Buddhi".

Jivanmukta (*Sk.*). An adept or yogi who has reached the ultimate state of holiness, and separated himself from matter; a *Mahatma,* or *Nirvânee,* a "dweller in bliss" and emancipation. Virtually one who has reached Nirvâna during life.

Jivatma (*Sk.*). The ONE universal life, generally; but also the divine Spirit in Man.

Jnânam (*Sk.*). The same as "Gnâna", etc., the same as "Jhâna" (*q.v.*).

Jnânendriyas (*Sk.*). The five channels of knowledge.

Jnâna Sakti (*Sk.*). The power of intellect.

K

Kadmon (*Heb.*). Archetypal man. See."Adam Kadmon".

Kaliyuga (*Sk.*). The fourth, the black or iron age, our present period, the duration of which us 432,000 years. The last of the ages into which the evolutionary period of man is divided by a series of such ages. It began 3,102 years B.C. at the moment of Krishna's death, and the first cycle of 5,ooo years will end between the years 1897 and 1898.

Kalpa (*Sk.*). The period of a mundane revolution, generally a cycle of time, but usually, it represents a "day" and "night" of Brahmâ, a period of 4,320,000,000 years.

Kama (*Sk.*) Evil desire, lust, volition; the cleaving to existence. Kama is generally identified with *Mara* the tempter.

Kamadeva (*Sk.*). In the popular notions the god of love, a Visva-deva, in the Hindu Pantheon. As the *Eros* of Hesiod, degraded into Cupid by exoteric law, and still more degraded by a later popular sense attributed to the term, so is Kama a most mysterious and metaphysical subject. The earlier Vedic description of Kama alone gives the key-note to what he emblematizes. Kama is the first conscious, *all embracing desire* for universal good, love, and for all that lives and feels, needs help and kindness, the first feeling of infinite tender compassion and mercy that arose in the consciousness of the creative ONE Force, as soon as it came into life and being as a ray from the ABSOLUTE. Says the *Rig Veda*, "Desire first arose in IT, which was the primal germ of mind, and which Sages, searching with their intellect, have discovered in their heart to be the bond which connects Entity with non-Entity", or *Manas* with pure *Atma-Buddhi*. There is no idea of sexual love in the conception. Kama is pre-eminently the divine desire of creating happiness and love; and it is only ages later, as mankind began to materialize by anthropomorphization its grandest ideals into cut and dried dogmas, that Kama became the power that gratifies desire on the animal plane. This is shown by what every *Veda* and some *BrahManas* say. In the *Atharva Veda*, Kama is represented as the Supreme Deity and Creator. In the Taitarîya Brahmana, he is the child of Dharma, the god of Law and Justice, of Sraddha and faith. In another account he springs from the heart of Brahmâ. Others show him born from water, i.e., from primordial chaos, or the "Deep". Hence one of his many names, *Irâ-ja*, "the water-born"; and *Aja*, "unborn" ; and *Atmabhu* or "Self-existent". Because of the sign of *Makara* (Capricornus) on his banner, he is also called " Makara Ketu". The allegory about Siva, the "Great Yogin ", reducing Kama to ashes by the fire from his *central* (or third) *Eye*, for inspiring the Mahadeva with thoughts of his wife, while he was at his devotions – is very suggestive, as it is said that he thereby reduced Kama to his primeval spiritual form.

Kamaloka (*Sk.*). The *semi*-material plane, to us subjective and invisible, where the disembodied "personalities", the astral forms, called *Kamarupa* remain, until they fade out from it by the complete exhaustion of the effects of the mental impulses that created these eidolons of human and animal passions and desires; (See "Kamarupa".) It is the Hades of the ancient Greeks and the Amenti of the Egyptians, the land of Silent Shadows; a division of the first group of the *Trailôkya*. (See "Kamadhâtu".)

Kamarupa (*Sk.*). Metaphysically, and in our esoteric philosophy, it is the subjective form created through the mental and physical desires and thoughts in connection with things of matter, by all sentient beings, a form which survives the death of their bodies. After that death three of the seven "principles" – or let us say planes of senses and consciousness on which the human instincts and ideation act in turn – viz., the body, its astral prototype and physical vitality, – being of no further use, remain on earth; the three higher principles, grouped into one, merge into the state of Devachan (*q.v.*), in which state the Higher Ego will remain until the hour for a new reincarnation arrives; and the *eidolon* of the ex-Personality is left alone in its new abode. Here, the pale copy of the man that was, vegetates for a period of time, the duration of which is variable and according to the element of materiality which is left in it, and which is determined by the past life of the defunct. Bereft as it is of its higher mind, spirit and physical senses, if left alone to its own senseless devices, it will gradually fade out and disintegrate. But, if forcibly drawn back into the terrestrial sphere whether by the passionate desires and appeals of the surviving friends or by regular necromantic practices – one of the most pernicious of which is medium- ship – the "spook" may prevail for a period greatly exceeding the span of the natural life of its body. Once the Kamarupa has learnt the way back to living human bodies, it becomes a vampire, feeding on the vitality of those who are so anxious for its company. In India these *eidolons* are called *Pisâchas,* and are much dreaded, as already explained elsewhere.

Kapila Rishi (*Sk.*). A great sage, a great adept of antiquity; the author of the Sankhya philosophy.

Karabtanos (*Gr.*). The spirit of blind or animal desire; the symbol of Kama-rupa. The Spirit "without sense or judgment" in the Codex of the Nazarenes. He is the symbol of matter and stands for the father of the seven spirits of concupiscence begotten by him on his mother, the "Spiritus" or the Astral Light.

Kârana (*Sk.*). Cause (metaphysically).

Kârana Sarîra (*Sk.*). The "Causal body". It is dual in its meaning. Exoterically, it is Avidya, ignorance, or that which is the cause of the evolution of a human ego and its reincarnation ; hence the lower *Manas* esoterically – the causal body or Kâranopadhi stands in the Taraka Raja yoga as corresponding to Buddhi and the Higher " *Manas,*" or Spiritual Soul.

Kâranopadhi (*Sk.*). The basis or *upadhi* of Karana, the "causal soul". In Taraka Rajayoga, it corresponds with both *Manas* and *Buddhi.* See Table in the *Secret Doctrine*, Vol. I, p. 157.

Karma (*Sk.*). Physically, action: metaphysically, the LAW OF RETRIBUTION, the Law of cause and effect or Ethical Causation. Nemesis, only in one sense, that of bad Karma. It is the eleventh *Nidana* in the concatenation of causes and effects in orthodox Buddhism ; yet it is the power that controls all things, the resultant of moral action, the meta physical *Samskâra*, or the moral effect of an act committed for the attainment of something which gratifies a personal desire. There is the Karma of merit and the Karma of demerit. Karma neither punishes nor rewards, it is simply *the one* Universal LAW which guides unerringly, and, so to say, blindly, all other laws productive of certain effects along the grooves of their respective causations. When Buddhism teaches that "Karma is that moral kernel (of any being) which alone survives death and continues in transmigration ' or reincarnation, it simply means that there remains nought after each Personality but the causes produced by it ; causes which are undying, i.e., which cannot be eliminated from the Universe until replaced by their legitimate effects, and wiped out by them, so to speak, and such causes – unless compensated during the life of the person who produced them with adequate effects, will follow the reincarnated Ego, and reach it in its subsequent reincarnation until a harmony between effects and causes is fully reestablished. No "personality" – a mere bundle of material atoms and of instinctual and mental characteristics – can of course continue, as such, in the world of pure Spirit. Only that which is immortal in its very nature and divine in its essence, namely, the Ego, can exist for ever. And as it is that Ego which chooses the personality it will inform, after each Devachan, and which receives through these personalities the effects of the Karmic causes produced, it is therefore the Ego, that *self* which is the "moral kernel" referred to and embodied karma, "which alone survives death."

Kartikeya (*Sk*), or *Kartika.* The Indian God of War, son of Siva, born of his seed fallen into the Ganges. He is also the personification of the power of the Logos. The planet Mars. Kartika is a very occult personage, a nursling of the Pleiades, and a Kumâra. (See *Secret Doctrine.*)

Kasyapa (*Sk.*). A Vedic Sage; in the words of *Atharva Veda*, "The self-born who sprang from Time". Besides being the father of the Adityas headed by Indra, Kasyapa is also the progenitor of serpents, reptiles, birds and other walking, flying and creeping beings.

Kosmos (*Gr.*). The Universe, as distinguished from the world, which may mean our globe or earth.

Krishna *(Sk.)..* The most celebrated avatar of Vishnu, the "Saviour" of the Hindus and their most popular god. He is the- eighth Avatar, the son of Devaki, and the nephew of Kansa, the Indian King Herod, who while seeking for him among the shepherds and cow-herds who concealed him, slew thousands of their newly-born babes. The story of Krishna's conception, birth, and childhood are the exact prototype of the New Testament story. The missionaries, of course, try to show that the Hindus stole the story of the Nativity from the early Christians who came to India.

Krita-Yuga *(Sk.).* The first of the four Yugas or Ages of the Brahmans; also called *Satya-Yuga*, a period lasting 1,728,000 years.

Kriyasakti (Gk.). The power of thought; one of the seven forces of Nature. Creative potency of the *Siddhis* (powers) of the full Yogis.

Kronos *(Gr.).* Saturn. The God of Boundless Time and of the Cycles.

Kshanti *(Sk.).* Patience, one of the *Paramîtas* of perfection.

Kshetrajna or *Kshetrajneswara* *(Sk.).* Embodied spirit, the Conscious Ego in its highest manifestations; the reincarnating Principle; the "Lord" in us.

Kumâra *(Sk.).* A virgin boy, or young celibate. The first Kumâras are the seven sons of Brahmâ born out of the limbs of the god, in the so-called ninth creation. It is stated that the name was given to them owing to their formal refusal to "procreate their species", and so they "remained Yogis", as the legend says.

Kundalini Sakti *(Sk.).* The power of life; one of the Forces of Nature; that power that generates a certain light in those who sit for spiritual and clairvoyant development. It is a power known only to those who practise concentration and Yoga.

L

Lanoo *(Sk.).* A disciple, the same as "chela".

Laya or *Layam* *(Sk.).* From the root *Li* "to dissolve, to disintegrate" a point of equilibrium (*zero-point*) in physics and chemistry. In occultism, that point where substance becomes homogeneous and is unable to act or differentiate.

Lha *(Tib.).* Spirits of the highest spheres, whence the name of Lhassa, the residence of the Dalaï-Lama. The title of Lha is often given in Tibet to some *Narjols* (Saints and Yogi adepts) who have attained great occult powers.

Lhamayin (*Tib.*). Elemental sprites of the lower terrestrial plane. Popular fancy makes of them demons and devils.

Linga or *Lingam* (*Sk.*). A sign or a symbol of abstract creation. Force becomes the organ of procreation only on this earth. In India there are 12 great Lingams of Siva, some of which are on mountains and rocks, and also in temples. Such is the *Kedâresa* in the Himalaya, a huge and shapeless mass of rock. In its origin the Lingam had never the gross meaning connected with the phallus, an idea which is altogether of a later date. The symbol in India has the same meaning which it had in Egypt, which is simply that the creative or procreative Force is divine. It also denotes who was the dual Creator – male and female, Siva and his Sakti. The gross and immodest idea connected with the phallus is not Indian but Greek and pre-eminently Jewish. The Biblical *Bethels* were real priapic stones, the " Beth-el" (phallus) wherein God dwells. The same symbol was concealed within the ark of the Covenant, the "Holy of Holies". Therefore the "Lingam" even as a phallus is not "a symbol of Siva" only, but that of every "Creator" or creative god in every nation, including the Israelites and their "God of Abraham and Jacob".

Linga Purâna (*Sk.*). A scripture of the Saivas or worshippers of Siva. Therein *Maheswara*, "the great Lord", concealed in the Agni Linga explains the ethics of life – duty, virtue, self-sacrifice and finally liberation by and through ascetic life at the end of the *Agni Kalpa* (the Seventh Round). As Professor Wilson justly observed "the Spirit of the worship (phallic) is as little influenced by the character of the type as can well be imagined. *There is nothing like the phallic orgies of antiquity; it is all mystical and spiritual.*"

Linga Sharîra (*Sk.*). The "body", i.e., the aerial symbol of the body. This term designates the *döppelganger* or the "astral body" of man or animal. It is the *eidolon* of the Greeks, the vital and *prototypal* body; the reflection of the men of flesh. It is born *before* and dies or fades out, with the disappearance of the last atom of the body.

Lipikas (*Sk.*). The celestial recorders, the "Scribes", those who record every word and deed, said or done by man while on this earth. As Occultism teaches, they are the agents of KARMA – the retributive Law.

Logos (*Gr.*). The manifested deity with every nation and people; the outward expression, or the effect of the cause which is ever concealed.

Thus, speech is the Logos of thought; hence it is aptly translated by the "Verbum" and "Word" in its metaphysical sense.

Loka (*Sk.*). A region or circumscribed place. In metaphysics, a world or sphere or plane. The Purânas in India speak incessantly of seven and fourteen Lokas, above, and below our earth; of heavens and hells.

Lotus (*Gr.*). A most occult plant, sacred in Egypt, India and else where; called "the child of the Universe bearing the likeness of its mother in its bosom". There was a time "when the world was a golden lotus" (*padma*) says the allegory. A great variety of these plants, from the majestic Indian lotus, down to the marsh-lotus (bird's foot trefoil) and the Grecian "Dioscoridis", is eaten at Crete and other islands. It is a species of nymphala, first introduced from India to Egypt to which it was-not indigenous. See the text of *Archaic Symbolism* in the Appendix Viii. "The Lotus, as a Universal Symbol".

Lucifer (*Lat.*). The planet Venus, as the bright "Morning Star". Before Milton, Lucifer had never been a name of the Devil. Quite the reverse, since the Christian Saviour is made to say of himself in *Revelations* (xvi. 22.) "I am . . . the bright morning star" or Lucifer. One of the early Popes of Rome bore that name; and there was even a Christian sect in the fourth century which was called the *Luciferians*.

Lunar Pitris (Gods). Called in India the Fathers, "Pitris" or the lunar ancestors. They are subdivided, like the rest, into seven classes or Hierarchies, In Egypt although the moon received less worship than in Chaldea or India, still Isis stands as the representative of Luna-Lunus, "the celestial Hermaphrodite". Strange enough while the modern connect the moon only with lunacy and generation, the ancient nations, who knew better, have, individually and collectively, connected their "wisdom gods" with it. Thus in Egypt the lunar gods are Thoth-Hermes and Chons; in India it is Budha, the Son of *Soma,* the moon; in Chaldea Nebo is the lunar god of Secret Wisdom, etc., etc. The wife of Thoth, *Sifix,* the lunar goddess, holds a pole with five rays or the five-pointed star, symbol of man, the Microcosm, in distinction from the Septenary Macrocosm. As in all theogonies a goddess precedes a god, on the principle most likely that the chick can hardly precede its egg, in Chaldea the moon was held as older and more venerable than the Sun, because, as they said, darkness precedes light at every periodical rebirth (or "creation") of the universe. Osiris although connected with the Sun and a Solar god is, nevertheless, born on Mount *Sinai*, because *Sin* is the Chaldeo-Assyrian word for the moon; so was Dio-Nysos, god of Nyssi or *Nisi*, which latter appelation was that of Sinai in Egypt, where it was called Mount Nissa. The *crescent* is not – as proven by many writers – an ensign of the Turks, but was adopted by Christians for their symbol before the Mahommedans. For ages the crescent was the emblem of the Chaldean Astarte, the Egyptian Isis, and the Greek Diana, all of them Queens of Heaven, and finally became the emblem of Mary the Virgin. "The Greek Christian Empire of Constantinople held it as their palladium. Upon the conquest by the Turks, the Sultan adopted it . . . and since that, the crescent has been made to oppose the idea of the *cross*". (*Eg. Belief.*)

M

Macrocosm (*Gr.*). The "Great Universe" literally, or Kosmos.

Macroprosopus (*Gr.*). A Kabalistic term, made of a compound Greek word: meaning the Vast or Great Countenance (See "Kabalistic Faces"); a title of Kether, the Crown, the highest Sephira. It is the name of the Universe, called *Arikh-Anpin*, the totality of that of which Microprosopus or *Zauir-Anpin* "the lesser countenance", is the part and antithesis. In its high or abstract metaphysical sense, Microprosopus is Adam Kadmon, the *vehicle of Ain-Suph*, and the crown of the Sephirothal Tree, though since Sephira and Adam Kadmon are in fact one under two aspects, it comes to the same thing. Interpretations are many, and they differ.

Madhyama (*Sk.*). Used of something beginningless and endless. Thus Vâch (Sound, the female Logos, or the female counterpart of Brahmâ is said to exist in several states, one of which is that of *Mâdhyama*, which is equivalent to saying that Vâch is *eternal* in one sense "the Word (Vâch) was with God, and *in* God", for the two are one.

Mâdhyamikas (Sk.). A sect mentioned in the *Vishnu Purâna*. Agreeably to the Orientalists, a "Buddhist sect, which is an anachronism. It was probably at first a sect of Hindu atheists. A later school of that name, teaching a system of sophistic nihilism, that reduces every proposition into a thesis and its antithesis, and then denies both, has been started in Tibet and China. It adopts a few principles of Nâgârjuna, who was one of the founders of the esoteric Mahayâna systems, not their *exoteric* travesties. The allegory that regarded Nâgârjuna's "Paramartha" as a gift from the *Nâgas* (Serpents) shows that he received his teachings from the secret school of adepts, and that the real tenets are therefore kept secret.

Mahâ Buddhi (*Sk.*). *Mahat*. The Intelligent Soul of the World. The seven

Prakritis or seven "natures" or planes, are counted from Mahâbuddhi downwards.

Mahâ Chohan (*Sk.*). The chief of a spiritual Hierarchy, or of a school of Occultism; the head of the trans-Himalayan mystics.

Mahâ Deva (*Sk.*). Lit., "great god"; a title of Siva.

Mahâ Guru (*Sk.*). Lit., "great teacher". The Initiator.

Mahâ Kâla (*Sk.*). "Great Time". A name of Siva as the "Destroyer", and of Vishnu as the "Preserver".

Mahâ Kalpa (*Sk.*). The "great age".

Mahâ Manvantara (*Sk.*). Lit., the great interludes between the "Manus". The period of universal activity. Manvantara implying here simply a period of activity, as opposed to Pralaya, or rest – without reference to the length of the cycle.

Mahâ Mâyâ (*Sk.*). The great illusion of manifestation. This universe, and all in it in their mutual relation, is called the great Illusion or *Mahâmâyâ* It is also the usual title given to Gautama the Buddha's Immaculate Mother – Mayâdêvi, or the "Great Mystery", as she is called by the Mystics.

Mahâ Pralaya (*Sk.*). The opposite of Mahâmanvantara, literally "the great Dissolution", the "Night" following the "Day of Brahmâ". It is the great rest and sleep of all nature after a period of active manifestation; orthodox Christians would refer to it as the "Destruction of the World".

Mahâ Vidyâ (*Sk.*). The great esoteric science. The highest Initiates alone are in possession of this science, which embraces almost universal knowledge.

Mahâ Yogin (*Sk.*). The "great ascetic". A title of Siva.

Mahâ Yuga (*Sk.*). The aggregate of four *Yugas* or ages, of 4,320,000 solar years; a "Day of Brahmâ", in the Brahmanical system ; lit., "the great age".

Mahat (*Sk.*). Lit., "The great one". The first principle of Universal Intelligence and Consciousness. In the Purânic philosophy the first product of root-nature or *Pradhâna* (the same as Mulaprakriti); the producer of *Manas* the thinking principle, and of *Ahankâra*, egotism or the feeling of "I am I" (in the lower *Manas*).

Mahâtma. Lit., "great soul". An adept of the highest order. Exalted beings who, having attained to the mastery over their lower principles are thus living unimpeded by the "man of flesh", and are in possession of knowledge and power commensurate with the stage they have reached in their spiritual evolution. Called in Pali Rahats and Arhats.

Maitreya Buddha (*Sk.*). The same as the *Kalki Avatar* of Vishnu (the "White Horse" Avatar), and of Sosiosh and other Messiahs. The only difference lies in the dates of their appearances. Thus, while Vishnu is expected to appear on his white horse at the end of the present *Kali Yuga* age "for the final destruction of the wicked, the renovation of creation and the restoration of purity", Maitreya is expected earlier. Exoteric or popular teaching making slight variations on the esoteric doctrine states that Sakyamuni (Gautama Buddha) visited him in Tushita (a celestial abode) and commissioned him to issue thence on earth as his successor at the expiration of five thousand years after his (Buddha's) death. This would be in less than 3,000 years hence. Esoteric philosophy teaches that the next Buddha will appear during the seventh (sub) race of this Round. The fact is that Maitreya was a follower of Buddha, a well-known Arhat, though not his direct disciple, and that he was the founder of an esoteric philosophical school. As shown by Eitel (*Sanskrit-Chinese Dict.*), "statues were erected in his honour as early as B.C. 350".

Manas (*Sk.*). Lit., "the mind", the mental faculty which makes of man an intelligent and moral being, and distinguishes him from the mere animal; a synonym of *Mahat. Esoterically*, however, it means, when unqualified, the Higher EGO, or the sentient reincarnating Principle in man. When qualified it is called by Theosophists *Buddhi-Manas* or the Spiritual Soul in contradistinction to its human reflection – *Kâma-Manas.*

Manas, Kâma (*Sk.*). Lit., "the mind of desire." With the Buddhists it is the *sixth* of the Chadâyatana (*q.v.*), or the six organs of knowledge, hence the highest of these, synthesized by the seventh called *Klichta*, the spiritual perception of that which defiles this (lower) *Manas*, or the "Human-animal Soul", as the Occultists term it. While the Higher *Manas* or the Ego is directly related to *Vijnâna* (the 10th of the 12 Nidânas) – which is the perfect knowledge of all forms of knowledge, whether relating to object or subject in the nidânic concatenation of causes and effects; the lower, the Kâma *Manas* is but one of the *Indriya* or organs (roots) of Sense. Very little can be said of the dual *Manas* here, as the doctrine that treats of it, is correctly stated only in esoteric works. Its mention can thus be only very superficial.

Manas Sanyama (*Sk.*). Perfect concentration of the mind, and control over it, during Yoga practices.

Manas Taijasi (*Sk.*). Lit., the "radiant" *Manas*; a state of the Higher Ego, which only high metaphysicians are able to realize and comprehend.

Mânasa or *Manaswin* (*Sk.*). "The efflux of the *divine* mind," and explained as meaning that this efflux signifies the *Manasa* or divine sons of Brahmâ-Virâj. Nilakantha who is the authority for this statement, further explains the term "*Manasa*" by *manomâtrasarira*. These *Manasa* are the *Arupa* or incorporeal sons of the Prajâpati Virâj, in another version. But as Arjuna Misra identifies Virâj with Brahmâ, and as Brahmâ is *Mahat*, the universal mind, the exoteric blind becomes plain. The Pitris are identical with the Kumâra, the Vairaja, the *Manasa*-Putra (mind sons), and are finally identified with the human "Egos".

Mânasa Dhyânis (*Sk.*). The highest Pitris in the *Purânas*; the Agnishwatthas, or Solar Ancestors of Man, those who made of Man a rational being, by incarnating in the senseless forms of semi-ethereal flesh of the men of the third race. (See Vol. II. of *Secret Doctrine*.)

Mânasas (*Sk.*). Those who endowed humanity with *Manas* or intelligence, the immortal EGOS in men. (See "*Manas*".)

Mantrika Sakti (*Sk.*). The power, or the occult potency of mystic words, sounds, numbers or letters in these Mantras.

Manus (*Sk.*). The fourteen Manus are the patrons or guardians of the race cycles in a Manvantara, or Day of Brahmâ. The primeval Manus are seven, they become fourteen in the *Purânas.*

Manushi or *Manushi Buddhas* (*Sk.*). Human Buddhas, *Bodhisattvas*, or incarnated Dhyan Chohans.

Manvantara (*Sk.*). A period of manifestation, as opposed to Pralaya (dissolution, or rest), applied to various cycles, especially to a Day of Brahmâ, 4,320,000,000 Solar years – and to the reign of one Manu – 308,448,000. (See Vol. II. of the *Secret Doctrine*, p. 68 *et. seq.*) Lit., *Manuantara* – between Manus.

Mârga (*Sk.*). "The "Path", The *Ashthânga mârga*, the "holy" or sacred path is the one that leads to Nirvâna. The eight-fold path has grown out of the seven-fold path, by the addition of the (now) first of the eight Marga; *i.e.*, "the possession of orthodox views"; with which a *real Yogâcharya* would have nothing to do.

Mârttanda (*Sk*.). The Vedic name of the Sun.

Mâyâ *(Sk.)*. Illusion ; the cosmic power which renders phenomenal existence and the perceptions thereof possible. In Hindu philosophy that alone which is changeless and eternal is called *reality* ; all that which is subject to change through decay and differentiation and which has therefore a begining and an end is regarded as *mâyâ* – illusion.

Mîmânsâ (*Sk*.). A school of philosophy; one of the six in India. There are two Mîmânsâ the older and the younger. The first, the "Pârva-Mîmânsâ", was founded by Jamini, and the later or "Uttara Mîmânsâ", by a Vyasa— and is now called the Vedânta school. Sankarâchârya was the most prominent apostle of the latter. The Vedânta school is the oldest of all the six *Darshana* (lit., "demonstrations"), but even to the Pûrva-Mîmânsâ no higher antiquity is allowed than 500 B.C. Orientalists in favour of the absurd idea that all these schools are "due to Greek influence", in order to have them fit their theory would make them of still later date. The *Shaddarshana* (or Six Demonstrations) have all a starting point in common, and maintain that *ex nihilo nihil fit*.

Moksha (*Sk*.). "Liberation." The same as Nirvâna; a post mortem state of rest and bliss of the "Soul-Pilgrim".

Monad (*Gr*.). The Unity, the *one* ; but in Occultism it often means the unified triad, Atma-Buddhi-*Manas*, or the duad, Atma-Buddhi, that immortal part of man which reincarnates in the lower kingdoms, and gradually progresses through them to Man and then to the final goal – Nirvâna.

Monas (*Gr*.). The same as the term *Monad* ; "Alone", a unit. In the Pythagorean system the duad emanates from the higher and solitary Monas, which is thus the "First Cause".

Moon. The earth's satellite has figured very largely as an emblem in the religions of antiquity; and most commonly has been represented as Female, but this is not universal, for in the myths of the Teutons and Arabs, as well as in the conception of the Rajpoots of India (see Tod, *Hist*.), and in Tartary the moon was male. Latin authors speak of Luna. and also of Lunus, but with extreme rarity. The Greek name is Selene, the Hebrew Lebanah and also Yarcah. In Egypt the moon was associated with Isis, in Phenicia with Astarte and in Babylon with Ishtar. From certain points of view the ancients regarded the moon also as Androgyne. The astrologers allot an Influence to the moon over the several parts of a man, according to the several Zodiacal signs she traverses; as well as a special influence produced by the house she occupies in a figure.

The division of the Zodiac into the 28 mansions of the moon appears to be older than that into 12 signs: the Copts, Egyptians, Arabs, Persians and Hindoos used the division into 28 parts centuries ago, and the Chinese use it still.

The Hermetists said the moon gave man an astral form, while Theosophy teaches that the Lunar Pitris were the creators of our human bodies and lower principles. (See *Secret Doctrine* 1. 386.) [w.w.w.]

Mukta and **Mukti** *(Sk.).* Liberation from sentient life; one beatified or liberated; a candidate for *Moksha*, freedom from flesh and matter, or life on this earth.

Mûlaprakriti *(Sk.).* The Parabrahmic root, the abstract deific feminine principle—undifferentiated substance. Akâsa. Literally, "the root of Nature" *(Prakriti)* or Matter.

Munis *(Sk.).* Saints, or Sages.

Mysteries. Greek *teletai,* or finishings, celebrations of initiation or the Mysteries. They were observances, generally kept secret from the profane and uninitiated, in which were taught by dramatic representation and other methods, the origin of things, the nature of the human spirit, its relation to the body, and the method of its purification and restoration to higher life. Physical science, medicine, the laws of music, divination, were all taught in the same manner. The Hippocratic oath was but a mystic obligation. Hippocrates was a priest of Asklepios, some of whose writings chanced to become public. But the Asklepiades were initiates of the Æsculapian serpent-worship, as the Bacchantes were of the Dionysia; and both rites were eventually incorporated with the Eleusinia. The Sacred Mysteries were enacted in the ancient Temples by the initiated Hierophants for the benefit and instruction of the candidates. The most solemn and occult Mysteries were certainly those which were performed in Egypt by "the band of secret-keepers", as Mr. Bonwick calls the Hierophants. Maurice describes their nature very graphically in a few lines. Speaking of the Mysteries performed in Philæ (the Nile-island), he says that "it was in these gloomy caverns that the grand and mystic arcana of the goddess (Isis) were unfolded to the adoring aspirant, while the solemn hymn of initiation resounded through the long extent of these stony recesses". The word "mysteries" is derived from the Greek *muô,* "to close the mouth", and every symbol connected with them had, a hidden meaning. As Plato and many other sages of antiquity affirm, the Mysteries were highly religious, moral and beneficent as a school of ethics. The Grecian mysteries, those of Ceres and Bacchus, were only imitations of the Egyptian; and the author of *Egyptian Belief and Modern Thought*, informs us that our own "word *chapel* or *capella* is said to be the *Caph-El* or college of *El,* the Solar divinity". The well-known *Kabiri* are associated with the Mysteries. In short, the Mysteries were in every country a series of dramatic performances, in which the mysteries of cosmogony and nature, in general, were personified by the priests and neophytes, who enacted the part of various gods and goddesses, repeating supposed scenes (allegories) from their respective lives. These were explained in their hidden meaning to the candidates for initiation, and incorporated into philosophical doctrines.

N

Nâga (*Sk.*). Literally "Serpent". The name in the Indian Pantheon of the Serpent or Dragon Spirits, and of the inhabitants of Pâtâla, hell. But as Pâtâla means the *antipodes*, and was the name given to America by the ancients, who knew and visited that continent before Europe had ever heard of it, the term is probably akin to the Mexican Nagals the (now) sorcerers and medicine men. The Nagas are the Burmese *Nats*, serpent-gods, or "dragon demons". In Esotericism, however, and as already stated, this is a nick-name for the "wise men" or adepts in China and Tibet, the "Dragons." are regarded as the titulary deities of the world, and of various spots on the earth, and the word is explained as meaning adepts, yogis, and narjols. The term has simply reference to their great knowledge and wisdom. This is also proven in the ancient Sûtras and Buddha's biographies. The Nâga is ever a wise man, endowed with extraordinary magic powers, in South and Central America as in India, in Chaldea as also in ancient Egypt. In China the "worship" of the Nâgas was widespread, and it has become still more pronounced since Nâgarjuna (the "great Nâga", the "great adept" literally), the fourteenth Buddhist patriarch, visited China. The "Nâgas" are regarded by the Celestials as "the tutelary Spirits or gods of the five regions or the four points of the compass and the centre, as the guardians of the five lakes and four oceans" (**Eitel**). This, traced to its origin and translated esoterically, means that the five continents and their five root-races had always been under the guardianship of "terrestrial deities", i.e., Wise Adepts. The tradition that Nâgas washed Gautama Buddha at his birth, protected him and guarded the relics of his body when dead, points again to the Nâgas being only wise men, Arhats, and no monsters or Dragons. This is also corroborated by the innumerable stories of the conversion of Nâgas to Buddhism. The Nâga of a lake in a forest near Râjagriha and many other "Dragons" were thus converted by Buddha to the good Law.

Nârada (*Sk.*). One of the Seven great Rishis, a Son of Brahmâ This "Progenitor" is one of the most mysterious personages in the Brahmanical sacred symbology. Esoterically Nârada is the Ruler of events during various Karmic cycles, and the personification, in a certain sense, of the great human cycle; a Dhyan Chohan. He plays a great part in Brahmanism, which ascribes to him some of the most occult hymns in the *Rig Veda*, in which sacred work he is described as "of the Kanwa family". He is called Deva-Brahmâ, but as such has a distinct character from the one he assumes on earth – or Pâtâla. Daksha cursed him for his interference with his 5,000 and 10,000 sons, whom he persuaded to remain Yogins and *celibates*, to be reborn time after time on this earth (*Mahâbhârata*). But this is an allegory. He was the inventor of the Vina, a kind of lute, and a great "lawgiver". The story is too long to be given here.

Nârâyana (*Sk.*). The "mover on the Waters" of space: a title of Vishnu, in his aspect of the Holy Spirit, moving on the Waters of Creation. (See *Mânu*, Book II.) In esoteric symbology it stands for the primeval manifestation of the *life-principle*, spreading in infinite Space.

Nâstika (*Sk.*). Atheist, or rather he who does not worship or recognize the gods and idols.

Nephesh (*Heb.*). Breath of life. *Anima, Mens, Vita,* Appetites. This term is used very loosely in the Bible. It generally means *prana* "life"; in the Kabbalah it is the animal passions and the animal Soul. [w.w.w.]. Therefore, as maintained in theosophical teachings, *Nephesh* is the synonym of the Prâna-Kâmic Principle, or the vital animal Soul in man. [H. P. B.]

Nidâna (*Sk.*). The 12 causes of existence, or a chain of causation, "a concatenation of cause and effect in the whole range of existence through 12 links". This is the fundamental dogma of Buddhist thought, "the understanding of which solves the riddle of life, revealing the insanity of existence and preparing the mind for Nirvâna". (Eitel's *Sans. Chin. Dict.*) The 12 links stand thus in their enumeration. (1) Jail, or birth, according to one of the four modes of entering the stream of life and reincarnation – or

Chatur Yoni (q.v.), each mode placing the being born in one of the six *Gâti* (q.v.). (2) *Jarârnarana*, or decrepitude and death, following the maturity of the *Skandhas* (q.v.). (3) *Bhava,* the Karmic agent which leads every new sentient being to be born in this or another mode of existence in the *Trailokya* and Gâti. (4) *Upâdâna*, the creative cause of *Bhava* which thus becomes the cause of *Jati* which is the effect; and this creative cause is the *clinging to life.* (5) Trishnâ, love, whether pure or impure. (6) *Vêdâna*, or sensation; perception by the senses, it is the 5th Skandha. (7) Sparsa, the sense of touch. (8) *Chadâyatana*, the organs of sensation. (9) *Nâmarûpa*, personality, i.e., a form with a name to it, the symbol of the unreality of material phenomenal appearances. (10) *Vijnâna*, the perfect knowledge of every perceptible thing and of all objects in their concatenation and unity. (11) *Samskâra*, action on the plane of illusion. (12) *Avidyâ*, lack of true perception, or ignorance. The Nidânas belonging to the most subtle and abstruse doctrines of the Eastern metaphysical system, it is impossible to go into the subject at any greater length.

Nimitta (*Sk.*). 1. An interior illumination developed by the practice of meditation. 2. The efficient spiritual cause, as contrasted with Upadana, the material cause, in Vedânta philosophy. See also *Pradhâna* in Sankhya philosophy.

Nirguna (*Sk.*). Negative attribute; unbound, or without *Gunas* (attributes), i.e., that which is devoid of all qualities, the opposite of Saguna, that which has attributes (*Secret Doctrine,* II. 95), e.g., Parabrahmam is Nirguna; Brahmâ, Saguna. Nirguna is a term which shows the impersonality of the thing spoken of.

Nirmânakâya (*Sk.*). Something entirely different in esoteric philosophy from the popular meaning attached to it, and from the fancies of the Orientalists. Some call the *Nirmânakâya* body "Nirvana with remains" (Schlagintweit, etc.) on the supposition, probably, that it is a kind of Nirvânic condition during which consciousness and form are retained. Others say that it is one of the *Trikâya* (three bodies), with the "power of assuming any form of appearance in order to propagate Buddhism" (Eitel's idea); again, that "it is the incarnate avatâra of a deity" (*ibid.*), and so on. Occultism, on the other hand, says: that Nirmânakâya, although meaning literally a transformed "body", is a state. The form is that of the adept or yogi who enters, or chooses, that *post mortem* condition in preference to the Dharmakâya or *absolute* Nirvânic state. He does this because the latter *kâya* separates him for ever from the world of form, conferring upon him a state of *selfish* bliss, in which no other living being can participate, the adept being thus precluded from the possibility of helping humanity, or even *devas*. As a Nirmânakâya, however, the man leaves behind him only his physical body, and retains every other "principle" save the Kamic – for he has crushed this out for ever from his nature, during life, and it can never resurrect in his post mortem state. Thus, instead of going into selfish bliss, he chooses a life of self-sacrifice, an existence which ends only with the life-cycle, in order to be enabled to help mankind in an invisible yet most effective manner. (See *The Voice of the Silence*, third treatise, "The Seven Portals".) Thus a Nirmânakâya is not, as popularly believed, the body "in which a Buddha or a Bodhisattva appears on earth", but verily one, who whether a *Chutuktu* or a *Khubilkhan,* an adept or a yogi during life, has since become a member of that invisible Host which ever protects and watches over Humanity within Karmic limits. Mistaken often for a "Spirit", a Deva, God himself, &c., a Nirmânakâya is ever a protecting, compassionate, verily a *guardian* angel, to him who becomes worthy of his help. Whatever objection may be brought forward against this doctrine; however much it is denied, because, forsooth, it has never been hitherto made public in Europe and therefore since it is unknown to Orientalists, it must needs be "a myth of modern invention" – no one will be bold enough to say that this idea of helping suffering mankind at the price of one's own almost interminable self-sacrifice, is not one of the grandest and noblest that was ever evolved from human brain.

Nirupadhi *(Sk.)*. Attributeless; the negation of attributes.

Nirvâna *(Sk.)*. According to the Orientalists, the entire "blowing out", like the flame of a candle, the utter extinction of existence. But in the esoteric explanations it is the state of absolute existence and absolute consciousness, into which the Ego of a man who has reached the highest degree of perfection and holiness during life goes, after the body dies, and occasionally, as in the case of Gautama Buddha and others, during life. (See "Nirvânî".)

Nirvânî (ee) (Sk.). One who has attained Nirvana – an emancipated soul. That Nirvâna means nothing of the kind asserted by Orientalists every scholar who has visited China, India and Japan is well aware. It is *"escape from misery"* but only from that of matter, freedom from *Klêsha*, or *Kâma,* and the complete extinction of animal desires. If we are told that *Abidharma* defines Nirvâna "as a state of absolute annihilation", we concur, adding to the last word the qualification "of everything connected with matter or the physical world", and this simply because the latter (as also all in it) is illusion, *mâyâ*. Sâkya-mûni Buddha said in the last moments of his life that "the spiritual body is immortal" (See *Sans. Chin. Dict.*). As Mr. Eitel, the scholarly Sinologist, explains it: "The popular exoteric systems agree in defining Nirvâna *negatively* as a state of absolute exemption from the circle of transmigration; as a state of entire freedom from all forms of existence; to begin with, freedom from all passion and exertion; a state of indifference to all sensibility" and he might have added "death of all compassion for the world of suffering". And this is why the *Bodhisattvas* who prefer the Nirmânakâya to the Dharmakâya vesture, stand higher in the popular estimation than the Nirvânîs. But the same scholar adds that: "Positively (and esoterically) they define Nirvâna as the highest state of spiritual bliss, as absolute immortality through absorption of the soul (spirit rather) into itself, but *preserving individuality* so that, e.g., Buddhas, after entering Nirvâna, may reappear on earth" – i.e., in the future Manvantara.

Nitya Pralaya (*Sk.*). Lit., "perpetual" Pralaya or dissolution. It is the constant and imperceptible changes undergone by the atoms which last as long as a Mahâmanvantara, a whole age of Brahmâ, which takes fifteen figures to sum up. A stage of chronic change and dissolution, the stages of growth and decay. It is the duration of "Seven Eternities". (See *Secret Doctrine* I. 371, II. 69, 310.) There are four kinds of Pralayas, or states of changelessness. The Naimittika, when Brahmâ slumbers; the Prakritika, a partial Pralaya of anything during Manvantara; Atyantika, when man has identified himself with the One Absolute synonym of Nirvâna; and Nitya, for physical things especially, as a state of profound and dreamless sleep.

Nitya Sarga (*Sk.*). The state of constant creation or evolution, as opposed to *Nitya Pralaya*—the state of perpetual incessant dissolution (or change of atoms) disintegration of molecules, hence change of forms.

Nous (*Gr.*). A Platonic term for the Higher Mind or Soul. It means Spirit as distinct from animal Soul – *psyche*; divine consciousness or mind in man: *Nous* was the designation given to the Supreme deity (third *logos*) by Anaxagoras. Taken from Egypt where it was called *Nout*, it was adopted by the Gnostics for their first conscious Æon which, with the Occultists, is the third *logos*, cosmically, and the third "principle" (from above) or *Manas*, in man. (See "Nout".)

Nout (*Gr.*). In the Pantheon of the Egyptians it meant the "One- only-One", because they did not proceed in their popular or exoteric religion higher than the third manifestation which radiates from the *Unknown* and the *Unknowable*, the first unmanifested and the second *logoi* in the esoteric philosophy of every nation. The Nous of Anaxagoras was the *Mahat* of the Hindu Brahmâ, *the first manifested* Deity – "the Mind or Spirit self-potent"; this creative Principle being of course the *primum mobile* of everything in the Universe – its Soul and Ideation. (See "Seven Principles" in man.)

Nyâya (Sk.). One of the six *Darshanas* or schools of Philosophy in India; a system of Hindu logic founded by the Rishi Gautama.

O

Occult Sciences. The science of the secrets of nature – physical and psychic, mental and spiritual; called Hermetic and Esoteric Sciences. In the West, the Kabbalah may be named; in the East, mysticism, magic, and Yoga philosophy, which latter is often referred to by the Chelas in India as the *seventh* "Darshana" (school of philosophy), there being only *six* Darshanas in India known to the world of the profane. These sciences are, and have been for ages, hidden from the vulgar for the very good reason that they would never be appreciated by the selfish educated classes, nor understood by the uneducated; whilst the former might misuse them for their own profit, and thus turn the divine science into *black magic*. It is often brought forward as an accusation against the Esoteric philosophy and the Kabbalah that their literature is full of "a barbarous and meaningless jargon" unintelligible to the ordinary mind. But do not exact Sciences – medicine, physiology, chemistry, and the rest – do the same? Do not official Scientists equally veil their facts and discoveries with a newly coined and most barbarous Græco-Latin terminology? As justly remarked by our late brother, Kenneth Mackenzie – "To juggle thus with words, when the facts are so simple, is the art of the Scientists of the present time, in striking contrast to those of the XVIIth century, who called spades spades, and not 'agricultural implements'." Moreover, whilst their facts would be as simple and as comprehensible if rendered in ordinary language, the facts of Occult Science are of so abstruse a nature, that in most cases no words exist in European languages to express them; in addition to which our "jargon" is a *double* necessity – (a) for the purpose of describing clearly these *facts* to him who is versed in the Occult terminology; and (b) to conceal them from the profane.

Occultist. One who studies the various branches of occult science. The term is used by the French Kabbalists (See Eliphas Lévi's works).

Occultism embraces the whole range of psychological, physiological, cosmical, physical, and spiritual phenomena. From the word occultus hidden or secret. It therefore applies to the study of the **Kabbalah**, astrology, alchemy, and all arcane sciences.

Oeaihu, or *Oeaihwu.* The manner of pronunciation depends on the accent. This is an esoteric term for the six in one or the mystic seven. The occult name for the "seven vowelled" ever-present manifestation of the Universal Principle.

Om or Aum (*Sk.*). A mystic syllable, the most solemn of all words in India. It is "an invocation, a benediction, an affirmation and a promise and it is so sacred, as to be indeed *the word at low breath* of occult, *primitive* masonry. No one must be near when the syllable is pronounced for a purpose. This word is usually placed at the beginning of sacred Scriptures, and is prefixed to prayers. It is a compound of three letters a,u,m, which, in the popular belief, are typical of the three Vedas, also of three gods — **A** (Agni) **V** (Varuna) and **M** (Maruts) or Fire, Water and Air. In esoteric philosophy these are the three sacred fires, or the "triple fire"in the Universe and Man, besides many other things. Occultly, this "triple fire" represents the highest *Tetraktys* also, as it is typified by the Agni named Abhimânin and his transformation into his three sons, Pâvana, Pavamâna and Suchi, "who drinks up water", i.e., destroys material desires. This monosyllable is called Udgîtta, and is sacred with both Brahmins and Buddhists.

Omkâra (Sk.). The same as Aum or Om. It is also the name of one of the twelve *lingams,* that was represented by a secret and most sacred shrine at Ujjain — no longer existing, since the time of Buddhism.

Ophiomorphos (*Gr.*). The same, but in its material aspect, as the Ophis-Christos. With the Gnostics the Serpent represented "Wisdom in Eternity".

Ouranos (*Gr.*). The whole expanse of Heaven called the "Waters of Space", the Celestial Ocean, etc. The name very likely comes from the Vedic Varuna, personified as the water god and regarded as the chief Aditya among the seven planetary deities. In Hesiod's Theogony, Ouranos (or Uranus) is the same as Cœlus (Heaven) the oldest of all the gods and the father of the divine Titans.

P

Padma Âsana (*Sk.*). A posture prescribed to and practised by some Yogis for developing concentration.

Padma Kalpa (*Sk.*). The name of the last Kalpa or the preceding Manvantara, which was a year of Brahmâ.

Pancha Kosha (*Sk.*). The five "sheaths". According to Vedantin philosophy, Vijnânamaya Kosha, the fourth sheath, is composed of Buddhi, or is Buddhi. The five sheaths are said to belong to the two higher principles—*Jivâtma* and *Sâkshi*, which represent the *Upathita* and *An-upahita,* divine spirit respectively. The division in the esoteric teaching differs from this, as it divides man's physical-metaphysical aspect into seven principles.

Para (*Sk.*). "Infinite" and "supreme" in philosophy – the final limit.

Parabrahm (*Sk.*). "Beyond Brahmâ", literally. The Supreme Infinite Brahma, "Absolute" – the attributeless, the secondless reality. The impersonal and nameless universal Principle.

Paracelsus. The symbolical name adopted by the greatest Occultist of the middle ages – Philip Bombastes Aureolus Theophrastus von Hohenheim – born in the canton of Zurich in 1493. He was the cleverest physician of his age, and the most renowned for curing almost any illness by the power of talismans prepared by himself. He never had a friend, but was surrounded by enemies, the most bitter of whom were the Churchmen and their party. That he was accused of being in league with the devil stands to reason, nor is it to be wondered at that finally he was murdered by some unknown foe, at the early age of forty-eight. He died at Salzburg, leaving a number of works behind him, which are to this day greatly valued by the Kabbalists and Occultists. Many of his utterances have proved prophetic. He was a clairvoyant of great powers, one of the most learned and erudite philosophers and mystics, and a distinguished Alchemist. Physics is indebted to him for the discovery of nitrogen gas, or **Azote.**

Paramapadha (*Sk.*). The place where—according to Visishtadwaita Vedantins—bliss is enjoyed by those who reach *Moksha* (Bliss). This "place" is not material but made, says the Catechism of that sect, "of *Suddhasatwa,* the essence of which the body of Iswara", the lord, "is made".

Paramartha (*Sk*) Absolute existence.

Paramâtman (*Sk.*). The Supreme Soul of the Universe.

Paranirvâna (*Sk.*). Absolute *Non-Being,* which is equivalent to absolute *Being* or "Be-ness", the state reached by the human Monad at the end of the great cycle (See *Secret Doctrine* I, 135). The same as *Paraniskpanna.*

Pâtanjala (*Sk.*). The Yoga philosophy; one of the six *Darshanas* or Schools of India.

Patanjali (*Sk.*). The founder of the Yoga philosophy. The date assigned to him by the Orientalists is 200 B.C.; and by the Occultists nearer to 700 than 600 B.C. At any rate he was a contemporary of Pânini.

Personality. In Occultism – which divides man into seven principles, considering him under the three aspects of the *divine*, the *thinking* or the *rational*, and the *animal* man – the lower *quaternary* or the purely astrophysical being; while by *Individuality* is meant the Higher Triad, considered as a Unity. Thus the *Personality* embraces all the characteristics and memories of one physical life, while the *Individuality* is the imperishable *Ego* which re-incarnates and clothes itself in one personality after another.

Phenomenon (*Gr.*). In reality "an appearance", something previously unseen, and puzzling when the cause of it is unknown. Leaving aside various kinds of phenomena, such as cosmic, electrical, chemical, etc., and holding merely to the phenomena of spiritism, let it be remembered that theosophically and esoterically every "miracle" – from the biblical to the theumaturgic – is simply a phenomenon, but that no phenomenon is ever a miracle, *i.e.*, something supernatural or outside of the laws of nature, as all such are impossibilities in nature.

Pitar Devata (*Sk.*). The "Father-Gods", the lunar ancestors of mankind.

Pitaras (*Sk.*). Fathers, Ancestors. The fathers of the human races.

Pitris (*Sk.*). The ancestors, or creators of mankind. They are of seven classes, three of which are incorporeal, *arupa,* and four corporeal. In popular theology they are said to be created from Brahmâ's side. They are variously genealogized, but in esoteric philosophy they are as given in the *Secret Doctrine*. In *Isis Unveiled* it is said of them "It is generally believed that the Hindu term means the spirits of our ancestors, of disembodied people, hence the argument of some Spiritualists that fakirs (and yogis) and other Eastern wonder-workers, are *mediums*. This is in more than one sense erroneous. The Pitris are not the ancestors of the present living men, but those of the human kind, or Adamic races; the spirits of human races, which on the great scale of descending evolution *preceded our races* of men, and they *were physically, as well as spiritually, far superior* to our modern pigmies. In *Mânava Dharma Shâstra* they are called the *Lunar Ancestors*." The *Secret Doctrine* has now explained that which was cautiously put forward in the earlier Theosophical volumes.

Planetary Spirits. Primarily the rulers or governors of the planets. As our earth has its hierarchy of terrestrial planetary spirits, from the highest to the lowest plane, so has every other heavenly body. In Occultism, however, the term "Planetary Spirit" is generally applied only to the seven highest hierarchies corresponding to the Christian archangels. These have all passed through a stage of evolution corresponding to the humanity of earth on other worlds, in long past cycles. Our earth, being as yet only in its fourth round, is far too young to have produced high planetary spirits. The highest planetary spirit ruling over any globe is in reality the "Personal God" of that planet and far more truly its "over-ruling providence" than the self-contradictory Infinite Personal Deity of modern Churchianity.

Plato. An Initiate into the Mysteries and the greatest Greek philosopher, whose writings are known the world over. He was the pupil of Socrates and the teacher of Aristotle. He flourished over 400 years before our era.

Pragna (*Sk.*) or *Prajna*. A synonym of *Mahat* the Universal Mind. The capacity for perception. (*S. D.*, I. 139) Consciousness.

Prajâpatis (*Sk.*). Progenitors; the givers of life to all on this Earth. They are seven and then ten – corresponding to the seven and ten Kabbalistic Sephiroth; to the Mazdean Amesha-Spentas, &c. Brahmâ the creator, is called Prajâpati as the synthesis of the Lords of Being.

Prakriti (*Sk.*). Nature in general, nature as opposed to Purusha – spiritual nature and Spirit, which together are the "two primeval aspects of the One Unknown Deity". (*Secret Doctrine*, I. 51.)

Pralaya (*Sk.*). A period of obscuration or repose – planetary, cosmic or universal – the opposite of Manvantara (*S. D.*, I. 370.).

Pramantha (*Sk.*). An accessory to producing the sacred fire by friction. The sticks used by Brahmins to kindle fire by friction.

Prâna (*Sk.*). Life-Principle ; the breath of Life.

Pranidhâna (*Sk.*). The fifth observance of the Yogis; ceaseless devotion. (See *Yoga Shâstras*, ii. 32.)

Pratyasarga (*Sk.*). In Sankhya philosophy the "intellectual evolution of the Universe" ; in the *Purânas* the 8th creation.

Prometheus (*Gr.*). The Greek *logos*; he, who by bringing on earth divine fire (intelligence and consciousness) endowed men with reason and mind. Prometheus is the Hellenic type of our Kumâras or *Egos,* those who, by incarnating in men, made of them latent gods instead of animals. The gods (or Elohim) were averse to men becoming "as one of us (*Genesis* iii., 22), and knowing "good and evil". Hence we see these gods in every religious legend punishing man for his desire to know. As the Greek myth has it, for stealing the fire he brought to men from Heaven, Prometheus was chained by the order of Zeus to a crag of the Caucasian Mountains.

Protogonos (*Gr.*). The "first-born"; used of all the manifested gods and of the Sun in our system.

Psyche (*Gr.*). The animal, terrestrial Soul; the lower *Manas.*

Purânas (*Sk.*). Lit., "ancient". A collection of symbolical and allegorical writings – eighteen in number now – supposed to have been composed by Vyâsa, the author of *Mahâbhârata.*

Purusha (*Sk.*). "Man", *heavenly man.* Spirit, the same as Nârâyana in another   aspect. "The Spiritual Self."

Pymander (Gr.). The "Thought divine". The Egyptian Prometheus and the personified Nous or divine light, which appears to and instructs Hermes Trismegistus, in a hermetic work called "Pymander".

Pythagoras (*Gr.*). The most famous of mystic philosophers, born at Samos, about 586 B.C. He seems to have travelled all over the world, and to have culled his philosophy from the various systems to which he had access. Thus, he studied the esoteric sciences with the *Brachmanes* of India, and astronomy and astrology in Chaldea and Egypt. He is known to this day in the former country under the name of Yavanâchârya ("Ionian teacher"). After returning he settled in Crotona, in Magna Grecia, where he established a college to which very soon resorted all the best intellects of the civilised centres. His father was one Mnesarchus of Samos, and was a man of noble birth and learning. It was Pythagoras. who was the first to teach the heliocentric system, and who was the greatest proficient in geometry of his century. It was he also who created the word "philosopher", composed of two words meaning a "lover of wisdom"— *philo-sophos.* As the greatest mathematician, geometer and astronomer of historical antiquity, and also the highest of the metaphysicians and scholars, Pythagoras has won imperishable fame. He taught reincarnation as it is professed in India and much else of the Secret Wisdom.

Q

Qadmon, Adam, or *Adam Kadmon (Heb.)*. The Heavenly or Celestial Man, the Microcosm *(q.v.)*, He is the manifested Logos; the *third* Logos according to Occultism, or the Paradigm of Humanity.

R

Râga (Sk). One of the five *Kleshas* (afflictions) in Patânjali's Yoga philosophy. In *Sânkhya Kârikâ*, it is the "obstruction" called love and desire in the physical or terrestrial sense. The five *Kleshas* are: *Avidyâ*, or ignorance; *Asmitâ*, selfishness, or "I-am-ness" ; *Râga*, love; *Dwesha*, hatred; and *Abhinivesa,* dread of suffering.

Râjas *(Sk.)*. The "quality of foulness" *(i.e.,* differentiation), and activity in the *Purânas.* One of the three *Gunas* or divisions in the correlations of matter and nature, representing form and change.

Rajasâs *(Sk.)*. The elder *Agnishwattas* – the Fire-Pitris, "fire" standing as a symbol of enlightenment and intellect.

Râkshasas *(Sk.)*. *Lit.,* "raw eaters", and in the popular superstition evil spirits, demons. Esoterically, however, they are the *Gibborim* (giants) of the Bible, the Fourth Race or the Atlanteans. (See *Secret Doctrine*, II., 165.)

Ratnâvabhâsa Kalpa *(Sk.)*. The age in which all sexual difference will have ceased to exist, and birth will take place in the *Anupâdaka* mode, as in the second and third Root-races. Esoteric philosophy teaches that it will take place at the end of the sixth and during the seventh and last Root-race in this Round.

Reincarnation. The doctrine of rebirth, believed in by Jesus and the Apostles, as by all men in those days, but denied now by the Christians. All the Egyptian converts to Christianity, Church Fathers and others, believed in this doctrine, as shown by the writings of several. In the still existing symbols, the human-headed bird flying towards a mummy, a body, or "the soul uniting itself with its *sahou* (glorified body of the Ego, and also the *kâmalokic shell*) proves this belief. "The song of the Resurrection" chanted by Isis to recall her dead husband to life, might be translated "Song of Rebirth", as Osiris is collective Humanity. "Oh! Osiris [here follows the name of the Osirified mummy, or the departed], rise again in holy earth (matter), august mummy in the coffin, under thy corporeal substances", was the funeral prayer of the priest over the deceased. "Resurrection" with the Egyptians never meant the resurrection of the mutilated mummy, but of the *Soul* that informed it, the Ego in a new body. The putting on of flesh periodically by the Soul or the Ego, was a universal belief; nor can anything be more consonant with justice and Karmic law.

Rishi Prajâpati (*Sk.*). *Lit.*, "revealers", holy sages in the religious history of Âryavarta. Esoterically the highest of them are the Hierarchies of "Builders" and Architects of the Universe and of living things on earth; they are generally called Dhyan Chohans, Devas and gods.

Rishis (*Sk.*). Adepts; the inspired ones. In Vedic literature the term is employed to denote those persons through whom the various Mantras were revealed.

Rudras (*Sk.*). The mighty ones; the lords of the three upper worlds. One of the classes of the "fallen" or incarnating spirits; they are all born of Brahmâ.

Rûpa (*Sk.*). Body; any form, applied even to the forms of the gods, which are subjective to us.

S

Sabda Brahmam (*Sk.*). "The Unmanifested Logos." The *Vedas*; "Ethereal Vibrations diffused throughout Space ".

Sacred Science. The name given to the *inner* esoteric philosophy, the secrets taught in days of old to the initiated candidates, and divulged during the last and supreme Initiation by the Hierophants.

Sakti (*Sk.*). The active female energy of the gods; in popular Hinduism, their wives and goddesses; in Occultism, the crown of the astral light. Force and the six forces of nature synthesized. Universal Energy.

Sama (*Sk.*). One of the *bhâva pushpas,* or "flowers of sanctity Sama is the fifth, or "resignation". There are eight such flowers, namely: clemency or charity, self-restraint, affection (or love for others), patience, resignation, devotion, meditation and veracity. Sama is also the repression of any mental perturbation,

Sâma Veda (Sk.). Lit., "the Scripture, or *Shâstra,* of peace". One of the four Vedas.

Samâdhâna (Sk.). That state in which a Yogi can no longer diverge from the path of spiritual progress; when everything terrestrial, except the visible body, has ceased to exist for him.

Samâdhi (*Sk.*). A state of ecstatic and complete trance. The term comes from the words *Sam-âdha*, "self-possession ". He who possesses this power is able to exercise an absolute control over all his faculties, physical or mental; it is the highest state of Yoga.

Samâdhindriya (*Sk.*). Lit., "the root of concentration"; the fourth of the five roots called Pancha Indriyâni, which are said in esoteric philosophy to be the agents in producing a highly moral life, leading to sanctity and liberation ; when these are reached, the two *spiritual roots* lying latent in the body (Atmâ and Buddhi) will send out shoots and blossom. *Samâdhindriya* is the organ of ecstatic meditation in Râj-yoga practices.

Samâpatti (*Sk.*). Absolute concentration in Râja-Yoga; the process of development by which perfect indifference (*Sams*) is reached (*apatti*). This state is the last stage of development before the possibility of entering into Samâdhi is reached.

Samskâra (*Sk.*). Lit., from *Sam* and *Krî*, to improve, refine, impress. In Hindu philosophy the term is used to denote the impressions left upon the mind by individual actions or external circumstances, and capable of being developed on any future favourable occasion—even in a future birth. The *Samskâra* denotes, therefore, the germs of propensities and impulses from previous births to be developed in this, or the coming *janmâs* or reincarnations. In Tibet, Samskâra is called Doodyed, and in China is defined as, or at least connected with, action or Karma. It is, strictly speaking, a metaphysical term, which in exoteric philosophies is variously defined; *e.g.*, in Nepaul as illusion, in Tibet as notion, and in Ceylon as discrimination. The true meaning is as given above, and as such is connected with Karma and its working.

Samvriti (*Sk.*). False conception—the origin of illusion.

Samvritisatya (*Sk.*). Truth mixed with false conceptions (Samvriti); the reverse of absolute truth – or *Paramârthasatya*, self-consciousness in absolute truth or reality.

Sanat Kumâra (*Sk.*). The most prominent of the seven Kumâras, the Vaidhâtra the first of which are called Sanaka, Sananda, Sanâtana and Sanat Kumâra; which names are all significant qualifications of the degrees of human intellect.

Sânkhya (*Sk.*). The system of philosophy founded by Kapila Rishi, a system of analytical metaphysics, and one of the six *Darshanas* or schools of philosophy. It discourses on numerical categories and the meaning of the twenty-five *tatwas* (the forces of nature in various degrees). This "atomistic school", as some call it, explains nature by the interaction of twenty-four elements with *purusha* (spirit) modified by the three gunas (qualities), teaching the eternity of *pradhâna* (primordial, homogeneous matter), or the self-transformation of nature and the eternity of the human Egos.

Sânkhya Yoga (*Sk.*). The system of Yoga as set forth by the above school.

Sanskrit (*Sk.*). The classical language of the Brahmans, never known *nor spoken in its true systematized form* (given later *approximately* by Pânini), except by the initiated Brahmans, as it was pre-eminently "a mystery language". It has now degenerated into the so-called Prâkrita.

Saptarshi (*Sk.*). The seven Rishis. As stars they are the constellation of 'the Great Bear, and called as such the *Riksha* and *Chitrasikhandinas,* bright-crested.

Satya Yuga (*Sk.*). The golden age, or the age of truth and purity; the first of the four Yugas, also called Krita Yuga.

Sattva (*Sk.*). Understanding; quiescence in divine knowledge. It follows 'generally the word *Bodhi* when used as a compound word, e.g., "Bodhisattva".

Sattva or *Satwa*, (*Sk.*). Goodness; the same as Sattva, or purity, one of the trigunas or three divisions of nature.

Satya (*Sk.*). Supreme truth.

Satya Loka (*Sk.*). The world of infinite purity and wisdom, the celestial abode of Brahmâ and the gods.

Satya Yuga (*Sk.*). The golden age, or the age of truth and purity; the first of the four Yugas, also called Krita Yuga.

Secret Doctrine. The general name given to the esoteric teachings of antiquity.

Sephira (*Heb.*) An emanation of Deity; the parent and synthesis of the ten Sephiroth when she stands at the head of the Sephirothal Tree; in the Kabbalah, Sephira,or the " Sacred Aged ", is the divine Intelligence (the same as Sophia or Metis), the first emanation from the "Endless" or Ain-Suph.

Sephiroth (*Heb.*). The ten emanations of Deity; the highest is formed by the concentration of the Ain Soph Aur, or the Limitless Light, and each: Sephira produces by emanation another Sephira. The names of the Ten Sephiroth are – 1. Kether – The Crown; 2. Chokmah – Wisdom; 3. Binah – Understanding; 4. Chesed- – Mercy; Geburah – Power; 6. Tiphereth – Beauty; 7. Netzach – Victory; 8. Hod – Splendour; 9. Jesod_Foundation; and 10. Malkuth – The Kingdom.

The conception of Deity embodied in the Ten Sephiroth is a very sublime one, and each Sephira is a picture to the Kabbalist of a group of exalted ideas, titles and attributes, which the name but faintly represents. Each Sephira is called either active or passive, though this attribution may lead to error; passive does not mean a return to negative existence; and the two words only express the relation between individual Sephiroth, and not any absolute quality. [w.w.w.]

Sharîra (Sarîra) *(Sk.)*. Envelope or body.

Siddhas *(Sk.)*. Saints and sages who have become almost divine also a hierarchy of Dhyan Chohans.

Siddhâsana *(Sk.)*. A posture in Hatha-yoga practices.

Siddha-Sena *(Sk.)*. Lit., "the leader of Siddhas"; a title of Kârttikeya, the "mysterious youth" *(kumâra guha)*.

Siddhis *(Sk.)*. Lit., "attributes of perfection"; phenomenal powers acquired through holiness by Yogis.

Sishta *(Sk.)*. The great elect or Sages, left after every minor *Pralaya* (that which is called "obscuration" in Mr. Sinnett's *Esoteric Buddhism*), when the globe goes into its night or rest, to become, on its re-awakening, the seed of the next humanity. Lit. "remnant."

Siva *(Sk.)*. The third person of the Hindu Trinity (the Trimûrti). He is a god of the first order, and in his character of Destroyer higher than Vishnu, the Preserver, as he destroys only to regenerate on a higher plane. He is born as Rudra, the Kumâra, and is the patron of all the Yogis, being called, as such, Mahâdeva the great ascetic, His titles are significant *Trilochana*, "the three-eyed", *Mahâdeva*, "the great god ", *Sankara*, etc., etc., etc.

Skandha or *Skhanda* *(Sk.)*. Lit., "bundles", or groups of attributes; everything finite, inapplicable to the eternal and the absolute. There are five—esoterically, *seven*—attributes in every human living being, which are known as the *Pancha Shandhas*. These are (1) form, *rûpa;* (2) perception, *vidâna;* (3) consciousness, *sanjnâ;* (4) action, *sanskâra;* (5) knowledge, vidyâna. These unite at the birth of man and constitute his personality. After the maturity of these Skandhas, they begin to separate and weaken, and this is followed by *jarâmarana,* or decrepitude and death.

Son-kha-pa (*Tib.*). Written also *Tsong-kha-pa.* A famous Tibetan reformer of the fourteenth century, who introduced a purified Buddhism into his country. He was a great Adept, who being unable to witness any longer the desecration of Buddhist philosophy by the false priests who made of it a marketable commodity, put a forcible stop thereto by a timely revolution and the exile of 40,000 sham monks and Lamas from the country. He is regarded as an Avatar of Buddha, and is the founder of the *Gelukpa* (" yellow-cap ") Sect, and of the mystic Brotherhood connected with its chiefs. The "tree of the 10,000 images" *(khoom boom)* has, it is said, sprung from the long hair of this ascetic, who leaving it behind him disappeared for ever from the view of the profane.

Soul. The **yuch,** or *nephesh* of the *Bible;* the vital principle, or the breath of life, which every animal, down to the infusoria, shares with man. In the translated Bible it stands indifferently for *life,* blood and soul. " Let us not kill his *nephesh* ", says the original text: "let us not kill *him* ", translate the Christians (*Genesis* xxxvii. 21), and so on.

Sparsa (*Sk*). The sense of touch.

Spirit. The lack of any mutual agreement between writers in the use of this word has resulted in dire confusion. It is commonly made synonymous with *soul;* and the lexicographers countenance the usage. In Theosophical teachings. the term "Spirit" is applied solely to that which *belongs directly to Universal Consciousness,* and which is its homogeneous and unadulterated emanation. Thus, the higher Mind in Man or his Ego (*Manas*) is, when linked indissolubly with Buddhi, a spirit; while the term "Soul", human or even animal (the lower *Manas* acting in animals as instinct), is applied only to Kâma-*Manas,* and qualified as the living soul. This is *nephesh,* in Hebrew, the "breath of life". Spirit is formless and *immaterial,* being, when individualised, of the highest spiritual substance – *Suddasatwa,* the divine essence, of which the body of the manifesting *highest* Dhyanis are formed. Therefore, the Theosophists reject the appellation " Spirits" for those phantoms which appear in the phenomenal manifestations of the Spiritualists, and call them "shells", and various other names. (See "Sukshma Sarîra".) Spirit, in short, is no entity in the sense of having form ; for, as Buddhist philosophy has it, where there is a form, there is a cause for pain and suffering. But each *individual* spirit – this individuality lasting only throughout the manvantaric life-cycle – may be described as a *centre of consciousness*, a self-sentient and self-conscious centre; a state, not a conditioned individual. This is why there is such a wealth of words in Sanskrit to express the different States of Being, Beings and Entities, each appellation showing the philosophical difference, the plane to which such *unit* belongs, and the degree of its spirituality or materiality. Unfortunately these terms are almost untranslatable into our Western tongues.

Sraddha (*Sk.*). Lit., faith, respect, reverence.

Sri Sankarâchârya (*Sk.*). The great religious reformer of India, and teacher of the Vedânta philosophy—the greatest of all such teachers, regarded by the *Adwaitas* (Non-dualists) as an incarnation of Siva and a worker of miracles. He established many *mathams* (monasteries), and founded the most learned sect among Brahmans, called the Smârtava. The legends about him are as numerous as his philosophical writings. At the age of thirty-two he went to Kashmir, and reaching Kedâranâth in the Himalayas, entered a cave alone, whence he never returned. His followers claim that he did not die, but only retired from the world.

Sthûla Sarîram (*Sk.*). In metaphysics, the gross physical body.

Sthûlopadhi (*Sk.*). A "principle" answering to the lower triad in man, i.e., body, astral form, and life, in the Târaka Râja Yoga system, which names only three chief principles in man. *Sthûlopadhi* corresponds to the *jagrata,* or waking conscious *state.*

Sûkshma Sarîra (*Sk.*). The dream-like, illusive body akin to *Mânasarûpa* or "thought-body ". It is the vesture of the gods, or the Dhyânis and the Devas. Written also *Sukshama Sharîra* and called *Sukshmopadhi* by the Târaka Râja Yogis. (*Secret Doctrine*, I.,157)

Sûkshmopadhi (*Sk.*). In Târaka Râja Yoga the "principle" containing both the higher and the lower *Manas* and *Kâma*. It corresponds to the *Manomaya Kosha* of the Vedantic classification and to the *Svapna* state. (See "Svapna ".)

Suras (*Sk.*). A general term for gods, the same as devas; the contrary to asuras or "no-gods".

Sûryâvarta (*Sk.*). A degree or stage of Samâdhi.

Sushupti Avasthâ (*Sk.*). Deep sleep; one of the four aspects of Prânava.

Sûtrâtman (*Sk.*). Lit., "the thread of spirit"; the immortal Ego, the Individuality which incarnates in men one life after the other, and upon which are strung, like beads on a string, his countless Personalities. The universal life-supporting air, *Samashti prau*; universal energy.

Svabhâvat (*Sk.*). Explained by the Orientalists as "plastic substance", which is an inadequate definition. Svabhâvat is the world-substance and stuff, or rather that which is behind it – the spirit and essence of substance. The name comes from *Subhâva* and is composed of three words – **su**, good, perfect, fair, handsome; **sva,** self; and **bkâva**, being, or *state of being.* From it all nature proceeds and into it all returns at the end of the life-cycles. In Esotericism it is called "Father-Mother". It is the plastic essence of matter.

Svapna Avasthâ (Sk.). A dreaming state; one of the four aspects of *Prânava*; a Yoga practice.

Svasam Vedanâ (*Sk.*). Lit., "the reflection which analyses itself "; a synonym of Paramârtha.

Svastikâsana (*Sk.*). The second of the four principal postures of the eighty-four prescribed in Hatha Yoga practices.

T

Taijasi (*Sk.*). The radiant, flaming—from *Tejas* "fire"; used sometimes to designate the *Mânasa-rûpa*, the "thought-body", and also the stars.

Tamas (*Sk.*). The quality of darkness, "foulness" and inertia; also of ignorance, as matter is blind. A term used in metaphysical philosophy. It is the lowest of the three *gunas* or fundamental qualities.

Tanha (*Pali*). The thirst for life. Desire to live and clinging to life on this earth. This clinging is that which causes rebirth or reincarnation.

Tanmâtras (*Sk.*). The types or rudiments of the five Elements; the subtile essence of these, devoid of all qualities and identical with the properties of the five basic Elements – earth, water, fire, air and ether; i.e., the *tanmâtras* are, in one of their aspects, smell, taste, touch, sight, and hearing.

Tapas (*Sk.*). "Abstraction", "meditation". "To perform *tapas*" is to sit for *contemplation.* Therefore ascetics are often called Tâpasas.

Târakâ Râja Yoga (*Sk.*). One of the Brahminical Yoga systems for the development of purely spiritual powers and knowledge which lead to Nirvâna.

Tattwa (*Sk.*). Eternally existing " That "; also, the different principles in Nature, in their occult meaning. *Tattwa Samâsa* is a work of Sânkhya philosophy attributed to Kapila himself.

Also the abstract principles of existence or categories, physical and metaphysical. The subtle elements—five exoterically, seven in esoteric philosophy——which are correlative to the five and the seven senses on the physical plane ; the last two senses are as yet latent in man, but will be developed in the two last root-races.

Theosophia (*Gr.*). Wisdom-religion, or "Divine Wisdom". The substratum and basis of all the world-religions and philosophies, taught and practised by a few elect ever since man became a thinking being. In its practical bearing, Theosophy is purely divine ethics; the definitions in dictionaries are pure nonsense, based on religious prejudice and ignorance of the true spirit of the early Rosicrucians and mediæval philosophers who called themselves Theosophists.

Theosophists. A name by which many mystics at various periods of history have called themselves. The Neo-Platonists of Alexandria were Theosophists; the Alchemists and Kabbalists during the mediæval ages were likewise so called, also the Martinists, the Quietists, and other kinds of mystics, whether acting independently or incorporated in a brotherhood or society. All real lovers of divine Wisdom and Truth had, and have, a right to the name, rather than those who, appropriating the qualification, live lives or perform actions opposed to the principles of Theosophy. As described by Brother Kenneth R. Mackenzie, the Theosophists of the past centuries – " entirely speculative, and founding no schools, have still exercised a silent influence upon philosophy; and, no doubt, when the time arrives, many ideas thus silently propounded may yet give new directions to human thought. One of the ways in which these doctrines have obtained not only authority, but power, has been among certain enthusiasts in the higher degrees of Masonry. This power has, however, to a great degree died with the founders, and modern Freemasonry contains few traces of theosophic influence. However accurate and beautiful some of the ideas of Swedenborg, Pernetty, Paschalis, Saint Martin, Marconis, Ragon, and Chastanier may have been, they have but little direct influence on society." This is true of the Theosophists of the last three centuries, but not of the later ones. For the Theosophists of the current century have already visibly impressed themselves on modern literature, and introduced the desire and craving for some philosophy in place of the blind dogmatic faith of yore, among the most intelligent portions of human-kind. Such is the difference between past and modern THEOSOPHY.

Thread Soul. The same as *Sutrâtmâ (q.v.).*

Thumos *(Gr.).* The astral, animal soul; the *Kâmas-Manas; Thumos* means passion, desire and confusion and is so used by Homer. The word is probably derived from the Sanskit *Tamas,* which has the same meaning.

To On *(Gr.).* The "Being", the "Ineffable All" of Plato. He" whom no person has seen except the Son".

Tretâ Yuga *(Sk.).* The second age of the world, a period of 1,296,000 years.

Triad, or *the Three.* The ten Sephiroth are contemplated as a group of three triads: Kether, Chochmah and Binah form the supernal triad; Chesed, Geburah and Tiphereth, the second; and Netzach, Hod and Yesod, the inferior triad. The tenth Sephira, Malkuth, is beyond the three triads. [w.w.w.]

The above is orthodox Western Kabalah. Eastern Occultists recognise but one triad – – the upper one (corresponding to Atmâ-Buddhi and the " Envelope" which reflects their light, the three in one) – and count seven lower Sephiroth, everyone of which stands for a " principle", beginning with the Higher *Manas* and ending with the Physical Body – of which Malkuth is the representative in the Microcosm and the Earth in the Macrocosm.

Trigunas *(Sk.).* The three divisions of the inherent qualities of differentiated matter—i.e., of pure quiescence *(satva),* of activity and desire *(rajas),* of stagnation and decay *(tamas)* They correspond with Vishnu, Brahmâ, and Shiva. (See " Trimûrti ".)

U

Upâdhi *(Sk.).* Basis; the vehicle, carrier or bearer of something less material than itself: as the human body is the *upâdhi* of its spirit, ether the *upâdhi* of light, etc., etc.; a mould; a defining or limiting substance.

Upanishad *(Sk.).* Translated as "esoteric doctrine ", or interpretation of the *Vedas* by the *Vedânta* methods. The third division of the *Vedas* appended to the *BrâhManas* and regarded as a portion of *Sruti* or "revealed" word. They are, however, as records, far older than the *BrâhManas* the exception of the two, still extant, attached to the *Rig -Veda* of the Aitareyins. The term *Upanishad* is explained by the Hindu pundits as "that which destroys ignorance, and thus produces liberation" of the spirit, through the knowledge of the supreme though *hidden* truth; the same, therefore, as that which was hinted at by Jesus, when he is made to say, "And ye shall know the truth, and the truth shall make you free " (*John* viii. 32). It is from these treatises of the *Upanishads*—themselves the echo of the primeval Wisdom-Religion—that the Vedânta system of philosophy has been developed. (See "Vedânta".) Yet old as the *Upanishads* may be, the Orientalists will not assign to the oldest of them more than an antiquity of 600 years B.C. The accepted number of these treatises is 150, though now no more than about twenty are left unadulterated. They treat of very abstruse, metaphysical questions, such as the origin of the Universe; the nature and the essence of the Unmanifested Deity and the manifested gods the connection, primal and ultimate, of spirit and matter; the universality of mind and the nature of the human Soul and Ego.

The *Upanishads* must be far more ancient than the days of Buddhism, as they show no preference for, nor do they uphold, the superiority of the Brahmans as a caste. On the contrary, it is the (now) second caste, the Kshatriya, or warrior class, who are exalted in the oldest of them. As stated by Professor Cowell in Elphinstone's *History of India*——"they breathe a freedom of spirit unknown to any earlier work except the *Rig Veda. . .* The great teachers of the higher knowledge and Brahmans are continually represented as *going to Kshatriya Kings to become their pupils.*" The " Kshatriya Kings" were in the olden times, like the King Hierophants of Egypt, the receptacles of the highest divine knowledge and wisdom, the *Elect* and the incarnations of the primordial divine Instructors—the Dhyâni Buddhas or Kumâras. There was a time, æons before the Brahmans became a caste, or even the *Upanishads* were written, when there was on earth but one "lip ", one religion and one science, namely, the speech of the gods, the Wisdom-Religion and Truth. This was before the fair fields of the latter, overrun by nations of many languages, became overgrown with the weeds of intentional deception, and national creeds invented by ambition, cruelty and selfishness, broke the one sacred Truth into thousands of fragments.

Uparati (*Sk*) Absence of outgoing desires; a Yoga state.

V

Vâch (Sk.). To call Vâch "speech" simply, is deficient in clearness. Vâch is the mystic personification of speech, and the female *Logos,* being one with Brahmâ, who created her out of one-half of his body, which he divided into two portions; she is also one with Virâj (called the "female" Virâj) who was created in her by Brahmâ. In one sense Vâch is "speech" by which knowledge was taught to man; in another she is the "mystic, secret speech" which descends upon and enters into the primeval Rishis, as the "tongues of fire" are said to have "sat upon" the apostles. For, she is called "the female creator ", the "mother of the Vedas ", etc., etc. Esoterically, she is the subjective Creative Force which, emanating from the Creative Deity (the subjective Universe, its "privation ", or *ideation*) becomes the manifested "world of speech ", i.e., the *concrete expression of ideation*, hence the "Word" or Logos. Vâch is "the male and female" Adam of the first chapter of *Genesis*, and thus called "Vâch-Virâj" by the sages. (See *Atharva Veda*.) She is also "the celestial Saraswatî produced from the heavens ", a "voice derived from *speechless* Brahmâ" *(Mahâbhârata)*; the goddess of wisdom and eloquence. She is called *Sata-rûpa,* the goddess of *a hundred forms.*

Vâhan(a) (*Sk.*). A vehicle, the carrier of something immaterial and formless. All the gods and goddesses are, therefore, represented as using vâhanas to manifest themselves, which vehicles are ever symbolical. So, for instance, Vishnu has during Pralayas, *Ânanta* the infinite" (Space), symbolized by the serpent Sesha, and during the Manvantaras – *Garuda* the gigantic half-eagle, half-man, the symbol of the great cycle; Brahma appears as Brahmâ, descending into the planes of manifestations on *Kâlahamsa,* the "swan in time or finite eternity"; Siva (phonet, Shiva) appears as the bull *Nandi*; Osiris as the sacred bull *Apis*; Indra travels on an elephant; Kârttikeya, on a peacock; Kâmadeva on *Makâra,* at other times a parrot; Agni, the universal (and also solar) Fire-god, who is, as all of them are, "a consuming Fire", manifests itself as a ram and a lamb, *Ajâ,* "the unborn"; Varuna, as a fish; etc., etc., while the vehicle of MAN is his body.

Vaikhari Vâch (*Sk.*). 'That which is uttered; one of the four forms of speech.

Vaisheshika (Sk.). One of the six *Darshanas* or schools of philosophy, founded by Kanâda. It is called the Atomistic School, as it teaches the existence of a universe of atoms of a transient character, an endless number of souls and a fixed number of material principles, by the correlation and interaction of which periodical cosmic evolutions take place without any directing Force, save a kind of mechanical law inherent in the atoms; a very materialistic school.

Vaishnava (*Sk.*). A follower of any sect recognising and worshipping

Vishnu as the one supreme God. The worshippers of Siva are called *Saivas*.

Vaivaswata (*Sk.*). The name of the Seventh Manu, the forefather of the post-diluvian race, or our own fifth humankind. A reputed son of Sûrya (the Sun), he became, after having been saved in an ark (built by the order of Vishnu) from the Deluge, the father of Ikshwâku, the founder of the solar race of kings. (See "*Sûryavansa*".)

Vâyu (*Sk.*). Air: the god and sovereign of the air; one of the five states of matter, namely the *gaseous*; one of the five elements, called, as wind, *Vâta*. The *Vishnu Purâna* makes Vâyu King of the Gandharvas. He is the father of Hanumân, in the *Râmâyana*. The trinity of the mystic gods in Kosmos closely related to each other, are " Agni (fire) whose place is on earth; Vâyu (air, or one of the forms of Indra), whose place is in the air ; and Sûrya (the sun) whose place is in the air (*Nirukta*.) In esoteric interpretation, these three cosmic principles, correspond with the three human principles, Kâma, Kâma-*Manas* and *Manas*, the sun of the intellect.

Vedânta (*Sk.*). A mystic system of philosophy which has developed from the efforts of generations of sages to interpret the secret meaning of the *Upanishads (q.v.)*. It is called in the *Shad-Darshanas* (six schools or systems of demonstration), *Uttara Mîmânsâ*, attributed to *Vyâsa*, the compiler of the *Vedas*, who is thus referred to as the founder of the Vedânta. The orthodox Hindus call Vedânta_a term meaning literally the "end of all (Vedic) knowledge " – *Brahmâ-jnâna*, or pure and spiritual knowledge of Brahmâ. Even if we accept the late dates assigned to various Sanskrit schools and treatises by our Orientalists, the Vedânta must be 3,300 years old, as Vyâsa is said to have lived I,400 years B.C. If, as Elphinstone has it in his *History of India*, the *BrahManas* are the *Talmud* of the Hindus, and the *Vedas* the Mosaic books, then the *Vedânta* may be correctly called the *Kabalah* of India. But how vastly more grand! Sankarâchârya, who was the popularizer of the Vedântic system, and the founder of the *Adwaita* philosophy, is sometimes called the founder of the modern schools of the Vedânta.

Vedas (*Sk.*). The "revelation". the scriptures of the Hindus, from the root *vid*, "to know ", or "divine knowledge". They are the most ancient as well as the most sacred of the Sanskrit works. The *Vedas* , on the date and antiquity of which no two Orientalists can agree, are claimed by the Hindus themselves, whose Brahmans and Pundits ought to know best about their own religious works, to have been first taught orally for thousands of years and then compiled on the shores of Lake Mânasa-

Sarovara (phonetically, *Mansarovara*) beyond the Himalayas, in Tibet.

The Vedic writings are all classified in two great divisions, exoteric and esoteric, the former being called *Karma-Kânda*, "division of actions or works ", and the *Jnâna Kânda*, "division of (divine) knowledge", the Upanishads (q.v.) coming under this last classification. Both departments are regarded as *Sruti* or revelation. To each hymn of the *Rig -Veda*, the name of the Seer or Rishi to whom it was revealed is prefixed. It, thus, becomes evident on the authority of these very names (such as Vasishta, Viswâmitra, Nârada, etc.), all of which belong to men born in various manvantaras and even ages, that centuries, and perhaps millenniums, must have elapsed between the dates of their composition.

Vidyâ (*Sk*.). Knowledge, Occult Science.

Vijnânam (*Sk*.). The Vedântic name for the principle which dwells in the *Vijnânamaya Kosha* (the sheath of intellect) and corresponds to the faculties of the Higher *Manas*.

Vishnu (*Sk*.). The second person of the Hindu Trimûrti (trinity), composed of Brahmâ, Vishnu and Siva. From the root **vish**, "to pervade". in the *Rig - Veda*, Vishnu is no high god, but simply a manifestation of the solar energy, described as "striding through the seven regions of the Universe in *three* steps and enveloping all things with the dust (of his beams ".) Whatever may be the six other occult significances of the statement, this is related to the same class of types as the seven and ten Sephiroth, as the *seven* and *three* orifices of the perfect Adam Kadmon, as the seven "principles" and the higher triad in man, etc., etc. Later on this mystic type becomes a great god, the preserver and the renovator, he "of a thousand names – Sahasranâma ".

W

Will. In metaphysics and occult philosophy, Will is that which governs the manifested universes in eternity. *Will* is the one and sole principle of abstract eternal MOTION, or its ensouling essence. " The will", says Van Helmont, "is the first of all powers. . . . The will is the property of all spiritual beings and displays itself in them the more actively the more they are freed from matter." And Paracelsus teaches that "determined will is the beginning of all magical operations. It is because men do not perfectly imagine and believe the result, that the (occult) arts are so uncertain, while they might he perfectly certain." Like all the rest, the Will is *septenary* in its degrees of manifestation. Emanating from the one, eternal, abstract and purely quiescent Will (Âtmâ in Layam), it becomes Buddhi in its Alaya state, descends lower as *Mahat* (*Manas*), and runs down the ladder of degrees until the divine Eros becomes, in its lower, animal manifestation, erotic desire. Will as an eternal principle is neither spirit nor substance but everlasting ideation. As well expressed by Schopenhauer in his *Parerga*, " in sober reality there is neither *matter* nor *spirit.* The tendency to gravitation in a stone is as unexplainable as thought in the human brain. . . If matter can—no one knows why——fall to the ground, then it can also— no one knows why—-think. . . . As soon, even in mechanics, as we trespass beyond the purely mathematical, as soon as we reach the inscrutable adhesion, gravitation, and so on, we are faced by phenomena which are to our senses as mysterious as the WILL."

Wisdom. The " very essence of wisdom is contained in the Non- Being ". say the Kabbalists; but they also apply the term to the WORD or Logos, the Demiurge, by which the universe was called into existence. "The one Wisdom is in the Sound ", say the Occultists; the Logos again being meant by Sound, which is the substratum of Âkâsa. Says the *Zohar,* the " Book of Splendour" "It is the Principle of all the Principles, the mysterious Wisdom, the crown of all that which there is of the most High". (*Zohar*, iii., fol. 288, Myers *Qabbalah*.) And it is explained, "Above Kether is the Ayin, or Ens, i.e., Ain, the NOTHING". "It is so named because we do not know, and it is impossible to know, *that which there is in that Principle,* because . . . it is above Wisdom itself." (iii., fol. 288.) This shows that the real Kabbalists agree with the Occultists that the essence, or that which is in the principle of Wisdom, is still above that highest Wisdom.

Wisdom Religion. The one religion which underlies all the now-existing creeds. That "faith" which, being primordial, and revealed directly to human kind by their *progenitors* and informing EGOS (though the Church regards them as the "fallen angels"), required no "grace", nor *blind* faith to believe, for it was *knowledge.* (See "Gupta Vidyâ", Hidden Knowledge.) It is on this Wisdom Religion that *Theosophy is based.*

Y

Years of Brahmâ. The whole period of "Brahma's Age" (100 Years). Equals 31I,040,000,000,000 years. (See "Yuga ".)

Yoga (*Sk.*). (1) One of the six Darshanas or schools of India; a school of philosophy founded by Patanjali, though the real Yoga doctrine, the one that is said to have helped to prepare the world for the preaching of

Buddha, is attributed with good reasons to the more ancient sage Yâjnawalkya, the writer of the *Shatapatha Brâhmana*, of *Yajur Veda*, the *Brihad Âranyaka*, and other famous works. (2) The practice of meditation as a means of leading to spiritual liberation. Psycho-spiritual powers are obtained thereby, and induced ecstatic states lead to the clear and correct perception of the eternal truths, in both the visible and invisible universe.

Yogâchârya (*Sk.*). (1) A mystic school. (2) Lit., a teacher (*âchârya*) of Yoga, one who has mastered the doctrines and practices of ecstatic meditation – the culmination of which are the *Mahâsiddhis*. It is incorrect to confuse this school with the Tantra, or Mahâtantra school founded by Samantabhadra, for there are two Yogâchârya Schools, one esoteric, the other popular. The doctrines of the latter were compiled and glossed by Asamgha in the sixth century of our era, and his mystic tantras and mantras, his formularies, litanies, spells and mudrâ would certainly, if attempted without a Guru, serve rather purposes of sorcery and black magic than real Yoga. Those who undertake to write upon the subject are generally learned missionaries and haters of Eastern philosophy in general. From these no unbiassed views can be expected. Thus when we read in the *Sanskrit - Chinese Dictionary* of Eitel, that the reciting of mantras (which he calls " spells"!) " should he accompanied by music and distortions of the fingers (mudrâ), that a state of mental fixity (*Samâdhi}* might he reached ' – one acquainted, however slightly,. with the real practice of Yoga can only shrug his shoulders. These distortions of the fingers or ,mudrâ are necessary, the author thinks, for the reaching of Samâdhi, "characterized by there being neither thought nor annihilation of thought, and consisting of six-fold bodily (*sic*) and mental happiness (*yogi*) *whence would result endowment with supernatural miracle-working power*". Theosophists cannot be too much warned against such fantastic and prejudiced explanations.

Yogi (*Sk.*). (1) Not "a state of six-fold bodily and mental happiness as the result, of ecstatic meditation" (Eitel) but a state which, when reached, makes the practitioner thereof absolute master of his six principles", *he now being merged in the seventh*. It gives him full control, owing to his knowledge of SELF and Self, over his bodily, intellectual and mental states, which, unable any longer to interfere with, or act upon, his Higher Ego, leave it free to exist in its original, pure, and divine state. (2) Also the name of the devotee who practises Yoga.

Yuga (*Sk.*). A 1,000th part of a Kalpa. An age of the World of which there are four, and the series of which proceed in succession during the manvantaric cycle. Each Yuga is preceded by a period called in the *Purânas* Sandhyâ, twilight, or transition period, and is followed by another period of like duration called Sandhyânsa, "portion of twilight". Each is equal to one-tenth of the Yuga. The group of four Yugas is first computed by the *divine* years, or "years of the gods" – each such year being equal to 360 years of mortal men. Thus we have, in "divine" years :

	AGE	YEARS
1	Krita or Satya Yuga	4,000
	Sandhyâ	400
	Sandhyansa	400
		4,800

	AGE	YEARS
2	Tretâ Yuga	3,000
	Sandhyâ	300
	Sandhyânsa	300
		3,600

	AGE	YEARS
3	Dwâpara Yuga	2,000
	Sandhya	200
	Sandhyânsa	200
		2,400

	AGE	YEARS
4	Kali Yuga	1,000
	Sandhyâ	100
	Sandhyânsa	100
		1,200
	Total =	**12,000**

This rendered in years of mortals equals:

4800	X	360	=	1,728,000
3600	X	360	=	1,296,000
2400	X	360	=	864,000
1200	X	360	=	432,000
		Total	=	**4,320,000**

The above is called a Mahâyuga or Manvantara. 2,000 such Mahâyugas, or a period of 8,640,000 years, make a Kalpa the latter being only a "day and a night", or twenty-four hours, of Brahmâ. Thus an "age of Brahmâ", or one hundred of his divine years, must equal 311,040,000,000,000 of our mortal years. The old Mazdeans or Magi (the modern Parsis) had the same calculation, though the Orientalists do not seem to perceive it, for even the Parsi Moheds themselves have forgotten it. But their "Sovereign time of the Long Period" (*Zervan Dareghâ Hvadâta*) lasts 12,000 years, and these are the 12,000 *divine* years of a Mahâyuga as shown above, whereas the *Zervan Akarana* (Limitless Time), mentioned by Zarathustra, is the *Kâla*, out of space and time, of Parabrahm.

INDEX

B

C

D

E

H

I

L

M

N

O

R

T

U

V

W

Y

Z

CPSIA information can be obtained
at www.ICGtesting.com
Printed in the USA
LVHW032337100221
679011LV00027BA/108